STRATHCLYDE

CHANGING HORIZONS

STRATHCLYDE

CHANGING HORIZONS

Edited by

JOHN BUTT and GEORGE GORDON

1985

SCOTTISH ACADEMIC PRESS

Published by
Scottish Academic Press Ltd,
33 Montgomery Street
Edinburgh EH7 5JX

SBN 7073 0423 7 (Casebound)
SBN 7073 0444 X (Paperback)

British Library Cataloguing in Publication Data

Butt, John, *1929–*
   Strathclyde: changing horizons.
   1. Strathclyde — Economic conditions
   I. Title   II. Gordon, George, *1939–*
   330.9414′10858   HC257.S4

ISBN 0–7073–0423–7

Printed in Great Britain by
Clark Constable, Edinburgh, London, Melbourne

CONTENTS

FOREWORD

Lord Todd, O.M., F.R.S.
Chancellor of the University of Strathclyde

The British Association for the Advancement of Science is no stranger to Glasgow, having held no fewer than seven of its annual meetings in the city, the most recent being in 1958. Nor is that surprising for this is the city of William Cullen, Adam Smith, Joseph Black, James Watt, John Anderson, Thomas Graham, William Thomson (Lord Kelvin), Lyon Playfair, James Young (founder of the shale oil industry), David Livingstone and John Logie Baird. This visit in 1985 is, however, especially significant for me. My first contact with the Association was in 1928 when as a newly graduated student I attended its annual meeting in Glasgow; many years later — in 1970 — I had the honour to be its President when it met in Durham and this year I am proud, as Chancellor, to welcome it to the University of Strathclyde, an institution peculiarly suited to be host to the Association for the first time.

For the University of Strathclyde is the oldest institution of higher education in the United Kingdom devoted to science and technology, having been in continuous operation (albeit with a number of changes of name) since its foundation in the year 1796 under the will of John Anderson, Professor of Natural Philosophy in the ancient University of Glasgow as Anderson's Institution or University in which 'men shall be taught the principles of the arts they practise'. Dr. Garnett, the first professor appointed to Anderson's Institution in 1796, became the first professor in Count Rumford's Royal Institution in London while George Birkbeck, the second professor in Anderson's, founded the first Mechanics Institution in England and his name is commemorated to this day in Birkbeck College, London.

For all these reasons, and being myself a native Glaswegian, I have particular pride in welcoming the British Association to Strathclyde. Here we still abide by the wish of John Anderson that 'men shall be taught the principles of the arts they practise'. Today we no longer bear his name but we are proud to display in our armorial bearings the crown and cinquefoils of the ancient Scottish kingdom of Strathclyde and to remain an integral part of the great city of Glasgow.

vii

Anderson's played a full part in the regeneration of Glasgow following the collapse of the tobacco trade after the American War of Independence by producing the technically trained men and women who enabled it to rise again to greatness by taking advantage of the first industrial revolution; today, as Glasgow seeks a new future following the decay of many of its traditional heavy industries, Strathclyde again stands ready to aid its drive into the new technologies of the second industrial revolution now in progress.

'Let Glasgow flourish' says the city's motto. To that in Strathclyde we say 'Amen' but add 'and so it shall'.

INTRODUCTION

When the title for this volume was discussed, the emphasis on change and the need for further developments in the West of Scotland dominated the thinking of the organising committee and after due consideration the objective of changing horizons for the Region crystallised as a suitable theme for our endeavours.

It was not the case, however, that the Region lacked tradition, even if it was only established as a local government unit in 1973. Ancient burghs and the great city of Glasgow have been joined by new towns such as East Kilbride, Cumbernauld and Irvine in recent decades. Established industries in the post-war era such as shipbuilding and heavy engineering have increasingly been under stress, and structural changes in the production of coal and iron and steel have reduced the Region's ability to compete on traditional lines. Industrialisation in other parts of the world has made it necessary for the human skills of the West of Scotland to be transferred into a wider range of high technology activities, dependent upon a strong educational base. Many of the themes of this volume occur because of the certainty that the Region is changing its economy and in the future will change even more, with implications for society and its institutions.

Population distribution is changing. It is not simply that the City of Glasgow has lost people; there have been changes associated with the building of the new towns; there has been interplay between the emergence of the city as a service centre for the Region and the development of small settlements of commuters beyond the periphery of Glasgow. It has been relatively easy to suggest that the drift of population out of Glasgow has led to a decline of the city's manufacturing base, but the truth may run counter to this simple proposition. Out migration may reflect the magnetism of industry which was locating elsewhere.

It is also easy to forget that the Region possessed an intrinsic cohesion which goes far back into history and that a reputation for heavy work, militant radicalism, educational excellence and social problems has been set in an almost mythological mould. Heritage is economic, social and cultural; it can be an incubus or potentially a substantial advantage. We hope that readers will form the impression that the editors believe it is the latter.

Traditional craft skills nurtured in an apprenticeship system had always depended upon a sound basic education, with an emphasis on breadth. Primary and secondary education are being reformed; further education is expanding and diversifying to take account of economic developments and the changing demand for trained personnel. The two universities, with their differing traditions, have been heavily concerned with the provision of advanced education in the Region and the supply of a scientific and professional elite; they are a fundamental resource, along with the other higher educational institutions, an agency for change and economic advance. Their commitment to collaboration, as symbolised by the creation of the Science Park, and their continued provision of highly educated and effectively trained graduates should operate to the considerable economic and social advancement of the community. Some of the direct benefits of research may be deduced from the selection of technical and scientific innovations at Strathclyde University discussed in this volume.

Enterprise does not need to be native-born and bred; capital more obviously can be international. It is central to social and economic change that the combination of capital and enterprise should occur in a favourable environment. The new main growth points in Strathclyde have been the towns of East Kilbride, Cumbernauld and Irvine, and science-based industries have located there under the benevolent aegis of Development Corporations. Their development and role is closely examined in this volume.

We do not propound the deterministic view of the inevitable progress of the Region nor do we suggest that there are no problems. The difficulties arising from structural economic change and world depression have reduced the advantages accruing from the accumulation of new firms and new jobs. The City of Glasgow and other urban industrial areas, despite the safety net provided by the Welfare State, are grappling with major problems affecting the quality of life of their inhabitants. A striking improvement in the regional economy would help but not solve these difficulties.

Nonetheless, the Region is blessed with a varied and stimulating physical environment and a diverse array of natural resources. The scenery and the heritage are two obvious important advantages, particularly in an age where greater stress is laid on recreation, leisure and the quality of life.

The way ahead is far from smooth. Our distinguished commentators do not pretend that it is. However, there are many grounds for optimism. The Regional Council is committed to implementing programmes designed to aid economic advance and to ameliorate social problems. So is the Scottish Office. The educational facilities from primary school to higher education are open enough to assist these processes. The skill, versatility and adaptability of the people represent major advantages which should not be lost in the myth of proletarian militancy. Strathclyde-made will replace Clyde-built as a motto of excellence.

JOHN BUTT
GEORGE GORDON

CHAPTER ONE

THE PHYSICAL ENVIRONMENT

K. Smith

Introduction

The Strathclyde region covers 13,850 km², which is approximately one-sixth of the total area of Scotland, and embraces a very wide range of environmental conditions. It extends from the rich machair sands of coastal Tiree to the arctic-alpine summit of Ben Cruachan; from the desolate peat bogs of Rannoch Moor to the city centre of Glasgow and from the expanse of Loch Lomond to the narrow headwaters of the Clyde. The area is not a coherent physical unit and has little natural focus. Indeed, as shown in Figure 1, the macro geology dictates a fragmentation into at least three major structural divisions — Western Highlands and Islands, Central or Midland Valley and Southern Uplands. About one-quarter of the area is occupied by the inland valley of the Clyde, which contrasts markedly with the sea lochs and indented, peninsular environment of the west coast and the islands.

This is not to say that environmental conditions are unimportant. On the contrary, the very nature and variety of the physical environment is of enormous historical and present-day significance. For example, the geological formations have supplied many economic minerals such as coal, fire clay and building stone. Abundant rainfall has endowed the area with plentiful water supplies and hydro-electric power. A combination of fertile land and climate results in the area producing over one-quarter of the Scottish agricultural output. More subtle environmental combinations provide landscapes of such outstanding natural beauty that 60 per cent of all holiday visitors specify scenery as the prime attraction (Anonymous, 1983).

In the short space available, it is only possible to sketch a rapid portrait of the physical composition of Strathclyde for those British Association visitors unfamiliar with the region. Consequently, this account will attempt to highlight the environmental diversity of the area in both time and space by concentrating on the broad evolution of the physical landscape and the major factors leading to such great internal variety today.

1

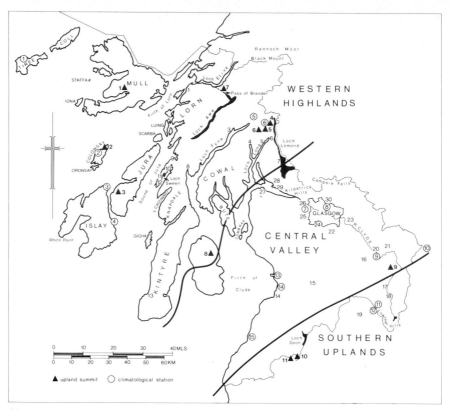

Fig. 1   The Strathclyde Region showing the major physical features and placenames mentioned in the text.

CLIMATOLOGICAL STATIONS

1	Tiree	6	Loch Sloy	11	Leadhills
2	Colonsay	7	Abbotsinch	12	Lowther Hill
3	Rhuvaal	8	Springburn	13	Troon
4	Islay	9	Bonnington	14	Prestwick
5	Allt na Lairige	10	Blyth Bridge	15	Girvan

PLACE NAMES

1	Oban	11	Taynish	21	Carstairs
2	Easdale	12	Kilmory	22	East Kilbride
3	Inveraray	13	Machrihanish	23	Motherwell
4	Lochgoilhead	14	Ayr	24	Giffnock
5	Ardgarten	15	Mauchline	25	Paisley
6	Arrochar	16	Lesmahagow	26	Renfrew
7	Luss	17	Abington	27	Port Glasgow
8	Lochgilphead	18	Crawford	28	Bonhill
9	Crinan	19	Sanquhar	29	Dumbarton
10	Tayvallich	20	Lanark	30	Bishopbriggs

UPLAND SUMMITS

1	Ben More	5	Ben Vane	9	Tinto
2	Carnan Eoin	6	Ben Ime	10	Mullwharchar
3	Beinn an Oir	7	Ben Cruachan	11	The Merrick
4	Ben Vorlich	8	Goatfell		

Geology and Relief

As shown in Table 1 and Figure 2, the emergence of Strathclyde can be traced back several hundred million years to the Archean platform of Lewisian gneiss. This complex basement of crystalline rock comprises some of the oldest geological formations in the world and forms the western extremities of the region in Coll, Tiree and the southern part of the Islay peninsula known as the Rhinns of Islay. In these areas the low landscape, never rising above 135 m OD on Coll and Tiree, is almost more typical of the Outer than the Inner Hebrides with outcrops of bare rock surrounded by peat bogs and acid pools. This is especially so on Coll, where the Lewisian gneiss is exposed over three-quarters of the surface, but on Tiree the Atlantic gales have buried most of the ancient platform under blown shell-sand.

The grits, shales and conglomerates of the overlying Torridonian sandstone also produce a topography of low coastal platforms, covered with peat and dotted with lochans, but the appearance is slightly greener and more fertile

TABLE 1   SIGNIFICANT GEOLOGICAL SUCCESSIONS

	Formation/Event	Absolute Timescale (b_p)	Main Features/Areas
Cainozoic — Quaternary — Holocene	Later Postglacial	5,000–present	Raised beaches, river erosion
	Early Postglacial	10,000– 5,000	Marine transgression
	Late Glacial Stadial	11,000–10,000	Hummocky moraine
	Late Glacial Interstadial	14,000–11,000	
	Late Devensian ice	27,000–14,000	Glacial erosion
	Pleistocene ice ages	1·6 m	
	Tertiary igneous	65–54 m	Vulcanicity on Mull/Arran
Mesozoic	Not widely represented		
Palaeozoic	New Red Sandstone	280–190 m	
	Hercynian Orogeny	300 m	Faulting and uplift
	Coal Measures and Grits	325–280 m	
	Carboniferous Limestone	345–325 m	Clyde Plateau lavas
	Old Red Sandstone	395–345 m	Volcanics and plutonics
	Caledonian Orogeny	400 m	Major faults and granites
	Silurian	430–395 m	Greywacke grits of
	Ordovician	500–430 m	Southern Uplands
Pre-Cambrian	Moinian/Dalradian	pre 600 m	Highland metamorphics
	Torridonian Sandstone	pre 600 m	Colonsay
	Lewisian Gneiss	2700 m	Coll/Tiree

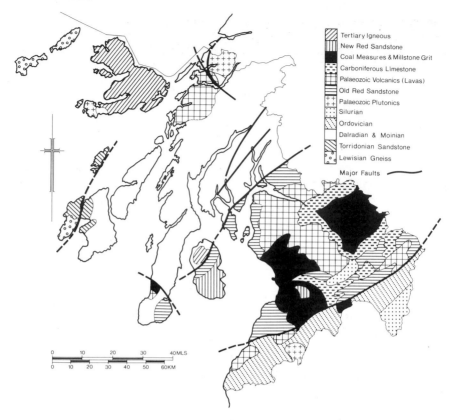

Fig. 2   The solid geology of the Strathclyde Region.

than the Lewisian areas owing to the lime content of the rocks. The main outcrops lie west of the faulted western peninsula of Islay, with the Loch Gruinart fault continuing up the eastern shores of Oronsay and Colonsay which, like the small island of Iona, are also Torridonian. As indicated in Figure 3, the relief is still subdued with the highest point on Colonsay, Carnan Eoin, only 143 m OD.

The extensive outcrops of Moinian and Dalradian rocks, covering approximately one-third of the region, provide a sharp contrast. Original deposits of sands, muds, limestones and pebbles laid down in a shallow sea stretching far to the south of our area (George, 1958) have been transformed by crustal pressure to produce the slates, quartzites and schists characteristic of the Western Highlands. These metamorphic rocks are too complicated for lithological differentiation but the less uniform Dalradian sediments are dominant in Strathclyde, thus giving maximum opportunity for topographic variety. Most of these rocks are resistant to erosion but important differences occur. For example, quartzite is highly resistant and forms the boldest relief in Knapdale, Islay and the spine of Jura which rises to 784 m OD on Beinn an Oir (Whittow, 1977). By comparison, the slates are often worn down to produce valleys as at Luss on Loch Lomondside.

Most of the scenery of Argyll has been carved from enormous recumbent folding in these rocks. The pattern of faults in Figure 2 is clearly reflected in the SW-NE grain of the relief due to Caledonian folding which, in turn, has led to the most indented stretch of coastline in Britain. Thus, the Loch Awe syncline can be traced south-westwards into the Sound of Jura and the three major peninsulas of Cowal, Knapdale and Kintyre all betray this trend. Much

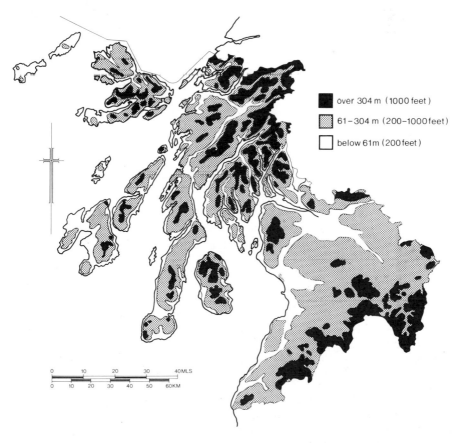

over 304 m (1000 feet)

61–304 m (200–1000 feet)

below 61m (200 feet)

Fig. 3   The relief of the Strathclyde Region.

of Argyll is influenced by the southern Grampian nappe complex, described by Whittow (1977). A major overfold has produced the inverted succession of the Cowal anticline, the axis of which can be traced topographically from the northern end of Loch Lomond, via the peaks of Ben Vorlich (941 m) and Ben Ime (1,012 m), through the Cowal hills and across Loch Fyne into Kintyre. In detail, each peninsula presents a different pattern of relief. Cowal, with the peaks of Arrochar, is much more Highland in character than Kintyre, the surface of which is further softened by outliers of Carboniferous and Old Red Sandstone rocks in the south. On the other hand, Knapdale is more rugged than Kintyre due to very tight folding of the rocks. The original fold structure has subsequently undergone a complete inversion of relief so that the axes of the weaker arches have been eroded to produce the inlets of Loch Sween and Loch Caolisport while the tougher synclines now appear as the peninsulas of Tayvallich and Kilmory, each formed of hard Crinan Grits. At an even smaller scale, the ridges around Loch Sween follow the outcrops of resistant epidiorite and parallel the innumerable ribbon lochs.

The Southern Uplands originated some 500 million years ago in Ordovician times with the deposition of thick beds of greywacke and mudstones. These rocks outcrop in the Abington–Leadhills-Sanquhar area adjacent to the principal Southern Uplands fault and along the coast south of Girvan. Sharp folding of some of the thinner beds may be partially responsible for the characteristically rounded shape of these hills. Silurian rocks have been less important as landscape makers but occur south of Crawford and as an inlier around Lesmahagow. Shortly after these rocks appeared, the Caledonian orogeny imposed its structural stamp on Scotland and created the Central Valley as a rift feature between the Highlands and the Southern Uplands in association with further folding and mineralisation.

At about the same time, the Southern Uplands were also modified by magmatic intrusions. On the southern boundary of Strathclyde the Loch Doon granites have greatly influenced relief although most of the summits — such as The Merrick (at 843 m OD the highest point in southern Scotland) — lie just outside the metamorphic aureole. Indeed, it is only at the Mullwharchar ridge (692 m) that the granite outcrop plays a direct topographic role.

Subsequent deposits of Old Red Sandstone were laid down as alluvial fans on the flanks of the eroding rift valley by torrents descending from the higher ground to north and south (George, 1958). Thus, as seen in Figure 2, this formation exists as a semi-continuous outcrop from Kintyre to Loch Lomond in the north and as a narrower, less continuous band south of a line from Ayr to Motherwell, although significant hills are restricted to the Highland border. Much more important topographically has been the contemporaneous Palaeozoic vulcanicity much farther north. In Lower Old Red Sandstone times one of the largest granitic emplacements in Britain occurred with the intrusion of the Loch Etive ring complex into the local country rock. The Pass of Brander fault-line is clearly related to the ring fracture and the resistant

Etive granites rise to the highest point in Strathclyde on Ben Cruachan at 1,125 m OD. Immediately south of Ben Cruachan, successive sheets of basaltic lava were also laid down to create the low lying, loch-scattered surface of the Lorn plateau south-east of Oban.

Apart from an outlier in Kintyre, which is responsible for the anomalous Machrihanish coalfield, the Carboniferous rocks are essentially confined to the Midland Valley. The so-called Carboniferous Limestone (actually composed mainly of mudstones and shales) is much less important topographically than the volcanic episodes of the period which produced the Clyde lavas. Overall, about 915 m of basaltic lava flows have combined to create the upland encirclement of Glasgow by the Kilpatricks, Campsies and Renfrew Heights plus the marked narrowing of the lower Clyde valley between Dumbarton and Port Glasgow. The resultant moorland scenery is perhaps best expressed in the Campsie Fells where no less than thirty-three separate lava flows exist in a steeply tiered and fault-guided edge almost overlooking the city (Bluck, 1973). In many cases, the last magma to cool and solidify in the volcanic vents was the most resistant to subsequent erosion. Consequently, as noted by Lawson and Lawson (1976), many of these volcanic rocks now form prominent hills around Glasgow with the 'Dun' or 'Dum' placename, e.g. Dumbuck, Dumgoyne, Duncryn, Duntreath and — most famous of all — the site of Dumbarton Castle on the dolerite plug of an ancient volcano.

The later Palaeozoic rocks have contributed rather less to the relief of Strathclyde, although the Coal Measures have proved to be economically important. Similarly, the Hercynian orogeny did little more than reactivate the main fault systems of the area and reinforce the Midland Valley syncline in which the New Red Sandstone is primarily limited to the Mauchline basin and the southern part of Arran.

The final geological episode of topographic importance, apart from the comparatively recent ice ages, was the Tertiary igneous phase which began around 65 million years before the present (bp). This activity is most extensively expressed on Mull, the northern part of which shows a distinctive stepped or tabular landscape arising from the dissection of successive Tertiary basalt flows some 1,800 m thick (Whittow, 1977). The central and southern areas of the island are dominated by complex igneous intrusions and concentric ring dykes which have broken through the earlier extrusive flows. The curved shape of the south-eastern coast betrays this central intrusion and, whilst lavas form the highest point of Ben More (966 m OD), the mountains and lochs are generally carved from the igneous intrusion. Amongst many well-known features are the basaltic lava columns forming Fingal's Cave on Staffa.

For its size, Arran is even more geologically complex than Mull (MacGregor, 1965). The northern half is rugged and mountainous, culminating in Goatfell (874 m), formed of a nearly circular mass of intruded Tertiary granite. As on Mull, the shape of the plutonic intrusion is reflected in the northern coastline and also in the path of the Highland boundary fault. By contrast, the southern half of Arran is an undulating tableland of New Red Sandstone sediments into which have been intruded numerous sills and dykes.

In addition to its topographic effects, it should be noted that the solid geology of Strathclyde has imparted a special character to Glasgow and other large towns through its use as building materials (Lawson, 1981). Thus, Carboniferous Sandstone from Bishopbriggs and Giffnock, Old Red Sandstone from Bonhill, New Red Sandstone from Mauchline, slates from Easdale and Luing and granites from Mull have all contributed to the architectural heritage of the city.

Quaternary Landforms

The last 1·5 million years have had a disproportionately important influence on the physical landscape of the Strathclyde region. This is due to the rapid environmental fluctuations associated with the sixteen or more major glaciations which are now known to have occurred and to have had profound effects on sea levels, coastlines and the detailed shaping of the land by erosion and deposition.

The most recent icesheet to overwhelm the region began to grow in Late Devensian times shortly after 30000 bp. The main accumulation zone lay in the Western Highlands, immediately to the north of our area, with a subsidiary centre in the Southern Uplands. It has been estimated that, at its maximum extent, the ice dome was some 1,500–2,000 m thick over central Scotland (Price, 1983). Every part of Strathclyde was, therefore, subject to glacial influence but the major erosive action was concentrated in the high energy areas represented by the greatest amplitudes of relief and the thickest accumulations of ice. In these areas the pre-glacial valleys were markedly over-deepened to produce glacial troughs and steep rock basins, now mainly occupied by either fresh or sea-water lochs. Loch Doon in the Southern Uplands and the upper stretch of Loch Lomond, which descends at its deepest point to 198 m below the water surface and 189 m below current sea level (Slack, 1957), are both fine examples. Where the rocks had been weakened by faulting, as in the Pass of Brander and Glen Etive localities, particularly steep valley sides result. The spectacular fiord of Loch Etive was subsequently created by rising sea levels whilst other coastal examples include Lochs Fyne and Long.

In other areas, glacial erosion had quite different effects. Many low-lying areas, such as those of Lewisian gneiss, were subjected to roughening and smoothing by the moving ice to produce the 'knob and lochan' scenery found on Islay and elsewhere. At much higher levels the northern and eastern slopes of most of the hill masses show at least partial development of corrie features.

The Devensian ice-sheet waned rapidly in the Late Glacial warming after 14000 bp and the evidence suggests that the Strathclyde region would have been de-glaciated by 12500 bp. The speedy melting of such large volumes of ice produced an appreciable rise in sea level since the ice wastage occurred much faster than the isostatic recovery of the land from glacial loading. One consequence was that the sea lochs of the Firth of Clyde and the Sound of Jura invaded the mainland well beyond the present coastline in two large embayments, one centred around Paisley to the south-west of Glasgow and the other between Crinan and Lochgilphead. However, the most obvious evidence for the high Late Glacial sea levels is found in the wave-cut platforms and cliff lines now stranded up to 30 m above present-day sea level. These features may be seen throughout the region but the most impressive staircase patterns are found on the western shores of Jura and Islay, possibly because this coastline was the first to be exposed to Atlantic waves while the seas farther east remained in the grip of the retreating mainland ice (Whittow, 1977). As isostatic recovery eventually overtook the eustatic effects of melting in the arctic sea, relative sea level began to fall but with a wide-spread pause which has left behind the common so-called 25 foot (7·6 m) raised beach.

The climatic amelioration of the Late Glacial Interstadial was brought to a sharp halt by a short period of intense cold from approximately 11000 to 10000 bp known as the Loch Lomond Stadial. As the name suggests, this new, mini-ice age grew from a glacier complex spreading out from the main West Highland spine so that valley glaciers, rather than a complete ice cover, produced lobes of ice extending to the west coast and central lowlands of Strathclyde. From the ample deposits of fresh 'hummocky moraine', it is fairly certain that smaller ice accumulation centres existed on Mull, Arran and in the Lowther Hills. According to Price (1983), the Loch Lomond glacier contained over 80 km^3 of ice and created an ice stream some 50 km long terminating in an end moraine which can be traced for about 40 km around the edge of the former lobe. As it retreated, the lobe held back several small pro-glacial lakes on the edge of our area in the dammed valleys of the Endrick, Blane and Fruin.

Moraines are found principally in the Highland glens and along the flanks of the Central Valley but this latter area is also extensively covered with glacial till and fluvio-glacial deposits which buried the pre-existing topography. For example, Price (1983) cites the Kelvin valley, north-east of Glasgow, where up to 60 m of sands and gravels are overlain by till 1–3 m thick from the last ice-sheet. In turn, the till is covered by up to 15 m of sands and gravels from outwash fans, kames and eskers. Glasgow itself is built in the middle of a broad drumlin field stretching north and south of the Clyde. These steep-sided features, up to 30 m high, have exerted an interesting influence on the city plan with Sauchiehall Street, for example, following a gap in this distinctive ENE-WSW orientated topography.

Despite these drumlins, and the remains of eskers and kame terraces near the city, some of the best depositional features are found farther south in the upper Clyde valley. Thus, Sissons (1967) has mapped the extensive glacial drainage system, including meltwater channels, eskers and kettle holes, which occupies the northern and eastern edge of the Tinto Hills alongside the Clyde. Even more celebrated is the large accumulation of fluvio-glacial materials near

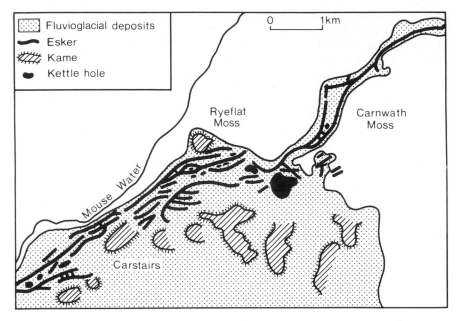

Fig. 4   The fluvioglacial deposits of sands and gravels near Carstairs in the Clyde valley (after
Price, 1983).

Carstairs. As shown in Figure 4, a complex topography of mounds and
hollows bears witness to the power of meltwater rivers at the close of an ice
age.

With the retreat of the Loch Lomond ice, more stable environmental
conditions began to prevail. In Early Postglacial times, the major landform
modifications were restricted to the coastal areas. As a result of the final
melting of the great northern hemisphere ice-sheets, sea levels rose to their
highest post-glacial level around 6000 bp. This rise promoted the
Holocene/Flandrian transgression marked by small marine embayments
around Girvan, Troon and Renfrew. During the last 5,000 years, the sea level
has fallen between 6–12 m exposing coastal marshes in the low-lying estuarine
areas and raised beaches along the steeper coasts. Inland, the main
geomorphological changes have been achieved by the rivers cutting down into
the wide valleys and transferring sediment to the lochs. In some cases, large
deltas have been formed such as that of the river Croe at Ardgartan near the
head of Loch Long.

Weather and Climate

Atmospheric conditions over Strathclyde vary systematically in space with
latitude (nearly 200 km from north to south), altitude (from sea level to over

1,000 m) and distance from the sea (about 80 km at maximum). Temporal variations are imposed by the rather uncertain march of the seasons and the even less predictable synoptic pattern of weather events. Of all these influences, the rapid deterioration of climate with altitude and the general exposure to imported air masses of great variety are probably the most important.

In view of the location of the region, it is not surprising that polar maritime air dominates the atmospheric circulation and that the circulation is often vigorous. The mean annual wind roses, depicted in Figure 5, show some tendency for predominant wind directions between south (170°–190°) and west (260°–280°), but exceptions do exist. For example, 140°–160° is most common at Tiree whilst Glasgow airport (Abbotsinch) is comparatively well sheltered from the north. In view of the Atlantic origin of most air masses, the humidity is characteristically high. Even in the middle of summer afternoons, the average relative humidity rarely falls below 60 per cent and rises to 90 per cent or more on most nights of the year.

Local topography exerts a significant control on both the direction and speed of the wind but the most exposed locations are invariably either on the coast or in the uplands. At an open, level site in Glasgow, the mean wind speed near the ground is little more than 8 kt and comparable to the average velocity in other cities, such as London or Birmingham (Plant, 1973). However,

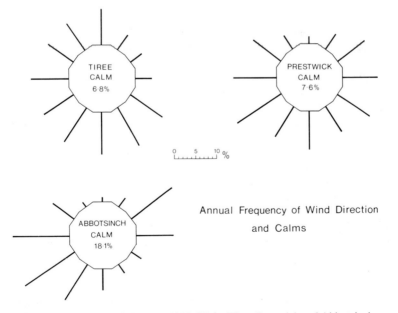

Annual Frequency of Wind Direction and Calms

Fig. 5 Mean annual wind roses (1957–71) for Tiree, Prestwick and Abbotsinch.

westerly gales, especially in winter, occur throughout the region and many locations have mean wind speeds more than double those experienced in Glasgow. For example, Tiree and Lowther Hill are two of the windiest places in Britain. Tiree is one of a handful of low-level stations ever to have recorded 60 kt or more as a mean hourly wind speed, with values of 67 kt in January 1968 and 65 kt in September 1961, and has an average of roughly 30 days per year with gales as opposed to about 5 per year at Abbotsinch. Even higher wind speeds occur in the uplands and Lowther Hill had a mean hourly value of 86 kt in January 1963. During the notorious 'Glasgow gale' of 15th January 1968, which caused 22 deaths and damaged 100,000 properties in the west of Scotland, gusts of 102 kt and 108 kt were measured at Tiree and Lowther Hill respectively.

The frequent passage of Atlantic depressions also results in a high degree of cloudiness, particularly in the uplands. But — again — there are exceptions, especially when it is appreciated that the best indication — the duration of bright sunshine — is one of the least variable of all the climatic elements. Thus, at Blyth Bridge (250 m OD near the regional border in the Clyde valley) the annual duration is reduced by upland cloud to only about 8 per cent less than at Abbotsinch (Anonymous, 1981). In the Glasgow area a combination of atmospheric pollution, surrounding high ground and the tendency for convective cloud to form inland during the afternoon produced a fairly modest mean annual duration of 1,266 hours of bright sunshine during the 1941–70 period. On the other hand, the Ayrshire coast is one of the sunniest locations on the western mainland of Scotland and, over the 1931–60 period, the 1,381 hours and 1,347 hours observed for Troon and Girvan respectively were equivalent to central London durations. Tiree is even more favourably endowed with about 1,420 hours of sunshine in an average year. In May, when anticyclonic conditions often prevail, the mean daily total exceeds 7 hours which is similar to the sunshine conditions on the south coast of England in that month.

Important secular changes in sunshine duration and visibility have occurred in the Glasgow area within recent decades as a result of reduced smoke pollution in the atmosphere. The Glasgow basin can occasionally experience sea fogs which are either carried inland from the Firth of Clyde with light winds in summer or, in the case of the east coast haar, are advected right through the Midland valley. More usually, local radiation fogs naturally result from the katabatic drainage of cold air into the Clyde valley from the surrounding hills on calm, cold winter nights. In the past, this process has been compounded by smoke particles trapped by the temperature inversion near to ground level. At high concentrations, such particles act as condensation nuclei and encourage the formation of so-called 'dry fog', i,e, visibility less than 1 km with a relative humidity of less than 95 per cent. Indeed, smoke pollution was so bad in Glasgow thirty years or more ago that visibilities of less than 100 m occurred with relative humidities as low as 75 per cent. Smoke pollution also had drastic consequences for sunshine. For example, in the 1931–60 period, the mean annual duration of bright sunshine was 8·3 per cent lower at Springburn (in the north-east of the city and directly in the path of the pollution plume) than at the airport only 10 km away to the west.

During the last two or three decades the situation has improved considerably with the advent of smoke control legislation and the trend in space-heating technology away from coal to oil or gas-fired systems. As shown in Figure 6, the mean winter (October–March) concentration of smoke in Glasgow has fallen by over 80 per cent from well over 400 μg/m³ to less than 50 μg/m³. As a result, the overall duration of fog at Abbotsinch has declined from more than half of all spells of light winds to around 15 per cent of such episodes (Harris and Smith, 1982).

The temperature regime over the Strathclyde region is highly complex. Although comparatively mild and maritime relative to some other areas of Scotland, the range of airmass experience ensures appreciable short-term variability. As noted by Halstead (1958), it is possible for the warmest winter day to have the same temperature as the coldest summer one, whilst summer nights are occasionally cooler than the warmer winter ones. The Glasgow area is sheltered from the coldest easterly and northerly winds of winter so that, under the more benign influence of the sea surface temperatures adjacent to the western seaboard, winters in Glasgow are rarely more severe than in places much farther south in England. However, for the remainder of the year, when latitude and solar radiation become more powerful factors than air mass characteristics, the temperatures are reduced compared to areas farther south.

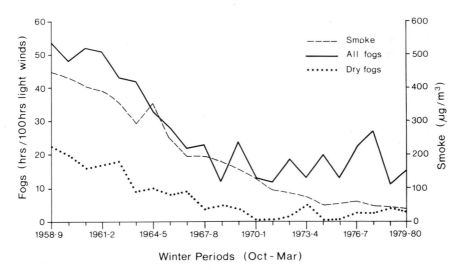

Fig. 6   The number of hours of all fogs and of 'dry' fogs per 100 hours of light winter winds at Abbotsinch related to the mean winter concentration of smoke pollution in Glasgow (after Harris and Smith, 1982).

If Glasgow airport (Abbotsinch) is taken as representative of low-level, inland conditions, the mean annual temperature of the period 1941–70 was 8·9°C with a mean maximum of 12·3°C and a mean minimum of 5·5°C. As elsewhere, the coldest and warmest months are usually January and July respectively with absolute extremes ranging from −17·4°C on 22nd January 1940 to 31·2°C on 4th August 1975. Ground frost can occur at any time of the year, although it is rare in July. Glasgow has about 60 air frosts per year which are confined essentially to the October–April period. The diurnal range of temperature is normally a good deal larger in summer than winter, varying from less than 2°C in January to an average of about 6°C in July.

Regional variations in temperature imposed by altitude and proximity to the sea are comparatively illustrated in Figure 7. Thus, Leadhills (387 m OD)

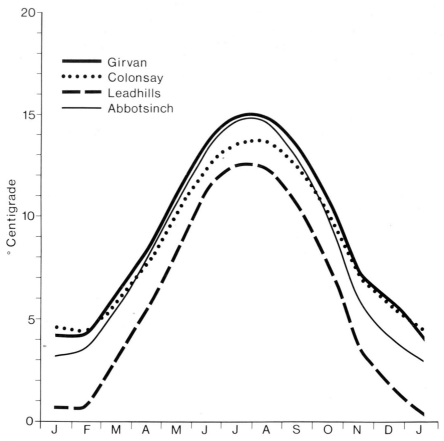

Fig. 7   The mean monthly temperature regime (1941–70) for Colonsay, Girvan, Abbotsinch and Leadhills.

has a mean annual temperature of only 6·5°C or almost 2·5°C less than Glasgow. Altitudinal differences are especially prominent on hot summer days and the absolute maxima at Leadhills are up to 4°C lower than those at Abbotsinch. Girvan is typical of mainland coastal conditions and experiences a much milder climate with an annual mean of 9·6°C. The main thermal differences between Girvan and Abbotsinch occur in winter when the relatively warm sea surface gives a mean monthly temperature advantage of at least 1°C to such coastal locations. In summer the differences are much less. Indeed, the development of sea breezes in July and August produces mean maximum temperatures at Girvan which are 0·5°C lower than the Abbotsinch values. An even more extreme maritime influence is represented by the thermal regime for Colonsay. Here the moderating effect of the sea not only results in a very low seasonal amplitude of temperature but also sufficient thermal inertia to lag the mean monthly extremes in February and August.

The most detailed relationships between topography and temperature are revealed on calm, clear winter nights when the maximum opportunity is provided for surface cooling. In such conditions the gravitational flow of cold air into topographic depressions of all sizes provides pronounced 'frost hollow' effects. These effects are well known in the Glasgow area which is predisposed to katabatic drainage from the surrounding moorlands on nights with strong terrestrial radiation. Abbotsinch airport, situated in a shallow depression at the foot of sloping ground, is itself a reasonably good example of a frost hollow. Therefore, although the minimum temperatures averaged over all nights are not dissimilar to those recorded elsewhere in the central lowlands, the absolute minima — observed on the coldest, clearest winter nights — are much lower and the overall incidence of frost is higher than at some other sites. For example, over the decade 1956–65, the airport recorded an average of 59 air frosts during the year as opposed to only 46 at Paisley a few kilometres away.

Frost hollow effects can contrast markedly with the artificially high temperatures characteristically found at night in built-up areas and universally termed the 'urban heat island'. For Glasgow all the evidence suggests a strong heat island with a rapid transition from the cold rural areas to the warm urban air on anticyclonic nights (Hartley, 1977). This pattern is well demonstrated in Figure 8 which shows the steep gradient of nocturnal isotherms found around the fringe of the built-up area under conditions of good back radiation. On this occasion the overall urban-rural temperature difference exceeded 8°C. This is fairly large compared to that reported for some other cities but it may well be explained by the topographic site of Glasgow and the compact development of the city as well as the favourable synoptic conditions during the early part of the night when the temperature traverses were undertaken.

Precipitation is usually considered to be the most variable of all the meteorological elements and, as might be expected, the Strathclyde region provides a wide range of experience. At the regional scale, spatial variation is

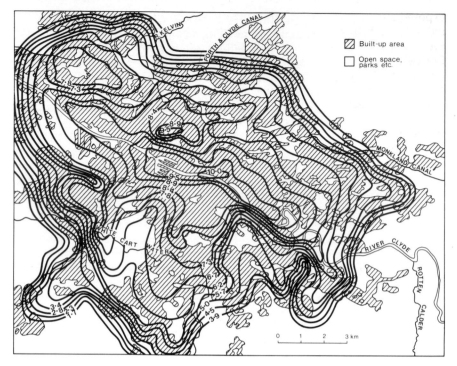

Fig. 8　The urban heat island in Glasgow recorded by traverses between 2130 and 0100 hours GMT on 19th–20th October 1975. Isotherms in degrees Celsius (after Hartley, 1977).

largely controlled by the tendency for both the rate and duration of rainfall to increase with altitude and nearness to the exposed west coast. Altitude is particularly effective in intensifying persistent frontal rain by promoting additional uplift and in encouraging convective showers in unstable airstreams. The result, as indicated in Figure 9, is a fairly close agreement between the relief of the region (Figure 3) and the mean annual precipitation.

The driest areas, which average less than 900 mm per year, are located in the middle Clyde valley around Lanark and along a short stretch of the Ayrshire coast near Prestwick. This latter area is one of the driest sections of the whole of the west coast of Britain and the whole of the Ayrshire plain has less precipitation than any other area of comparable size in the western half of Scotland (Plant, 1971). Immediately to the north of Glasgow, which experiences rather more than 1,000 mm each year, mean annual values increase rapidly. An extensive area of high rainfall (exceeding 2,500 mm per annum) extends throughout the Western Highlands from Loch Lomond to the northern boundary of the Strathclyde region. On the highest and most exposed slopes, mean yearly totals will be greater than 4,000 mm. Another index of wetness is the duration of rainfall. This also shows wide variations, even at sea level. For example, in the 10 years from 1951–60, it rained at Prestwick (9 m OD) for an average of only 702 hours per year whilst at Loch Sloy on Loch Lomondside the annual duration was more than doubled to 1,422 hours each year.

The mean monthly pattern of precipitation is illustrated for six representative stations in Figure 10. Allt na Lairige and Leadhills have been chosen to represent upland sites in the Western Highlands and Southern Uplands respectively. Girvan and Bonnington Power Station are characteristic of the Ayrshire coast and the Clyde valley, whilst Tiree and Islay supply a picture for the islands. Most of the stations exhibit the general west coast feature of

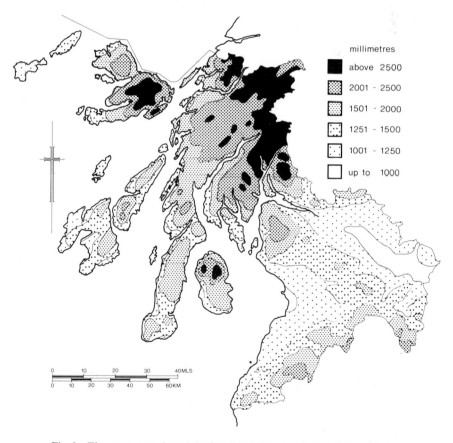

millimetres

■ above 2500

▨ 2001 - 2500

▦ 1501 - 2000

▣ 1251 - 1500

□ 1001 - 1250

□ up to 1000

0 10 20 30 40MLS
0 10 20 30 40 50 60KM

Fig. 9   The mean annual precipitation (1916–50) over the Strathclyde Region.

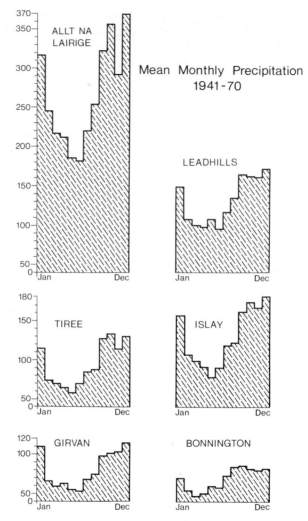

Fig. 10   The mean monthly rainfall regime (1941–70) for six representative stations in the
Strathclyde Region.

maximum values in early winter (often December) and minimum monthly
totals in late spring or early summer (usually May or June). On average the
first half of the calendar year is drier than the last six months.

The areas which experience large annual precipitation totals receive a
substantial proportion of intense daily falls. These are often concentrated in
the uplands but, even in the centre of Glasgow at Glasgow Green, there was a

total of 66 days in the 35-year period from 1931–65 when the rainfall equalled or exceeded 25 mm. The maximum daily falls range from about 50 mm in the vicinity of Glasgow to the massive 238 mm recorded at Loch Sloy on 17th January 1974 in the warm sector of a very active depression. This fall constitutes a daily record for Scotland and compares with the maximum one-day fall of 279 mm ever observed in Britain.

A particular feature of precipitation in Strathclyde is the combination of heavy rainfall with high wind speeds. Lacy and Shellard (1962) showed that the worst wind direction for such 'driving rain' in Glasgow is from the south-west and that the city suffers from this phenomenon more than any other comparably sized settlement in Britain. On the other hand, it must be admitted that the rainfall regime is also responsible for the abundant water resources of the Strathclyde region. The river Clyde, as well as several of the major fresh-water lochs, provides both water supplies and hydro-electric power. Loch Awe is the focus of a major power scheme and three other developments, known collectively as the Sloy-Shira complex, are found between Loch Lomond and the sea lochs of the Firth of Clyde. In recent years Loch Lomond has been increasingly developed for water supply purposes. The loch covers an area of over 70 km² and gathers water from a natural catchment about ten times as large, thus ensuring massive reserves stored conveniently near to the central Lowlands.

The erratic incidence of both snowfall and snow-cover reflect the vagaries of the Scottish winter and the degree of control exerted by local topography. In view of Strathclyde's latitude, the lowland and coastal parts of the region are remarkably snow-free. Snowfall is mainly confined to January and February but can fall on low ground in the Glasgow area as late as May or as early as October. On average, there are some 25 days per year with sleet or snow falling around Glasgow with probably less than half that number of days with snow lying at 0900 hours. Except in the uplands, accumulations tend to be slight. Thus, Lowndes (1971) showed that, in the 1954–69 period, Prestwick experienced fewer substantial snowfalls (at least 7 mm water equivalent) than the Isles of Scilly. However, conditions change abruptly with altitude. Over the 20-year period 1957–58 to 1976–77, the mean number of days with snow lying at 0900 GMT varied from 1 at Rhuvaal (20 m OD on Islay) to 39 at Leadhills (387 m OD in the Southern Uplands). The temporal variability of snow may be illustrated by the fact that at Leadhills in two consecutive winters (1962–63 and 1963–64) the number of days with snow lying ranged from 79 to 15 respectively.

Soils and Vegetation

The soils and vegetation of the region are relatively young since they have formed after the retreat of the last ice-sheet about 10,000 years ago. Some grasses and heathland species, together with dwarf birch, were able to colonise the mineral soils of Late Glacial times but it was not until the climatic recovery following the Loch Lomond Advance that a complete vegetation cover evolved. Forest colonisation was probably rapid in the early Post Glacial period and most of the region was covered with trees by 5000 bp. Brown forest soils were dominant and the main woodland cover was oak with significant stands of pine in the north. About 7500 bp the Atlantic phase of climate ushered in warmer and wetter conditions which led to the growth of blanket peat in the flatter areas. The spread of peat, combined with progressive forest clearance by man, produced a wide-spread decrease in tree cover which has only been reversed by afforestation in the present century.

Soil development has been mainly determined by natural drainage rather than the variety of rock types. Podsolisation has been the most common process and, together with the extensive occurrence of acidic rocks, this has produced imperfectly drained, base-poor soils in many areas. Much of Argyll, for example, is composed of peaty and iron-pan podsols. On the highest summits shallow particles of coarse mineral 'Alpine' soil may be found. Varying degrees of gley phenomena exist and such fine textured soils, with poor or very poor drainage, are characteristic of the wetter parts of the Central Valley around Glasgow. The most extensive area of fertile soil is coincident with the Ayrshire plain. This is principally covered with a grey-brown podsolic soil of variable drainage, although a well-drained brown soil of moderate base status is located in a coastal strip nearly 10 km wide in places. Blanket peat, occasionally over 3 m deep and dominated by sphagnum, is common in the uplands. In complete contrast, the calcareous sands of the machair form a narrow, wind-driven deposit on the low Atlantic coasts of several of the islands.

Owing to the impact of man, only a few rather remote or infertile sites now retain any semi-natural vegetation cover. Forest clearance has been mainly for agricultural purposes but the woodland had intrinsic industrial value and in many areas — e.g. around the Firth of Clyde — oak coppice was managed for charcoal with the bark used for tanning. Only fragments of the climax woodland vegetation can still be found as in the oak-ash complex of the Nethan gorge in the Clyde valley, the patches of pine wood in Glen Falloch north of Loch Lomond, the oakwoods around Taynish in Argyll and the relict survivals on a few islands in the boggy plain of Rannoch Moor.

Mostly the land is either built-over or dominated by agriculture. Sheep grazing and moor burning have been major factors in creating what are — essentially — anthropogenic moorlands and grasslands throughout the uplands. This is nowhere more apparent than in the Southern Uplands where trees have been replaced by rough grasslands, often with considerable amounts of heather and bilberry on the slopes and cotton grass, sedges and mosses in the poorly drained areas. The hills of Cowal have been similarly dedicated to sheep.

Farther north and west, the vegetation is slightly more diverse. For example, the peninsulas of Knapdale and Kintyre have some well-wooded slopes. Admittedly much of the cover is of introduced conifers but some natives survive in the steep tributary valleys. Oak and birch is the climax vegetation on the poorer valley soils, intermixed with rowan and holly (Ratcliffe, 1977). Alder and willow are found adjacent to the streams and in these wet, western woodlands, a rich ground flora of ferns, mosses and lichens exists. Near the highest, steepest summits, arctic-alpine species may be found.

The islands have a broadly similar vegetation pattern. Woodland is comparatively extensive, fringing the coast of Jura, Islay and Mull with oak, birch and hazel. Many island interiors have little to offer other than rather drab moorland but their prime botanical joy is the richly diverse flora of the machair. These are basically grasslands but provide a wealth of colour from other herbaceous plants such as buttercups, primroses, daisies and dandelions.

Commercial forestry has had an important influence on vegetation and landscape throughout Strathclyde. According to James (1958), the first substantial re-planting was undertaken privately around Inveraray in the seventeenth century but widespread activity awaited the establishment of the Forestry Commission in 1919. The most extensive plantations lie on the Cowal peninsula where the Commission began its work in Scotland with the purchase of the Glenbranter estate in 1921. Fourteen years later sufficient land had been added to allow designation of the Argyll Forest Park. This was Britain's first forest park and extends to over 250 km² between Loch Fyne and Loch Long. The main coniferous specimens are spruces, with Sitka and Norway spruce forming about 80 per cent of the plantations (Edlin, 1976). Lodgepole pine, Scots pine and three species of larch are also used. Poor soil drainage has been a major impediment to good root penetration and the wind throw of shallow rooted trees in winter gales has occasionally imposed limitations on timber production. For example, the gale of January 1968, estimated by Fraser (1971) to have a return period of 75 years, levelled in one night timber equivalent to five years of normal production in Argyll alone.

Despite such setbacks, commercial forestry is re-creating a woodland cover in Strathclyde. At the present time some 14 per cent of the region is under commercial forestry and, on current planting trends, this will have risen to 20 per cent by the year 2000. Thus, by the end of the century, the Strathclyde region will begin — at least in parts — to acquire landscapes not seen for several thousand years.

REFERENCES

Anonymous (1981), *Glasgow and the Clyde Valley*. Climatological Memorandum No. 124, Meteorological Office, Edinburgh. 17 pp.
Anonymous (1983), *Strathclyde Structure Plan 1981 — Consultative Draft* (Second Review and Alteration). Strathclyde Regional Council, Glasgow. 215 pp.
Bluck, B. J. (Ed.) (1973), *Excursion Guide to the Geology of the Glasgow District*. Geological Society of Glasgow, Glasgow. 181 pp.

Edlin, H. L. (Ed.) (1976), *Argyll Forest Park*. Her Majesty's Stationery Office, Edinburgh. 114 pp.

Fraser, A. I. (1971), Meteorology. In Holtam, B. W. (Ed.), *Windblow of Scottish Forests in January 1968*. Forestry Commission Bulletin No. 45. Edinburgh, HMSO, 3–7.

George, T. N. (1958), The geology and geomorphology of the Glasgow district. In Miller, R. and Tivy, J. (Eds.), *The Glasgow Region*. British Association for the Advancement of Science, Glasgow, 17–61.

Halstead, C. A. (1958), The climate of the Glasgow region. In Miller, R. and Tivy, J. (Eds.), *The Glasgow Region*. British Association for the Advancement of Science, Glasgow, 62–72.

Harris, B. D. and Smith, K. (1982), Cleaner air improves visibility in Glasgow. *Geography, 67*, 137–139.

Hartley, M. (1977), Glasgow as an urban heat-island. *Scottish Geographical Magazine, 93*, 80–89.

James, J. E. (1958), Forestry. In Miller, R. and Tivy, J. (Eds.), *The Glasgow Region*. British Association for the Advancement of Science, Glasgow, 88–96.

Lacy, R. E. and Shellard, H. C. (1962), An index of driving rain. *Meteorological Magazine, 91*, 177–184.

Lawson, J. A. (1981), *The Building Stones of Glasgow*. Geological Society of Glasgow, Glasgow. 29 pp.

Lawson, J. A. and Lawson, J. D. (1976), *Geology Explained around Glasgow and South West Scotland, including Arran*. David & Charles, Newton Abbot. 176 pp.

Lowndes, C. A. S. (1971), Substantial snowfalls over the United Kingdom, 1954–69. *Meteorological Magazine, 100*, 193–207.

Macgregor, M. (1965), *Excursion Guide to the Geology of Arran*. Geological Society of Glasgow, Glasgow. 192 pp.

Plant, J. A. (1971), *The Climate of the Ayr–Kilmarnock–Irvine Region of Ayrshire*. Climatological Memorandum No. 67, Meteorological Office, Edinburgh. 104 pp.

Plant, J. A. (1973), *The Climate of Glasgow*. Climatological Memorandum No. 60, Meteorological Office, Edinburgh. 21 pp. plus tables and illustrations.

Price, R. J. (1983), *Scotland's Environment during the Last 30,000 Years*. Scottish Academic Press, Edinburgh. 224 pp.

Ratcliffe, D. (1977), *Highland Flora*. Highlands and Islands Development Board, Inverness. 111 pp.

Sissons, J. B. (1967), *The Evolution of Scotland's Scenery*. Oliver & Boyd, Edinburgh. 259 pp.

Slack, H. D. (1957), *Studies on Loch Lomond I*. Blackie & Son Limited, London. 133 pp.

Whittow, J. B. (1977), *Geology and Scenery in Scotland*. Penguin Books, Harmondsworth. 362 pp.

CHAPTER TWO

THE RISE OF THE STRATHCLYDE REGION

S. G. E. Lythe

Origins and Early History

Strathclyde has been the sleeping giant of Scottish history. For the best part of seven centuries the very word almost ceased to have currency. One seeks it in vain, for example, on the early maps of Scotland: thus on the anonymous Italian map of *c.* 1566 the only 'regional' label south of the lower Clyde is 'Gallovidia'; Mercator, a generation later, has 'Cuningham' and 'Clidesdaill' but no Strathclyde. The loss of identity was so complete by the nineteenth century that the entry in the mid-Victorian *Imperial Gazetteer of Scotland* runs 'STRATHCLYDE. See General Introduction and the articles CLYDESDALE and LANARKSHIRE', and it does not even warrant a separate entry in Groome's *Ordnance Gazetteer* of 1901.

Yet today Strathclyde has become a household word, and not only within Scotland. The obvious landmarks in its revival have been the approval by the Privy Council of the title of the University, the designation of the administrative region created in the reorganisation of Scottish local government in the early 1970's, and the incorporation of the word in the titles of European Parliamentary constituencies. The extent to which commercial and social organisations have joined the band-wagon can be judged from the telephone directories where entries under 'Strathclyde' range from aluminium suppliers and caterers to pressure washing and rape crisis. And, partly through the publicity (or should one say prestige?) of the University and Region, the name has spread furth of Scotland. There is, for example, a growing tendency south of the Border to assume, by false analogy with the English system, that the Scottish regions have become postal districts and it is now common in the English press to see a town, maybe Kilmarnock, described as 'in Strathclyde'.

So, after centuries of slumber, the giant has reawakened. The study of its first incarnation is fraught with such difficulty that even the best authorities hedge their pronouncements with a liberal scattering of 'possibly', 'perhaps' and 'circa'. What is indisputable is that, a thousand years ago, there was a

23

recognisable political unit which, at its greatest extent (to quote Barrow, 1973), 'stretched between two famous boundary marks, the Clach nam Breatann in Glen Falloch, above the head of Loch Lomond, and the Rere or Rey Cross on the Western edge of Stainmore Common in the North Riding of Yorkshire'. Furthermore, as we shall endeavour to show, the nature and evolution of this territory had major implications for its later cultural and economic life.

The ancient heartland of this early kingdom of Strathclyde was the home of the British tribe known to the Romans as the Damnonii. In shorthand, we can call them the Dumbarton Britons. Much of their land had remained immune from Roman penetration in any sustained fashion; similarly they were to resist infiltration or takeover by either Scots or Picts and, culturally, they remained more akin to Wales than to most of Scotland. The rise of Strathclyde to become what Smyth (1984) has called 'the premier kingdom of the north' was signalised by the Battle of Strathcarron (c. 642) when, under their King Owen, the Strathclyde Britons overthrew the Scots of Dal Riata and when, thirty years later, the Northumbrian massacre of the Pictish warriors emasculated a potential rival.

Indeed the first major weakening of the independent Strathclyde kingdom was to come not so much from internal rivals as from the Vikings. In 870 a huge combined Viking force laid siege to the Strathclyde capital on Dumbarton Rock, a siege allegedly lasting the then phenomenal length of four months, ending only when the attacking forces cut off the defenders' water supply. The outcome was near-catastrophic. Apart from the slain, two hundred shiploads of captives were borne off to slavery in the Viking capital of Dublin, and though the Strathclyde king escaped he was, soon after, murdered with at least the connivance of Constantine I, King of Scots.

Within a short time the native dynasty in Strathclyde ended. But Strathclyde survived both as a recognisable political unit and as a kingship. Thus, at the famous Border Conference with Athelstan in 927, the King of Scots attended along with Owen, King of Strathclyde. The relationship is complex to the point of obscurity, but there seems no doubt that, partly through marriage, partly through military weakness, the kings of Strathclyde had become subordinate to those of the Scots and this form of client-kingship survived into the early eleventh century. Owen the Bald, King of Strathclyde, fought with the Scots to defeat the Northumbrians at Carham in 1018, but thereafter there is no clear evidence of even a client king.

It has been cogently argued, for example by Jackson (1969), that the termination of the native British dynasty in Strathclyde had far-reaching consequences involving, in effect, the obliteration of a northern enclave of Welsh-type culture. Taking up the theme, Smyth (1984) has produced evidence of a substantial migration of members of the upper social strata in Strathclyde who 'fled down the Irish Sea ... because they refused to be subsumed in the new Scottish realm'. Their destination was Wales with which Strathclyde had ancient links based on cultural and racial affinity, and with them they took the stock of literature and lore, of history and genealogy, which had nurtured the cultural identity of Strathclyde.

But, despite the loss of native rulers and cultural identity, Strathclyde was on the eve of the thrust south which carried its nominal frontier to the edge of Stainmore. Cumbria — in round terms much the same territory as the present English region — because of its marginal location had kept relatively clear of the internal conflicts in England and, if the archaeological evidence is any guide, had enjoyed a measure of material prosperity. As such it must have been a temptation to the native rulers of Strathclyde, and some historians, for example Duncan (1975), have detected indications that in the early 900's Owen may have pressed his rule temporarily as far south as the river Eamont in Cumberland. At all events, within a few decades the economic considerations were submerged beneath the strategic as the Danes increasingly used Cumbria as a stepping-stone between their kingdoms in Dublin and York. So in 948 Edmund (Athelstan's successor) overran much of Cumbria and granted it to Malcolm King of Scots in return for assurances of action against the Danish war-bands and longships, but clearly this compromise was unlikely to last for it left Cumbria as a Scottish-ruled salient thrusting into England, a threat unacceptable to the later Saxon, Norman and Angevin kings whose aim was the consolidation of the realm of England. It would be both tedious and confusing even to summarise the ebbs and flows of Scottish rule south of the Solway with critical changes in 1092 when Rufus occupied Carlisle and built the castle and in 1136 when (the English monarchy being in a state of confusion) David I restored at least nominal Scottish rule. What is clear is that by the latter half of the twelfth century the concept of a Strathclyde running south of the Solway was being abandoned: perhaps we might cite the Treaty of York of 1237 as the final admission of the facts of political life.

Nevertheless the long existence of Strathclyde as a political unit — whether independent or client — had consequences for its evolution and way of life in the centuries ahead. Barrow (1973) has argued that the most striking expression of this was the great extent and elevated status of the diocese of Glasgow 'whose cathedral was the cult-centre of Cumbria's patron saint, Kentigern or Mungo'. Until the southern end was lopped off to form the see of Carlisle, the Glasgow diocese included most of modern Cumberland and Westmorland; indeed as late as 1267 its bishop (no doubt as a bargaining counter) claimed that his authority still stretched to the Rere Cross on Stainmore. Even in its attenuated form, this great ecclesiastical unit did much to keep alive something of that sense of difference from the rest of Scotland which might otherwise have perished along with the end of the old British kingdom of Strathclyde. In short, the East–West divide in Scotland is rooted in the Dark Ages and in medieval history.

The effective take-over of Strathclyde by the kings of the Scots, driving out, as we have seen, the traditional British culture, created a vacuum, filled partly by the new ecclesiastical structure, partly by the equally alien system of feudalism. By the time it reached Scotland, roughly the twelfth century, feudalism was already a highly honed instrument at the disposal of kings and barons, and its imposition in Strathclyde was a rapid and deliberative process involving grants of immense territories to English or Flemish incomers. It created — or, perhaps more accurately, perpetuated — a pattern of large territorial holdings as when the first of the Stewarts in Scotland was granted virtually the whole of what was later the sheriffdom of Renfrew and when David Oligard (or Oliphant) acquired the 'land between the Calders' which became the core of the great medieval lordship of Bothwell. In this kind of way the feudalising process, whereby Strathclyde was more firmly integrated within the kingdom of Scotland, established a pattern of landholding which was to influence the social and economic development of the countryside down to the present century.

It will be immediately apparent that the Strathclyde of today, the administrative Region, embraces only the northern end of the ancient 'Kingdom' but reaches north and west into mainland and island territory which, historically and physically, belongs to the Highland sector of Scotland. Whereas Dumbarton lay near the northern frontier of the Kingdom, it lies today less than halfway on the long axis of the Region which runs from the headwaters of the Clyde in the south-east to Tobermory and beyond to Tiree and Coll in the north-west. In other words, that classic divide in Scottish geography and culture, the Highland Line, cuts north-east–south-west across modern Strathclyde, splitting it into two parts of roughly equal area: to the south a zone which (in Scottish terms) can be broadly classified as 'Lowland'; to the north and west areas of genuine mountain, land- and sea-lochs, firths and sounds, peninsulas and islands which just as evidently belong to 'Highland' Scotland. In short, modern Strathclyde is a reduced version of Scotland.

This picture is fairly reflected in population distribution, for north of Dumbarton there neither is nor ever has been any major urban development and the patches of dense rural settlement have been few and far between. But against that we must emphasise the abundant evidences both of early settlement and of high levels of cultural attainment. Because of easy access by sea, the islands and western coastlands were always highly vulnerable to invasion — often with dire consequences — but equally they were open to the infiltration of alien cultural influences. So, over much the same period as that when the old Kingdom of Strathclyde was waxing and waning, the history of Iona epitomises the clash of Irish Christianity and Viking longboats. The unrivalled collection of 'Dark Age' and medieval carved stones on Iona encapsulates the whole story: for example the stone carved on the Isle of Man from local slate and then imported to Iona, showing a ship and a smith with hammer and tongs forging a sword, but clearly acceptable in the heart of the Christian community. Regardless, apparently, of changes in social order or of religious belief, carvings on stone survive as testimony to the skill of craftsmen, ranging in time from the cup and ring markings of the Bronze Age to the late medieval monumental slabs (Figure 1). In the light of material evidence of this quality and quantity, the familiar bloodcurdling accounts of life in the northern and western part of the Region must be regarded as but one side of the story.

Nevertheless, just as the old Kingdom's quasi-independence bred a feeling of difference from the rest of Scotland, so this Highland sector was for long a debated territory not fully integrated with the Kingdom of Scotland until well

Fig. 1   The slab cross at Kilchoman on Islay (J. R. Hume).

within the reach of documented history. Crucial in this context was the existence, from the twelfth century to the end of the fifteenth, of the Lordship of the Isles, a powerful regime owing — at best — doubtful loyalty to the King of Scots. The Lordship arose under Somerled — his origin is obscure but his name might suggest Norse parentage — who effectively broke the dominance of the Manx-based Norwegian rulers and who, according to the plaque erected by the Clan Donald Society in the ruins of Saddell Abbey, was the progenitor of their Clan. Though periodically an embarrassment to the Scottish Crown (for example as a possible ally of the English), the Lordship became a relatively stable and sophisticated organisation with a calendar of ceremonies and councils on Islay and with charters (some in Gaelic, some in Latin) of a quasi-feudal nature. It is, therefore, a not unreasonable proposition that its ultimate suppression in 1494–96 created an administrative vacuum which the central authority in Edinburgh was not able to occupy, save, in the long run, by bloodshed and repression.

In fact the political history of these northern and western parts of the Region was to be dominated, down anyhow to the mid-eighteenth century, by inter-clan rivalry and by the manipulation of particular clans by the Scottish — and later, British — central government. Once the royal writ began to acquire real significance in the western fringes of the kingdom, the survival of clan territory and influence came to depend as much on diplomacy and 'pull' as on sheer physical strength. So, as Mitchison (1970) has written, 'the Macdonalds, though still a great clan, failed to show these qualities and therefore declined'. Lawlessness, especially on the fringe of the settled Lowlands, could bring fearful retribution as in the outlawing of the Macgregors and the banning of the clan name after their assault on the Colquhouns in Glenfruin in 1603. Yet throughout this calendar of feuding, the one clear thread is the rise of the Campbells whose head, notwithstanding temporary lapses from royal favour, advanced over the centuries from Earl of Argyll to Marquess and eventually to Duke.

The Western Fringe

So long as the clan system, with its hereditary jurisdictions and semi-military structure, remained the dominant feature of society, as it did to the mid-eighteenth century, its twin material foundations were territory and manpower. We can form only the haziest impression of population distribution before the eighteenth century, but Alexander Webster's 'census', compiled in the few years before 1755, provides a reasonably reliable basis for comparison with the official figures of 1801 onwards. The immediate deduction is that the northern and more remote island areas of the Region experienced much the same pattern of population rise and decline as characterised the Highlands generally. Argyll as a whole, with 66,286 in Webster's time, rose to a peak of just over 100,000 in 1831 and then fell off (sharply especially in the 1850's) to 73,665 at the end of the nineteenth century.

The smaller distant islands suffered even worse: Coll, with 1,193 in 1755, had only 432 in 1901; Colonsay over the same period fell from 1,097 to 313. But farther south the trend was different. Islay, with 6,891 in 1901, had grown by over 1,500 since Webster's day; Campbeltown, with over 10,000 in 1901, had doubled in size; whilst, to move into Bute, Rothesay had risen from 2,222 to 9,376 and the small island of Cumbrae from 259 to 1,769. It is plain that much of the north and west of the Region, whilst historically and culturally more Highland than Lowland, was subject to factors which enabled it to survive the traumas of the eighteenth century and to adjust to changing economic and social circumstances: the more effective exploitation of the natural resources of the land and the adjacent seas and, in selected cases, a measure of industrialisation based often on imported capital; servicing the relatively wealthy incomers who established either 'weekend' or retirement homes; and, thirdly, catering for the whole gamut of holiday-makers and tourists.

The more skilful employment of natural resources can be well illustrated for the closing decades of the eighteenth century from the instructions issued by the fifth Duke of Argyll to his chamberlains of Mull and Morven and of Tiree. 'The Instructions', writes Cregeen (1964) who edited them for the Scottish History Society, 'show us one of the most able and energetic landlords of his day, moving populations, setting down towns and villages, founding industries, meticulously controlling the life of the inhabitants of his estate.' The motive was financial, for without rationalisation he would almost certainly have suffered that insolvency which overtook many contemporary Scottish landowners, but to him emigration was not the answer. In language which Robert Owen might have used, he enunciated a policy based on the disciplined employment of the well affected: 'I'm resolved', he wrote, 'to keep no tenant but such as will be peaceable and apply to industry' — an injunction to be intimated from all church pulpits within his control. Essentially he aimed at more productive land use and the creation of related industries. Thus tenants on Tiree were required to grow flax to feed the new linen factory at Dunoon whilst local wool was to be sent to the new cloth and carpet factory at Clunary near the ducal capital of Inveraray.

Nowhere, perhaps, is the impact of proprietorial dominance more clearly illustrated than on Arran. Milne (1981) develops the central theme that Arran was 'roughly torn from the highlands and islands' and dragged protesting into the lifestyle of the lowlands. There were two very well-defined phases. In the first, the Dukes of Hamilton — the owners — undertook an economic exercise in the demolition of the old communal subsistence farming in favour of greater productivity and, hence, higher rents. Simultaneously, and largely in consequence, the island began its transformation from Gaelic- to English-speaking, and with that a great deal of its ancient culture faded into the mists of legend. This fusion of economic and cultural change, coinciding with an upward trend in population, led in the short run to both emigration and to island resistance, notably in the remarkable 'Revival' of 1812 when the Reverend Neil McBride emerged from years of obscurity to preach so forcefully at Kilmory that even the island smugglers temporarily abandoned their trade.

Nevertheless the full integration of Arran in the life of mainland Clydeside was delayed, partly through inadequacy of transport but mainly by the restrictive policy of the Hamiltons in keeping out speculative builders and expressly forbidding tenants to take in visitors. The break came in the last thirty years of the nineteenth century, beginning in 1872 when the appalling landing facilities underwent their first uplift by the building of Brodick pier, when steamboat proprietors and the Caledonian Railway vied or combined to take trippers from Glasgow in ninety minutes and when the Hamiltons began feuing sites for home-building by outsiders. Then, says Milne (1981), Arran was 'launched on its career as Scotland's Holiday Isle'.

By and large the attempts to raise industrial production in these northern and western areas beyond the level of the cottage spinning-wheel and handloom were visionary. The whole trend of industrial development — concentration, power, economies of scale, integration of processes — was against them. Nevertheless there were exceptions which created pockets of employment and enhanced local purchasing power. Thus outside capital, largely English, came in to exploit some of the more accessible wooded areas for the provision of charcoal for iron-smelting. The furnace at Bonawe (Figure 2), a classic example of the process and now happily preserved as an ancient monument, remained in blast until the 1870's. The making of whisky, an activity influenced in the eighteenth century by a complex of economic, social and legal influences, moved from the small and often well-hidden still to the conspicuous and indeed self-conscious distillery, proudly advertising its name and the unique characteristics of its product. Thus, Moss and Hume (1981), under the title 'Islay Malt', identify twenty-four licensed distilleries operating at various dates since the 1790's; Campbeltown had a similar cluster; John Sinclair set up a distillery at Tobermory in 1798, that at Oban dates from 1794 and that on Jura from *c.* 1810.

The development of these areas never suffered from the lack of 'expert' advisers, who, almost to a man, pinned their faith in fisheries as the great potential growth point. 'The whole coast of Scotland', wrote Knox (1785), 'may be considered one continual fishery', but it was not exploited with conspicuous efficiency and even where the governing legislation was sympathetic its administration was often clumsy and inconvenient. Nevertheless at a few points, most notably at Campbeltown, fishing combined with other employments (some allied to it) to produce genuine industrial town growth in an area where any form of urban development had been virtually unknown. Bitterly contested by the Macdonalds and Campbells in the sixteenth century, Campbeltown became a stronghold of the latter who repopulated it with loyal immigrants to such effect that by the 1750's — now enjoying royal burgh status — it already had a population of about 4,600 which, as we have already noted, doubled in the following 150 years.

But, by and large, urban concentration was associated with tourism or

Fig. 2 Bonawe Iron Works, Taynuilt, in 1976, with the charcoal-fired blast furnace in the centre, iron ore shed to the left and charcoal sheds in the background (J. R. Hume).

residential development and these, in turn, hinged on transport. With the coming of steam locomotion and steam navigation we can begin to detect — albeit localised and patchy — an element of integration between the two major parts of the modern Region. Faster and almost all-weather transport enabled the northern parts and the islands to draw on the Clyde for coal, building materials and household requirements on a scale and with a frequency impossible in the days of sail and horses. Places which, as late as the 1770's, were visited (and often written up) only by intrepid travellers, were, a century later, advertising their tourist and holiday facilities. It is significant how often hotel advertisements emphasised local transport facilities: the 'Argyll' at Dunoon was 'within one minute of the pier'; the 'Ardlui' on Loch Lomond had 'four arrivals and departures of steamboats daily'; whilst the 'Grand' at Oban had 'conveyance awaiting steamers'. Oban, in fact, is a fine instance of a transport-created town: its prosperity, according to Groome's *Gazetteer* of 1901, having been 'much enhanced by this perfecting of its communications with the south', the town fulfilling an essentially transit function for 'tourists go to Oban simply for the purpose of getting to somewhere else'.

Whilst the scenic attractions, fishing, sailing and stalking drew tourists from far afield, the major human flow, in terms of numbers, came from what — by the nineteenth century — had become the industrial heartland of modern Strathclyde. At the most popular level it meant short trips down the Clyde estuary (Figure 3) or to Loch Lomond with a huge concentration during the annual 'Fair' holidays. As family financial resources increased (both within the social structure at any moment and within society generally over time) so holiday plans became more ambitious, embracing, say, a week on Arran. And, as indeed has been the experience in most holiday resorts, the logical next step was the permanent weekend or 'second' house, at the top level a mock baronial castle for the shipowner at Rhu, for the more modest a villa for retirement at Dunoon or Rothesay. The effect was to create a view of the Region as the territory for both work and recreation, an attitude not seriously challenged until the promotion of cheap package flights to exotic beaches around the coasts of Iberia. The result persists: the typical Glaswegian will know Dunoon, Brodick and the Costa Brava, but — apart from the football grounds — anything north of Stirling is unknown alien territory.

The Heartland

In terms of the major indices of social and economic growth — accumulation of capital, expansion and concentration of population, rise of business units and so on — the developments within the northern part of the ancient Kingdom of Strathclyde were of such magnitude as to revolutionise the entire economy of Scotland and to influence the lives of men and women in every part of the world. Down to the eighteenth century the mainsprings of Scottish economic and social life had been the coastal and riparian burghs of the East Coast, largely because of their European links. To a quite remarkable

Fig. 3 The *Columba* of David MacBrayne & Son calling at Rothesay Pier in about 1885 (McLean Museum, Greenock).

extent Edinburgh was able to counter the loss of political functions following the Act of Union by establishing a near monopoly within the Scottish legal system and by generating — behind the image of 'the Athens of the North' — the cultural and literary output which is the most obvious evidence of the Scottish Enlightenment. But the dominant theme in Scottish Economic History and the most dramatic change in terms of population distribution was the great swing to the west, notably to Clydeside.

Down to the late seventeenth century Glasgow, still recovering from the loss of prestige with the break-up of its great diocese in the previous century, was not more than one of the group of medium-sized burghs in the southern part of the present Region. Nearby Rutherglen and, twenty or thirty miles away, Lanark and Ayr, were old-established urban centres with their own traditions and burghal paraphernalia. Even then, however, there were signs of vitality in Glasgow with the emergence of a stronger mercantile element, made up in part at least of families who had profited from the redistribution of pre-Reformation Church lands, and who, well before the legalising of the trade in 1707, were beginning to edge their way into trans-Atlantic colonial commerce. So whilst the popular image of Clydeside is one of heavy industry, and whilst the overseas trade of the Clyde has today shrunk to minor proportions, it must be emphasised that the initial impetus to the rise of Glasgow above its neighbouring burghs and ultimately to the status of the second biggest city in Britain came from overseas commerce.

As aspects of this have already been examined in recent scholarly works, by Devine (1975), Slaven (1975) and others, and as a more comprehensive examination is promised in the Glasgow History project currently under way in the University of Strathclyde, we may attempt to focus on headlines only. The first major triumph came when, after a hesitant start, the Glasgow merchants established something like a monopoly of the American tobacco trade to Britain, and, because much of the activity was of *entrepôt* nature, a major foothold in the supply of tobacco to France and Holland. Though the merchants and shippers involved continued to handle tobacco after the American War of Independence, the direct physical participation of the Clyde ports shrank after 1776 to a mere shadow of the level attained in the previous three decades, but the boom had had a decisive influence in accelerating the emergence of Glasgow as a major growth point in the British economy generally. Though the precise implications for Glasgow await fuller examination, it is plain that the boom had demonstrated the importance of efficiency in merchanting; it had led to the establishment of a network of Glasgow-controlled agencies in North America; it had provided a market for local industrialists; its profits had enormously enhanced the capital resources of the leading merchant families; it had triggered off the first positive measures to improve the Clyde waterway which, continued into the nineteenth century, eventually enabled deep sea-going vessels to reach the Broomielaw, so diminishing Glasgow's traditional dependence on Port Glasgow and the outports farther down the river.

Threatening as the disruption of the tobacco trade may have been, the overall level of commerce on the Clyde recovered rapidly, based, in part anyhow, on a switch to the West Indies and to sugar and cotton and in part to the expansion of coastal traffic, itself a reflection of expanding local industrial output. It may come as something of a surprise to those who picture Clydeside industry in terms of shipbuilding and heavy engineering to discover that its strength in the eighteenth and early nineteenth centuries lay in textiles. Because it enjoyed a measure of state subsidy, the output of linen cloth from the 1720's to the 1820's is unusually well documented and the statistics, organised on a county basis, reveal a quite remarkable pattern of regional shifts. In 1727/28 the County of Forfar produced *c*. 23 per cent by quantity of Scotland's marketable linen: in 1821 it produced *c*. 62 per cent of a total which had increased by a factor of over 16. By contrast, the share of the counties around the Clyde which represented *c*. 20 per cent in 1727 and had climbed to 25–30 per cent by 1755–75, fell to a quite negligible figure by 1821. The Clydeside sector of the industry, though always second to Forfar in terms of quantity, was in general at the 'fine' end of the trade so that, in the peak years around 1760, it was producing at least 40 per cent of Scotland's output by value. Furthermore, because of its commercial links, Glasgow controlled much of the trade with a sophisticated market in handkerchiefs, 'bengals', 'carolines', cambrics and thread.

The sharp decline in Clydeside linen production after *c*. 1780, far from being a retreat from textiles, reflected a swing to cotton. Because, apart from bleaching, production was still carried out by small units not far removed from the traditional 'cottage' level but depending increasingly on imported raw material and external markets, the real control (and the mobile capital) lay in the hands of merchants who were highly sensitive to opportunities and to developments elsewhere. To a quite remarkable extent the pioneers in the West of Scotland cotton industry — the Finlays, Dale, the Buchanans, James Monteith and so on — all had experience of flax or linen marketing, all were aware of the potentialities and merits of American raw cotton and all were informed of the technical changes in power spinning in England. Sometimes in collaboration with local lairds, sometimes drawing on England for managerial backing (notably in Robert Owen), they created the first major industrial concentrations at — originally — water-power sites some of which (notably New Lanark, Figure 4) survive virtually intact for the attention of the industrial archaeologists. Steam, first for spinning and then, slowly, for weaving, completed the process both of mechanisation and concentration until, by the mid-nineteenth century, the Scottish cotton industry was itself falling victim to the even more vigorous concentration in Lancashire. Though there were flickers of revival of cotton in Glasgow in the 1870's and '80's the trend can be summarised in the history of one of the great mills, Houldsworths in Anderston: built *c*. 1804, extended 1854–64, became a bonded warehouse 1878, demolished 1969. In so far as textile production survived the late nineteenth-century collapse of straight cotton manufacture it was by

Fig. 4 New Lanark village in 1965. To the left is part of the School for Children with numbers three and one mills beyond. In the centre is the Institution for the Formation of Character and on the right Caithness Row with the bell-towered New Buildings beyond (J. R. Hume).

concentration on specialities: carpets in Glasgow and Kilmarnock, thread in Paisley.

In his challenging book *The Upas Tree*, Checkland (1976) took that legendary tree — which had the power to destroy all other growth within a fifteen-mile radius — as a symbol of the heavy industries which arose in and dominated the economy of Glasgow and its industrial periphery. Its roots were originally nourished by the widespread local deposits of coal and iron ore. Coal had been dug for centuries on a small scale for local use and for export coastwise and to Ireland, but output had never matched that of the Forth and Fife coalfields which commanded the valuable Dutch market. Coalmining's first significant growth came towards the end of the eighteenth century when the smelting of iron by coal fuel was introduced to the area (for example at Wilsontown in 1779, Clyde Ironworks in 1786 and Muirkirk in 1787) and when one of the great obstacles to the use of coal — high haulage costs — was being relieved by transport improvements such as the Monkland Canal. Even then there was no prospect of a major iron-producing industry until David Mushet found that the nodules of black stone which were often banded between seams of local coal were in fact rich in iron ore and until the introduction of the hot blast (commonly associated with the name of J. B. Neilson) led both to enormous economy in fuel consumption and to a better grade of pig iron. With this new technology, coupled with the advantage of low mineral royalties and cheap labour, the ironmasters (many of them also coalmine owners) rapidly assumed a commanding position in the British pig iron market. At the peak *c.* 1870, their output was 1·2 million tons of which over one-half was sent out of Scotland, and of the 126 Scottish furnaces in blast no fewer than 108 were in the counties of Lanark and Ayr.

In part because of this attractive export market for pig iron, the normal logical advance into wrought iron and thence into fabrication other than casting came relatively late. The ironmasters, willing enough to integrate backwards into coalmining, were slow to venture forward and, as Slaven (1975) points out, it is significant that when the first steelworks was established (near Cambuslang in 1871–73) its promoters came from the chemical industry, from potential customers in engineering and from science in the person of C. W. Siemens. In fact the lag arose not simply from the attitude of the ironmasters; by the later nineteenth century local ore (which in any event was unsuitable for the Bessemer process of steelmaking) was running low, the English had already practically cornered the lucrative market in railway metals, the lack of integration with pig-iron production increased costs and the shipbuilders, the great potential market, were exacting in their specifications.

Readers unfamiliar with the minutiae for Clydeside history may wonder why reference to shipbuilding has been so long delayed. The simple fact is that down to the nineteenth century the Clyde was no more associated with shipbuilding than several Scottish rivers and a good deal less than some. The first inklings of possible expansion came, appropriately in the area where

James Watt spent his early creative years, with experiments in the application of steam power to navigation. The first major surge forward followed relatively quickly, thanks largely to the engineering talents of the Napiers, so that by 1850 the Clyde was building two-thirds of Britain's steam tonnage output and almost all of that was in iron hulls. In other words, this was a 'new technology' industry, owing little to tradition at a time when traditionalists in wood and sail elsewhere were fighting for survival. In the second, and greater, surge, Clyde shipbuilding (Figure 5) was to assume global significance, its output by 1913 representing 18 per cent of all the world's new tonnage. Whilst it is obvious that the industry drew some strength from the local production of steel and coal, its success stemmed from a combination of favourable factors: the abundant labour supply from which it could select and train a permanent cadre of skilled craftsmen; the rapid evolution of interrelated specialisations — brass-founding, cabin-fitting and the like; the value of the label 'Clyde built' as a token of quality; the employment of new designs in hull construction and in marine engines. It is no accident that the Departments of Naval Architecture in both Glasgow's universities were among the pioneers in the technological application of science to a particular industry.

In agriculture, as in manufacturing industry, the trend in the nineteenth century was inexorably towards specialisation. As we have seen, the lowland part of the Region — in effect the northern end of the ancient Kingdom — emerged from the Middle Ages as an area of great estates, virtually all in lay hands after the break-up of the old Diocese of Glasgow and the dissolution of the religious houses. As Strawhorn (1975) points out, Ayrshire in the eighteenth century had seven earls and, hence, a 'social hierarchy' dominated by great landowners. Reinforced by local small-scale industrial production of textiles, leather and the like, arable and pastoral farming supported a modest rural population serviced by and servicing the local burghs. Because of climatic conditions, notably the relatively high rainfall and relatively mild winters, the emphasis in the agrarian 'improving' movement lay principally on rationalisation of the field pattern and of holdings generally and on the evolution of the Ayrshire breed of cattle. So the natural endowments of the area were linked to demand: the frost-free coastlands produced the early potatoes, the inland pastures produced the raw material for the 'Dunlop' and other cheese which farmers carted to Glasgow and then, especially as urban cow-keeping declined, the flood of milk which (contrary to scurrilous legend) Glasgow drank daily. To quote again from Strawhorn (1975), 'Ayrshire farming entered the twentieth century with a dairy economy producing cheese, liquid milk, bacon and pedigree cattle'.

Conclusion

The interrelationship between economic change and population growth is so complex that cause and effect are not easily identified. Similarly there is no simple formula to explain the balance between the 'push' and 'pull' forces

Fig. 5   Berths at the Greenock and Grangemouth Dockyard Co., 1910. The vessel on the far left is framed and is being plated. The next one is having the floors (vertical plates) attached to the keel, and the ship on the right, fully plated, is being prepared for launching (Collection of J. R. Hume).

which have induced hundreds of thousands of people to move into the Strathclyde area over the past two centuries. The rise of Glasgow and its immediate environs over this period has been the most dramatic manifestation of human mobility. It is true that, partly because it escaped the worst excesses of the Civil Wars, Glasgow in the seventeenth century recovered from the loss of its medieval ecclesiastical status; but, even so, its population around 1750 was not much more than one-half of that of Edinburgh. Then, within two generations, the flood began: by 1821, with 147,000, it already exceeded Edinburgh; by 1871 it had passed the half-million mark and around the First World War it had reached the magical million after which the curve flattened until the decline of the last twenty years. The upsurge is all the more remarkable when set against Glasgow's history of mortality (for example the cholera of the 1830's) and the persistently high incidence of various illnesses so that life expectation in Glasgow has normally been about four years below the Scottish average; against the environmental conditions of overcrowding, slum dwelling and polluted atmosphere, and against the very considerable emigration.

In part the population increase was self-generated, for, at least since reliable statistics have been maintained, Glasgow's birthrate has been appreciably above the national average, but in the early stages of growth the major contribution came from immigration to such an extent that, in the opening decades of the nineteenth century, only one resident in four could claim to be a Glaswegian by birth. So late as the mid-nineteenth century the balance between natural increase and immigration was still about half and half, and much the same pattern prevailed in the peripheral industrial centres. This was the greatest population shift in Scottish history, the incoming flood supported by tributary streams from the neighbouring rural districts, from the Highlands and Isles, from Ireland and, continuing in time, from Lithuania and Eastern Europe. They came as the labour force for employment by mainly local entrepreneurs and to construct the greatest Industrial Revolution/Victorian complex in Scotland. The great nineteenth-century flood, almost entirely European, diversified religious life, most conspicuously in the strength of Roman Catholicism with its own schools and its own sporting loyalties. Yet some catalyst converted them into Glaswegians, speaking the common tongue, observing the common way of life. When unemployment and frustration threw up the notorious 'gangs' of the 1920's, they did not necessarily divide on ethnic or religious grounds. Even, as Checkland (1976) points out, the Gorbals, that classic melting pot of races, 'was a true community assimilating a succession of immigrant groups — Irish, Jews, Lithuanians, bringing colour, and perhaps coherence'.

It would be untrue, and indeed insulting to other places, to equate Glasgow with the Region as a whole. Nevertheless in the higher echelons of economic life, in financial and commercial institutions, in the provision of advanced education, in the theatre and the arts and in politics, the Glasgow of the early 1900's exercised the leadership and dominance inevitable in the light of its sheer size and wealth. To the eye of the visitor (and indeed to many of its more sensitive citizens) it presented a jigsaw pattern ranging from magnificence to sheer disaster. Of the medieval town little survived save the Cathedral, for the other great landmark, the Old College lower down the High Street axis, was falling into dilapidation after its abandonment by Glasgow University's removal to Gilmorehill. The glories of the colonial trade, the merchant premises south of George Square, had sunk to the level of warehouses, their original association remembered only in the street names. With the centrifugal expansion on both sides of the Clyde, old and once-independent communities such as Gorbals served briefly as middle-class residential suburbs and then, as foundries and factories overshadowed them, succumbed to the insidious process of sub-division and sank to slum areas. One stage farther out the planned residential districts such as Pollokshields, where Alexander Thomson and the like displayed their eclectic architectural talents, survived as enclaves as industry and mass housing carried the conurbation yet farther from the traditional centre of Glasgow Cross. It would have been a bold man who, in the opening decades of the present century, would have dared to suggest a halt, let alone a reversal, in the expansion of Glasgow and its dominance of the surrounding area. Yet with 'overspill' of population, with the run-down of much of Glasgow's industry, with the decline in Clyde commerce and with the relegation of Glasgow to the status of a 'District' within Strathclyde Region, a reverse swing has in fact taken place stemming initially from the economic trends described by Nairn and Kirwan. Much of the effort of Glasgow's leaders in recent years — some of it plain to the eye of the beholder — has been directed to a fight-back: the aggressive publicity (for example the punning slogan 'Glasgow's Miles Better'); the creation of pedestrian shopping precincts; the drive to acquire international status for Glasgow airport; the 'facelift', i.e. stone-cleaning, of smoke-blackened frontages; the injection of new vigour into cultural life, notably in music, opera, the ballet and — with the Burrell Gallery — in the fine arts; the heady expansion of the University of Strathclyde — its very name implying a boast — and the revitalising of the University of Glasgow. So whilst the population of Glasgow proper may have fallen back by 20 or even 25 per cent, whilst Dixon's Blazes and Tennant's St. Rollox works and the railway shops of Cowlairs have been demolished and whilst that jewel of the industrial crown, Clyde shipbuilding, survives both attenuated and tenuously, Glasgow retains the central position in both the economic and social life of the Region which it has held since the days of Watt and Neilson.

REFERENCES

Barrow, G. W. S. (1973), *The Kingdom of the Scots*. Arnold, London.
Barrow, G. W. S. (1981), *Kingship and Unity*. Arnold, London.
Butt, J. (1967), *The Industrial Archaeology of Scotland*. David & Charles, Newton Abbot.
Campbell, M. (1977), *Argyll, The Enduring Heartland*. Turnstile Books, London.
Checkland, S. G. (1976), *The Upas Tree, Glasgow 1875–1975*, University of Glasgow Press, Glasgow.
Cregeen, E. R. (1964), *Argyll Estate Instructions*. Scottish History Society, Edinburgh.
Devine, T. (1975), *The Tobacco Lords*. Donald, Edinburgh.
Duncan, A. A. M. (1975), *Scotland: The Making of a Kingdom*. Oliver & Boyd, Edinburgh.
Flinn, M. *et al.* (1977), *Scottish Population History*. Cambridge University Press, Cambridge.
Gomme, A. and Walker, D. (1968), *Architecture of Glasgow*. Lund Humphries, London.
Hume, J. R. (1976), *Industrial Archaeology of Scotland (1) — Lowlands and Borders*. Batsford, London.
Jackson, K. H. (1969), *The Gododdin: The Oldest Scottish Poem*. Cambridge University Press, Cambridge.
Knox, J. (1785), *A View of the British Empire more especially of Scotland*.
Kydd, J. G. (1952), *Scottish Population Statistics*. Scottish History Society, Edinburgh.
Milne, A. P. (1981), *Arran, An Island's Story*.
Mitchison, R. (1970), *A History of Scotland*. Methuen, London.
Moss, M. S. and Hume, J. R. (1981), *The Making of Scotch Whisky*. James & James, London.
Reports of the Royal Commission on the Ancient and Historical Monuments of Scotland, especially *Lanarkshire* (1978) and *Late Medieval Monumental Sculpture in the West Highlands* (1977). HMSO.
Slaven, A. (1975), *The Development of the West of Scotland, 1750–1960*. Routledge & Kegan Paul, London.
Smyth, A. P. (1984), *Warlords and Holy Men, Scotland AD 80–100*. Arnold, London.
Statistical Accounts of Scotland, especially the new edition of the 'Old', *Lanarkshire and Renfrewshire* (1973) and the 'Third', e.g. *Glasgow* (1958). Collins, Glasgow.
Strawhorn, J. (1975), *Ayrshire in the Time of Burns*.
Youngson, A. J. (1973), *'After the Forty-five.'* Edinburgh University Press, Edinburgh.

CHAPTER THREE

LOCAL GOVERNMENT IN STRATHCLYDE

Arthur Midwinter

Structure

The basis of the present structure of local government in Strathclyde was established by the Local Government (Scotland) Act 1973, which created one Regional and nineteen District Councils in the area. In theory, the two tiers of government are not to be regarded as upper and lower tiers. In practice, Strathclyde Region provides the major services, and with a population of 2·4 million people (just under half the population of Scotland), a geographic area of 5,350 square miles, a staff of 110,000, a revenue budget of £1·4 billion and a capital budget of around £110 million in 1984–85, is big by normal standards of local government. The region also has the biggest District Council, the City of Glasgow, with a population of around 750,000, revenue spending of over £200 million, and capital expenditure of around £70 million in 1984–85.

The structure of local government was hotly contested during the passage of the Act. There was considerable opposition from within the existing structure to both the creation of Strathclyde Region, and the proposed incorporation of Bearsden and Eastwood areas within Glasgow (Keating, 1975). The former lobby was unsuccessful, but the second achieved its goals. The result was that the city-region concept, which dominated the Wheatley Report, remained intact, but tighter boundaries were drawn around Glasgow, and housing became a district rather than a regional function.

Regional functions are as follows:

Assessor (Rateable Valuation)	Fire Services
Chemist and Analyst	Industrial Development
Children's Panel	Police
Coastal Protection	Public Transport
Consumer Protection	Regional Parks
Diseases of Animals and	Registration of Births,
Plant Health	Deaths and Marriages
Education	Roads and Streets
Electoral Registration	Sewerage and Flood
Estates	Prevention

Social Work
Strategic Planning
Street Lighting

Trading Standards
Water
Weights and Measures

At district level, the councils have functional responsibility for another set of services. Housing is the major service, and they deal with the let, maintenance and repair of all local authority houses. The full range of District services is as follows:

Baths and Wash-houses
Building Warrants
Burial Grounds
Cleansing and Refuse
Clearance and Rehabilitation
District Courts
District Golf Courses
District Halls
District Parks
Environmental Health
Factories
Food Hygiene

Housing
Libraries
Licensing
Local Planning and
    Development Control
Markets
Museums and Art Galleries
Offices, Shops and Railway
    Premises
Public Conveniences
Public Health
Slaughterhouses
Tourism

The opposition which existed to the creation of Strathclyde Region continued till around 1978–79. Strathclyde was described as a 'bureaucratic monster' (Keating and Midwinter, 1983), and there was a school of thought that such a large authority could not co-exist peacefully with the proposed Scottish Assembly. Regions in particular were seen as being too big, too remote, and too bureaucratic and inefficient. Secondly, it was argued that the division of responsibilities between region and district was causing problems of co-ordination and duplication.

We can examine the first proposition by looking at the evidence that the creation of Strathclyde Region has increased costs and manpower. There is no doubt that real increases in expenditure occurred between 1975 and 1976. The growth in rates during this period was, however, due mainly to two factors: high levels of inflation and changes in government grant income. This needs some explanation. Local government is heavily labour intensive. Social services, like police, social work, or education (which account for a large proportion of total expenditure), are personal services, where local authority *manpower* is a key element in service provision. In the year 1975–76, when wage settlements were high, rates would have had to rise by 25 per cent merely to keep pace with inflation. Secondly, the post-reorganisation period was marked by a dramatic change in contributions from central government.

As I have shown elsewhere, whereas there was high growth in expenditure from 1972 to 1975, about 75 per cent of this increase was funded by growth in central grants. However, although increases of the same magnitude were incurred in the first two years of the new system, only 44 per cent of the additional expenditure was financed by government grant, a marked contrast (Page and Midwinter, 1980).

The key point here is that assessments about the impact of reorganisation on costs, rates and manpower need to take account of the dramatic change in the financial environment in which the Region was operating, from one of growth in expenditure and grant, to one of fiscal retrenchment, which became even more marked after 1977. Before 1977 there was a period of expenditure growth dating back to 1971, and indeed stimulated by the then Heath Government's economic and fiscal policy. 1975 did not mark any great discontinuity in the trends to growth of both spending and manpower, but the period since 1977 did. For example, capital expenditure, which is controlled by the Secretary of State for Scotland, fell by £107 million (46·7 per cent) between 1976/77 and 1982/83. During the same period, there was a considerable growth in the major client groups for local services in Strathclyde, the unemployed, the elderly, and families on low income, with the exception of primary school population (Strathclyde Regional Council, 1984).

Figure 1 displays the change in local authority manpower. The trends are consistent with central government policies over the period, with the only period of growth coming from 1978/79 when the Labour Government had restored modest growth in its public expenditure plans. Since 1976/77 manpower has fallen by nearly 5,000, from 98,666 to 93,899.

There is, in effect, little evidence to support the contention that the *creation* of regional councils led to a costly and inefficient system of local government. The changes in spending, local taxation and manpower are clearly related to

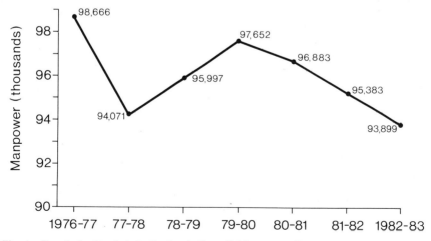

Fig. 1   Trends in Strathclyde Regional Council Manpower (Source: Strathclyde Regional Council Annual Report and Financial Statement for 1982/83.

other major national factors, such as inflation, and government policies on public expenditure. The arrival of retrenchment, however, could have an effect on how the public perceive the local government system. Given the complexities of local government finance, it is not surprising that ratepayers associated high rates increases with the major structural reform which had taken place. The end of growth also had an important effect in constraining the ability of local authorities to respond to demands for new public goods. The 46 per cent cut in capital expenditure has to be compared to a situation before reorganisation where central government consent to capital projects was always forthcoming.

This view was certainly shared by the Scottish Office in 1979, when the remit for the newly elected Conservative Government's manifesto included a commitment to review the local government system.

'With a view to improving the effective discharge of functions by Regional, Island and District Authorities —
  (i) to review the working relationships among the new authorities since 15th May 1975;
  (ii) to recommend whether any transfer or rationalisation of functions between them is desirable and consistent with fully maintaining the viability of the existing authorities' (Stodart, 1981).

Major upheaval was therefore ruled out from the outset, and the Committee's recommendations concentrated on concurrent or overlapping powers. Minor changes were recommended for functions such as planning, leisure and recreation and industrial development, but problems continue to occur because of the structural separation of responsibility for housing and social work, and for the other main infrastructure services, roads, water and sewerage.

The two areas which the Committee examined were the aspirations of the City of Glasgow District Council and Argyll and Bute District Council to become most purpose authorities. Glasgow's case was particularly well argued, and indeed commended a solution not at all dissimilar from the Government's proposals for the abolition of the Metropolitan Counties. The basis of their case was three-fold. First of all, that the concept of a region depended upon the acceptability of there being a legitimate strategic planning role at local level, which experience has shown *not* to be the case as all the key issues required approval from central government. Secondly, the case for expanded boundaries for Glasgow had been made in the sixties when population loss from the city was being encouraged. It was no longer the case that a wide strategic context was needed for Glasgow's housing stress. Thirdly, that the city was of a size that made it a convenient area for the administration of services currently provided by regions.

The Committee did not dissent from the latter point. Glasgow was seen as being quite capable of providing the functions it sought. Their acceptance, however, would have made a nonsense of the concept of Strathclyde as a coherent Region, and therefore the Committee ruled that they would be acting outwith their remit.

Argyll and Bute's submission is interesting, because of the patent differences between that District, as a sparse, rural area, with the urban dominance of the rest of Strathclyde. The District argued that the area had benefited in terms of public resources and the development of services by being part of Strathclyde Region. The only improvement they could imagine would be a single-tier authority, but this would require additional financial support from the Government. This gave the Committee a way out. They replied:

> 'If the District Council had told us that they were prepared to accept whatever financial disadvantages might ensue as a result of their request, our examination might have been made in a different light. . . . We are quite clear that, without major adjustment in the Rate Support Grant, the cost of keeping services at their current levels could not be contained. . . . We are therefore unable to accept the financial basis upon which the submission by Argyll and Bute was made to us' (Stodart, 1981).

In practice, authorities have been coming to terms with the structure. Strains are inevitable where organisational, professional and political priorities and loyalties diverge. Not all would disappear with the creation of a single-tier system. The recommendations of the Morris Committee (1975) on the need for joint committees between housing and social work authorities has had less impact than informal working arrangements between professionals at the operational level. Region and several districts have co-operated by trying to align policies and programmes in tackling problems of urban deprivation (Keating and Midwinter, 1982).

Authorities have, moreover, attempted through their organisation and management systems to counter the charges of remoteness. Services in Strathclyde, for instance, are divided into six sub-regions, largely corresponding to the six former County and City Authorities which amalgamated to form the Region in 1975 — Argyll and Bute, Ayrshire, Dunbartonshire, Glasgow, Lanarkshire and Renfrewshire. The sub-regions have a great deal of autonomy in the day-to-day running of services but at all times they operate under the policy and financial guidelines laid down by the Council.

In the City of Glasgow, a comprehensive area-based system of management has been brought into operation, whereby strong central policy direction at the corporate level operates alongside (with tensions) a local area structure concerned with monitoring and improving services at the point of delivery. The structure covers the whole city and operates through eight management areas. Each area is represented by a committee comprising District and Regional Councillors, MPs and community groups. Area management teams support this structure, with representatives of the main service departments and led by Area Co-ordinators (Keating and Midwinter, 1982).

Unless there is a major upturn in the national fortunes of the SNP or the Alliance, it would seem that the present structure will be with us for at least the next eight to ten years. The Conservatives have had their review, and Labour are more concerned with implementing a devolved legislative assembly than tinkering with local government, particularly when the present structure lends itself to dominance by the Labour Party, because three of the Regions are predominantly urban (Strathclyde, Fife and Central), providing extensive areas of Labour control over local services.

Local Elections in Strathclyde

Local government is a unique institution within the British system of government, as the only elected level of government outside Parliament. In Scotland there tends to be two distinct traditions with regard to local government, the 'Party Government' and 'Consensus' models of local government (Bochel and Denver, 1977). The Consensus approach assumes that local politics is basically a question of generally like-minded individuals overseeing the administration of local affairs. Candidates should be supported on the basis of their personal qualities and characteristics and, once elected, should represent local communities, not a party viewpoint. By contrast, the Party Government view suggests that local issues are matters over which there is, and should be, overt partisan conflict. This approach sees the 'party' as being more important than the 'individual', and local elections being a means of choosing a particular 'government' for the locality. Manifestos with local policy statements provide the means of ensuring responsible government, by providing choices for voters, and a means of accountability for performance. With the exception of Argyll and Bute, the Party Government approach is the dominant one in Strathclyde. This results in a greater degree of party competition and contested seats in local elections.

Strathclyde local politics are dominated by the Labour Party. The Regional Council has been Labour controlled since reorganisation, and Labour has increased its majority in each of the subsequent elections. This is reflected in Table 1.

The 1978 elections were interesting for two reasons. First, they marked the beginning of a period of nationalist decline, falling from seven seats (two had been gained in by-elections) to two seats. Second, that both Labour and the Conservatives had gains. In 1974 the Conservatives clearly suffered from

TABLE 1   NUMBER OF SEATS WON IN STRATHCLYDE
REGIONAL ELECTIONS

	Labour	Conservative	Liberal	SNP	Other
1982	79	15	4	3	2
1978	72	25	2	2	2
1974	71	20	2	5	5

being in national government. This is consistent with the research evidence on local elections in general.

'Local elections are widely interpreted as important and reliable between general election indicators of trends in the popularity of major parties. Underlying this is the assumption that local electoral behaviour is largely "nationalised" in that it reflects voters' concerns with national issues, personalities and governmental performance' (Bochel and Denver, 1985).

Labour's performance cannot be clearly explained by this phenomenon, as Labour was in government in 1978. What does seem likely is that Strathclyde Region is a relatively homogeneous area in terms of social and economic

TABLE 2   PARTIES' SHARES (PERCENTAGE) OF THE VOTES IN
         STRATHCLYDE REGION

	Labour	Conservative	Liberal	SDP	SNP	Others
1982	45·8	22·5	9·5	7·6	12·5	2·1
1978	43·0	30·0	1·8	–	22·6	1·0

characteristics. There are few of the marginal seats on which elections are won and lost. The same is true of several other Scottish regions, Lothian being the key exception.

Labour is also helped by the first past the post electoral system. Whilst it has always held around 75 per cent of the seats, it has only had between 40 and 45 per cent of the vote. Increased party competition has affected this little. The increased intervention of the new Alliance had more adverse effect on the Conservatives and the SNP than it did on Labour. This is shown in Table 2.

Strathclyde looks likely to remain a Labour stronghold for the foreseeable future. Labour has strengthened its control at a period when nationally its fortunes are in decline.

Similar patterns are found at District level. In 1980 Labour made sweeping gains and won control of fifteen of the Districts, losing control of only one of these in 1984. This is demonstrated in Table 3.

In Glasgow, Labour gained 60 per cent of the poll, an increase of 6 per cent. This resulted in the Party winning 59 out of the 66 seats. Again, there was an Alliance advance at the expense of the Conservatives and the SNP. The extent of Labour's dominance in Strathclyde, therefore, is in part due to the electoral system. The Party has succeeded in maintaining and increasing its popular support, in terms of votes, seats and, more importantly, in terms of councils under its control. The wider social change which has dramatically altered voting patterns in the rest of Britain has had little impact yet on local government in Strathclyde.

TABLE 3   PARTY CONTROL OF STRATHCLYDE DISTRICTS

	1974	1977	1980	1984
Argyll and Bute	*Ind.	*Ind.	*Ind.	*Ind.
Dumbarton	*Lab.	Con.	*Lab.	*Lab.
City of Glasgow	*Lab.	Lab.	*Lab.	*Lab.
Clydebank	Lab.	SNP	*Lab.	*Lab.
Clydesdale	Ind.	Ind.	Lab./Ind.	Lab.
Bearsden and Milngavie	Con.	*Con.	*Con.	*Con.
Strathkelvin	Lab.	SNP	*Lab.	*Lab.
Cumbernauld and Kilsyth	*SNP	*SNP	*Lab.	*Lab.
Monklands	*Lab.	*Lab.	*Lab.	*Lab.
Motherwell	*Lab.	*Lab.	*Lab.	*Lab.
Hamilton	*Lab.	*Lab.	*Lab.	*Lab.
East Kilbride	SNP	*SNP	*Lab.	*Lab.
Eastwood	*Con.	*Con.	*Con.	*Con.
Renfrew	*Lab.	Lab.	*Lab.	*Lab.
Inverclyde	*Lab.	*Lib.	*Lab.	*Lab.
Cunninghame	*Lab.	SNP	*Lab.	*Lab.
Kilmarnock and Loudoun	*Lab.	Lab./Con.	*Lab.	*Lab.
Kyle and Carrick	*Con.	*Con.	*Lab.	*Con.
Cumnock and Doon Valley	*Lab.	*Lab.	*Lab.	*Lab.

* Party of group with clear majority.

What Future for Local Government Services in Strathclyde?

The period since local government reorganisation has been dominated by the problems of managing retrenchment. Successive governments have sought to restrain and reduce local government expenditure. Unfortunately, the public debate about local spending focuses around expenditure, rates and manpower levels, rather than detailed analysis of needs and services. Strathclyde Region identified the two major problems in the area as unemployment and deprivation(and of course the two are related). Despite considerable administrative and political effort to tackle such problems (Strathclyde Regional Council, 1982), their solution is clearly beyond the scope of local authorities. The stark facts are that unemployment and poverty have increased in Strathclyde, and indeed, it is arguable the increase in urban deprivation is partly a consequence of the Government's public expenditure policy. Unemployment in Strathclyde has increased rapidly since 1979. It is now over 200,000, or 18 per cent of the working population, with 41 per cent of these classified as long-term (unemployed for more than a year). Similarly, the number of supplementary benefit claims increased by 59 per cent between 1979 and 1982. In terms of regional population, there are two significant trends, the growth of the elderly (plus 75) and the decline in school population.

These environmental trends have considerable implications for local government services, particularly in the light of the Government's continuing desire to cut local government expenditure and manpower. It is obvious that local government can only have a limited direct impact on unemployment and poverty as an employer and provider of services. Many services are provided for the community as a whole (e.g. fire, sewerage, roads) and not directly to specific client groups. Even education is discussed professionally and politically in terms of standard levels of service, with deprivation seen as a marginal issue. Authorities, however, are being asked to reduce spending and services in areas such as leisure and recreation when there are more people with leisure time, e.g. the unemployed and the elderly, who have less ability to pay for such services.

Realistically, what authorities can do themselves (i.e. in areas where they exercise managerial control) is re-order their priorities. In practice, this will mean changes at the margins. Strathclyde Region, faced with declining school rolls, has benefited in its ability to recruit and deploy staff across the Region, and thus achieve national standards in areas of deprivation. Community Work and Welfare Rights have expanded tenfold in Social Work. Community Involvement by the Police now gets a higher profile.

Problems arise, however, in managing retrenchment because of factors outwith the control of authorities. For example, the rate support grant distribution formula for education does not take adequate account of areas with acute population decline, especially when, as the Audit Commission report (1984) noted about secondary school closures, there are 'protracted timetables for statutory consultation and inevitable difficulties in "carrying" any reorganisation proposals through the communities affected by them'. For Strathclyde, this means a resource loss of around £2 million of grant income in addition to any general reduction in government support.

Government housing policy also has significant implications for local government. Since 1979 there have been two main thrusts of the policy: cuts in public housing expenditure, and attempts to promote home ownership through council house sales and increased grants to private sector housing. The result is an imbalanced policy which does nothing for those most in need, who generally live in the least attractive council housing, and cannot afford to buy their houses anyway. This amounts to over 40 per cent of Strathclyde's population.

Capital expenditure on housing has been cut by over 40 per cent since 1979, and it is to be maintained at present levels for the next few years. Public sector housing in Strathclyde still has considerable expenditure need. There are a wide variety of needs for modernisation and repair. Some 43 per cent of pre-war council housing in Strathclyde (59,000 houses) still need modernising; 78 per cent of the non-traditional post-war houses need modernising (21,000); 96,000 houses suffer from condensation and dampness.

A Strategic Review of Public Sector Housing Finance in Strathclyde Region concluded that the capital allocations to district councils in 1983–84 provided for only 30 per cent of the need, and that in many areas of deprivation, housing conditions will continue to deteriorate.

Faced with such severe problems of unemployment, poverty and bad housing, it is little wonder that many of those working in local government view as unnecessary aberrations the recent developments in government controls, such as rate-capping. There is little doubt, however, that the reorganised system of local government has allowed more sensitive managerial responses to retrenchment. The next ten years will provide further challenge for those who work in local government, and for those who depend on their services.

REFERENCES

Audit Commission (1984), The Impact of Local Authorities' Economy, Efficiency and Effectiveness of the Block Grant Distribution System. London, HMSO.

Bochel, J. M. and Denver, D. T. (1977), The Scottish District Elections. Department of Political Science, University of Dundee.

Bochel, J. M. and Denver, D. T. (1985), The District Elections 1984 — A One Plus Three Party System. In McCrone, D. (Ed.), *The Scottish Government Yearbook 1985*. Research Centre for Social Sciences, University of Edinburgh.

Keating, M. (1975), The Scottish Local Government Bill. *Local Government Studies*.

Keating, M. and Midwinter, A. (1982), Region-District Relations: Lessons from Glasgow. In McCrone, D. (Ed.), *The Scottish Government Yearbook 1983*. Research Centre for Social Sciences, University of Edinburgh.

Keating, M. and Midwinter, A. (1983), *The Government of Scotland*. Edinburgh, Mainstream Publishing.

Midwinter, A. (1984), *The Politics of Local Spending*. Edinburgh, Mainstream Publishing.

Morris (1975), Housing and Social Work — A Joint Approach. Edinburgh, HMSO.

Page, E. and Midwinter, A. (1980), Remoteness, Efficiency, Cost and the Reorganisation of Scottish Local Government. *Public Administration* (58), Winter.

Stodart, A. (1981), Committee of Inquiry into Local Government in Scotland. *Report*, Cmnd 8115. Edinburgh, HMSO.

Strathclyde Regional Council (1982), Social Strategy for the Eighties.

Strathclyde Regional Council (1984), Annual Report and Financial Statement 1983/84.

CHAPTER FOUR

THE CITY OF GLASGOW

George Gordon

Popular perceptions of a city are invariably particular, partial and imprecise or even inaccurate. Such a situation is scarcely surprising because the images are mental simplifications of a complex reality, involving the interplay, in time and space, of the web of relationships connecting economy, society and built-environment.

Like other great cities, Glasgow has been variously labelled. At the peak of the industrial era it laid claim to the title Second City of the Empire. At that time, the products of shipbuilding, locomotive construction and engineering were sold throughout the world and Clydeside was a leading British and international manufacturing region. Yet the success and prosperity encapsulated in that image was not a true indicator of the quality of life of many citizens who lived in small, unhealthy and overcrowded tenement flats and had poorly paid, insecure jobs. Subsequently, the recognition of these social problems earned the city less flattering images, such as in *No Mean City* and in several post-1945 reports on housing and social conditions. Paradoxically whereas Victorian boosterism tended to stress economic success and relegate social problems and deficiencies of the built-environment to lesser importance, modern imagery has witnessed the opposite swing of the pendulum with equally unfortunate distorting influences. The Glasgow's Miles Better campaign is a much-needed attempt to redress the balance and draw attention to recent achievements and successes. There is always a potential danger that the projection of positive images is used as an excuse to conceal some unpalatable truths. Nonetheless, there are substantial economic and social benefits to be derived from an upsurge in the confidence of the community, as witnessed by the recent growth of the tourist industry in Glasgow.

The following account investigates the topics of economy, society and built-environment from the medieval origins of the burgh to the present-day city.

The Pre-Industrial City

Modern Glasgow occupies most of the undulating lowland encompassed by the lava-based uplands of the Kilpatrick Hills, Campsie Fells, Gleniffer Braes and Cathkin Braes. Within this hollow much of the topographic variation stems from a product of glaciation, some 180 drumlins, with their distinctive steep stoss and gentler lee slopes indicating the direction of ice movement. A further topographic feature, but of variable dimensions, is the flood plain of the Clyde.

During the last quarter of the twelfth century the Bishop of Glasgow received royal charters conferring burghal status on the settlement and conveying rights to hold weekly markets and an annual July fair. Glasgow became one of a small number of ecclesiastical burghs until such rights were abolished in the wake of the Reformation.

Medieval Glasgow developed on a sloping site formed by a raised beach and a marine terrace above the flood-plain and to the north of the Clyde and west of the Molendinar Burn. A pre-burghal nucleus centred on the Cathedral. Gibb (1983) suggested that the shrine of Kentigern attracted pilgrims which fostered a small pre-charter market in the vicinity of the Cathedral. By the end of the twelfth century the principal urban focus was located closer to the edge of the flood-plain at the intersection of the route from the Cathedral to a ford across the Clyde and an east–west track following the alignment of the raised shoreline. The commercial core of the burgh displayed a distinctive T-shaped plan and was spatially separated from the religious district on the upper terrace. Gibb (1983) outlined a convincing conjectural reconstruction of the growth of medieval Glasgow involving marked expansion of the T-shaped core of the burgh, modest increment around the Cathedral and substantial urban development of the intervening land. In addition to the expanding built area of the burgh there was also large tracts of agricultural land and undivided waste or common land controlled by the burgh. These lands were located beside the Clyde, on the eastern fringes of Gallowmuir and, more extensively, to the north of the burgh on the Wester and Easter Commons (Gibb, 1983).

In addition to the religious landholdings in the Cathedral precinct, religious houses were major landowners in other parts of the late medieval burgh. Thus in the second half of the fifteenth century the monastery of the Blackfriars occupied a substantial site on the eastern side of the High Street immediately north of the original location of Glasgow University. The remaining burgage plots were of a more typical linear form with a narrow 'head' fronting the street. Originally the house was located at the head of the plot but subsequent infilling of the rear of burgage plots created a more complex morphology, access occurring by means of closes or wynds. Land uses were sorted into broad groupings based upon function but both workshop and dwelling place were normally coincident. Medieval Glasgow was much smaller than medieval Edinburgh, a fact which had a number of influences on the urban morphology of the settlement. Firstly, there was less pressure on space than occurred in medieval Edinburgh, resulting in a lesser degree of overbuilding, infilling and multi-storey development. Secondly, the pattern of land use may have been less complex than that in Edinburgh. For example, by the fifteenth century the latter had a detailed locational plan of market sites authorised by royal decree.

After the Reformation, Glasgow became a Royal Burgh. Pryde (1958) suggested that municipal powers had developed from the mid-fifteenth century, citing as evidence the creation of the first provost of the city in 1453 and the fact that royal confirmation in 1492 of burghal privileges was addressed to the burgh rather than the bishop. Early in the sixteenth century Glasgow ranked eleventh amongst Scottish towns in the amount of stent tax levied but by the end of the century it had risen to fifth place (Pryde, 1958). By the later date only Edinburgh, Dundee, Aberdeen and Perth stood higher, beneficiaries of the geography of contemporary trade routes and the disposition of international markets. Thus the evidence appears to suggest that Glasgow experienced a major phase of economic growth during the sixteenth century. It is tempting to correlate this prosperity with the abolition of clerical authority, but some of the evidence of economic growth pre-dates the Reformation, although there does seem to have been an upsurge in the local economy in the second half of the century.

There is little evidence to indicate that Glasgow suffered in terms of the rate of economic and physical growth as a result of almost four centuries of church control. Indeed, Pryde (1958) postulated that, on balance, it had probably benefited from the situation. Nevertheless, the post-Reformation growth of Glasgow does raise interesting questions about the effects of a change in power and about the generative forces operating in the local economy. Smout (1960) pointed to the emergence of Glasgow as the major urban centre (Figure 1) in western Scotland, drawing upon the resources of a substantial rural hinterland and trading with Ireland as the principal factors stimulating economic growth. It was also a phase of population growth from an estimated total of 4,500 in 1556 to more than 7,600 people in 1610 (Pryde, 1958). The later figure may seem modest by modern standards or when compared to the statistics for the city between 1851 and 1951, but it represented the status of a substantial market town in the context of the first decade of the seventeenth century. Subsequent population increase can be measured by estimates for 1712 and 1755 which respectively numbered the residents of the city to be 13,800 and 23,500.

This phase has been described as the growth of the Merchant City. In fact, the early years were associated with increasing power of both merchants and trades and with the struggle between the two factions to gain control of the Town Council, although it was not until 1690 that the town council acquired the right to choose the magistrates. Traditionally the latter had been selected by the archbishop although for a period in the seventeenth century this privilege was awarded to the Duke of Lennox. In addition to the evolution of municipal politics, the period of the Merchant City coincided with a quickening of the pace of economic and urban development. By the middle of the seventeenth century Glasgow had become a major Scottish port, in spite of the deficiencies of the Clyde as a waterway. Indeed the city was forced to use

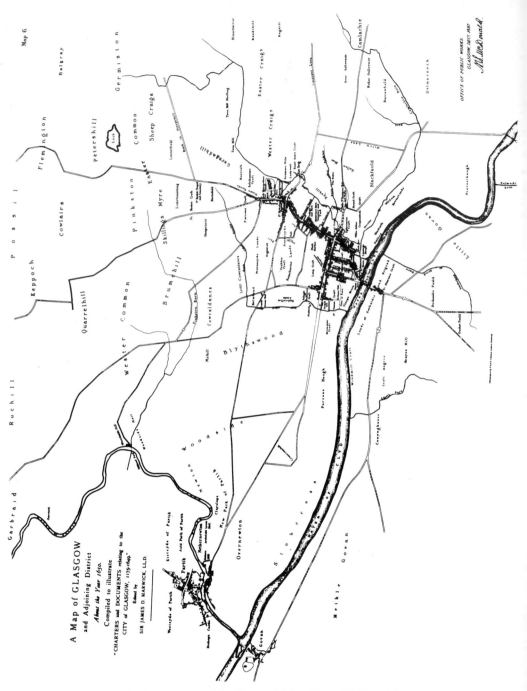

Fig. 1   Glasgow *c.* 1650. Source: J. Marwick and R. Renwick.
Charters and Documents relating to the City of Glasgow.

outports on the Ayrshire coast because shoals and silting impeded the Clyde. A thriving local trade was supplemented by increasing contacts with Ireland and Europe. For example, Glasgow imported wine and salt from France and in return supplied furs, linens, tartans and skins (Gibb, 1983).

In the later decades of the century Glasgow merchants engaged in the Atlantic trade, with tobacco featuring amongst the new imports. Glasgow subscribers figured prominently in the abortive Darien scheme, an event which illustrated the high risks associated with some of the new trading initiatives. Equally, the projects could also produce great profits and a new wealthy class emerged, the merchant families.

Early in the seventeenth century a quay had been built at Broomielaw but the river channel was of inadequate depth and obstructed by shoals and bars. With the increase in maritime trade the council acquired land near Greenock on the south bank and developed a new outport, Port Glasgow. This solution still necessitated transhipment of goods but it was several decades before an adequate shipping channel was created, as a result of engineering works designed by John Golbourne, and ocean-going vessels could unload at Broomielaw.

Commerce and manufacturing benefited from increased trade. Gibb (1983) refers to woollen- and linen-making, silk weaving, candle-making, soap-making and sugar refining. Some activities introduced foreign expertise whilst others were based upon imported raw materials. Additionally Glasgow acquired characteristic port industries such as ropeworks and glassworks. Demographic and economic growth also stimulated local crafts, commerce and construction. Between 1550 and 1700 there was a small extension of the built-up area, notably with the development of land between Saltmarket and Stockwellgate and to a lesser degree on lands east and west of the High Street.

The flowering of the tobacco trade in the eighteenth century broadly coincided with the transformation phase from pre-industrial to the industrial city of the ages of cotton, iron and shipbuilding (Gordon, 1983).

Devine (1983) discussed the importance of the emergence of a strong mercantile class in the late seventeenth and early eighteenth centuries in providing the business foundations for the rapid expansion of the industrial economy of Scotland in the second half of the eighteenth century. In Glasgow one major new section of the pre-industrial mercantile class were the tobacco lords (Devine, 1975). From modest levels of tobacco imports at the start of the eighteenth century, by 1771 the volume handled had risen to over 46 million lbs., equivalent to 54 per cent of the total British imports of tobacco. Most of the tobacco was re-exported to Europe without further processing. Other imports from America included rum, sugar, cotton and ginger (Gilfillan and Moisley, 1958), whilst Glasgow merchants despatched a wide range of manufactured goods to the American colonies and the West Indies, e.g. textiles, iron goods, earthenware, stoneware, soap and glass. The Clyde ports also conducted a vigorous trade with Europe and Ireland but by 1771 it was tobacco which dominated, accounting for 38 per cent of Scottish imports.

Industry prospered with more than a score of new branches of industry commencing operation. Several banks and money houses were formed to handle the increased scale and complexity of financing trade and industry.

The urban area also grew. In the first half of the eighteenth century the principal directions of growth were to the south, south-west and south-east of the old heart of the city, with King Street being one of the most notable new developments. However, the scale of urban increment was modest, particularly when compared to the major phase of westward expansion which occurred during the Georgian era. Within the span of a few decades a series of streets (Figure 2) were laid out to the north and west of Stockwell Street, tentatively at first but soon in the creation of middle-class residential suburbs. Speculative ventures on the eastern periphery of the city and to the south of the river in the independent settlement of Gorbals failed to become established as middle-class residential districts, leaving the western zone virtually unchallenged in the emerging segregated social topography of Georgian Glasgow.

The Industrial City

The highlights of the industrial economy of late Georgian, Victorian and Edwardian Glasgow have been described elsewhere in this volume and in many other works (Cunnison and Gilfillan, 1958; Miller and Tivy, 1958; Checkland, 1964; Kellett, 1967; Lythe and Butt, 1975; Slaven, 1975; Daiches, 1977; Adams, 1978; Gibb, 1983; Gordon, 1983). Broadly, three industries, cotton, iron and shipbuilding, successively wore the mantle of leading activity. In detail, however, the story is more complex. There were, for example, several major downswings in the economy, which had particularly marked effects upon activities prone to the cyclical state of the market such as the construction industry. These oscillations had a sharp effect on the workforce which was laid off during a recession or, at best, experienced short-time working or spasmodic employment (Treble, 1979; Rodger, 1985).

Industrialisation fostered economic and social change but at variable pace in terms of structural and spatial manifestations. Several decades passed before changes to the production process affected each facet of textile manufacturing. In general, small firms continued to exist and play an important role in the urban economy, but the large employer became an increasingly significant feature of the labour market. Some occupations declined or ceased to exist, many new specialised functions developed. Temporal analysis of employment statistics provides an insight into these changes.

In 1841 37·56 per cent of the industrial workforce was engaged in textiles and clothing. By 1911 the figure had fallen to 16·86 per cent, the exact equal to employment in metalworking, engineering and toolmaking. In 1841 only 7·17 per cent of industrial labour worked in those industries (Rodger, 1985). Marked, though less spectacular, decline occurred in the proportion engaged

Map 4.

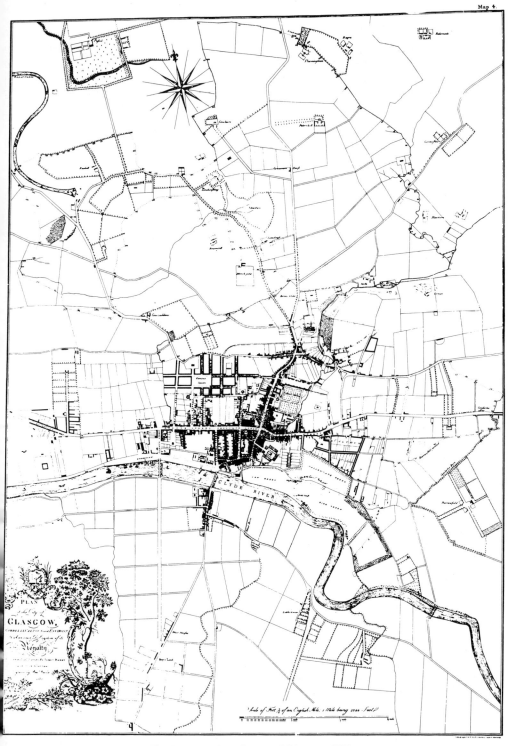

Fig. 2   James Barry's map of Glasgow, 1782.

in general labouring and steady growth in share of employment associated with the food, drink and tobacco industrial grouping. Throughout the Victorian era the sectoral balance between employment in industry, commerce, professional and personal services was comparatively stable. Industrial employment fluctuated from a peak in 1851 of 77·53 per cent of the male workforce to a minimum, in 1901, of 70·50 per cent (Rodger, 1985). A sectoral shift was apparent in the 1911 census data with a substantial increase in professional employment and decline in the proportions occupied in the other major sectors. However, one caveat must be attached to that deduction, namely that the results may have been affected by a series of boundary extensions to the area of the city in the first decade of the twentieth century. It should also be noted that, even in 1911, less than 2 per cent of the industrial workforce was directly employed in shipbuilding. Part of the explanation lay in the fact that many shipyards were not within the city boundary. If location quotients are used as a measure of occupational specialisation then, in 1911, the leading male activities were associated with tobacco manufacture and sale, the cotton industry, metal manufacturing and commerce. For female employment, the principal specialisms were the dress industries, cotton industry and tobacco manufacture and sale (Rodger, 1985).

The total labour force increased, matching the massive growth of the urban population which experienced almost a tenfold increment within the compass of the nineteenth century. Initially migration exceeded natural increase as the city attracted thousands of people from rural backgrounds, particularly from the Highlands and from Ireland. However, in the second half of the nineteenth century there were phases when natural increase was the primary cause of continuing demographic growth. The decisive variable was the fluctuating scale and direction of net migration in the late Victorian era. Another factor in the equation was the substantial proportion of population growth in the period 1872–1912 which resulted from several boundary extensions. For example, extensions between 1891 and 1912 added more than 300,000 people to the total, with some 224,000 incorporated in the sweeping annexations of the 1912 Boundaries Act. By 1912 Glasgow had more than one million inhabitants, it accounted for more than one-fifth of the population of Scotland and some 46 per cent of the regional total (Gibb, 1983). By comparison, in 1841 the city housed less than 10 per cent of the Scottish and about one-third of the regional population.

The addition of more than 900,000 people in one hundred and fifty years had major repercussions upon the built environment of the city. Successive waves of urban growth spawned a series of residential and industrial districts. Initially expansion involved a middle-class western sector between the Merchant City and Blythswood estate, and several industrial and working-class districts such as Anderston, Calton, Bridgeton and Port Dundas. Speculative residential and industrial development occurred at Hutchesontown, Laurieston and Gorbals on the south side of the river, although the middle-class venture at Laurieston suffered as a result of the subsequent industrial development of adjoining districts. Nonetheless, in the Victorian period a substantial number of middle-class families lived there before the declining social reputation of the area and the challenge from the newer late-Victorian suburbs of Pollokshields, Pollokshaws and Newlands left Laurieston, Hutchesontown, Tradeston, Gorbals and Kinning Park as an inner industrial and working-class zone (Robb, 1983). Another small Victorian villa district was created to the east of the Merchant City at Dennistoun. However, throughout the Georgian and Victorian years the principal middle-class districts were developed to the west of the old urban nucleus. The Georgian and early Victorian areas consisted of terraced properties in the vicinity of George Square, at Garnethill and on the Blythswood estate. Subsequent developments which occurred on more westerly sites at Woodside, Woodlands, Hillhead, Kelvinside, Partickhill and Dowanhill variously involved terraces, tenements and villas. It was not a simple temporal progression of house styles for tenements and terraces were built at both the start and finish of the Victorian period. Simpson (1977) and Dicks (1985) have written detailed accounts of the development of Glasgow's middle-class West End. It was flanked to the south and north by working-class industrial districts focused respectively around the river Clyde and the Forth and Clyde Canal. These were dominated by tenemental townscapes, a ubiquitous feature of late Victorian and Edwardian working-class neighbourhoods.

Economic, demographic and physical growth led to the spread of the central business district. The first western suburbs were soon invaded by shops, offices, workshops and industrial premises. Progressively, the invasion by commercial land users marched up the slope towards Blythswood Square and onward, in the first decades of the twentieth century, to the Victorian residential properties at Park Circus and Park Terrace. As the core of the central area migrated westward, the Merchant City declined in functional and social importance. In the 1870's the University of Glasgow abandoned the site on the High Street and moved to a new location at Gilmorehill in the developing West End. The old urban core was dominated by slums and industries although retailing continued to occupy sites in Trongate and Saltmarket. But these premises served the poorer citizens as more westerly streets such as Buchanan Street became the location of the department stores and outfitters serving the successful Victorian middle-class Glaswegians. Segregation of land uses was emerging but imperfectly. Even in the fashionable shopping and office districts of the late Victorian city, industries and workshops could be found occupying premises in back lanes and minor streets. Conversion of use did not necessarily lead to rebuilding but various innovations in shop and office-building did promote that outcome. Shops and warehouses dominated Victorian redevelopment whereas offices were characteristic of change in the Edwardian period. The latter represented the implementation of an innovation, the multi-storey office block, during a phase of economic recovery when a surge in supply apparently satisfied a

Fig. 3   Jamaica Bridge in 1924. Source: Annan, Glasgow.

substantial, possibly delayed, demand for new purpose-built premises (Whitehand, 1978).

Many industries were attracted to transport-oriented sites on the fringe of the urban area. The complex at Port Dundas on the Forth and Clyde Canal was a late eighteenth-century example of this trend which could be illustrated in the Victorian era by the locomotive engineering works at Springburn and the shipyards at Partick and Govan. Often housing development followed some years after the opening of the industrial premises, so, in certain sectors, industry was an important pioneer of urban advance into the adjoining countryside. Nevertheless, many industrial firms were located centrally. *Pigot's Commercial Directory* (1823) revealed a pronounced concentration of textile concerns at the western edge of the Merchant City, notably in the Candleriggs, Brunswick Street, Glassford Street and Wilson Street quarter (Gibb, 1983).

Further improvements to the navigation channel of the Clyde and the construction of a series of docks in the late-Victorian period enhanced the capacity of the port. Increased trade — gross tonnage handled multiplied tenfold between 1861–1908 (Marwick, 1909) — attracted additional commercial and industrial development at Broomielaw and in the vicinity of Kingston, Queen's and Princes Docks.

Kellett (1969) investigated the impact of the railways on Victorian Glasgow and Hume (1983) presented a wide-ranging discussion of the influence of transport on Victorian urban settlements in Scotland. Debate continues about the causal role of transport in urban development and change, but the innovations in water transport and the introduction of railways and tramways certainly had a profound effect upon the economy, functioning and structure of urban areas. For example, considerable central redevelopment resulted from the construction of Central and St. Enoch Stations. Improved means of moving goods and materials was an essential ingredient for industrialisation. Similarly, as cities grew in size and area, intra-urban passenger transport developed through the medium of tramways and suburban railways. The latter generated the growth of extra-mural suburbs whilst the former primarily served the contiguous urban area. In the last decade of the nineteenth century an underground circuit was constructed linking Govan and Hillhead on opposite sides of the river with the centre of Glasgow. Contemporaneously cluthas, river water buses, plied the Clyde between Whiteinch and the city centre, but the service was withdrawn in 1903 in the face of competition from the rapidly expanding electric tramway system (Hume, 1983). Intra-urban movement of goods depended upon horses and carts in such numbers that they frequently choked the streets of the central area (Figure 3).

Despite the extension of the built area, Glasgow remained comparatively compact (Figure 4). Particularly high population densities were found in the central neighbourhoods and 70 per cent of citizens lived within three square miles of Glasgow Cross. Yet redistribution and decentralisation, involving

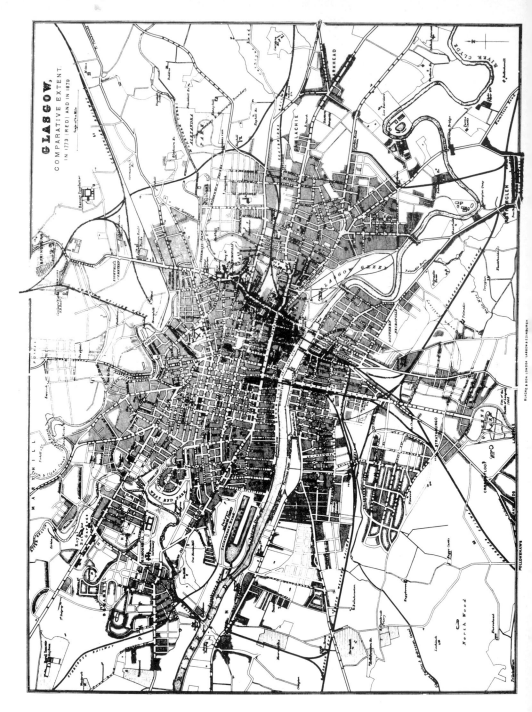

Fig. 4   The Growth of Glasgow 1773–1879. Source: A. McGeorge.
Old Glasgow — the Place and the People, 1880.

some 54,600 people between 1871–81, followed in the wake of the clearance of many central slums (Figure 5) by the City Improvement Trust (Allan, 1965), and residential displacement arising from the process of commercial redevelopment. Nevertheless, central and inner industrial districts were characterised by high densities and squalid living conditions. Russell (1886), the medical officer of Glasgow, reported that in 1881 the highest densities (408 persons per acre) and highest death rate (38·3 per 1,000) were found in

Fig. 5   136 Saltmarket in the 1860's. Source: Annan, Glasgow.

Bridgegate and the adjoining wynds. That district also had the highest rate of infant mortality and the second largest proportion of people living in one-apartment houses (49 per cent). Primacy in the latter went to High Street East where 53 per cent of houses consisted of only one room. The nineteenth-century cholera epidemics did not respect social class divisions, but the benefits of public health measures were noticeable in later decades when the death rate in the middle-class West End was about half that of the central slums.

Throughout the nineteenth century demand for low rent housing outpaced supply, leading to inevitable overcrowding and squalor. Nonetheless, tens of thousands of new tenements were constructed under legislation designed to impose at least minimal standards for ventilation, space and services. National and local government played an increased role in dictating housing standards and various acts authorised direct intervention by demolition of unfit and unsafe properties and redevelopment of cleared sites. Attitudes changed slowly as these remarks by a local official to the Municipal Commission on Housing in 1903 indicated: 'I would say that with cleanliness and good ventilation, a one apartment house may be healthy and comfortable, and in many cases, quite sufficient for the humble occupants . . .' (Butt, 1983). However, the considerable weight of evidence presented to the Royal Commission on Housing, appointed in 1912, revealed the scale of inadequacy of the provision of working-class housing and questioned the ability of the market to provide for this area of demand.

The Twentieth-Century City

Several trends cumulatively distinguished the modern city from that of the industrial era. Manufacturing occupied a smaller share of the population with textiles, shipbuilding and heavy engineering being adumbrated since the 1950's. The tertiary sector expanded and dominated urban employment. Indicators of economic stress and change were evident in the late Victorian period. Shipbuilding faced some difficulties because of the comparative high costs of steel and other materials (Warren, 1965). In retrospect even more disquieting was the absence of signs of the growth of a new star in the manufacturing firmament to assume the mantle of leader and maintain the cycle of succession which had occurred previously. Clydeside industry seemed to be locked into a mould which industrialists did not wish to break. The ebbing tide of these activities fluctuated, with a nadir in the slump of the 1930's recession and false optimism in the immediate post-Second War recovery, but the origins of shrinkage dated from the start of the century (Checkland, 1981). Elsewhere in this volume Nairn and Kirwan examine in greater detail the changes in the urban economy.

The city also experienced changes in various demographic trends. Population growth was modest and fuelled by natural increase. There were reductions in the birth rate and death rate. Outmigration dominated, both furth of Scotland and to outer parts of the metropolitan area. The latter involved voluntary suburbanisation and also the planned dispersal and overspill policies which originated in the proposals of the Clyde Valley Plan (Abercrombie and Matthew, 1949). New Towns (see Wannop), suburbs and metropolitan villages (see Pacione) were products of these centrifugal processes. In aggregate, between 1961–81, the population of the city declined by more than 350,000 (Rhind, 1983).

The implementation of the Addison Act 1919 introduced the era of local authority housing. By 1951 that sector had constructed 74,035 houses in Glasgow (Butt, 1983). Most of these dwellings were situated in the urban periphery on land acquired by boundary extensions, notably those of 1926 and 1938 which doubled the area under municipal control. In the 1950's such areas became sites of vast local authority estates at Drumchapel, Easterhouse and Castlemilk. By comparison, between 1919–51, some 10,000 properties were built in the private sector, particularly at King's Park and Croftfoot on the southern margin of the city. With middle-class expansion confined to the suburbs a social schism developed between the city and the surrounding residential districts.

In 1919 the civic authorities estimated that Glasgow needed an additional 57,000 new dwellings. About 37 per cent of the demand was required to relieve overcrowding and 27 per cent to accommodate population growth. Subsequently the estimates were increased as the scale of the housing crisis unfolded. In 1915 one household in five consisted of one apartment, and more than half of all families shared common water closets. At the prevailing standard of three persons per room, over 200,000 people were classed as living in overcrowded conditions (Butt, 1983).

The first fruits of local authority housing produced attractive areas of flatted and semi-detached villas (e.g. Mosspark) which continue to enjoy a prestigious ranking in consumer preferences. However, the rate of construction failed to match demand. In 1933 the city had 80,000 names on its housing list. Overcrowded and inadequate houses, in terms of size and amenities, continued to constitute a slowly declining but persistently unacceptable proportion of the total stock. A succession of policies were directed towards this problem. The 1935 Housing Act offered a special subsidy designed to encourage rehousing of families from slums and the clearance of such districts. Unfortunately, the measure created a socio-economic distinction between slum clearance and general needs tenants. Moreover, in time, the spatial concentration of transference of slum clearance families in specific estates resulted in the social stigmatisation of these areas.

Cessation of house-building during the Second War left the city with an accumulated demand totalling some 90,000 families. The civic authorities and the authors of the Clyde Valley Plan presented similar diagnoses of the housing and planning problems confronting Glasgow, but they differed in terms of solutions. The former believed that redevelopment and dispersal could be managed within the municipal area, whereas Abercrombie and

Matthew (1949) advocated overspill of population and the development of New Towns (see Wannop). Both strategies demanded the speedy development of a series of substantial peripheral local authority estates in order to reduce the massive housing list and generate the decanting space for inner city redevelopment. Estates such as Drumchapel, Easterhouse, Castlemilk, Pollok and Priesthill ultimately accommodated more than 46,000 families (Gibb, 1983). Nonetheless, by the mid-1950's the waiting list had grown to 100,000 names and the city was rapidly exhausting its supply of building land.

In 1957 the Planning Officer proposed that the emphasis should switch to redevelopment through the mechanism of twenty-nine comprehensive development areas. This strategy was a logical extension of planning policy with a co-ordination of clearance and redevelopment as well as dispersion and peripheral construction. In fact only nine comprehensive development areas were formally approved, involving inner city or industrial districts. The process proved to be more complex than the development of New Towns. Considerable delays often occurred in the initial stages because of problems over acquisition of properties, and cleared sites could then remain vacant for several years awaiting redevelopment. Communities were disrupted, indus-

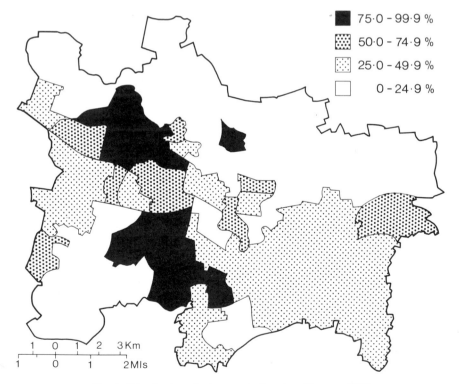

75·0 - 99·9 %

50·0 - 74·9 %

25·0 - 49·9 %

0 - 24·9 %

Fig. 6   Distribution of private sector housing, Glasgow, 1983.

tries displaced. By the 1970's concern about these problems and inefficiencies led to a re-evaluation of the policy of redevelopment. A new initiative introduced the concept of Action Areas which were much smaller than comprehensive development areas. Wherever possible, improvement through rehabilitation would be applied rather than wholesale demolition.

Moss Heights, 1957, were an earlier example of the high-rise solution to the housing problem. Stimulated by subsidy, Glasgow in the 1960's, along with other major cities, adopted the high-rise approach and by 1982, 321 blocks, ranging from eight to thirty-one storeys, had been constructed, 263 by the local authority and fifty-eight by the Scottish Special Housing Association. Escalating costs and an array of social problems resulted in the abandonment of the high-rise strategy and the introduction of revised allocation policies and enhanced levels of supervision in existing blocks.

In 1983 of a total of 297,000 dwellings, 109,000 were privately rented or owner-occupied, and the remainder were let by the local authority or other public agencies (Glasgow District Council, 1983). The private sector (Figure 6) accounted for a majority of properties in twenty-three of the seventy-two wards of the city. Of the fifteen wards in which owner-occupation (Figure 7)

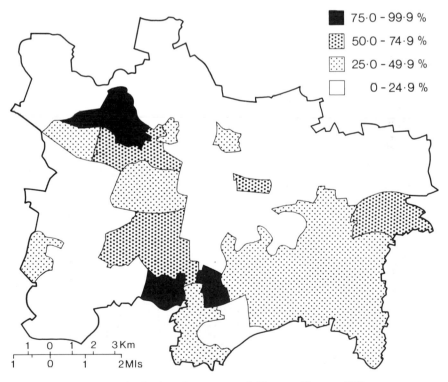

Fig. 7   Distribution of owner-occupied houses, Glasgow, 1983.

dominated the tenurial structure, seven were located in a southern zone between Pollokshields and King's Park, and six were situated in the West End of the city. Two outliers were the Victorian speculation at Dennistoun and the post-war housing at Baillieston/Garrowhill. With the exception of King's Park, the major concentrations primarily consisted of pre-1914 properties. Although the range of house-type included tenements, terraces and villas, clustering tended to result in spatial dominance by one type, e.g. tenements in Mount Florida and villas in Newlands.

The distribution of local authority housing (Figure 8) reflects the spatial and temporal evolution of that sector. Sixteen wards had more than 90 per cent of houses in that tenure category, of which only one, Cowcaddens, reflected the process of inner-city redevelopment. However, evidence of a gathering tide was provided by the fact that a further five inner city wards had over 70 per cent of properties in the public sector. Particularly high concentrations of Scottish Special Housing Association dwellings occurred in Wyndford (49·3 per cent), Prospecthill (35·8 per cent), Hutchesontown (23·5 per cent), Calton (22·3 per cent) and Darnley (20·4 per cent) wards.

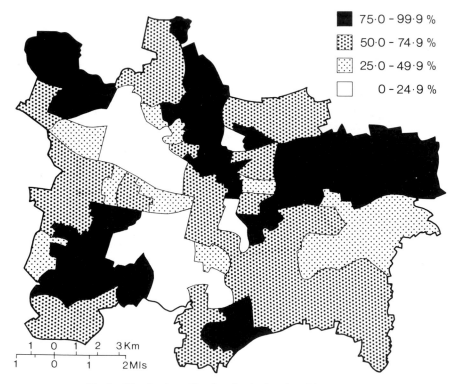

■ 75·0 - 99·9 %

▨ 50·0 - 74·9 %

▦ 25·0 - 49·9 %

□ 0 - 24·9 %

Fig. 8   Distribution of local authority housing, Glasgow, 1983.

From the mid-1970's diversification of housing and planning policies fostered the intervention by housing associations in the field of rehabilitation and the resuscitation of the private sector through the release of land to builders in a desperate attempt to reverse or stem the prevailing centrifugal movement to the suburban fringe. Rehabilitation and improvement encouraged residential stability and also linked with planning initiatives in conservation and environmental enhancement which were directed towards the preservation of the historic fabric and the attainment of a better quality of life for both residents and visitors.

In 1983 some forty Housing Associations were engaged in programmes funded by the Housing Corporation. Twenty-six associations were involved in inner area renewal of tenement properties, mostly in Housing Action Areas. At March 1983, Housing Associations had acquired 13,900 properties in Housing Action Areas and work was either completed or in progress in about 70 per cent of the properties. More than a quarter of the improved stock of Housing Associations was situated within the GEAR area (Glasgow District Council, 1983).

The Glasgow Eastern Area Renewal Project was launched in 1976 with an initial eight-year budget of £120 million. An extensive programme of urban renewal is planned, under the direction of the Scottish Development Agency in partnership with the District and Regional Council and the Scottish Special Housing Association, to staunch outmigration, introduce new industries, reclaim derelict land and create an attractive physical, economic and social environment in an area suffering from the symptoms of advanced urban decay. Progress has been made, particularly in relation to housing and land renewal, but the prevailing adverse economic climate has hampered attempts to capture a substantial injection of new jobs. Questions have been raised about the vagueness of the goals of the project (Booth, Pitt and Money, 1982) and the consequences of differential rates of success of policies of urban-renewal and socio-economic rejuvenation. It seems likely that if the blight of high levels of unemployment persists, an associated matrix of social problems will remain unresolved.

GEAR is a major response to the inner-city problems and urban deprivation which confronted the newly elected Strathclyde Regional Council. Local and national studies (Holtermann, 1975) identified unacceptable concentrations of deprivation in particular parts of the city, notably in the inner city and in certain overcrowded inter-war and post-war local authority housing schemes. The precise characteristics of deprivation vary between tenurial groups and districts, but normally involve some combination of disadvantage in relation to housing, health, welfare and security. Danson (1984) has argued that deindustrialisation and recent changes in social policy have caused a deepening and widening of poverty and deprivation amongst groups most at risk. Macro-scale trends have certainly affected the situation, but the Regional Council has implemented an extensive programme of initiatives directed at the problem of deprivation. The major strands of the policy are the designation of areas of priority treatment, improved service delivery and the development of client-based and community programmes (Yates, 1984). Division of functions between authorities (see Midwinter) has meant that the Education and Social Work departments have been the principal agents of the Regional Council, although transport, planning and industrial promotion have also featured in the strategy.

'In many ways the policies to date have relied upon the action of the above departments, but in themselves these departments are incapable of resolving the basic problems which confront the Region's deprived communities. Any list of priorities produced by a community would highlight five major issues as jobs, family income, housing, transport and health and, with the exception of transport, these are mainly outwith the direct control of the Council' (Yates, 1984, 42).

Greater Glasgow Health Board has conducted a detailed cartographic analysis of the social geography of Glasgow using data from the 1981 Census (GGHB, 1984). The spatial distribution of various demographic and socio-economic characteristics has consequences for demand for, delivery of, and access to, health services. For example, Figures 9 to 14 illustrate the social geography of the city in relation to particularly high levels of concentration

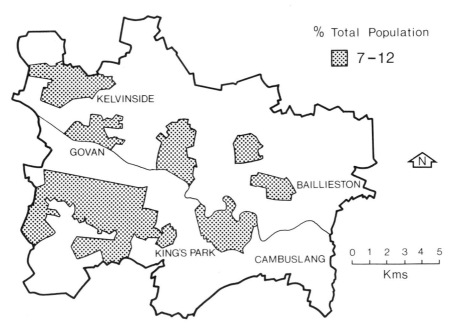

Fig. 9   Distribution of the elderly, Glasgow, 1981.
Source: Greater Glasgow Health Board Information Services Unit.

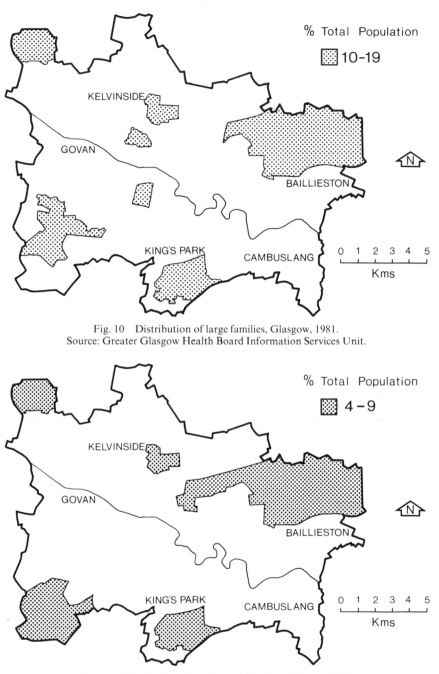

Fig. 10   Distribution of large families, Glasgow, 1981.
Source: Greater Glasgow Health Board Information Services Unit.

Fig. 11   Distribution of single-adult families, Glasgow, 1981.
Source: Greater Glasgow Health Board Information Services Unit.

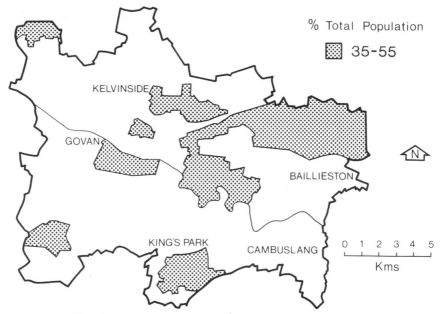

Fig. 12   Distribution of overcrowded households, Glasgow, 1981.
Source: Greater Glasgow Health Board Information Services Unit.

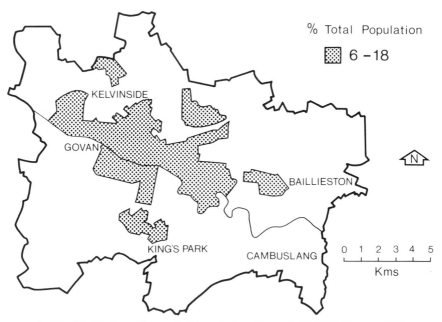

Fig. 13   Distribution of houses lacking a bath and/or an inside WC, Glasgow, 1981.
Source: Greater Glasgow Health Board Information Services Unit.

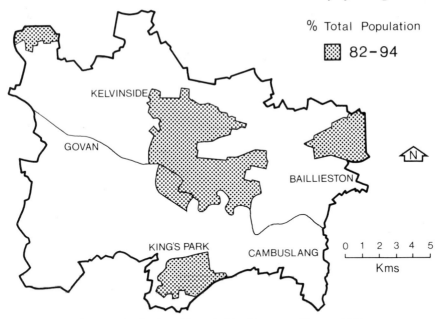

Fig. 14 Distribution of households with no car, Glasgow, 1981.
Source: Greater Glasgow Health Board Information Services Unit.

respectively of the elderly, large families, single adult families, overcrowding, dwellings lacking basic amenities and households without use of a car. For emphasis, only values in the uppermost quintile have been shown. The chapter by Butt offers an extended discussion of the topic of quality of life.

The processes of redevelopment and renewal, of peripheral construction and suburbanisation outlined earlier, have promoted a considerable degree of residential mobility in recent decades and a redrawing of the social geography of the city. Forbes and Robertson (1981) conducted a detailed investigation into residential mobility in Greater Glasgow in 1974 which extended our understanding of migrational processes and patterns. The results revealed that different sectors of the housing market and districts within each sector had distinctive migration fields, although the Clyde acted as a powerful barrier to intra-urban movement. Inter-censal comparisons (Tivy, 1958; Forbes and Robertson, 1984) indicate areas of growth and decline, thereby providing a measure of intra-urban migration. Such analyses can raise issues of policy. For example, Forbes and Robertson (1984) in an inter-censal study, 1971–81, of population change in Glasgow, discuss the implications for inner city initiatives.

'It is an announced objective of the GEAR project to stem the decline of population from the area. There is perhaps a basic assumption here which ought to have been questioned first: is numerical decline within an arbitrarily defined sector of a large city necessarily indicative of something bad which must be reversed? Substantial migration of GEAR households took place to the adjacent public authority housing areas in the 1970's. In the context of Glasgow city some of the loss to GEAR is not necessarily a city loss' (Forbes and Robertson, 1984, 67).

In the 1950's Glasgow started to receive a new and distinctive international migration emanating from the Indian sub-continent. By 1981 just over one per cent of the residents of Greater Glasgow listed the New Commonwealth or Pakistan as their place of birth. Initially many immigrants settled in Gorbals, but subsequent residential diffusion occurred into tenement properties at East Pollokshields and Woodlands, which now constitute the principal foci (Kearsley and Srivastava, 1974; GGHB, 1984). These migrants have played an important, although inadequately quantified, role in certain sectors of commerce, and the new mosque on the south bank of the river is a visible symbol of the impact of their religion and culture.

Concluding Remarks
   Physical and functional change has occurred in the central area. Office and institutional redevelopment has been concentrated primarily on the western and northern fringe, in the vicinity of the Inner Ring Road. The shatter belt created by the development of the latter and the subsequent magnetic attraction of improved accessibility were probably more influential than the desire to escape the restrictions imposed in the 1970's with the designation of the Central conservation area. The processes of change also led to the abandonment of parts of the eastern and southern fringe of the Central Business District as markets, warehouses and industries moved to peripheral locations or ceased operations. A report (Eve, 1971) forecast contraction of the C.B.D., especially in relation to shopping. Whilst there was a phase of store closures, the shopping district has proved to be remarkably resilient. New shopping centres have been developed in Sauchiehall Street and there have been major extensions to both branches of the nation's leading retailer. Pedestrianisation has been introduced in the principal shopping thoroughfares and improvements made to public transport, including the complete refurbishment of the underground system and the reopening of a city-centre rail link. With the shift in emphasis from decentralisation to containment and implosion planning initiatives have been introduced to entice people to live, shop and work in the central area. The revivification of the Merchant City is only in embryo but, in combination with plans for other parts of the central area, fruition of the policy could lead to a significant regeneration of centripetal forces with a strengthened central core and central community.
   Industrial and commercial change has created a surfeit of vacant sites which are now being landscaped or developed. Within a decade a series of riverside projects could transform a depressing scene of dereliction into one of

imaginative functional growth. Notable in this context is the development of the Exhibition Centre and Britoil offices on the site of the abandoned Queen's Docks and the probable Garden Festival 1988 complex on disused land at Princes Docks.

The net product of these strategies, coupled with those of renewal of inner city and old industrial areas, the modernisation and improvements to local authority houses, the experiments with homesteading and co-operative management of difficult-to-let properties, the amelioration of deprivation and the revitalisation of the urban economy, should be the more attractive, wealthier and healthier city of the twenty-first century. Many obstacles might intervene to delay progress and divert policies, but the greatest potential impediment must be the prospect of continued high rates of unemployment. Just as many of the present problems have been inherited from past events, so some of the solutions echo earlier measures. Glasgow, as the site of International Exhibitions in 1888 and 1901 and the Empire Exhibition of 1938, knows the financial and psychological benefits which would accrue from holding an international exhibition and establishing the city as a conference centre. Success cannot depend upon such limited and fragile instruments of revival but, apart from the direct generative boost to the local economy, there would be a resurgence of confidence which would represent the rejection of the inevitability of decline. That is why it is important that the present plans and policies succeed.

REFERENCES

Abercrombie, P. and Matthew, R. (1949), *The Clyde Valley Regional Plan 1946*. HMSO, Edinburgh.

Adams, I. H. (1978), *The Making of Urban Scotland*. Croom Helm, London.

Allan, C. M. (1965), The Genesis of British Urban Redevelopment with special reference to Glasgow, *Economic History Review* XVIII, 598–613.

Booth, S., Pitt, D. and Money, W. J. (1982), Organisational Redundancy: A Critical Appraisal of the GEAR Project, *Public Administration, 60,* 56–72.

Butt, J. (1983), Working Class Housing in the Scottish Cities 1900–1950. In Gordon, G. and Dicks, B. (Eds.), *Scottish Urban History*. Aberdeen University Press, Aberdeen, 233–267.

Checkland, S. G. (1964), The British industrial city as history: The Glasgow case, *Urban Studies, 1*, 34–54.

Checkland, S. G. (1981), *The Upas Tree*. University of Glasgow Press, Glasgow. Second Edition.

Cunnison, J. and Gilfillan, J. B. S. (1958), *The City of Glasgow*, Vol. V. Third Statistical Account of Scotland. Collins, Glasgow.

Daiches, D. (1977), *Glasgow*. Deutsch, London.

Danson, M. (1984), Poverty and Deprivation in the West of Scotland. In Pacione, M. and Gordon, G. (Eds.), *Quality of Life and Human Welfare*. Geo-Books, Norwich, 23–24.

Devine, T. M. (1983), The Merchant Class of the Larger Scottish Towns in the Seventeenth and Early Eighteenth Centuries. In Gordon, G. and Dicks, B. (Eds.), *Scottish Urban History*. Aberdeen University Press, Aberdeen, 92–111.

Dicks, B. (1985), Choice and Constraint: Further Perspectives of Socio-Residential Segregation in Nineteenth Century Glasgow with particular reference to its West End. In Gordon, G. (Ed.), *Perspectives of the Scottish City*. Aberdeen University Press, Aberdeen, 91–123.

Eve, G. and Co. (1971), *Glasgow: Report on Aspects of Future Shopping Provision.*

Forbes, J. and Robertson, I. M. L. (1981), Patterns of Residential Movement in Greater Glasgow, *Scottish Geographical Magazine 97*, 85–97.

Forbes, J. and Robertson, I. M. L. (1984), Population Changes and their Implications in Inner City Glasgow. In Jones, H. (Ed.), *Population Change in Contemporary Scotland.* Geo-Books, Norwich, 53–70.

Gibb, A. (1983), *Glasgow — The Making of a City.* Croom Helm, London.

Gilfillan, J. B. S. and Moisley, H. A. (1958), Industrial and Commercial Developments to 1914. In Miller, R. and Tivy, J. (Eds.), *The Glasgow Region.* British Association, Glasgow, 150–189.

Glasgow District Council (1983), *Annual Housing Review.* Glasgow District Council Housing Department.

Gordon, G. (1983), Industrial Development *c.* 1750–1980. In Whittington, G. and Whyte, I. D. (Eds.), *An Historical Geography of Scotland.* Academic Press, London, 165–190.

Greater Glasgow Health Board (1984), *Census 1981: Maps for Community Medicine Areas.* Greater Glasgow Health Board Information Services Unit.

Holtermann, S. (1975), Areas of urban deprivation in Great Britain: an analysis of 1971 Census data, *Social Trends, 6.* C.S.O.

Hume, J. R. (1983), Transport and Towns in Victorian Scotland. In Gordon, G. and Dicks, B. (Eds.), *Scottish Urban History.* Aberdeen University Press, Aberdeen, 197–232.

Kearsley, G. W. and Srivastava, S. R. (1974), The Spatial Evolution of Glasgow's Asian Community, *Scottish Geographical Magazine, 90*, 110–24.

Kellett, J. R. (1967), *Glasgow: a concise history.* Blond, London.

Kellett, J. R. (1969), *The Impact of Railways on Victorian Cities.* Routledge & Kegan Paul, London.

Lythe, S. G. E. and Butt, J. (1975), *An Economic History of Scotland 1100–1939.* Blackie, Glasgow.

Marwick, J. D. (1909), *The River Clyde and the Clyde Burghs.* Glasgow.

Miller, R. and Tivy, J. (Eds.) (1958), *The Glasgow Region.* The British Association, Glasgow.

Pryde, G. S. (1959), The City and Burgh of Glasgow 1100–1750. In Miller, R. and Tivy, J. (Eds.), *The Glasgow Region.* British Association, Glasgow, 134–149.

Rhind, D. (Ed.) (1983), *A Census User's Handbook.* Methuen, London.

Robb, J. G. (1983), Suburb and Slum in Gorbals: Social and Residential Change 1800–1900. In Gordon, G. and Dicks, B. (Eds.), *Scottish Urban History.* Aberdeen University Press, Aberdeen, 130–167.

Rodger, R. (1985), Employment, Wages and Poverty in the Scottish Cities 1841–1914. In Gordon, G. (Ed.), *Perspectives of the Scottish City.* Aberdeen University Press, Aberdeen, 25–63.

Russell, J. B. (1886), *The Vital Statistics of the City of Glasgow.* Glasgow.

Simpson, M. A. (1977), The West End of Glasgow, 1830–1914. In Simpson, M. A. and Lloyd, T. H. (Eds.), *Middle Class Housing in Britain.* David & Charles, Newton Abbot, 44–85.

Slaven, A. (1975), *The Development of the West of Scotland.* Routledge & Kegan Paul, London.

Smout, T. C. (1960), The development and enterprise of Glasgow 1556–1707, *Scottish Journal of Political Economy, vii*, 194–212.

Tivy, J. (1958), Population Distribution and Change. In Miller, R. and Tivy, J. (Eds.), *The Glasgow Region.* British Association, Glasgow, 242–269.

Treble, J. H. (1979), The Market for Unskilled Male Labour in Glasgow 1891–1914. In MacDougall, I. (Ed.), *Essays in Scottish Labour History: a Tribute to W. H. Marwick.* Donald, Edinburgh, 115–142.

Warren, K. (1965), Locational problems of the Scottish iron and steel industry since 1760, *Scottish Geographical Magazine, 81*, 18–36 and 87–103.

Whitehand, J. W. R. (1978), Long-Term Changes in the Form of the City Centre; The Case of Redevelopment, *Geografiska Annaler, 60B*, 79–96.

Yates, K. (1984), Strathclyde's Strategy to Combat Deprivation. In Pacione, M. and Gordon, G. (Eds.), *Quality of Life and Human Welfare.* Geo-Books, Norwich, 35–48.

CHAPTER FIVE

THE NEW TOWNS OF STRATHCLYDE

U. A. Wannop

Their Origins and Changing Roles
Almost three centuries prior to the arrival of the modern generation of new
towns of East Kilbride in 1947, Cumbernauld in 1955 and Irvine in 1966,
Strathclyde's mercantile and industrial growth had seen the launch of earlier
new towns and new communities including Port Glasgow in 1667,
Helensburgh in 1776 and New Lanark in 1785. The history of absorption of
this earlier generation of economic and social initiatives into the urban fabric
of the region and their changing relationships with their region, begs questions
as to how far the twentieth century new towns remain 'new' after forty years of
comprehensive urban renewal on Clydeside and, also, of whether their roles
may now be distinctive and similar more in their political significance than in
their economic or social contribution to regional development.

   Initiated at intervals of a decade between each, the twentieth century new
towns began each in different circumstances. East Kilbride followed from the
Scottish Office's acceptance of the strategy of the Clyde Valley Regional Plan
1946 (Abercrombie and Matthew, 1949), which foresaw the need to help
people decentralise from congested and overcrowded housing to new
locations to be of the order of 550,000 persons from Glasgow and 166,500
from the rest of Clydeside. Against the objections of Glasgow Corporation
and without its formal acceptance by the Clyde Valley Regional Planning
Advisory Committee, the Plan's strategy of up to four new towns for
Clydeside was initially limited to the launch of East Kilbride. Glenrothes in
the East of Scotland, begun in 1948, foreshadowed the primarily economic
role later adopted for the new towns in the West by its basis in the intended
opening of the Rothes colliery, although linked to the West by its expected
attraction for miners from the declining Lanarkshire coalfield. By the early
1950's, Glasgow Corporation came to accept the need for new towns in
conjunction with its own programme of rehousing in peripheral estates and,
subsequently, by progressive redevelopment of the Victorian city. By 1955 the
Corporation agreed to make a financial contribution for each Glasgow

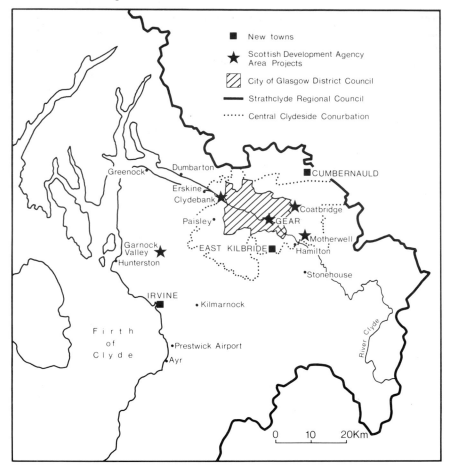

Fig. 1   Location of new towns and of Scottish Development Agency Area Projects.

household accepted to the tenancy of a house in Cumbernauld; the designation of this new town proceeded with Cabinet approval on grounds of Glasgow's still desperate housing needs and it was the only new town launched in the United Kingdom in the 1950's. By the mid-1960's, the rising tide of the national birth rate and the arguments of the Scottish Office for the economic stimulus provided by new towns in regional development, brought Livingston and Irvine as components of the Scottish Office's strategy for Central Scotland (Scottish Development Department, 1963). These new towns were located beyond the easy commuting range of Glasgow which made East Kilbride and Cumbernauld so considerably dependent upon the city's prosperity to support their living standards. Yet, Strathclyde's population and employment levels were both to reach their historic peaks in the mid-1960's, falling continuously thereafter and drastically undermining the assumptions of need for housing, building land and urban infrastructure upon which the new town programme for Central Scotland had been extended.

Acceptance by the Scottish Office that the new town programme was being stretched beyond the capacity of the Development Corporations to fulfil came in 1976, with the termination of the barely-begun new town at Stonehouse. Emerging from criticism by the Scottish Office of standards of redevelopment in Glasgow and from an assessed shortfall in the regional public housing programme, Stonehouse's initial basis in housing need had been shifted towards economic development when the new town was designated in 1973. Contemporaneously, the West Central Scotland Plan (1974) proposed Stonehouse's deferral against a background of declining regional population and economic prospects; whether sufficient new employment could be created to match the combined target populations of the new towns was debatable enough, but even if this could be done the prospect had gone of population growth in the region sufficient to fill so many jobs. Stonehouse was terminated after the new Strathclyde Regional Council assumed its responsibilities in 1975, adopting the analyses and planning strategy of the West of Scotland Plan; within a year, the Secretary of State had acceded to the Council's pressure to limit the call for investment in new infrastructure outside the renewal of established urban areas.

Over the post-war period since East Kilbride's inception in 1947, the new towns have had to adjust to perhaps four major phases of redirection of strategy for the development of metropolitan Clydeside and of Strathclyde. Overlapping in time and purpose, in each of these phases the relationships of the new towns to their region and to their social and economic roles have been considerably redefined. First, there was the period in which the post-war housing drive required the local, planned overspill and redistribution of households from the congested and overcrowded tenements of Clydeside and North Lanarkshire, when Glasgow continued its historic economic and political dominance over the West of Scotland. This phase reached a peak in the early 1960's, had lost much of its impetus by the early 1970's but was not formally concluded by the Secretary of State until the latter part of that decade. East Kilbride and Cumbernauld were launched in this period; Livingston was to adopt a partial role in attracting Glaswegians for a brief time, but Irvine shunned such a connection.

Second, the era of 'growth area' strategy, emerging in the late 1950's, was formally incorporated in the White Paper on Central Scotland: A Programme for Development and Growth (Scottish Development Department, 1963). Livingston and Irvine were wholly of this strategy to which East Kilbride and Cumbernauld would be grafted.

Third, although 'growth area' strategy was to be severely criticised in the 1970's for conceptual weaknesses as applied to Central Scotland and other advanced industrial or de-industrialising economies, elements of the concept remained in Scottish Office policy statements even after the demise of Stonehouse in 1976, following Government's acceptance that the strategy was over-extended and could never be fulfilled in its higher ambitions. By this time, however, Glasgow had no longer an overwhelming dominance on Clydeside by weight of population nor, in Strathclyde, by weight of employment; politically, Glasgow lost its pre-eminence in 1975 when Strathclyde Regional Council was established, from which time might be arbitrarily dated the emergence of a regional city which reversed the old order and now dominated Glasgow in important respects. Even so, while Glasgow and the older areas of Clydeside were continuing to lose their economic dominance through the 1970's, they gained ascendancy in regional development strategy in a decade from 1974 to 1984, which came to be preoccupied with urban renewal rather than with the new towns and extra-metropolitan economic initiatives.

Fourth, there was a phase commencing in the late 1970's in which it became very evident that the Development Corporations had a political role, which Government was sustaining after the new towns' significance in planning and economic strategy had become much reduced. In retrospect, Stonehouse's initiation in the late 1960's might now be seen as less a late flowering of overspill strategy than as the start of this phase, in which Government came to increasingly prefer its own agencies to the local authorities as channels for not only public investment in the physical renewal of the West of Scotland but, also, as leaders for change in housing policy, in economic initiatives and in both the physical and the social face of Clydeside. But Government's agents for change in its increasing intervention in the renewal of Glasgow and of the infrastructure of the mature urban areas of the region were primarily the Scottish Development Agency, the Scottish Special Housing Association and the Housing Corporation. By the time of its Policy Statement on the New Towns of 1981 (Scottish Economic Planning Department, 1981), inconsistencies in Scottish Office attitudes left the new towns to face growing problems of demographic and economic structure and, possibly, unattainable targets for growth, without prospect of a sufficient revival of Government investment. In this fourth phase, Strathclyde's new towns of the period 1947–66 have had intimations of a future in which they may take a fully proportionate share in the problems of social and economic adaptation characteristic of old towns, at a time when accelerated urban and environmental renewal has greatly narrowed the age disadvantage of the longer-established urban areas of Strathclyde.

THE NEW TOWNS IN THE 1980's

Their Policy Context

The Policy Statement on the Scottish New Towns published by the Scottish Economic Planning Department in September 1981, reaffirmed that because of the concentration on the new towns' 'role as industrial growth points their housing activities should be at a distinctly lower level than in the past' (para. 13). It was said that 'Whatever the future economic outlook, the new towns will still have a major part to play as central government instruments for stimulating employment and underpinning the economy. In particular, the new towns structure as a form of local administration as well as of urban development, provides an environment, backed with administrative resource, which has shown itself to be eminently successful in the attraction of foreign investment ... there can be no doubt that the new towns as presently constituted, offer an environment which they find very attractive' (para. 6). Future policy would be that 'the new towns will have to continue to demonstrate their ability to produce a high rate of industrial growth' (para. 8) and that 'the development corporations therefore will not remain for their own sakes but only for as long as they are necessary to promote and achieve further industrial growth. When each new town has reached the stage of growth necessary to establish it as a viable, economic and social entity, within the physical framework provided in the designated area, then the purpose of the Corporation will be fulfilled and the town can cease to be "new"; it can undergo the more gradual process of change experienced in other towns' (para. 9).

Although from its initial drift, the Policy Statement might seem to have been leading to economic criteria by which the economic performance of the new towns could have been measured, to be compared with the record of other parts of their region, the Statement did not go so far. It concluded that the economic contribution of the new towns would cease only when they had reached the populations for which they were designed. The Statement did not consider whether these targets established up to twenty years or more previously would still be relevant to the demographic and economic circumstances of the 1990's — before which it recognised that none of the new towns would be completed — or, indeed, whether regional and new towns' economic opportunities in the 1990's and early twenty-first century would be appropriate to the remaining physical opportunities in the new towns. The Statement suggested, however, that arrangements to withdraw the development corporations would commence when the towns had grown to within 5,000 of their target populations.

In July 1982, the Secretary of State announced that he was inviting the development corporations to prepare Development Profiles (Cumbernauld, East Kilbride and Irvine Development Corporations, 1983), to be aimed at establishing the Corporations' views upon the investment programmes required to complete their growth. Now recognising the advice forcefully presented by Strathclyde Regional Council, the Secretary of State modified his formula of a year previously which would determine the date for withdrawal of the development corporations. The Regional Council had suggested that the decline of population already occurring in East Kilbride through shrinkage of household size, would prevent any possibility of its reaching its target by the end of the 1980's, as the 1981 Statement had anticipated. The 1982 announcement accordingly stated 'that winding-up should begin when a specified percentage of the new town's present designated population has been reached. Different percentages may be appropriate according to the circumstances, prospects and unique characteristics of each new town.' There was no recognition in the announcement of projections by the Regional Council, which suggested that Cumbernauld and Irvine might be some twenty-three years and forty-one years respectively from the date at which they would be completed.

Submitted in 1983, the Development Profiles recognised the scale of the task remaining if the corporations were to achieve the standards and targets they sought. Although the town now had a slowly falling population, East Kilbride's Development Profile suggested that 'Uniquely among the Scottish New Towns, East Kilbride can realistically hope to achieve its target population'. Neither Irvine nor Cumbernauld Development Corporations conceded this view of East Kilbride's uniqueness, but neither could foresee when in the twenty-first century they might reach their targets and both were prepared to accept that balance and self-containment might be reached at a point short of prior intentions. The programmes of investment for which the Secretary of State had asked so as to foresee the remaining needs to complete the towns were lengthy, revealing sharply the disparity between the corporations' view of their needs and the trends in public and private investment from which the new towns had been suffering from the early 1970's.

The Secretary of State announced his decision on the evidence of the Development Profiles in November 1984 (Secretary of State for Scotland, 1984), when he tacitly accepted that the inconsistencies between resources and expectations for the new towns were unbridgeable. While none of their targets were formally retracted, all were effectively superseded by lower 'trigger' population levels at which the five-year process of winding-up development corporations would commence (Table 1). East Kilbride's trigger was set at an increase of population of 71,850 above that existing when the new town began, or 11 per cent below its now irrelevant target; Cumbernauld's trigger was at 24 per cent below its target increase and Irvine's trigger was as much as 53 per cent less than the growth incorporated in its designated target. The new towns were assured that none would begin to wind-up before 1990 but, broadly, all were expected to do so at different dates in the 1990's. In view of the difficulty of predicting demographic trends, however, the Secretary of State said that all trigger levels and timings of wind-up would be reviewed in 1989.

The Secretary of State's announcement was politically dexterous. Although their designated targets remained, all had effectively been cut and Government was implicitly withdrawing guarantees of investment in the new towns soon after attainment of their trigger populations. Furthermore, although under the terms of the announcement the trend to real declines of population in the new towns could be taken to imply a possibly indefinite life for the corporations, the Secretary of State had left open another course of action. He

TABLE 1   NEW TOWN POPULATION TARGETS AND GROWTH[1]

	East Kilbride	Cumbernauld	Irvine
Year of designation	1947	1955	1966
Population at designation	2,400	3,000	34,600
Targets at designation	40,000–45,000	50,000	95,000
Subsequent revisions of targets	50,000 (1956) 70,000 (1960) 82,500 (1963)	70,000 (1960)	—
Population growth: Residents on Census night			
Census 1951	5,136	2,929	29,324
1961	31,970	4,924	32,716
1971	64,123	32,213	42,451
1981	71,737[2]	48,413	55,436
1983 Development Profile projections	78,900– 83,100 in 1992	64,000 in 2003	75,000 in 1999
Secretary of State's 1984 Announcement on Wind-up			
Trigger per cent	90	77	66
Trigger population	74,250	54,000	63,000

[1] All statistics for designated area, not local authority.
[2] Boundary change since preceding Census.

had given no guarantee in his announcement that any corporation would continue beyond 1995 and, in 1989, he had opened the possibility that trigger populations could be further reduced to achieve that.

Their Economic Record

The administrative and physical advantages of the new towns have often been held to be principal explanations for their better-than-average employment performance in a region declining since the mid-1960's (Coopers and Lybrand, 1979). Is this equally true of all three Strathclyde new towns and are they distinctive in relation to all parts of the region, or only to the regional average? Henderson (1982) demonstrates that in 1960–70, firms in the Scottish new towns created employment in new manufacturing enterprises three times faster than firms in other areas which also had a relatively plentiful supply of industrial and advance factories; in the period 1970–76, the new towns did even better on this comparison, although in the national employment downturn of the later 1970's the new towns lost their capacity to create jobs in new enterprises more rapidly than did other areas of Scotland. Of course, during their greatest growth in the 1960's, the Scottish new towns drew only one in six of jobs created in new manufacturing enterprises in Scotland and barely 5 per cent of jobs in expanding firms. In the West of Scotland, the new towns drew a higher proportion of closer to one in four jobs in new firms, but Henderson suggests that the new towns had priority for public investment in infrastructure including some 50 per cent of new advance factory floorspace, by which they were helped to attract consistently about 20 per cent of Scottish employment in incoming industry. Once established, however, differences in employment performance between plants in the new towns and established plants in many other parts of Scotland generally ceased to be statistically significant. The contribution of the new towns to regional policy has been by their attraction of new industries, rather than any additional contribution to regional stability and growth which these industries demonstrated subsequently. This begs the question of whether the relative advantages which the new towns held in industrial attraction up to the late 1970's will remain in future conditions. Enterprise Zones at Clydebank, Dundee, Arbroath and Invergordon, and a Freeport at Prestwick, offer new and marked financial advantages which the new towns cannot match; furthermore, the area projects launched by the Scottish Development Agency in Motherwell, Coatbridge, the East End of Glasgow and other parts of Scotland, together with the rapid growth of local economic initiatives amongst local authorities, have in the 1980's come to introduce much of the style and substance of economic promotion in the new towns, extending its benefits to areas hitherto incapable of competing on equal terms. Even so, the evidence is that the Region has depended overwhelmingly on new employment created in Glasgow and places other than the new towns, whose success has been significant but not unmatched by localised economic developments elsewhere.

Individually, the economies of the three Strathclyde new towns have had separate and distinctive histories. Cumbernauld's improving advantages as a strategic centre for distribution and service industries for Central Scotland have contributed to a much lower emphasis on manufacturing than in East Kilbride. Irvine was implanted in a District with an already established economy of small towns servicing a population which still dominates that of the new town and, for different reasons, its service base compares with that of Cumbernauld. Even so, all three new towns have a manufacturing emphasis at least matching that of older industrial towns like Clydebank and Coatbridge. The opportunism of Irvine and East Kilbride (Smith, 1979) in the periods of the 1960's when inward manufacturing investment to Scotland ran at a relatively high level, fostered their most rapid economic expansion. Irvine's most vigorous growth actually preceded the town's translation from an old but expansive burgh to a new but struggling town, launched into the tide of national economic difficulty which swelled through the 1970's. East Kilbride's most vigorous period of growth saw employment increase between 1966 and

TABLE 2   PERCENTAGE RATES OF EMPLOYMENT GROWTH IN
THE SCOTTISH NEW TOWNS

	1971–74	1974–78	1978–83	Date of Designation
Livingston	101·3	34·0	12·3	1962
Irvine	47·3	5·5	−30·9	1966
Cumbernauld	11·9	17·4	−10·8	1955
Glenrothes	41·9	4·0	−0·8	1950
East Kilbride	26·1	1·4	−17·9	1947
All New Towns	37·0	8·0	−10·7	

Source: Town and Country Planning.

1974 by 11,700 or 65 per cent, supported by an effort between 1965 and 1970 when half the dwellings in the town were completed. During the 1970's, the signs (Table 2) were that East Kilbride's industrial structure was maturing to the point at which its rate of employment growth would persist as the lowest amongst those Scottish new towns not based upon a substantial existing local economy, as Irvine is; East Kilbride's peak of employment was reached at 31,500 in 1978, but losses in the next five years reduced employment to 26,000 in 1983, following a decline as rapid as the growth of the town's most expansive period. As the oldest of the Scottish new towns with more manufacturing employment than any other, shrinking employment amongst East Kilbride firms suffering ageing and the downturn of their product cycles was particularly acute, significantly countering new growth. The correlation between the maturity of the local economy and a weaker capacity to offset closures and decline persisted into the 1980's, when in 1983–84 East Kilbride contributed only 150 of the net increase of 1,500 jobs in the three Strathclyde new towns, the weakest recovery in the emergence of the new towns from their unprecedented decline of employment of the early 1980's. The effects on economic growth of ageing is shared by new towns throughout Britain; Fothergill *et al.* (1982a) show that the new towns started prior to 1950 had by 1967 ceased to show manufacturing growth above the rate of all other towns of similar size and, by 1974, this was true for all generations of new towns. The vulnerability of maturing manufacturing economies in the new towns has been emphasised by Hood and Young (1977, 179–85), who have compared the dependence of the new towns on multi-national and other externally controlled firms with that of inner city areas upon declining industries.

Evidence of this vulnerability which surfaced in 1978–83 is given in Table 3, which shows the sharp decline of manufacturing in all three new towns. Whereas even prior to 1978 the rate of closures amongst new town manufacturing firms had, for many years, closely compared to that of Glasgow, it was no longer obscured by higher gains of new firms as the mobility of industry and

TABLE 3   MANUFACTURING EMPLOYMENT CHANGE IN THE STRATHCLYDE
NEW TOWNS AND THE INNER CONURBATION

	Manufacturing Employment			Percentage Change	
	1971	1978	1983	1971–78	1978–83
Cumbernauld	4,501	5,084	3,488	+12·9	−31·4
East Kilbride	11,871	14,614	9,305	+23·1	−36·3
Irvine	7,200	9,505	6,462	+32·0	−32·0
Inner Clydeside Conurbation	172,847	135,181	98,490	−21·8	−27·2

Sources: Industry Department for Scotland.
Glasgow District Council: District Profile 1984.

industrial production fell so rapidly from the late 1970's new town manufacturing employment fell more steeply between 1978 and 1983 than in Glasgow and the Inner Conurbation. East Kilbride's decades of manufacturing growth led it first into steep recession. A younger town in the expansive decade of the 1960's Cumbernauld had been less well prepared than East Kilbride to provide for the higher flow of firms and activities available to draw on in this period; nor at an earlier stage in the evacuation from Scottish cities of wholesaling and service industries and their increasing centralisation within Scotland, did Cumbernauld enjoy such a favourable strategic position as the development of the Scottish motorway network provided it with in the 1970's. Initially dominated by the Burroughs' factory, Cumbernauld's manufacturing base was drastically undermined for the first time when Burroughs completed work on the adaptation of calculating machines at the introduction of decimal currency to the United Kingdom. Even Government's contribution of offices to reinforce the economies of the new towns went awry when, in 1971, the Conservative administration rescinded the previous Labour administration's proposals for a Land Commission, which was to administer for the United Kingdom from headquarters in Cumbernauld. Replaced by the Inland Revenue Computer Centre in 1977, Government's contributions to Cumbernauld had less continuity than in East Kilbride, where the National Engineering Laboratory had been established from its designation as a new town, the Scottish PAYE Centre of the Inland Revenue followed in 1968 and offices of the Overseas Development Administration transferred in 1981. Irvine's was already an established economy at its translation to a new town in 1966, expanding rapidly with the stimulus of vigorous promotion by its Town Clerk. As a new town, it was to be perhaps relatively less successful than as a Small Burgh; its impetus from the expanding regional economy of the early 1960's inevitably lost pace as the regional and national economies turned towards recession in the 1970's, although its British Telecom international exchange came as a gesture of Government commitment. More distant than Cumbernauld and East Kilbride from the Clydeside economy, Irvine's unemployed could less readily turn to commuting and its unemployment rate grew by July 1984 to 19·9 per cent, higher than existed in Motherwell, Greenock, Paisley, Clydebank or the Vale of Leven, and exceeding the rates of 14·2 per cent in Cumbernauld and 11·7 per cent in East Kilbride.

Because surveys of residents customarily show them to have been drawn by the prospect of new houses even more than by new employment (e.g. Livingstone and Sykes, 1972), the new towns have local economies which are far from being self-sufficient or self-contained. Their labour markets are unusually open, integrated and dependent upon the wider economy of the West of Scotland to an exceptional degree. Of the residents in employment living in 1981 in the new towns, 38 per cent in East Kilbride, 52 per cent in Cumbernauld and 21 per cent in Irvine worked outside their area. Each new town drew in workers from other areas, but East Kilbride possessed a total employment equivalent to only 74 per cent of its economically active residents, Cumbernauld for the equivalent of 57 per cent and Irvine for 76 per cent. But for this very considerable dependence upon commuting to employment provided by Glasgow and areas beyond, unemployment in the new towns would have become notably higher — in East Kilbride and Cumbernauld in particular.

Unemployment in the 1980's is closely related to socio-economic status, of course, and when socio-economic profiles are compared with unemployment rates in Strathclyde, it can be seen (Table 4) that the new towns have no less unemployment than their weight of professional and skilled residents would make likely. This further indicates the overwhelming extent to which the new towns are bound by the laws of the regional economy and their regulation of opportunities for local populations. Looking to the future, the strong representation in the new towns of teenagers and young people who suffer particularly high unemployment rates, suggests that the demographic structure of the new towns may appreciably add to their problems in the re-creation of employment. After losing an estimated 5,000 jobs in the period 1979–82, East Kilbride's Development Profile had foreseen need to more than replace these by expanding an employment of 26,500 in 1982 by a quarter within a decade. Cumbernauld's target of population growth had implied a necessary increase of a third in employment in the same period. In facing a rather larger proportionate need for a job-increase than Cumbernauld, Irvine recognised that since the mid-1970's its attraction of new industries had been almost exactly countered by the annual average loss of jobs by closure or contraction of firms on its industrial estates; amongst industries in Irvine outside the Corporation's estates, there had been a major decline of employment. The Secretary of State's subsequent substitution of lower 'trigger' populations implicitly recognised the unlikelihood that employment growth could be found to meet the targets.

Despite Government's gestures to reinforce the component of white-collar office employment, the structure of employment in the new towns continues to reflect the emphasis which development corporations have put on manu-

TABLE 4   UNEMPLOYMENT AND SOCIO-ECONOMIC
STRUCTURE, RANKING OF STRATHCLYDE DISTRICTS.
1981 CENSUS

	Population in Social Classes I, II and III (N)		Unemployment	
	%	Rank	%	Rank
Eastwood	55	1	5	1 =
Bearsden and Milngavie	53	2	5	1 =
Strathkelvin	41	3	8	3
*East Kilbride	35	4	11	5
Kyle and Carrick	30	5	12	6 =
*Cumbernauld and Kilsyth	29	6	12	6 =
Clydesdale	28	7	10	4
Dumbarton	27	8 =	14	10
Renfrew	27	8 =	12	6 =
Hamilton	25	10	17	13 =
Kilmarnock and Loudoun	24	11	13	9
*Cunninghame	23	12	17	13 =
Inverclyde	19	13 =	16	11 =
Monklands	19	13 =	19	17 =
Glasgow	18	15 =	19	17 =
Motherwell	18	15 =	18	16
Clydebank	17	17	17	13 =
Cumnock and Doon	16	18	16	11 =

* Districts containing new towns.

facturing industry. It also reflects the tendency for people in the new as well as in surrounding towns to look to established county towns for the offices of solicitors, estate agents and other local personal services, which have been slow to transfer to the new towns. Indeed, amongst the opportunities for service employment in the new towns, Cameron (1979, 30) emphasises their significant dependence upon public service posts in teaching, nursing, social services and the civil service, amongst which there is substantial salaries and wage investment by Strathclyde Regional Council, whose important contribution to new town employment has not commonly been recognised by the Development Corporations.

The employment record of the new towns was placed in a fresh light in the 1980's not only by the evidence of their marked vulnerability to the recession in British manufacturing industry, but by experience from new economic initiatives in older areas of Clydeside and particularly those associated with the Scottish Development Agency. The new initiatives were displaying a record for attracting and locating new employment which was favourably comparable to the best of the Strathclyde new towns. In the period 1980–84, the Clydebank Task Force claimed the generation of 1,750 jobs in newly located and expanding firms, while East Kilbride and Cumbernauld appear to have generated some 2,100 jobs each of these kinds; the GEAR project in Glasgow's East End claimed over 3,200 jobs in newly located industry between 1976 and 1984.

Do the New Towns Harm the Regeneration of Metropolitan Clydeside?
When from the inception of Strathclyde Regional Council in 1975, its resistance to the introduction of Stonehouse new town became a trial of strength in the Council's assertion of its strategic planning policies, its attitude to the social and economic impact of the new towns was seen as incorporating several strands of argument and assumption. The Council translated the proposition of the West Central Scotland Plan (1974) that Stonehouse should be postponed into a determination that it should be permanently abandoned. There was an implication in the Council's position that the new towns had contributed to the 'flow of employment and population from the established urban centres' (Strathclyde Regional Council, 1981). This implication incorporated assertions arising in the metropolitan regions of Britain from the late 1960's, where many allied to the interests of the mature conurbations considered that new towns were depriving the central cities, drawing out people and jobs and exacerbating endemic problems of poverty and economic decline, which were becoming increasingly obvious as urban congestion was succeeded by spreading dereliction and vacancy of urban land. This critical view of the new towns was not taken by the West Central Scotland Plan, which became strongly influential in the development of policies in regional planning, social deprivation and employment creation in the new Regional Council, but whose analysis of the new towns did not incorporate any tension between their interests and those of Glasgow and the Clydeside conurbation. To the contrary, the Plan had seen tension only in competition between the new towns themselves, whose remaining capacity was evidently sufficient for the needs of the remainder of the century, when a slackened demand for rented houses was foreseen by comparison with the high pressure of the 1960's. The Plan's recommendation that Stonehouse should be postponed was because of the risk that, in proceeding, it would divert potential employment or population from the longer established new towns.

In the decade following the analysis of the West Central Scotland Plan, new understanding of social and economic change within British metropolitan regions and changing Government policy towards the new towns, has borne out the Plan's understanding that new towns are perhaps more in competition

Fig. 2   East Kilbride new town. Electronic industry established in the early 1970's and expanding with new investment ten years later.

Fig. 3   Irvine new town. The Development Corporation's extension of the shopping and commercial centre of the historic burgh of Irvine.

Fig. 4 Cumbernauld new town. New housing environment for the 1980's at Balloch.

Fig. 5 Templeton Business Centre, Glasgow. Economic regeneration by the Scottish Development Agency in the GEAR project in inner Glasgow. The former carpet factory overlooking Glasgow Green has been converted for professional and commercial offices, workshops and community businesses.

TABLE 5   NEW TOWN AND SCOTTISH DEVELOPMENT AGENCY EXPENDITURE

Current prices (£'000)

	1976/77	1977/78	1978/79	1979/80	1980/81	1981/82	1982/83	1983/84
Scottish New Towns:								
Capital Expenditure	53,162	42,342	46,541	53,579	61,551	59,609	54,780	57,946
Scottish Development Agency: Expenditure								
Urban Renewal	81	787	2,237	4,156	12,172			
Land Renewal	1,273	14,472	19,505	26,386	22,767			
Land Reclamation					} 28,703	{ 8,368	15,718	10,355
Site and Environmental Improvements						12,508	17,958	18,730

Note: change in presentation of Scottish Development Agency accounts from 1981 precludes exact comparisons before and after. Data for 1980/81 compared under the separate forms of presentation.

Sources: Development Corporation Annual Reports.
Scottish Development Agency Annual Reports.

with one another than they are with Glasgow. In terms of Government policy, the new towns have experienced a major reduction in the rate of Treasury investment. Although this has coincided (Table 5) with a contemporaneous increase in Government investment in urban renewal and land reclamation through the Scottish Development Agency and other Government agencies, this has been countered in the 1980's in particular by the considerable cuts in allocations for renewal and improvement of the public housing stock of the urban councils. That the population growth and housebuilding programmes of the new towns have been curtailed has, therefore, been overwhelmingly a consequence of Treasury cuts in housing expenditure nationally, particularly in the life of the Conservative Government since 1979. In their economic growth, the consequences of the declining manufacturing base of the British economy have become as evident in the new towns as they were earlier obvious in Glasgow, Paisley or Clydebank. Notwithstanding the very notable rise since 1976 in Government involvement in the economic and physical renewal of Glasgow and the older parts of Clydeside, an even-handed view would find it as hard to see that their rapid physical improvement in the past decade should be blamed for the deteriorating growth and economic record of the new towns, as that in an earlier period the new towns can be seen to deserve blame for the evacuation and decline in physical condition of their parent metropolitan area. Despite dispute over Strathclyde Regional Council's Structure Plan, it is not possible to see any restrictions on the corporations by the Regional Council as more than marginal to a decade of overwhelming restraints associated with Government, exerted through Treasury cuts, response to international recession in macro-economic policy for national industrial restructuring, major modifications to United Kingdom inter-regional policy and the assertion of the private housing sector at the expense of the public sector, which dominated the calculations of housing need underlying the target populations for the new towns. Whatever the new emphasis on rebuilding Clydeside from 1975, any lessened emphasis on the new towns in public policy reflected more than caused their slowing growth.

Although Clydesiders moving to the new towns have been biased to the young, to the skilled and semi-skilled, to the socially mobile and away from those deprived of education or income, the new towns together with all other official overspill projects drew no more than 32 per cent of net out-migration of people from Glasgow in the peak decade of overspill from 1961 to 1971 (Farmer and Smith, 1975, 158). However, Liverpool, Manchester and Newcastle, which lacked the drawing power of a new town until the later 1960's, all lost population more considerably than Glasgow during the 1950's and 1960's. It cannot be clearly established that the relatively greater availability of new towns on Clydeside significantly exacerbated overspill during the period of Glasgow's heaviest population loss. The new towns may accordingly be seen to have drawn from a vigorous flow from Glasgow, but to have done so to a much lesser extent than had been expected by the Clyde Valley Regional Plan of 1946 or, indeed, by the city's calculations in reviews of planning and housing policy during the 1960's. Only East Kilbride published a practice of discrimination in favour of tenants who were economically active and in demand by local employers but, while it lasted, the practice was to become in retrospect more damaging to East Kilbride than to Glasgow. Later, the accentuated bulge of the 1960's in the town's age structure amongst the most active working ages would become an accentuated bulge of prospective retirals, exacerbating a problem of housing elderly people for whom little provision had been made at times of readier investment in housing. Sim (1983) shows that 6,696 families were rehoused from Glasgow to East Kilbride in the period from 1959 to 1978, under the official scheme whereby the city paid a fixed contribution for each family. Others of Glasgow origin also moved to East Kilbride outwith the official scheme, but together with the much larger migration of Glaswegians to Cumbernauld — some 74 per cent of whose incomers had been of Glasgow origin when the new town's expansion had reached 46,200 in 1983, it remained that the new towns were merely representative of the many towns and communities to which Glasgow people were moving in the 1960's and 1970's, whether in Strathclyde, the rest of Scotland, England or overseas.

In the 1980's, the pull of the new towns, of Bishopbriggs, of Eastwood, of Erskine and of the other communities fringing the Clydeside Conurbation was being challenged more considerably than in the preceding thirty years. The relationship of the new towns to the regional housing market and to conditions in the regional economy had changed. In conjunction with these changes, there was a shift in the profile of households and people moving to the new towns. Sim shows families with young children to no longer form such a disproportionately large share of migrant families moving into East Kilbride, as prior to the 1970's. In contrast to the earlier period when the Development Corporation reserved dwellings only for incomers with employment in East Kilbride, elderly households had by the late 1970's become notably more common amongst migrants to the town than amongst all migrants from Glasgow to all other places; a quarter of households arriving in East Kilbride in the late 1970's were wholly or partially constituted of pensioners. An accompanying shift away from skilled and towards semi-skilled migrants, again contrasted with the dominance of skilled workers still evident amongst migrants within the United Kingdom as a whole.

These trends which had emerged in the late 1970's may be appreciably affected in the 1980's by the new towns' replacement of their programmes of rented housing by a concentration on private housebuilding. What was being seen was, however, the consolidation of a new balance of relations between the new towns and the renewing areas of Clydeside. There was an equalisation both in the quality of domestic environments — which was a progressive shift — and in the distribution of opportunities for employment — which was not. Glasgow and renewed parts of older Clydeside were increasingly able to offer younger, ambitious and economically competitive households the choice of a fit house in a good environment, a choice previously largely confined to Bishopbriggs, Cumbernauld, East Kilbride, Eastwood, Erskine and the newer communities and housing estates on the periphery of the Conurbation. In the 1970's, the belated programme of rehabilitation of the best of the inheritance of Victorian tenements was beginning to offer younger households a quality of house hitherto insufficiently available within the Conurbation; in the early 1980's, the opportunities were rapidly extended by the revival of low-cost private housebuilding in parts of inner Glasgow where it had been absent for seventy years or more. Coupled to this increasing equalisation of housing opportunities across the Conurbation, the new towns were losing impetus in new job creation. For the minority of migrants for whom the main reason for moving to a new town had been job-related, there were rapidly diminishing opportunities. Within the Conurbation, opportunities were also diminishing; notwithstanding localised economic initiatives frequently associated with the Scottish Development Agency, which were helping equalise the kind of opportunities for new employment previously disproportionately associated with the new towns, unemployment was rising in Glasgow, inner Clydeside, North Ayrshire, North Lanarkshire and other areas from which the new towns had drawn most of their populations. To a significant extent, therefore, the slowing flow of people from older to newer urban areas in the late 1970's was also probably associated with a reduced ability to afford a move. There was accordingly a reducing impetus to leave Glasgow and older urban areas coincident with a reducing attraction in the new towns.

If it can be argued that the new towns have damaged the social and demographic health of Glasgow less than the difficult and protracted history of the city's post-war renewal, it can similarly be suggested that the new towns have not been a principal reason for the economic difficulties of the inner Conurbation, whose economic history since 1945 has been paralleled both in other British conurbations and in the old industrial cities of the north central and north eastern United States. Indeed, unlike some new towns around London, the Strathclyde new towns have drawn relatively few firms to relocate where, undoubtedly, new premises and co-operation have been more readily available for a longer period than across most of the region. As late as the 1960's, the Corporation of Glasgow sought to help industries to move out from the congested city. Yet the loss of manufacturing employment in Glasgow was overwhelmingly due to the closure or contraction of industries, coupled to a weak replacement by new activity. A tentative assessment by Fothergill *et al.* (1982a) suggests that 20 per cent of Clydeside's loss of manufacturing jobs in 1960–78 could have been due to the diversionary effect of the new towns, at most. Henderson (1974, 77) shows that redevelopment was relatively much less significant in the city's employment decline than was probably true of its population loss, and he also shows that firms tended to relocate within the City rather than to move outside. For inward investment, of course, the opportunities for new firms to obtain land or premises in inner areas were few, although Lever (1981) suggests that there appears to have been higher value added per employee in inner city locations on Clydeside, where outer locations gained employment which was not justified solely on grounds of any decisive operating cost advantage. Glasgow Corporation completed a flatted factory at Finnieston in the early 1960's, a small gesture to such firms as were displaced by comprehensive redevelopment schemes; yet the Corporation was still encouraging firms to leave for the new towns and outlying industrial estates but with small success. Finnieston remained one of the most prominent gestures in matching the new towns' industrial attractions until the 1970's, when the Scottish Development Agency brought financial and technical support for the sudden burgeoning of initiatives for economic regeneration amongst the urban Districts. Of course, in the field of offices and regional administration, the new towns have scarcely challenged the pre-eminence of Glasgow in the private sector; the significant offices which have established in the new towns have depended upon public sector decisions.

When the employment record of Glasgow and the new towns is closely compared with the records of other British conurbations, it can be seen that inner Clydeside has tended to lose employment at a rather faster rate than others, yet at a markedly lower rate than inner London, in whose region new towns are relatively less numerous than on Clydeside. Fothergill and Gudgin (1982b) suggest that the degree to which manufacturing employment has fallen in recent decades in older urban areas of the United Kingdom and grown in rural areas and small towns, has been closely related to the size of urban populations. London, of all urban areas, has declined most considerably. The notable feature of Clydeside, however, has not been that Glasgow has tended to any greater loss of employment than the cities central to other British conurbations; this has not been the case. What is distinctive about Clydeside is that outer parts of the Conurbation and its rural periphery have failed to compensate. Strathclyde's weakest characteristic has been the inability of peripheral locations to provide new growth sufficient to compensate for employment loss in the inner Conurbation, falling short of the larger replacement evident in several English metropolitan regions. Although Cumbernauld and East Kilbride have contributed disproportionately large shares to the new growth of the outer Conurbation, they can be seen (Cameron, 1979, 48) to have been well supported by growth at a number of other strategically advantageous locations to the east and south of Clydeside. Yet, this concentration of growth in and around North Lanarkshire was unable to match the strength seen in comparable locations in other conurbations.

Notwithstanding that the people of East Kilbride and Cumbernauld depend upon work in Glasgow and other Districts to a degree exceptional for towns of their size, it remains that their growth of population and of employment appears to have been complementary to plans to renew the Conurbation. Assertions that the new towns have particularly damaged Glasgow cannot be convincingly sustained. Nor is there any convincing evidence to show that Irvine has damaged the towns of North Ayrshire. If, however, the new towns may remain complementary to urban renewal within the development of urban Strathclyde, the issue of competition between the new towns for people and jobs may be seen as one which can be less readily denied. Similarly, when housing expansion in the new towns has become largely dependent upon attracting house owners of a kind for whom the inner city may offer few alternatives, the new towns appear less likely to demand public investment which could have been saved to apply to the problems of financing urban renewal.

The Political Significance of the New Towns

If the new towns are highly integrated with the regional economy by their exceptionally open labour markets, by their notable dependence upon other areas to generate income for their commuting residents — which more than offsets the income they provide to the residents of neighbouring communities — by the origins in Glasgow or other older towns of most of the adult populations, and by the association of much of their employment with the wider economy of the region, the new towns are notably segregated in their administration. When their much reduced rate of growth from the late 1970's has altered the balance of their investment considerably, shifting it towards problems of maintenance and management, longer characteristic of the older communities, the preoccupations of administration in the development corporations are closer than ever before to those of the District Councils of

Strathclyde. The Development Profiles indicate the growing extent to which rehabilitation and renewal will come to feature in the work of the corporations. In these circumstances, the Regional Council and East Kilbride District Council particularly sought an earlier withdrawal of the development corporations than the Secretary of State has been prepared to countenance. The retention of the corporations has rested primarily on a view of their special merits in economic development; alongside this case, there appear to have been other, unstated political reasons. The continuation of the corporations stands with the increased strategic intervention of Government development agencies in the economic and physical renewal of Strathclyde, which the Scottish Development Agency, the Scottish Special Housing Association and the Housing Corporation made from the mid-1970's.

Government's political responsibility for the new towns has persisted through both Labour and Conservative administrations, with sustained encouragement from civil servants of the Scottish Office. Under the supervision of the economic planning arm of the Industry Department, the Scottish new towns have continued to hold an eminence in the Scottish Office which the English new towns have failed to hold, located as they have been within the responsibility of the Department of the Environment. Whereas English new towns suffered downward revisions in their target populations in 1977 which were sometimes major, no reductions occurred in Scotland apart from the abandonment of Stonehouse until the substitution of 'trigger' populations in 1984. Stonehouse, however, was the opportunity for the Government to transfer some new town methods to Glasgow and older urban areas and, to this extent, its end anticipated an extension of government agency influence. This extended influence followed the inauguration of the new local government system in 1975 which, in its central analysis, was intended to provide a superior means of planning for regional development than the fragmented system which had previously inhibited strategic planning. The continuation of separate administration for the new towns and maintenance of population targets lying far beyond the horizon of the Regional Council's structure plan (1981) and, indeed, beyond the structure plan's belief that the targets were achievable in foreseeable circumstances, reflected a political importance to Government of the development corporations which was greater than was admitted in policy statements by the Scottish Office and Secretaries of State.

The advantages to Government of the new town development corporations have been various. Their presence has provided opportunities for economic promotion by the corporations and by Government itself, free of the distractions which arise by the political and administrative divisions of interest more prevalent in local authorities. The greater ability of the corporations to be single-minded about economic development was clearly evident up to the 1970's, but has become less distinctive as the influence of the Scottish Development Agency has spread into Clydeside and urban and some rural areas beyond; from 1980, annual capital investment by the Scottish

Development Agency in their Area Projects alone in Strathclyde ran at about £25 million, by comparison with investment by the development corporations of about £30 million per annum in the three new towns of the region. Furthermore, since local government reorganisation in 1975, economic initiatives by Strathclyde Regional Council and by Glasgow and other District Councils have also frequently been innovative, sometimes in directions and with influence which has led the new towns. In the fields of design and of housing standards, the new towns have also come to be more closely matched by the quality of work in older urban areas since the early 1970's and, in problems and standards of contemporary rehabilitation, Glasgow and the older areas have been unable to turn to the new towns for examples of innovation so influential in earlier periods.

While no longer so significant to Government as exemplars in architecture and environmental planning, the new towns remain significant when Government pursues changes in social policy to which local authorities may be unsympathetic. Accelerated pressures by Governments to sell publicly owned houses and to narrow the gap between Scottish and English rent levels were, of course, earlier and more readily reflected in the new towns than in local authorities. The level of new town house rents is higher on average than for tenants of Scottish local authorities or the Scottish Special Housing Association, although because a higher proportion of new town houses were built at times of high building costs and high interest rates, their occupants are subsidised by the Treasury to a markedly higher extent than tenants of either Glasgow District Council or the Scottish Special Housing Corporation (Table 6).

Whatever housing benefits come to new town residents in the mid-1980's, their experience of the previous decade had been that their economic environment was shared with others of their status and skills elsewhere in their region. When the Scottish Economic Planning Department (1981, 2) had stated that the new towns' population targets constituted 'an article of faith on

TABLE 6   AVERAGE SUBSIDIES TO TENANTS

	New Towns £	Glasgow £	S.S.H.A. £
1979–80	569	358	340
1980–81	615	460	328
1981–82	611	445	286
1982–83	619	448	279
1983–84	628	342	245

Note: Glasgow data includes rebates.

Sources: Hansard, written answers 13.12.83 c.424: PQ 70.
Glasgow District Annual Housing Reviews.

the basis of which individuals and enterprises had been induced to settle in the towns', the depth of faith required over the remainder of the century was already more than the Treasury or the national economy seemed likely to sustain. Three years later, the Secretary of State (1984) would implicitly recognise that the targets involved a larger expectation than was fair to place on the development corporations. The new towns had already matured to share the problems of readjustment to the changing international economy which had been longer familiar in other towns in Strathclyde; this was a task in which the development corporations had much to learn from the experience of the older parts of their region.

REFERENCES

Abercrombie, P. and Matthew, R. (1949), *The Clyde Valley Regional Plan.* HMSO,Edinburgh.

Cameron, G. C., McCallum, J. D., Adams, J. G. L., Coopers and Lybrand (1979), *An Economic Study Conducted for East Kilbride Development Corporation.*

Coopers and Lybrand Associates (1979), *Economic Impact Analysis of Cumbernauld.* Cumbernauld Development Corporation.

Coopers and Lybrand Associates (1979), *Economic Impact Analysis of Irvine.* Irvine Development Corporation.

Cumbernauld, East Kilbride and Irvine Development Corporations (1983), *Development Profiles.* Separate profiles for each of the new towns.

Farmer, E. and Smith, R. (1975), Overspill Theory: a metropolitan case study, *Urban Studies, 12,* 135–149.

Fothergill, S., Kitson, M. and Monk, S. (1982a), The Impact of the New and Expanded Town programmes on Industrial Location in Britain 1960–78, *Industrial Location Research Project, Working Paper No. 3.* Department of Land Economy, University of Cambridge.

Fothergill, S. and Gudgin, G. (1982b), *Unequal Growth.* Heinemann, London.

Henderson, R. A. (1974), Industrial Overspill from Glasgow, 1958–68, *Urban Studies, 11,* 61–79.

Henderson, R. A. (1982), *The Employment Performance of Established Manufacturing Industry in the Scottish New Towns.* ESU Discussion Paper No. 16, Industry Department for Scotland, Edinburgh.

Hood, N. and Young, S. (1977), The Long-Term Impact of Multinational Enterprise on Industrial Geography: The Scottish Case, *Scottish Geographical Magazine, 93, No. 3,* Dec. 1977.

Lever, W. F. (1981), *Operating Costs as an Explanation of Employment Change in the Clydeside Region.* Paper presented to 'Industry and the Inner City' conference, University of Newcastle upon Tyne, May 1981.

Livingstone, J. M. and Sykes, A. J. M. (1972), *East Kilbride 70: an economic and social survey.* University of Strathclyde.

Secretary of State for Scotland (1984), Written Answer to Parliamentary Question, 14th November 1984. *Hansard,* Columns 279–80.

Scottish Development Department (1963), *Central Scotland: A Programme for Development and Growth.* HMSO, Edinburgh, Cmnd. 2188.

Scottish Economic Planning Department (1981), *New Towns in Scotland: A Policy Statement.* Edinburgh.

Sim, D. (1983), Some Changes in New Town Migration. *Planning Outlook, 26, No. 1.*

Smith, R., *East Kilbride: the biography of a Scottish new town 1947–73.* Department of Environment: HMSO.

Strathclyde Regional Council (1981), *Strathclyde Structure Plan 1981.*

West Central Scotland Plan Team (1974), *West Central Scotland: a programme of action.* Glasgow.

CHAPTER SIX

THE SMALLER URBAN SETTLEMENTS OF STRATHCLYDE

M. Pacione

The Strathclyde Region encompasses an area of 5,000 sq. mls. and contains within its boundaries 2·4 million, or almost 50 per cent, of the Scottish population. While the majority of inhabitants are concentrated in the city of Glasgow, a significant proportion are located in the hundreds of smaller urban centres which form the body and tail of the settlement hierarchy. The definition of 'smaller urban places' employed here included all 170 settlements with a population of 1,000 or more, and reached an upper limit of 82,524 in Paisley — the largest settlement in the Region outside Glasgow. Below this, at the lower end of the settlement size pyramid, are 155 rural places with a combined population of 59,500 (2·5 per cent of the regional total). These lay outwith the scope of the present investigation. This chapter sets out to illustrate the nature of the smaller urban places by first identifying the social, economic and demographic structure of each settlement and then classifying the settlements in terms of their principal characteristics.

Selection of Social Indicators
   Social indicators are measures of the social position, characteristics and living conditions of people or households in an area and as such provide a key tool for social geographers. The principal advantage of the national census as a source of social, economic and demographic data is that small area statistical information is available for a wide range of topics at the enumeration district level. As a listing of census-based social indicators can extend to over five hundred items selectivity is essential (Hakim, 1978). Most studies have found that an adequate coverage can be provided by a selection of around fifty indicators but the particular indices employed clearly depend on the objectives of the investigation. The present study included the measures indicated in Table 1.

Demographic indicators (variables 1–5)
   These recorded the population and age-structure of each settlement. Some demographic indicators can be useful measures of particular types of need in

102

TABLE 1   LIST OF SOCIAL INDICATOR VARIABLES EMPLOYED

V1	All Present Residents 1981
V2	% All Persons Aged 0–4
V3	% All Residents Aged 5–14
V4	% All Residents of Working Age in Private Households (males 15–64; females 15–59)
V5	% Residents of Pensionable Age
V6	% Economically Active Males Unemployed
V7	% Economically Active Females Unemployed
V8	% All Males 16 + who are Economically Active
V9	% All Females 16 + who are Economically Active
V10	% Those in Employment who are Self-employed
V11	% Households in Owner-Occupied Accommodation
V12	% Households in Local Authority Rented Accommodation
V13	% Households in Private Rented Unfurnished Accommodation
V14	% Households in Private Rented Furnished Accommodation
V15	% Households with more than 1·5 Persons Per Room
V16	% Households with between 1 and 1·5 Persons Per Room
V17	% Households with No Car
V18	% Households which Lack Bath or Inside W.C.
V19	% Households which Share Bath or Inside W.C.
V20	% Households with Two or More Cars
V21	% Households with One or Two Rooms
V22	% Households with Six or More Rooms
V23	% Households spaces Vacant
V24	% Households with Six or More Persons
V25	% Households Not in Self-Contained Accommodation
V26	% Households with One Pensioner Living Alone
V27	% Households containing Persons of Pensionable Age Only
V28	% One Person Households
V29	% Lone Parent Households
V30	% Residents Aged 16 + in Employment Working in Agriculture
V31	% Residents Aged 16 + in Employment Working in Energy and Water
V32	% Residents Aged 16 + in Employment Working in Manufacturing
V33	% Residents Aged 16 + in Employment Working in Construction
V34	% Residents Aged 16 + in Employment Working in Distribution and Catering
V35	% Residents Aged 16 + in Employment Working in Transport
V36	% Residents Working Outside District of Residence
V37	% Residents Aged 16 + in Employment who Travel to Work by Car
V38	% Residents Aged 16 + in Employment who Travel to Work by Bus
V39	% Residents Aged 16 + in Employment who Travel to Work by Train
V40	% Residents Aged 16 + in Employment who Travel to Work on Foot
V41	% Residents Aged 16 + in Employment who Travel to Work by Other Means
V42	% Households with Head in S.E.G. 1, 2, 3, 4 (Professional Workers, Employers and Managers)
V43	% Households with Head in S.E.G. 7, 10, 11 (Personal Service Workers, Semi-Skilled and Manual Workers)
V44	% Households with Head in S.E.G. 8, 9 (Foremen, Supervisors and Skilled Manual)
V45	% Households with Head in S.E.G. 13 (Farmers — Employers and Managers)
V46	% Households with Head in S.E.G. 14 (Farmers — own account)
V47	% Households with Head in S.E.G. 15 (Agricultural Workers)
V48	% Population which Speaks, Reads or Writes Gaelic
V49	% Households Living in House that is Detached or Semi-Detached
V50	% Households Living in House that is Two-Storey or Low-Rise
V51	% Households Living in House that is High-Rise

an area and may be of considerable value in the planning of service provision by public and private agencies. An ageing population, for example, is likely to make an increasing demand on social services and may reduce an area's ability to support or attract employment opportunities. A youthful population, on the other hand, will make heavy demands on education, recreational and paediatric services and may require additional employment opportunities if the indigenous population is to be encouraged to remain.

Employment indicators (variables 6–10, 30–35)

These cover a range of topics including economic activity rates, occupation, proportion of working women, educational qualifications, job mobility, and the industrial composition of the labour force. Information on unemployment has been used as a particularly useful indicator of industrial decline in a town and of the attendant social and financial problems faced by families in an area of high unemployment. While male unemployment had traditionally been considered more important than the unemployment of women, the latter appears to perform better as a social indicator, being more closely correlated with other indicators of social malaise.

Housing indicators (variables 11–16, 18, 19, 21–24, 49–51)

This important suite of indicators covers topics such as housing tenure, standards, size and type. Information on the proportion of households lacking exclusive use of the basic facilities of hot water, bath and inside toilet is generally accepted as an indicator of low housing quality. A limitation of this measure is that it does not take into account factors related to structural defects or dampness which would form part of any definition of sub-tolerable housing. A second important indicator refers to overcrowding. As housing conditions have improved so measures of overcrowding have also changed. In 1951 a commonly used indicator was the percentage of households with two or more persons per room. For the 1961 census the figure of 1·5 persons per room was used. By 1971 the criterion had fallen again and currently a value of over 1·0 ppr is used to indicate overcrowding, with over 1·5 ppr indicative of acute overcrowding. Indicators of household size, which measure the number of persons and number of rooms per dwelling unit, normally focus on identifying the extreme cases, i.e. those which are well above or below the average. As in the case of overcrowding, the cut-off points vary. Some studies identify large households as those with six or more persons while others use a figure of seven and over, and the former is employed in this study.

Affluence indicators (variables 11, 12, 17, 20)

Since the British census does not collect income data, both housing and economic indicators have been used as a source of income-surrogates, with particular attention given to car ownership and household tenure. The proportion of households with or without the use of a car is often employed but this measure is not completely reliable when considering both urban and rural areas given the degree of enforced ownership in the latter as a result of the poor provision of public transport. A more accurate proxy-measure of affluence is the proportion of households with two or more cars. Household tenure has also been used as a broad measure of social status. The distinction between owner-occupied and council housing is particularly marked in Scotland where the majority of the population occupy housing rented from the local authority.

Household structure indicators (variables 24–29)

These provide information on the living arrangements and social structure of households or families to complement the information on their housing conditions. Special attention is focused on the identification of families with a large number of children, one-parent families, and pensioner households. One-parent families, for example, constitute one of the most deprived social groups and this indicator can assist local authorities in planning nursery school programmes. Similarly, the utility of identifying concentrations of pensioner households with their attendant needs is readily apparent.

Social class indicators (variables 42–47)

The census classification of household heads into seventeen socio-economic groupings is one of the most important social indicators, having been found to correlate highly with non-census indicators of social malaise. The seventeen socio-economic groupings are normally aggregated to form a smaller number of categories as in Table 1. A related source of information on the social composition of the labour force is the transport to work data which identify the proportion using various modes of travel to work.

Procedure

Since the census does not provide information on these indicators for individual settlements it was first necessary to collect data on the 100 per cent (e.g. population and housing) and 10 per cent (e.g. economic activity) topics at the enumeration district level. Individual enumeration districts were then aggregated to form the 170 settlements under investigation. Values for the 51 indicator variables were then computed from the raw cell tabulations. The data set therefore consisted of a matrix of 51 measures on each of the 170 settlements. This was then subjected to analysis at several levels of statistical sophistication.

Settlement Structure

Univariate Analysis

Univariate statistical techniques are often ignored by researchers who have been 'seduced by the greater sophistication of bivariate and multivariate analysis' (Evans, 1983, p. 115). Yet, consideration of the statistical and spatial distribution of individual social indicators can reveal important patterns in a data set. Even when a group of variables is of interest, such as indicators related to housing, each should be studied individually before the application of multivariate techniques. Univariate analysis should be regarded as an essential preliminary phase in the analysis and mapping of census-derived variables. This procedure is adhered to in the present paper. Table 2 presents simple statistical measures for each variable, while Figures 1–8 indicate the distribution of settlements with extreme values on a selection of indicators. Figure 1, for example, shows these places with a well above average proportion of (a) pre-school age children and (b) old age pensioners. While it is not sensible to draw general conclusions from one measure only there does appear to be a core-periphery spatial distinction between the two patterns. The concentration of 'elderly' settlements in Argyll, on the Clyde coast and in the southernmost parts of the old counties of Ayrshire and Lanarkshire is suggestive of both the phenomenon of rural geriatrification and the residential preferences of retired people. Further insight into the reasons behind these distributions, however, requires more detailed consideration of the social structure of the settlements involved. Figures 2 and 3 indicate another distinctive pattern underlying the social geography of the region, with a strong correlation between the distribution of places with well above average proportions of households in socio-economic groupings 1–4 (professionals, employers and managers) and the locations of settlements with well above average proportions of owner-occupied housing. Thus, for example, the predominantly working-class area of north Lanarkshire in the east of the conurbation may be contrasted with the more affluent settlements to the north, south and west of Glasgow. This pronounced socio-spatial division is readily apparent in Figures 4 and 5 which also highlight the annular zone of commuter settlements around Glasgow. The prime loci of the problems associated with multiple deprivation and social malaise are clearly demonstrated in Figure 6 which plots the distribution of settlements with a disproportionate share of overcrowded households. Finally, the indicators of male and female unemployment (Figures 7 and 8) confirm those places with levels of disadvantage well above the regional average.

Similar univariate distribution maps can be prepared for each of the 51 social indicators employed but the range of examples shown in Figures 1–8 is sufficient to indicate the general situation. While each of these distributions is of academic and practical utility in itself it is clear that some degree of statistical correlation and spatial overlap exists among the revealed patterns. Examination of the 51×51 correlation matrix confirmed a degree of multicollinearity, with particularly high levels of association existing between certain variables, as shown in Table 3. Thus, for example, variables 10 (% self-employed), 11 (% owner-occupied housing), 20 (% households with two or more cars), 22 (% households with six or more rooms), 37 (% who travel to work by car), 42 (% households in S.E.G. 1–4), and 49 (% detached or semi-

TABLE 2   SIMPLE SUMMARY STATISTICS FOR INDIVIDUAL VARIABLES AT THE
REGIONAL LEVEL

	Variable	Mean	Standard Deviation	Maximum Value	Minimum Value
V1	(Population)	7830	11831	82524	1000
V2	(Aged 0–4)	6·6	1·4	12·0	3·0
V3	(Aged 5–14)	16·5	2·0	22·0	11·0
V4	(Working Age)	59·6	2·6	65·0	46·0
V5	(Pensioners)	14·8	4·5	36·0	4·0
V6	(Male Unemployment)	13·6	5·9	33·0	3·0
V7	(Female Unemployment)	9·4	3·6	23·0	1·0
V8	(Econ. Active Males)	79·5	4·5	89·0	57·0
V9	(Econ. Active Females)	46·0	5·4	62·0	30·0
V10	(Self-employed)	6·5	3·9	30·0	1·0
V11	(Owner-occupied)	31·9	23·6	99·0	1·0
V12	(Council)	63·3	25·1	98·0	0·0
V13	(Rented Unfurnished)	1·6	2·0	11·0	0·0
V14	(Rented Furnished)	0·7	1·3	7·0	0·0
V15	(Over 1·5 ppr)	3·3	2·4	13·0	0·0
V16	(1–1·5 ppr)	13·0	4·5	24·0	4·0
V17	(No car)	46·5	13·6	77·0	5·0
V18	(Lack Bath/W.C.)	0·5	0·9	8·0	0·0
V19	(Share Bath/W.C.)	0·02	0·2	1·0	0·0
V20	(Two or more Cars)	11·0	6·9	44·0	2·0
V21	(One or Two Rooms)	9·6	4·6	26·0	0·0
V22	(Six or More Rooms)	7·4	6·5	38·0	0·0
V23	(Spaces Vacant)	3·7	2·3	19·0	1·0
V24	(Six or more Persons)	5·3	2·4	15·0	2·0
V25	(Not Self-Contained)	0·2	0·4	1·0	0·0
V26	(Lone Pensioner)	13·3	4·3	29·0	1·0
V27	(Pensionable Age Only)	21·0	6·4	49·0	5·0
V28	(One Person Household)	2·1	1·1	6·0	0·0
V29	(Lone Parent)	0·1	0·3	1·0	0·0
V30	(Agriculture)	1·0	2·1	18·0	0·0
V31	(Energy and Water)	5·1	7·3	39·0	0·0
V32	(Manufacturing)	27·7	10·3	56·0	2·0
V33	(Construction)	8·5	3·5	19·0	2·0
V34	(Distribution/Catering)	17·8	5·1	38·0	3·0
V35	(Transport)	6·7	3·1	20·0	0·0
V36	(Work Outside District)	33·0	20·4	·84·0	0·0
V37	(Car Travel)	50·0	11·8	85·0	21·0
V38	(Bus Travel)	23·6	11·1	53·0	0·0
V39	(Train Travel)	3·5	4·2	21·0	0·0
V40	(Foot Travel)	17·1	9·5	53·0	0·0
V41	(Other Means)	4·3	2·7	17·0	0·0
V42	(S.E.G. 1–4)	15·1	10·5	44·0	0·0
V43	(S.E.G. 7, 10, 11)	19·6	8·0	45·0	0·0
V44	(S.E.G. 8, 9)	25·7	8·1	46·0	8·0
V45	(S.E.G. 13)	0·2	0·5	3·0	0·0
V46	(S.E.G. 14)	0·1	0·5	5·0	0·0
V47	(S.E.G. 15)	0·4	0·9	6·0	0·0
V48	(Gaelic)	1·0	3·3	39·0	0·0
V49	(Detached/Semi)	38·5	18·7	89·0	0·0
V50	(Two Storey/Low Rise)	29·2	15·7	81·0	0·0
V51	(High Rise)	1·5	4·0	27·0	0·0

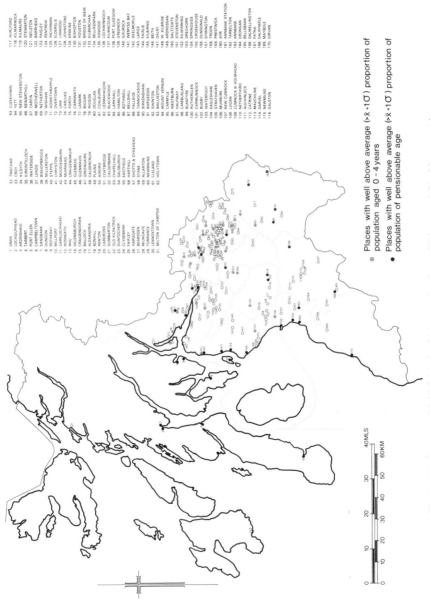

1. OBAN
2. LOCHGILPHEAD
3. ARDRISHAIG
4. TARBERT
5. PORT ELLEN
6. CAMPBELLTOWN
7. SANDBANK
8. DUNOON
9. ROTHESAY
10. MILLPORT
11. GARELOCHHEAD
12. ROSNEATH
13. RHU
14. HELENSBURGH
15. CRAIGENDORAN
16. BALLOCH
17. ALEXANDRIA
18. BONHILL
19. RENTON
20. CARDROSS
21. DUMBARTON
22. OLD KILPATRICK
23. DUNTOCHER
24. CLYDEBANK
25. FAIFLEY
26. HARDGATE
27. MILNGAVIE
28. TORRANCE
29. LENNOXTOWN
30. KILSYTH
31. MILTON OF CAMPSIE

32. TWECHAR
33. CROY
34. KILSYTH
35. KIRKINTILLOCH
36. WATERSIDE
37. LENZIE
38. BISHOPBRIGGS
39. MILLERSTON
40. STEPPS
41. CHRYSTON
42. MOODIESBURN
43. MUIRHEAD
44. CRAIGENDMUIR
45. GLENBOIG
46. GLENMAVIS
47. GREENGAIRS
48. CALDERCRUIX
49. PLAINS
50. AIRDRIE
51. COATBRIDGE
52. CALDERBANK
53. CHAPELHALL
54. SALSBURGH
55. EASTFIELD
56. HARTHILL
57. SHOTTS & DYKEHEAD
58. ALLANTON
59. STANE
60. NEWMAINS
61. CLELAND
62. HOLYTOWN

63. CLEEKHIMIN
64. YETT
65. NEW STEVENSTON
66. NEWARTHILL
67. CARFIN
68. MOTHERWELL
69. NETHERTON
70. WISHAW
71. GOWKTHRAPPLE
72. OVERTOWN
73. LAW
74. CARLUKE
75. FORTH
76. CARNWATH
77. LANARK
78. BIGGAR
79. RIGSIDE
80. DOUGLAS
81. COALBURN
82. LESMAHAGOW
83. BLACKWOOD
84. LARKHALL
85. HAMILTON
86. BOTHWELL
87. BELLSHILL
88. FALLSIDE
89. TANNOCHSIDE
90. BIRKENSHAW
91. BARGEDDIE
92. BAILLIESTON
93. MOUNT VERNON
94. CARMYLE
95. WESTBURN
96. HALFWAY
97. CAMBUSLANG
98. BLANTYRE
99. RUTHERGLEN
100. CARMUNNOCK
101. BUSBY
102. WATERFOOT
103. EAGLESHAM
104. STRATHAVEN
105. STONEHAVEN
106. MUIRKIRK
107. NEW CUMNOCK
108. LOGAN
109. CUMNOCK & HOLMHEAD
110. NETHERTHIRD
111. AUCHINLECK
112. CATRINE
113. MAUCHLINE
114. DARVEL
115. NEWMILNS
116. GALSTON

117. HURLFORD
118. KILMARNOCK
119. KILMAURS
120. STEWARTON
121. NEILSTON
122. BARRHEAD
123. PAISLEY
124. RENFREW
125. INCHINNAN
126. ELDERSLIE
127. LINWOOD
128. JOHNSTONE
129. ERSKINE
130. BISHOPTON
131. HOUSTON
132. BRIDGE OF WEIR
133. KILBARCHAN
134. MILLIKENPARK
135. HOWWOOD
136. LOCHWINNOCH
137. KILMACOLM
138. PORT GLASGOW
139. GREENOCK
140. GOUROCK
141. WEMYSS BAY
142. SKELMORLIE
143. LARGS
144. FAIRLIE
145. KILBIRNIE
146. BEITH
147. DALRY
148. W. KILBRIDE
149. ARDROSSAN
150. SALTCOATS
151. STEVENSTON
152. KILWINNING
153. DREGHORN
154. SPRINGSIDE
155. CROSSHOUSE
156. DUNDONALD
157. SYMINGTON
158. TROON
159. PRESTWICK
160. AYR
161. ANNBANK STATION
162. TARBOLTON
163. ANNBANK
164. DRONGAN
165. BELLSBANK
166. DALMELLINGTON
167. PATNA
168. DALRYMPLE
169. MAYBOLE
170. GIRVAN

⊛ Places with well above average (>x̄ +1σ) proportion of
   population aged 0 – 4 years

● Places with well above average (>x̄ +1σ) proportion of
   population of pensionable age

Fig. 1   Settlements with high levels of (a) pre-school age children, and (b) old-age pensioners.

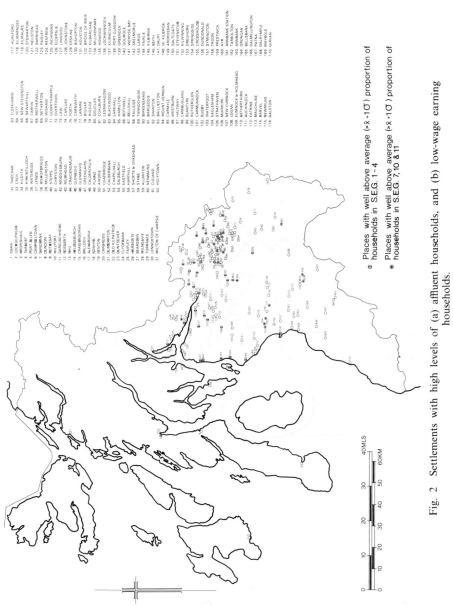

Fig. 2 Settlements with high levels of (a) affluent households, and (b) low-wage earning households.

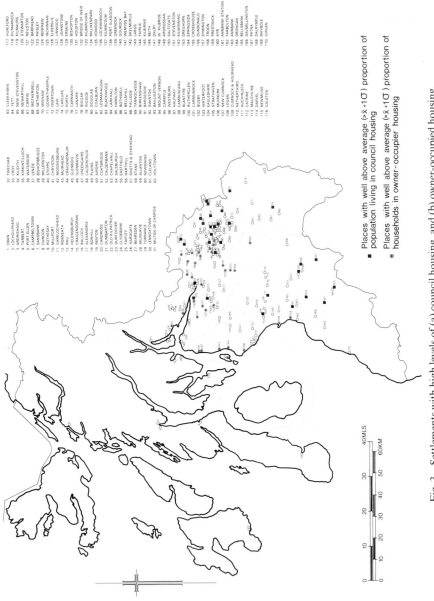

Fig. 3   Settlements with high levels of (a) council housing, and (b) owner-occupied housing.

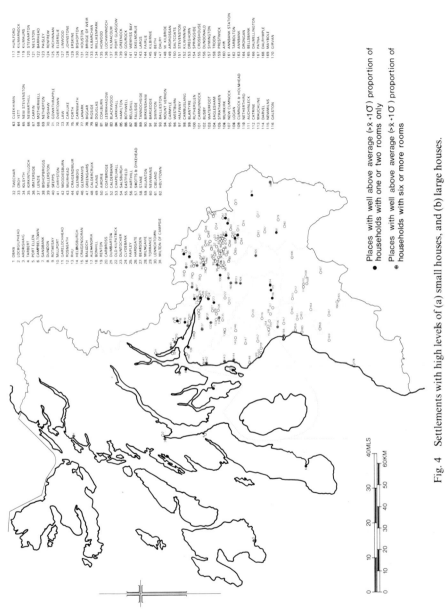

Fig. 4   Settlements with high levels of (a) small houses, and (b) large houses.

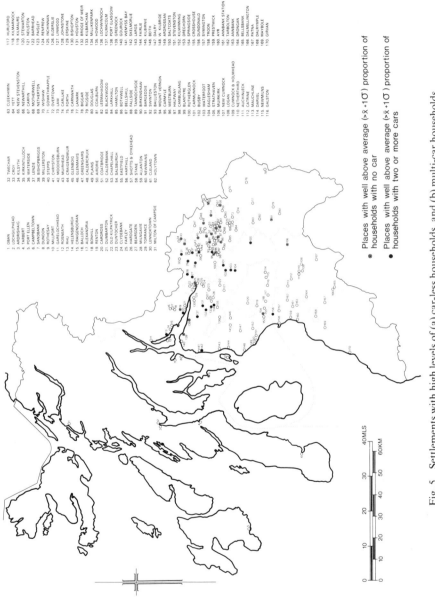

1 OBAN	32 TWECHAR	63 CLEEKHIMIN	117 HURLFORD
2 LOCHGILPHEAD	33 YETT	64 YETT	118 KILMARNOCK
3 ARDRISHAIG	34 KILSYTH	65 NEW STEVENSTON	119 KILMAURS
4 TARBERT	35 KIRKINTILLOCH	66 NEWARTHILL	120 STEWARTON
5 CAR-ELLEN	36 CARFIN	67 CARFIN	121 DUNLOP
6 CAMPBELTOWN	37 LENZIE	68 MOTHERWELL	122 BARRHEAD
7 SANDBANK	38 BISHOPBRIGGS	69 NETHERTON	123 PAISLEY
8 DUNOON	39 MILLERSTON	70 WISHAW	124 RENFREW
9 ROTHESAY	40 STEPPS	71 GOWKTHRAPPLE	125 INCHINNAN
10 MILLPORT	41 CHRYSTON	72 OVERTOWN	126 ELDERSLIE
11 GARELOCHHEAD	42 MOODIESBURN	73 LAW	127 LINWOOD
12 ROSNEATH	43 MUIRHEAD	74 CARLUKE	128 JOHNSTONE
13 RHU	44 CRAIGENDMUIR	75 FORTH	129 ERSKINE
14 HELENSBURGH	45 GLENBOIG	76 CARNWATH	130 BISHOPTON
15 CRAIGENDORAN	46 GLENMAVIS	77 LANARK	131 HOUSTON
16 BALLOCH	47 GREENGAIRS	78 BIGGAR	132 BRIDGE OF WEIR
17 ALEXANDRIA	48 CALDERCRUIX	79 RIGSIDE	133 KILBARCHAN
18 BONHILL	49 PLAINS	80 DOUGLAS	134 MILLIKENPARK
19 RENTON	50 AIRDRIE	81 COALBURN	135 HOWWOOD
20 CARDROSS	51 COATBRIDGE	82 LESMAHAGOW	136 LOCHWINNOCH
21 DUMBARTON	52 CALDERBANK	83 BLACKWOOD	137 KILMACOLM
22 OLD KILPATRICK	53 CHAPELHALL	84 LARKHALL	138 PORT GLASGOW
23 DUNTOCHER	54 SALSBURGH	85 HAMILTON	139 GREENOCK
24 CLYDEBANK	55 EASTFIELD	86 BOTHWELL	140 GOUROCK
25 FAIFLEY	56 HARTHILL	87 BELLSHILL	141 WEMYSS BAY
26 HARDGATE	57 SHOTTS & DYKEHEAD	88 FALLSIDE	142 SKELMORLIE
27 BEARSDEN	58 STANE	89 TANNOCHSIDE	143 LARGS
28 MILNGAVIE	59 ALLANTON	90 BIRKENSHAW	144 FAIRLIE
29 TORRANCE	60 NEWMAINS	91 BARGEDDIE	145 KILBIRNIE
30 LENNOXTOWN	61 CLELAND	92 SWINTON	146 BEITH
31 MILTON OF CAMPSIE	62 HOLYTOWN	93 BAILLIESTON	147 DALRY
		94 MOUNT VERNON	148 W. KILBRIDE
		95 CARMYLE	149 ARDROSSAN
		96 WESTBURN	150 SALTCOATS
		97 HALFWAY	151 STEVENSTON
		98 CAMBUSLANG	152 KILWINNING
		99 BLANTYRE	153 DREGHORN
		100 RUTHERGLEN	154 SPRINGSIDE
		101 CARMUNNOCK	155 CROSSHOUSE
		102 BUSBY	156 DUNDONALD
		103 WATERFOOT	157 SYMINGTON
		104 EAGLESHAM	158 TROON
		105 STRATHAVEN	159 PRESTWICK
		106 MUIRKIRK	160 AYR
		107 NEW CUMNOCK	161 ANNBANK STATION
		108 LOGAN	162 TARBOLTON
		109 CUMNOCK & HOLMHEAD	163 ANNBANK
		110 NETHERTHIRD	164 DRONGAN
		111 AUCHINLECK	165 BELLSBANK
		112 CATRINE	166 DALMELLINGTON
		113 MAUCHLINE	167 PATNA
		114 DARVEL	168 DALRYMPLE
		115 NEWMILNS	169 MAYBOLE
		116 GALSTON	170 GIRVAN

⊛ Places with well above average (>x̄ +1σ) proportion of
    households with no car

● Places with well above average (>x̄ +1σ) proportion of
    households with two or more cars

0   10   20   30   40MLS
0   10   20   30   40   50   60KM

Fig. 5   Settlements with high levels of (a) car-less households, and (b) multi-car households.

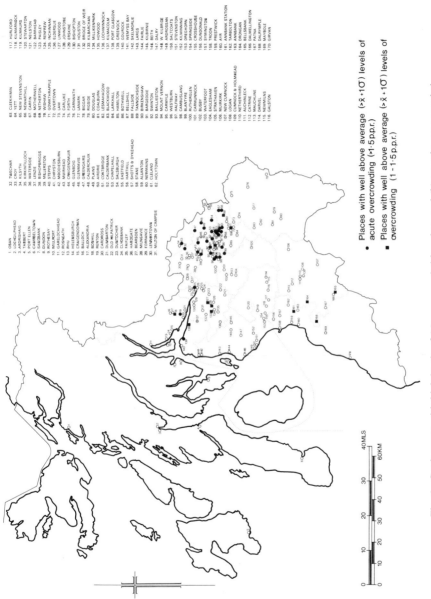

Fig. 6   Settlements with high levels of (a) overcrowded housing, and (b) acutely overcrowded housing.

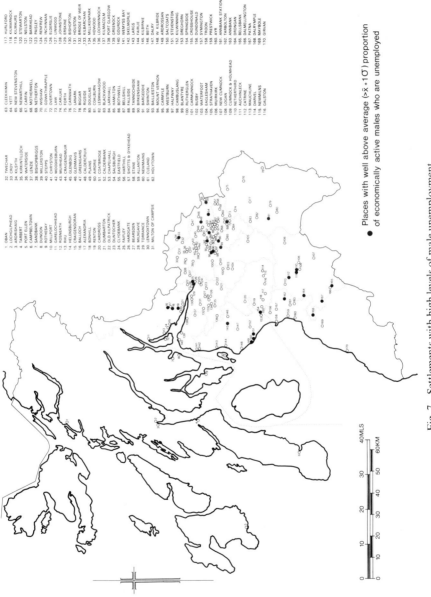

1 OBAN	32 TWECHAR	63 CLEEKHIMIN	117 HURLFORD
2 LOCHGILPHEAD	33 CROY	64 YETT	118 KILMARNOCK
3 ARDRISHAIG	34 KILSYTH	65 NEW STEVENSTON	119 KILMAURS
4 TARBERT	35 KIRKINTILLOCH	66 NEWARTHILL	120 STEWARTON
5 PORT ELLEN	36 WATERSIDE	67 CARFIN	121 NEILSTON
6 CAMPBELTOWN	37 LENZIE	68 MOTHERWELL	122 BARRHEAD
7 SANDBANK	38 BISHOPBRIGGS	69 NETHERTON	123 PAISLEY
8 DUNOON	39 MILLERSTON	70 WISHAW	124 RENFREW
9 ROTHESAY	40 STEPPS	71 GOWKTHRAPPLE	125 INCHINNAN
10 MILLPORT	41 CHRYSTON	72 OVERTOWN	126 ELDERSLIE
11 GARELOCHHEAD	42 MOODIESBURN	73 LAW	127 LINWOOD
12 ROSNEATH	43 MUIRHEAD	74 CARLUKE	128 JOHNSTONE
13 RHU	44 CRAIGENDMUIR	75 FORTH	129 ERSKINE
14 HELENSBURGH	45 GLENBOIG	76 CARNWATH	130 BISHOPTON
15 CRAIGENDORAN	46 GLENMAVIS	77 LANARK	131 HOUSTON
16 BALLOCH	47 GREENGAIRS	78 BIGGAR	132 BRIDGE OF WEIR
17 ALEXANDRIA	48 CALDERCRUIX	79 RIGSIDE	133 KILBARCHAN
18 BONHILL	49 PLAINS	80 DOUGLAS	134 MILLIKENPARK
19 RENTON	50 AIRDRIE	81 COALBURN	135 HOWWOOD
20 CARDROSS	51 COATBRIDGE	82 LESMAHAGOW	136 LOCHWINNOCH
21 DUMBARTON	52 CALDERBANK	83 BLACKWOOD	137 KILMACOLM
22 OLD KILPATRICK	53 CHAPELHALL	84 LARKHALL	138 PORT GLASGOW
23 DUNTOCHER	54 SALSBURGH	85 HAMILTON	139 GREENOCK
24 CLYDEBANK	55 EASTFIELD	86 BOTHWELL	140 GOUROCK
25 FAIFLEY	56 HARTHILL	87 BELLSHILL	141 WEMYSS BAY
26 HARDGATE	57 SHOTTS & DYKEHEAD	88 FALLSIDE	142 SKELMORLIE
27 BEARSDEN	58 STANE	89 TANNOCHSIDE	143 LARGS
28 MILNGAVIE	59 ALLANTON	90 BIRKENSHAW	144 FAIRLIE
29 TORRANCE	60 NEWMAINS	91 BARGEDDIE	145 KILBIRNIE
30 LENNOXTOWN	61 CLELAND	92 SWINTON	146 BEITH
31 MILTON OF CAMPSIE	62 HOLYTOWN	93 BAILLIESTON	147 DALRY
		94 MOUNT VERNON	148 W. KILBRIDE
		95 WESTBURN	149 ARDROSSAN
		96 HALFWAY	150 SALTCOATS
		97 BLANTYRE	151 STEVENSTON
		98 CAMBUSLANG	152 KILWINNING
		99 RUTHERGLEN	153 DREGHORN
		100 CAMBUSNETHAN	154 SPRINGSIDE
		101 BUSBY	155 CROSSHOUSE
		102 WATERFOOT	156 DUNDONALD
		103 EAGLESHAM	157 SYMINGTON
		104 STRATHAVEN	158 TROON
		105 MUIRKIRK	159 PRESTWICK
		106 AYR	160 AYR
		107 NEW CUMNOCK	161 ANNBANK STATION
		108 LOGAN	162 TARBOLTON
		109 CUMNOCK & HOLMHEAD	163 ANNBANK
		110 NETHERTHIRD	164 DRONGAN
		111 AUCHINLECK	165 BELLSBANK
		112 CATRINE	166 DALMELLINGTON
		113 MAUCHLINE	167 PATNA
		114 DARVEL	168 DALRYMPLE
		115 NEWMILNS	169 MAYBOLE
		116 GALSTON	170 GIRVAN

● Places with well above average (>x̄ + 1σ) proportion of economically active males who are unemployed

Fig. 7   Settlements with high levels of male unemployment.

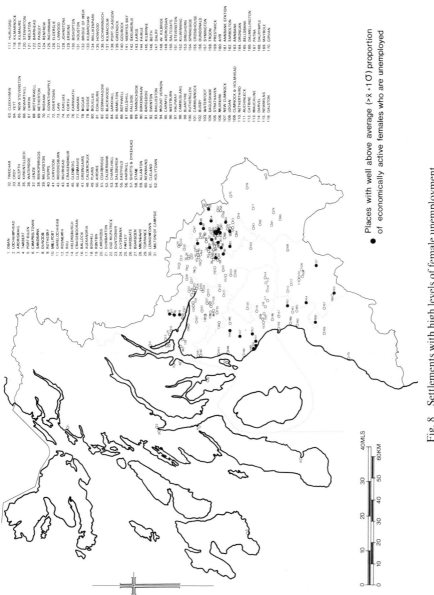

Fig. 8 Settlements with high levels of female unemployment.

● Places with well above average ($> \bar{x} + 1\sigma$) proportion of economically active females who are unemployed

1 OBAN
2 LOCHGILPHEAD
3 ARDRISHAIG
4 TARBERT
5 PORT ELLEN
6 CAMPBELTOWN
7 SANDBANK
8 DUNOON
9 ROTHESAY
10 MILLPORT
11 GARELOCHHEAD
12 ROSNEATH
13 RHU
14 HELENSBURGH
15 CRAIGENDORAN
16 CRAIGMORE
17 ALEXANDRIA
18 BONHILL
19 RENTON
20 CARDROSS
21 DUMBARTON
22 OLD KILPATRICK
23 DUNTOCHER
24 CLYDEBANK
25 FARLEY
26 HARDGATE
27 BEARSDEN
28 MILNGAVIE
29 TORRANCE
30 LENNOXTOWN
31 MILTON OF CAMPSIE
32 TWECHAR
33 CROY
34 KILSYTH
35 KIRKINTILLOCH
36 PORT ELLEN
37 WATERSIDE
38 BISHOPBRIGGS
39 MILLERSTON
40 STEPS
41 CHRYSTON
42 MOODIESBURN
43 MUIRHEAD
44 CRAIGENDMUIR
45 GLENBOIG
46 GLENMAVIS
47 GREENGAIRS
48 CALDERCRUIX
49 PLAINS
50 AIRDRIE
51 COATBRIDGE
52 CALDERBANK
53 CHAPELHALL
54 SALSBURGH
55 EASTFIELD
56 HARTHILL
57 SHOTTS & DYKEHEAD
58 STANE
59 ALLANTON
60 NEWMAINS
61 CLELAND
62 HOLYTOWN
63 CLEEKHIMIN
64 YETT
65 NEW STEVENSTON
66 NEWARTHILL
67 CARFIN
68 MOTHERWELL
69 NETHERTON
70 WISHAW
71 GOWKTHRAPPLE
72 OVERTOWN
73 LAW
74 CARLUKE
75 FORTH
76 CARNWATH
77 LANARK
78 BIGGAR
79 ROSIDE
80 DOUGLAS
81 COALBURN
82 KIRKMANAGLOW
83 BLACKWOOD
84 LARKHALL
85 HAMILTON
86 ROTHWELL
87 BELLSHILL
88 FALLSIDE
89 TANNOCHSIDE
90 BIRKENSHAW
91 BARGEDDIE
92 SWINTON
93 BAILLIESTON
94 MOUNT VERNON
95 CARMYLE
96 WESTBURN
97 HALFWAY
98 CAMBUSLANG
99 BLANTYRE
100 RUTHERGLEN
101 CARMUNNOCK
102 BUSBY
103 WATERFOOT
104 EAGLESHAM
105 STRATHAVEN
106 MUIRKIRK
107 NEW CUMNOCK
108 LUGAR
109 CUMNOCK & HOLMHEAD
110 NETHERTHIRD
111 AUCHINLECK
112 CATRINE
113 MAUCHLINE
114 DARVEL
115 NEWMILNS
116 GALSTON
117 HURLFORD
118 KILMARNOCK
119 KILMAURS
120 STEWARTON
121 NEILSTON
122 BARRHEAD
123 PAISLEY
124 RENFREW
125 INCHINNAN
126 ELDERSLIE
127 LINWOOD
128 JOHNSTONE
129 ERSKINE
130 BISHOPTON
131 HOUSTON
132 BRIDGE OF WEIR
133 KILBARCHAN
134 MILLIKENPARK
135 HOWWOOD
136 LOCHWINNOCH
137 KILMACOLM
138 PORT GLASGOW
139 GREENOCK
140 GOUROCK
141 WEMYSS BAY
142 SKELMORLIE
143 LARGS
144 FAIRLIE
145 KILBIRNIE
146 BEITH
147 DALRY
148 W. KILBRIDE
149 ARDROSSAN
150 SALTCOATS
151 STEVENSTON
152 KILWINNING
153 DREGHORN
154 SPRINGSIDE
155 CROSSHOUSE
156 DONDONALD
157 SYMINGTON
158 TROON
159 PRESTWICK
160 AYR
161 ANNBANK STATION
162 TARBOLTON
163 ANNBANK
164 DRONGAN
165 BELLSBANK
166 DALMELLINGTON
167 PATNA
168 DALRYMPLE
169 MAYBOLE
170 GIRVAN

40MLS
60KM

TABLE 3   LEVELS OF ASSOCIATION AMONG SELECTED VARIABLES EXTRACTED FROM THE MAIN CORRELATION MATRIX

I.

		Variables									
		6	7	12	15	16	17	24	28	38	43	44
	6											
	7	0·7741										
	12	0·7864	0·6720									
	15	0·5928	0·6204	0·6287								
Variables	16	0·6499	0·6302	0·8013	0·6254							
	17	0·8341	0·6918	0·7991	0·6268	0·6254						
	24	0·6114	0·5711	0·6218	0·8087	0·7417	0·5335					
	28	0·6805	0·5755	0·6014	0·3786	0·5503	0·5863	0·3651				
	38	0·6198	0·4407	0·6788	0·4989	0·6700	0·5900	0·5489	0·4150			
	43	0·7242	0·6820	0·7936	0·6244	0·6744	0·7289	0·5296	0·4954	0·5102		
	44	0·5366	0·3991	0·7258	0·3761	0·6170	0·5293	0·3953	0·4114	0·6227	0·4517	

II.

		Variables						
		10	11	20	23	38	43	50
	10							
	11	0·5870						
Variables	20	0·5206	0·8275					
	23	0·6722	0·7572	0·8179				
	38	0·3244	0·6476	0·7693	0·5569			
	43	0·6162	0·8971	0·9067	0·8469	0·6862		
	50	0·3941	0·8010	0·7398	0·5944	0·6406	0·7534	

detached housing) were all highly correlated. Clearly, further examination of the correlation matrix would uncover other groupings of associated variables. In order to pursue these linkages among variables it is necessary to employ multivariate techniques.

Multivariate Analysis

The main correlation matrix was subjected to an R-type principal components analysis. This procedure was employed to reduce the size of the initial data set and to extract a smaller set of components to account for most of the variance in the original data. The principal components algorithm has been employed extensively in geographic research and the mechanics and algebra of the technique have been described by several authors (Harman, 1960; Johnston, 1978).

Table 4 indicated the relative significance of the successive components. The first twelve components extracted exhibited well-defined structures and together accounted for 76 per cent of the variance. It was decided to consider the first four components in detail. These accounted for 55 per cent of the total variance and represented a cut-off point of 2·6 in terms of eigenvalues. The character of the four components is indicated in Table 5 which shows the most important loadings for each.

TABLE 4 RELATIVE IMPORTANCE OF COMPONENTS WITH EIGENVALUES
GREATER THAN 1·0

Component Number	Eigenvalue	Percentage of Variance	Cumulative Percentage of Total Variance
01	13·49415	26·5	26·5
02	8·73590	17·1	43·6
03	3·08746	6·1	49·6
04	2·55992	5·0	54·7
05	1·93451	3·8	58·5
06	1·73343	3·4	61·9
07	1·42128	2·8	64·6
08	1·41032	2·8	67·4
09	1·25579	2·5	69·9
10	1·14679	2·2	72·1
11	1·10808	2·2	74·3
12	1·00017	2·0	76·3

The first component accounted for 26·5 per cent of the total variance and loaded highly in a positive direction on variable 12 (proportion of dwelling stock rented from local authority), variable 17 (households without a car), variable 6 (male unemployment), variable 43 (personal service, semi-skilled and manual workers), variable 16 (households with between 1 and 1·5 persons per room), variable 7 (female unemployment), variable 44 (foremen, supervisors and skilled manual workers), variable 38 (travel to work by bus), variable 24 (households with six or more persons) and variable 50 (two-storey or low-rise housing). This could be clearly interpreted as a measure of general social well-being with *high* component scores indicative of *less* affluent households. Component II exhibited significant positive loadings on variables 5 (proportion of residents of pensionable age), 27 (households with persons of pensionable age only), 26 (lone pensioner households), 21 (households with one or two rooms only), and 40 (travel to work on foot) and was clearly indicative of an aged demographic structure. The loadings of greatest magnitude on component III referred to variables 23 (proportion of household spaces vacant), 14 (private-rented furnished accommodation), 13 (private-rented unfurnished accommodation) and 18 (households lacking bath or inside W.C.). This measure accounted for 6 per cent of the variance and was closely associated with the privately rented housing sector. The characteristic structure of component IV was based on its high association with variables 48 (Gaelic speakers), 45 (proportion of household heads in S.E.G. 13: farmers — employers and managers), 30 (agricultural workers) and 19 (households sharing a bath or W.C.), and was interpreted as an indicator of a 'rural Scots' dimension. The structure of the component matrix also enabled a clear interpretation to be placed on components V–XII; however, as component V accounted for only 4 per cent of the variance, the cut-off point

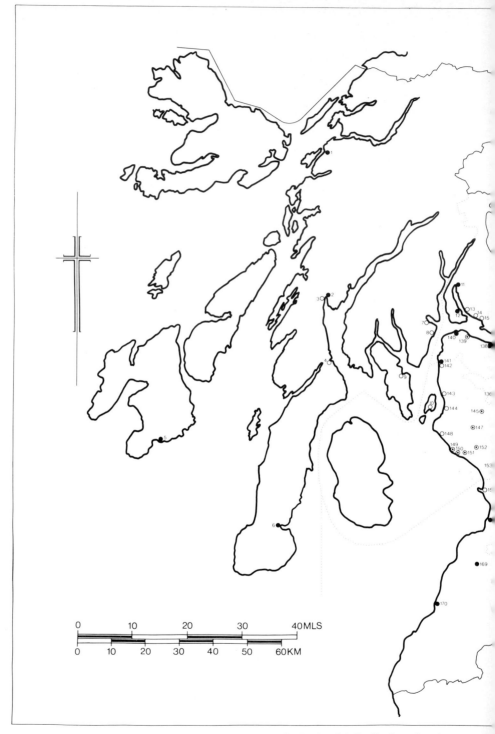

Fig. 9   Spatial distribution of settlement score

1. OBAN	32. TWECHAR	63. CLEEKHIMIN	117. HURLFORD
2. LOCHGILPHEAD	33. CROY	64. YETT	118. KILMARNOCK
3. ARDRISHAIG	34. KILSYTH	65. NEW STEVENSTON	119. KILMAURS
4. TARBERT	35. KIRKINTILLOCH	66. NEWARTHILL	120. STEWARTON
5. PORT ELLEN	36. WATERSIDE	67. CARFIN	121. NEILSTON
6. CAMPBELTOWN	37. LENZIE	68. MOTHERWELL	122. BARRHEAD
7. SANDBANK	38. BISHOPBRIGGS	69. NETHERTON	123. PAISLEY
8. DUNOON	39. MILLERSTON	70. WISHAW	124. RENFREW
9. ROTHESAY	40. STEPPS	71. GOWKTHRAPPLE	125. INCHINNAN
10. MILLPORT	41. CHRYSTON	72. OVERTOWN	126. ELDERSLIE
11. GARELOCHHEAD	42. MOODIESBURN	73. LAW	127. LINWOOD
12. ROSNEATH	43. MUIRHEAD	74. CARLUKE	128. JOHNSTONE
13. RHU	44. CRAIGENDMUIR	75. FORTH	129. ERSKINE
14. HELENSBURGH	45. GLENBOIG	76. CARNWATH	130. BISHOPTON
15. CRAIGENDORAN	46. GLENMAVIS	77. LANARK	131. HOUSTON
16. BALLOCH	47. GREENGAIRS	78. BIGGAR	132. BRIDGE OF WEIR
17. ALEXANDRIA	48. CALDERCRUIX	79. RIGSIDE	133. KILBARCHAN
18. BONHILL	49. PLAINS	80. DOUGLAS	134. MILLIKENPARK
19. RENTON	50. AIRDRIE	81. COALBURN	135. HOWOOD
20. CARDROSS	51. COATBRIDGE	82. LESMAHAGOW	136. LOCHWINNOCH
21. DUMBARTON	52. CALDERBANK	83. BLACKWOOD	137. KILMACOLM
22. OLD KILPATRICK	53. CHAPELHALL	84. LARKHALL	138. PORT GLASGOW
23. DUNTOCHER	54. SALSBURGH	85. HAMILTON	139. GREENOCK
24. CLYDEBANK	55. EASTFIELD	86. BOTHWELL	140. GOUROCK
25. FAIFLEY	56. HARTHILL	87. BELLSHILL	141. WEMYSS BAY
26. HARDGATE	57. SHOTTS & DYKEHEAD	88. FALLSIDE	142. SKELMORLIE
27. BEARSDEN	58. STANE	89. TANNOCHSIDE	143. LARGS
28. MILNGAVIE	59. ALLANTON	90. BIRKENSHAW	144. FAIRLIE
29. TORRANCE	60. NEWMAINS	91. BARGEDDIE	145. KILBIRNIE
30. LENNOXTOWN	61. CLELAND	92. SWINTON	146. BEITH
31. MILTON OF CAMPSIE	62. HOLYTOWN	93. BAILLIESTON	147. DALRY
		94. MOUNT VERNON	148. W. KILBRIDE
		95. CARMYLE	149. ARDROSSAN
		96. WESTBURN	150. SALTCOATS
		97. HALFWAY	151. STEVENSTON
		98. CAMBUSLANG	152. KILWINNING
		99. BLANTYRE	153. DREGHORN
		100. RUTHERGLEN	154. SPRINGSIDE
		101. CARMUNNOCK	155. CROSSHOUSE
		102. BUSBY	156. DUNDONALD
		103. WATERFOOT	157. SYMINGTON
		104. EAGLESHAM	158. TROON
		105. STRATHAVEN	159. PRESTWICK
		106. MUIRKIRK	160. AYR
		107. NEW CUMNOCK	161. ANNBANK STATION
		108. LOGAN	162. TARBOLTON
		109. CUMNOCK & HOLMHEAD	163. ANNBANK
		110. NETHERTHIRD	164. DRONGAN
		111. AUCHINLECK	165. BELLSBANK
		112. CATRINE	166. DALMELLINGTON
		113. MAUCHLINE	167. PATNA
		114. DARVEL	168. DALRYMPLE
		115. NEWMILNS	169. MAYBOLE
		116. GALSTON	170. GIRVAN

Settlement Scores on Component I

○ Places with well below average (>x̄ +1σ) scores

● Places with below average (x̄ -1σ) scores

⊙ Places with above average (x̄ -1σ) scores

■ Places with well above average (>x̄ +1σ) scores

ponent measuring general social well-being.

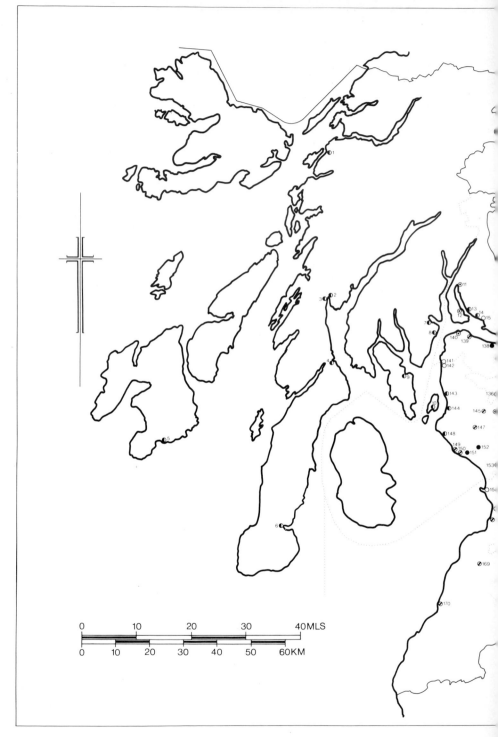

Fig. 10   Multi-variate classificati

1. OBAN	32. TWECHAR	63. CLEEKHIMIN	117. HURLFORD
2. LOCHGILPHEAD	33. CROY	64. YETT	118. KILMARNOCK
3. ARDRISHAIG	34. KILSYTH	65. NEW STEVENSTON	119. KILMAURS
4. TARBERT	35. KIRKINTILLOCH	66. NEWARTHILL	120. STEWARTON
5. PORT ELLEN	36. WATERSIDE	67. CARFIN	121. NEILSTON
6. CAMPBELTOWN	37. LENZIE	68. MOTHERWELL	122. BARRHEAD
7. SANDBANK	38. BISHOPBRIGGS	69. NETHERTON	123. PAISLEY
8. DUNOON	39. MILLERSTON	70. WISHAW	124. RENFREW
9. ROTHESAY	40. STEPPS	71. GOWKTHRAPPLE	125. INCHINNAN
10. MILLPORT	41. CHRYSTON	72. OVERTOWN	126. ELDERSLIE
11. GARELOCHHEAD	42. MOODIESBURN	73. LAW	127. LINWOOD
12. ROSNEATH	43. MUIRHEAD	74. CARLUKE	128. JOHNSTONE
13. RHU	44. CRAIGENDMUIR	75. FORTH	129. ERSKINE
14. HELENSBURGH	45. GLENBOIG	76. CARNWATH	130. BISHOPTON
15. CRAIGENDORAN	46. GLENMAVIS	77. LANARK	131. HOUSTON
16. BALLOCH	47. GREENGAIRS	78. BIGGAR	132. BRIDGE OF WEIR
17. ALEXANDRIA	48. CALDERCRUIX	79. RIGSIDE	133. KILBARCHAN
18. BONHILL	49. PLAINS	80. DOUGLAS	134. MILLIKENPARK
19. RENTON	50. AIRDRIE	81. COALBURN	135. HOWOOD
20. CARDROSS	51. COATBRIDGE	82. LESMAHAGOW	136. LOCHWINNOCH
21. DUMBARTON	52. CALDERBANK	83. BLACKWOOD	137. KILMACOLM
22. OLD KILPATRICK	53. CHAPELHALL	84. LARKHALL	138. PORT GLASGOW
23. DUNTOCHER	54. SALSBURGH	85. HAMILTON	139. GREENOCK
24. CLYDEBANK	55. EASTFIELD	86. BOTHWELL	140. GOUROCK
25. FAIFLEY	56. HARTHILL	87. BELLSHILL	141. WEMYSS BAY
26. HARDGATE	57. SHOTTS & DYKEHEAD	88. FALLSIDE	142. SKELMORLIE
27. BEARSDEN	58. STANE	89. TANNOCHSIDE	143. LARGS
28. MILNGAVIE	59. ALLANTON	90. BIRKENSHAW	144. FAIRLIE
29. TORRANCE	60. NEWMAINS	91. BARGEDDIE	145. KILBIRNIE
30. LENNOXTOWN	61. CLELAND	92. SWINTON	146. BEITH
31. MILTON OF CAMPSIE	62. HOLYTOWN	93. BAILLIESTON	147. DALRY
		94. MOUNT VERNON	148. W. KILBRIDE
		95. CARMYLE	149. ARDROSSAN
		96. WESTBURN	150. SALTCOATS
		97. HALFWAY	151. STEVENSTON
		98. CAMBUSLANG	152. KILWINNING
		99. BLANTYRE	153. DREGHORN
		100. RUTHERGLEN	154. SPRINGSIDE
		101. CARMUNNOCK	155. CROSSHOUSE
		102. BUSBY	156. DUNDONALD
		103. WATERFOOT	157. SYMINGTON
		104. EAGLESHAM	158. TROON
		105. STRATHAVEN	159. PRESTWICK
		106. MUIRKIRK	160. AYR
		107. NEW CUMNOCK	161. ANNBANK STATION
		108. LOGAN	162. TARBOLTON
		109. CUMNOCK & HOLMHEAD	163. ANNBANK
		110. NETHERTHIRD	164. DRONGAN
		111. AUCHINLECK	165. BELLSBANK
		112. CATRINE	166. DALMELLINGTON
		113. MAUCHLINE	167. PATNA
		114. DARVEL	168. DALRYMPLE
		115. NEWMILNS	169. MAYBOLE
		116. GALSTON	170. GIRVAN

Settlement Classification

- ● Cluster I
- ◑ Cluster II
- ⊘ Cluster III
- ⊙ Cluster IV
- ○ Cluster V

metropolitan urban places in Strathclyde.

TABLE 5   THE COMPONENT LOADINGS

COMPONENT I

Professional workers, employers and managers	−0·93392
Owner-occupied housing	−0·93193
Council-rented housing	0·92885
Households with two or more cars	−0·91018
Households without car	0·90067
Male unemployment	0·84239
Houses with six or more rooms	−0·82599
Personal service, semi-skilled and manual workers	0·82241
Overcrowded housing	0·82135
Detached or semi-detached housing	−0·82083
Travel to work by car	−0·78216
Female unemployment	0·76147
Severely overcrowded housing	0·72112
Foremen and skilled manual workers	0·68584
Travel to work by bus	0·68154
Households with six or more persons	0·66800
Self-employed	−0·57756
Two storey or low-rise housing	0·43665

COMPONENT II

Population of pensionable age	0·96012
Households with persons of pensionable age only	0·95606
Lone pensioner households	0·91972
Economically active males	−0·91928
Residents of working age	−0·82138
Economically active females	−0·71573
Persons aged 0–4	−0·67885
Persons aged 5–14	−0·61904
Households with one or two rooms	0·47718
Travel to work on foot	0·39422

COMPONENT III

Household spaces vacant	0·77272
Private rented furnished accommodation	0·75402
Private rented unfurnished accommodation	0·71888
Households lacking bath or W.C.	0·44300

COMPONENT IV

Gaelic speakers	0·81385
Farmers — employers and managers	0·74331
Agricultural workers	0·64528
Households sharing bath or W.C.	0·47309

was retained at component IV. The spatial expression of the first of these principal components is portrayed in Figure 9.

Inclusion of similar maps for all components would complete the presentation of the principal unrelated patterns of socio-spatial variation in the region. Individual maps, however, are not able to reveal the position of each settlement in terms of the *overall* concept of social well-being (Pacione, 1982). Clearly, to identify a place's social structure by its scores on only the first few components, despite their relative importance, would result in an excessively narrow definition and a considerable loss of information. What was required was a means of assessing each settlement by its score on all significant components. This requirement was fulfilled by the taxonomic procedure known as cluster analysis.

Settlement Classification

Methodology
Techniques of numerical taxonomy such as cluster analysis seek to devise a classification scheme for grouping a sample of N objects of individuals, each measured on p variates, into g classes where g < N. The clustering method thus simplifies the description of a large set of multivariate data and searches for natural groupings in the data which permit the definition of phenomena classes about which general statements may be made. Techniques of cluster analysis have been widely employed in both the natural and social sciences (Parks, 1966; Meyer, 1972), and the alternative procedures are well described by Everitt (1974). The agglomerative hierarchical algorithm was selected for use here (Johnston, 1976), but whichever method is employed the major problem requiring researcher decision is when to halt the grouping process. This decision is normally made by inspection of the dendrogram or by consideration of the degree of increase in the error sum of squares at each step (Ward, 1963).

A further difficulty was that hierarchical grouping procedures always group groups without enquiring whether at certain steps the criteria for classification would be better met if one of the pre-existing clusters was dismantled. Thus when the required number of clusters has been achieved it is still necessary to verify that the resultant grouping is optimal. The test for mis-classification of objects can be achieved by a subsequent multiple linear discriminant analysis (Ahmed, 1965). Alternatively, as in the present investigation, the integrity of the cluster solution can be tested by an iterative relocation procedure of the type suggested by Wishart (1978).

Settlement Types
The five-cluster grouping of settlements shown in Figure 10 proved to be the optimum solution. The definitive characteristic of places in each cluster may be identified by comparing the group mean score on each indicator with the regional average score for all settlements (Table 6). In general, while the five clusters cannot be regarded as a continuum from 'worst' to 'best', it is clear that settlements in cluster I exhibit most problems while those in cluster V offer the highest levels of life quality, with the intervening clusters showing varying combinations of social conditions and degrees of well-being.

TABLE 6 REGIONAL AND CLUSTER CHARACTERISTICS

Variable	All Settlements	Cluster I	Cluster II	Cluster III	Cluster IV	Cluster V
1. (Population)	7830	7578	3510	12709	4592	5611
2. (Aged 0–4)	6·6	7·2	5·8	6·1	6·7	7·4
3. (Aged 5–14)	16·5	18·2	15·1	15·7	16·8	16·1
4. (Working Age)	59·6	60·5	55·2	59·3	60·9	60·2
5. (Pensioners)	14·8	11·9	21·7	16·3	13·0	18·9
6. (Male Unemployment)	13·6	26·3	9·9	15·6	10·8	6·1
7. (Female Unemployment)	9·4	13·3	7·6	10·1	7·8	5·1
8. (Econ. Active Males)	79·5	81·0	73·5	78·4	81·8	80·5
9. (Econ. Active Females)	46·0	47·3	38·4	45·2	49·1	46·5
10. (Self-employed)	6·5	3·6	13·6	5·0	6·2	9·5
11. (Owner-occupied)	31·9	8·9	43·4	22·3	38·8	72·0
12. (Council)	63·3	88·9	43·4	74·0	56·5	22·6
13. (Rented unfurnished)	1·6	0·5	5·2	1·4	1·4	1·5
14. (Rented furnished)	0·7	0·0	3·3	0·4	0·4	1·2
15. (Over 1·5 ppr)	3·3	6·1	1·8	3·4	2·5	1·1
16. (1–1·5 ppr)	13·0	18·1	8·6	13·7	12·3	7·1
17. (No car)	46·5	58·9	44·9	53·3	37·8	24·8
18. (Lack Bath/W.C.)	0·5	0·3	1·5	0·6	0·4	0·4
19. (Share Bath/W.C.)	0·0	0·0	0·2	0·0	0·0	0·0
20. (Two or More Cars)	11·0	5·4	11·7	7·7	13·1	23·3
21. (One or Two Rooms)	9·6	8·9	10·3	11·9	8·8	6·6
22. (Six or More Rooms)	7·4	2·5	14·2	4·5	6·5	18·0
23. (Spaces Vacant)	3·7	2·7	7·3	3·6	3·1	3·4
24. (Six or More Persons)	5·3	8·2	3·4	5·1	4·7	3·6
25. (Not Self-contained)	0·2	0·2	0·4	0·2	0·2	0·0
26. (Lone Pensioner)	13·3	11·1	19·1	15·1	11·5	11·4
27. (Pensionable Age Only)	21·0	17·0	30·3	23·4	18·4	19·5
28. (One Person Household)	2·1	3·2	1·7	2·3	1·6	1·2
29. (Lone Parent)	0·1	0·4	0·2	0·1	0·0	0·0
30. (Agriculture)	1·0	0·4	4·0	0·9	0·6	0·4
31. (Energy and Water)	5·1	6·3	4·1	7·2	2·5	3·2
32. (Manufacturing)	27·7	34·3	13·4	30·7	27·6	21·0
33. (Construction)	8·5	8·5	10·3	8·6	8·8	6·7
34. (Distribution/Catering)	17·8	17·2	23·4	16·8	17·6	17·2
35. (Transport)	6·7	6·5	7·8	5·9	7·7	6·8
36. (Work Outside District)	33·0	35·4	12·2	26·9	37·7	51·3
37. (Car Travel)	50·0	41·8	48·1	45·5	55·9	66·1
38. (Bus Travel)	23·6	33·3	11·1	26·4	21·2	13·7
39. (Train Travel)	3·5	3·7	1·8	2·8	3·6	5·3
40. (Foot Travel)	17·1	16·3	28·6	20·4	14·0	9·5
41. (Other Means)	4·3	4·2	6·8	3·8	3·9	4·2
42. (S.E.G. 1–4)	15·1	5·8	20·4	9·8	18·0	33·8
43. (S.E.G. 7, 10, 11)	19·6	26·8	14·6	22·7	17·6	8·1
44. (S.E.G. 8, 9)	25·7	31·5	16·7	29·5	25·0	16·1
45. (S.E.G. 13)	0·2	0·1	0·3	0·1	0·8	0·2
46. (S.E.G. 14)	0·1	0·1	0·3	0·2	0·0	0·2
47. (S.E.G. 15)	0·4	0·2	1·4	0·4	0·4	0·3
48. (Gaelic)	1·0	0·3	4·9	0·3	0·8	1·0
49. (Detached/Semi)	38·5	21·2	40·7	33·9	44·8	68·0
50. (Two Storey/Low Rise)	29·2	36·0	35·3	33·6	21·1	15·8
51. (High Rise)	1·5	1·7	0·4	2·7	0·4	0·8

* With the exception of variable 1 all figures are percentages.

Cluster I — The 41 settlements in the first cluster were characterised primarily by lower than average proportions of pensioner households, male unemployment levels at twice the regional average, and high rates of female unemployment. In terms of housing, only 9 per cent of dwellings were owner-occupied (cf. a regional average of 32 per cent), with a correspondingly high proportion of 89 per cent rented from the local authority. Levels of overcrowding and of acute overcrowding were pronounced, as was the proportion of households with six or more persons. This generally low-status profile was confirmed by the high proportion of unskilled manual workers, and low numbers of self-employed. The employment base of towns in this cluster was predominantly in the manufacturing sector. Spatially, as Figure 10 shows, settlements in cluster I were concentrated in the north Lanarkshire area of the conurbation where economic fortunes have traditionally relied upon industries related to coal-mining, iron and steel making and heavy engineering, all of which have experienced severe retrenchment in the post-war period. Typical towns include some of ancient origin like Bothwell, and a majority of more recent industrial creations such as Bellshill, Bargeddie, New Stevenston and Newmains. Smaller groupings of 'type 1' settlements also occur in the old coalfield areas of Ayrshire, e.g. Kilwinning, and in the Leven valley of Dunbartonshire, as at Renton and Bonhill.

Cluster II — The settlements which comprise cluster II exhibit a population pyramid biased towards the top end of the scale with the proportion of persons of pensionable age 50 per cent above the regional average. This was supported by a high proportion of single pensioner and pensioner-only households. Both male and female unemployment levels and female activity rates were significantly below average. In contrast the proportion of self-employed was twice the norm, and the proportion of household heads in S.E.G. 1–4 was, at 20·4 per cent, the second highest of the five clusters. These trends were supported by a well above average proportion of owner-occupied housing, many of which had six or more rooms. Provision of privately rented accommodation was also significantly higher than the average while the level of local authority housing was, at 43 per cent, well below the regional norm of 63 per cent. Overcrowding was not a significant problem, but an above average proportion of houses lacked a bath or inside toilet. The employment structure was characterised by a high proportion of agricultural occupations, an above average involvement in distribution and catering trades, and a correspondingly low participation in manufacturing industry. By far the largest proportion of employees worked locally, i.e. within their District of residence, with a significant number travelling to work on foot. In spatial terms these 18 settlements are located on the periphery of the region, being concentrated primarily in Argyll but with representatives in Ayrshire and south Lanarkshire.

Cluster III — This forms the largest cluster, comprising 52 settlements with an average population size of 12,700 persons, and includes larger places such as Paisley, Motherwell, Kilmarnock and Dumbarton. Settlements in this cluster also exhibited a distinctive mix of characteristics, some of which were held in common with the previous two groupings. There is, for example, an above average proportion of pensioner households as in cluster II. However, while the direction of several indicators is the same as that for places in cluster I, the magnitude of the trends identified is much less. Thus, for example, levels of male and female unemployment are only just above the regional average. Also the proportion of owner-occupied and local authority housing is more akin to the norm than in cluster I, as are the proportions of large and small houses, and carless and two-car families. In terms of social class, towns in this cluster have a higher proportion of household heads in S.E.G. 1–4 than do places in cluster I although the level is well below the figure recorded by cluster II. The difference in socio-economic health between 'type 3' and 'type 1' places is underlined by the indicator of housing type which reveals a significantly higher proportion of detached and semi-detached dwellings in cluster III. These characteristics were represented in the distribution of settlements which, as Figure 10 indicates, were essentially located on the margins of the industrial heart of the conurbation. The major concentration of 'type 3' settlements is found in the south of the region in the mixed agricultural and now-depleted coal-mining centres of the Darvel valley (e.g. Rigside, Coalburn, Douglas, Lesmahagow). Other examples include local agricultural centres like Catrine and Tarbolton, as well as groupings of larger settlements to the west of Glasgow, e.g. Barrhead–Paisley–Renfrew, and the Balloch–Alexandria–Dumbarton axis in the Leven valley.

Cluster IV — Settlements in this cluster are generally of a small size with a mean population of only 4,600. Unemployment rates are below the regional average for both males and females and, as Table 6 indicates, there is an above average provision of owner-occupied housing, family cars and numbers of professional workers. Levels of overcrowding are below average and the proportion of detached or semi-detached accommodation is higher than the norm. A higher than average proportion of residents travel to work outside their District of residence, most by private car. Several of the group characteristics are similar to those of cluster II and, as Figure 10 illustrates, this cluster could be regarded, in many respects, as a less peripheral representation of cluster II. Typical settlements include Lochwinnoch, Kilmaurs, Carluke and Muirhead.

Cluster V — The social, economic and demographic profiles of places in cluster V are the most advantageous in the region. Settlements in this cluster consistently record above average scores on all indicators of prosperity. For example, unemployment levels are half the regional average, with male unemployment less than 25 per cent of that in cluster I. These towns also recorded the *highest* proportions of owner-occupied housing (72 per cent), of multi-car households (23 per cent), and of detached or semi-detached dwellings (68 per cent); and the *lowest* levels of local authority housing, overcrowding, carless families, small houses and numbers of manual workers. A further indication of the nature of these settlements is provided by the fact that over 50 per cent of those employed work outside their District of residence with two-thirds travelling by car. These factors are clearly represented in the locational pattern depicted in Figure 10 which identifies a ring of affluent commuter settlements around Glasgow occupied by people who work in the city but live elsewhere. Such settlements occur both close to the metropolitan edge (as at Stepps and Bishopbriggs) as well as beyond the green belt (e.g. at Milton of Campsie and Torrance). Thus, to the north of the city lie the prosperous dormitory settlements of Bearsden, Milngavie and Lenzie, to the west are places like Houston and Bridge of Weir, and to the south, Eaglesham and Strathaven. The general prosperity of these settlements stands in marked contrast to the relatively low levels of social and environmental well-being found to the east of the conurbation centre, as typified by settlements in cluster I.

The cluster-analytic procedure thus produced a five-fold classification of the 170 non-metropolitan settlements in the Strathclyde Region, based on a wide range of 51 census-based social indicators. Overall the powerful combination of univariate, multivariate and taxonomic procedures employed provides both individual vignettes of each settlement and a more general portrait of contemporary conditions in the smaller urban places of Strathclyde.

REFERENCES

Ahmed, A. (1965), *Indian Cities: Characteristics and Correlates*. Department of Geography Research Paper 102, University of Chicago.

Evans, I. S. (1983), Univariate analysis: presenting and summarizing single variates. In Rhind, D. (Ed.), *A Census User's Handbook*, 115–148. Methuen, London.

Everitt, B. S. (1974), *Cluster Analysis*. Heinemann, London.

Hakim, C. (1978), *Social and community indicators from the census*. O.P.C.S. Occasional Paper No. 5.

Harman, H. (1960), *Modern Factor Analysis*. University of Chicago Press.

Johnston, R. J. (1976), *Classification in Geography*. CATMOG 6, Geo Books, Norwich.

Johnston, R. J. (1978), *Multivariate Statistical Analysis in Geography*. Longman, London.

Meyer, D. R. (1972), Classification of U.S. metropolitan areas by the characteristics of their non-white population. In Berry, B. J. L. (Ed.), *City Classification Handbook*, 61–94. Wiley, New York.

Pacione, M. (1982), The use of objective and subjective measures of life quality in human geography. *Progress in Human Geography, 6 (4)*, 495–514.

Parks, J. M. (1966), Cluster analysis applied to multi-variate geological problems. *Journal of Geology, 74*, 703–715.

Ward, J. H. (1963), Hierarchical groupings to optimise an objective function. *Journal of the American Statistical Association, 58*, 236–244.

Wishart, D. (1978), *Clustan User Manual* (3rd edition). Inter University Research Councils Series Report No. 47. London.

CHAPTER SEVEN

THE QUALITY OF LIFE

John Butt

The quality of modern life has become a major issue for many social scientists in the last twenty years, indeed roughly in the period since the British Association last met in Glasgow. It seems as though contemporary society in the advanced industrial countries (Campbell *et al.*, 1976) has been faced with a considerable dilemma arising from the fact that their total material wants (as distinct from requirements) can be met by the technical means of production, and yet non-material goals then assume a greater significance. The general purposes of life and the conditions surrounding their pursuit become more important: ecology, conservation, 'natural living' and a 'higher quality of life' loom larger in the vocabulary of the more affluent, and city governments and politicians generally have to be aware that the creation and accumulation of wealth alone does not necessarily produce public contentment (Bateson, 1972).

The phrase, 'the quality of life', poses an immediate problem of definition (Pacione, 1984b): it differs in its meaning almost according to its user, but here it is used to assess the environment in which the people in Strathclyde live and work and also to describe their relative well-being. The latter involves the concepts of welfare and deprivation, i.e. some measurement of the Region's capacity (or lack of it) to provide an acceptable mode of living for most of its inhabitants. Although a material standard of life is plainly fundamental to well-being, a number of other circumstances condition any answer to the questions posed by the concepts outlined above. Obviously, a sense of well-being, satisfaction or dissatisfaction with life may derive first and foremost from such bases as income and employment, but private gratification is a psychological, not an economic, state. Individual perceptions of material status may be more important than reality in society, and this has been recognised by scholars (Wingo, 1973; Abrams, 1973).

If definition of the quality of life is fraught with difficulty, it is perhaps easier to establish its elements likely to receive wide acceptance. Theory in psychology and sociology can, unfortunately, help very little, and most

124

studies have turned to empirical analysis of social surveys (Kreiger, 1969; Allardt, 1973; Abrams, 1973; Andrews and Withey, 1976; Pacione, 1980). Defining human well-being is bound to be an ambiguous exercise otherwise; so-called 'expert' opinion, for example, may not convey the actual attitudes and opinions of a wider community. It is, therefore, most important to isolate the concerns of the population being studied. However, some indicators seem unexceptionable, although their relative weighting might provoke considerable controversy: a sufficient diet; satisfactory housing; good health; employment and income; job satisfaction; amenity and leisure; educational facilities for self and family; a sense of security within a local community. Pacione (1980) in his study of Milton of Campsie used five major life concerns: housing, health, job, standard of living and leisure time.

These will be the main concern of this chapter but inevitably some use of surrogates is necessary. For instance, patterns of income depend largely upon the historical development of patterns of employment and the economic structure of the Region. The standard of living involves the quantitative assessment of unemployment, poverty and deprivation; the use of leisure time at its most extreme may involve a judgement of the extent of alienation — alcoholism, drug abuse and vandalism — as well as of the growth of leisure activities and of their variety. Housing and health tend to overlap. The housing stock and its state and occupancy levels have implications for health, mortality and preventative medicine. Residential patterns often reflect levels of income and type of employment and these, in turn, may convey attitudes of families to educational opportunities.

Broadly these surrogates and indicators fall into two categories — social and economic. Although they interact, the economic elements seem of first importance. The history of the Region has been traced by Lythe and a contemporary dimension provided by Nairn and Kirwan; the place of the new towns has been assessed by Wannop and of the smaller urban settlements by Pacione; the city of Glasgow is treated by Gordon. All convey the significance of the decline of the Region's traditional economic activities and the necessity to replace or supplement these by more advanced industries. This is also the view of the Secretary of State for Scotland.

As Slaven (1975) and Campbell (1980) show, the economic structure of the Region, with the exception of the two world wars, has been under strain since the beginning of this century, and Checkland (1981) propounded the view that the earlier success of heavy industry drained the capital, entrepreneurial energies and capacity for economic diversification from the Region, leaving it a heritage of obsolete and obsolescent industries and a deficient social environment in which adequate new development was unlikely to occur. Certainly, economic revival after 1945 was largely a product of the traditional industrial structure which had helped to meet Britain's defensive requirements in two world wars but could not bring regional prosperity in peacetime.

Regional policy increasingly followed a 'growth-point' philosophy. For instance, government support for new towns from 1963 was deliberately designed to assist in the diversification of the regional economy and to aid the movement of labour from low productivity/low wage jobs to high productivity/high wage occupations (Johnston, Buxton and Mair, 1971). This policy was advocated by government advisers such as Sir Alec Cairncross and the Toothill Committee (1961). Industries supplying products in world demand requiring a labour force which was either highly skilled or able to operate an advanced level of technology were regarded as most desirable, and implants such as the car industry at Linwood were characteristic of this economic rationale. Employment in Glasgow reflected the increasing growth of the tertiary sector; more and more jobs were created in the service industries (Butt, 1985).

Under the pressures generated by government attempts to control inflation and world competition and depression, this implant strategy has been under severe strain. The steel-strip mill at Ravenscraig is the principal survivor of deliberate government enterprise which successfully countered the reluctance of Colvilles to proceed with it (Payne, 1979). Government initiatives, direct and through the Scottish Development Agency, have concentrated on high technology industries, especially in electronics, where the Region possesses some comparative advantages. However, the growth in the labour force has compounded cyclical difficulties, and jobs especially for school-leavers have been difficult to generate. Moreover, successes have often been accompanied by the closure of established businesses.

Unemployment in Strathclyde Region is difficult to chart accurately but differentially has depressed the quality of life for many people, young and not-so-young. The regional council's economic and industrial development committee received a report (September 1984) indicating that the official total of unemployed in Strathclyde at that date was 196,464 or 18·6 per cent of the working population. Taking into account, however, over 78,600 who were not on the register because they were not receiving unemployment benefit or were working temporarily on government schemes for the unemployed, a more accurate figure of 275,000 (26 per cent) was reached. Unemployment was highest in the city of Glasgow districts of Bridgeton-Dalmarnock (38·6 per cent) and Garngad-Blackhill (35·2 per cent) and lowest in Eastwood (7·1 per cent). In only two other areas of Strathclyde was it below 10 per cent, Bearsden and Milngavie (7·6 per cent) and Bishopbriggs (9·8 per cent). Male unemployment is particularly acute in parts of Ayrshire and Lanarkshire, and in some council housing schemes approaches 50 per cent. In the Garnock valley, with the second worst unemployment record in Ayrshire, Glengarnock's Longbar scheme, built in the 1930s to house steel workers and their families, has 42 per cent of men out of work. Youth unemployment is even more severe in some of Glasgow's areas. For instance, in Possilpark, 53 per cent of youths have been unable to find jobs.

Although the dimensions of these problems within unemployment have altered marginally in the 1980's, their significance for family and individual incomes have been constant since the mid-1970's. More households within the

Region have come to depend upon state benefits. The contours of this problem can be traced from the activity rate among those of working age as given in the 1981 Census (Danson, 1984). 89·9 per cent of Strathclyde's males of working age were economically active, a low figure nationally, with Glasgow's figure (89·1 per cent) the lowest in the Region. The female (single, widowed and divorced) rate at 73·9 per cent was, on the other hand, high compared with experience in the Region as a whole (71·4 per cent), no doubt reflecting the comparative strength of the city's service sector. The married women's rate at 56·8 per cent was also high; only in the new towns was it higher. This evidence suggests that many families depend on a second wage earner in order to keep out of a state of poverty and many others, especially in Glasgow, rely on state benefits for existence. Danson (1984) suggests that about 25 per cent of all households in Glasgow and its surrounding area in 1981 were 'on the poverty line' and to these have to be added those in receipt of sickness, unemployment and supplementary benefits, making a minimum of 37 per cent of all Glasgow households and probably slightly fewer for the Region as a whole.

Economic and social indicators of poverty and deprivation range wider than unemployment, economic activity rates or the receipt of state benefits (Gordon, 1984). The low level of self-employment has concerned the Scottish Development Agency, but local enterprise groups in many parts of the Region have endeavoured to generate more activities of this type. Low wages and a high incidence of poverty militate against this, for disposable income among communities has to form the basis for small business formation. A prosperous regional economy is, therefore, a *sine qua non* for the generation of new business opportunities unless special financial assistance is provided.

Poverty and standards of living are affected by such variables as family size, lack of a second income, single parent families as well as low wages and unemployment. Against all these indicators Scotland as a whole emerges badly, Strathclyde worse and the city of Glasgow worst. Strathclyde Regional Council's analysis (1981) of vital statistics (1976–78) by post code districts showed that of the worst thirty areas in the Region, twenty-five were in Glasgow. About half the city's population live in neighbourhoods of multiple deprivation. Indicators such as high concentration of old-aged pensioners, young mothers, illegitimate children and manual workers are all associated with poverty and deprivation, and Glasgow's twenty-five areas revealed these features. Elsewhere in the Region pockets of deprivation existed in most areas of high male unemployment in places such as Greenock, Kilmarnock, Airdrie and Coatbridge, and Motherwell.

As Wannop demonstrates, even the new towns have felt the pinch in the 1980's; the competition for firms able to provide additional employment is intense. Generally, Glasgow has assumed a service centre role for the Region; there has been a considerable loss of jobs in manufacturing since the late 1960's and a trend towards the deskilling of the labour force. The exodus of population has been partly occasioned by the outward drift of jobs in manufacturing and the decline of the building trades since 1980. Deindustrialisation within the city has not been matched by a sufficient increase in service jobs, and one especially worrying feature since 1981 has been a marginal decline in service employment.

There has been much analysis of the problem of deprivation in the Region. The Scottish Development Department's investigation (1973) concluded that about one-third of the city of Glasgow consisted of areas of multiple deprivation. The Regional Council sponsored a special study (1976) upon which a policy of priority treatment for particular areas was based: 52 areas were designated, varying greatly in size. However, initial action was confined to 45 APTs (Areas of Priority Treatment), although policy was reviewed in 1981 and the number of APTs more than doubled. The scale of the problem is so immense that vast public expenditure will be necessary if it is to be solved (Holtermann, 1975). Government counter-inflationary policy is one obvious constraint on regional policy.

Yet a strategy has been developed by the Region (Yates, 1984). As a consequence of national surveys the significance of unemployment, low wages, adverse family circumstances and poor housing in preventing children from having equal opportunities in education and life was recognised (Wedge and Prosser, 1973). Whereas in Britain as a whole one in fourteen children suffered from a mixture of these factors, in Strathclyde it was one in six. Holtermann (1975) demonstrated that in terms of urban deprivation, the Clydeside conurbation was the most severely affected in Great Britain. The statistical basis of these studies was beyond argument, and thus the new Regional Council was committed almost from its inception to formulating a strategy of effective land use, and social and economic development which, it was hoped, would lay the basis for dealing with deprivation. Regional policies earlier had not dealt adequately with local problems. Community aid programmes involving local people became part of a wider planning policy which included positive discrimination, a continuous and comprehensive monitoring of existing policies, an energetic programme of staff training designed *inter alia* to change bureaucratic and community attitudes, more co-ordination between central, local and community institutions and other agencies such as Health Boards (Strathclyde Regional Council, 1976).

In the APTs male unemployment rates over 30 per cent were present by the early 1980's, over 10 per cent of households were headed by single parents, and 15 per cent of births were illegitimate. Sixty per cent of children taken into care came from APTs and 70 per cent came from households whose head was unemployed and/or a single parent. Children in care from APTs have very much less chance of being fostered, the clearest indication of social inequality and deprivation.

Housing was a major issue since the APTs were largely districts dominated by public sector housing. In Glasgow this problem was of paramount importance, as Gordon shows. Within the rest of the Region the quality of residential environment was also a major issue. Pre-war housing stock was only slowly being replaced until the 1950's (Butt, 1983) but thereafter the question of poor quality often centred on post-war developments, some of them of relatively recent date and usually high-rise. Multi-storey living, according to Pacione (1984a), has deep-felt disadvantages in the minds of residents, three-quarters of whom wished to leave the particular Glasgow development which he investigated. Such negative reactions included 31·2 per cent who disliked multi-storey living generally and wanted their 'own front door and garden'; 16 per cent who missed relatives and friends and who wished to move nearer to them; 13·5 per cent who regarded the size of their dwellings as unsuitable for large families (too small) or for the elderly (too large); 12·1 per cent were repelled by poor environment with particular reference to dirty streets and untidy and litter-strewn communal areas. All residents complained of vandalism, crime and drunkenness and added a further range of local deficiencies varying from lack of play areas and entertainment facilities to defective lifts and poor maintenance services.

However, great progress has been made in the provision of housing. The Regional Council has adopted a Housing Plan System which establishes housing needs, reviews allocation policies and assesses priorities in association with the nineteen district councils. Families thought to be at risk, i.e. 'problem families', were often concentrated on one council estate in each district; this policy has been greatly modified. Special need housing (for single people, the elderly, large families) has received higher priority. The major change has been rehabilitation rather than build and/or demolish. A major problem has arisen over damp houses, the dampness commonly occurring through poor ventilation and condensation. Energetic improvement of such houses has been, and continues to be, the policy of the councils, but tight financial constraints have slowed progress.

Seven area initiatives have been launched since 1978, each headed by an area co-ordinator and designed to improve the pace of positive discrimination, but the most important element in this policy has been the Government's Urban Programme which provides £15 million in current expenditure and £5 million for new capital projects each year. Voluntary groups and local communities have become more actively involved in targeting areas of special deprivation and providing locally supported policies of amelioration.

Health studies increasingly focus upon environmental factors which clearly show an interaction within the concept of the quality of life. The unhealthy and ill are often poor, unemployed or low-paid, poorly housed over a long period, and exist at the margin of survival in terms of civilised standards. Gordon Stewart (1984) and Melvyn Howe (1984) both stress how powerless the doctors really are in the face of so many adverse environmental circumstances. The Greater Glasgow Health Board Report (1984) surveying health within the major conurbation over a ten-year period, noted that the city has the highest death rate for adults under the age of sixty-five in the civilised world. In spite of an increased life expectancy Glaswegians face a higher risk of death before the age of sixty-five than other Scots and 50 per cent higher than the average for

England. Heart disease, cancer, stomach disorders and accidents form the main hazards.

However, the incidence of 'premature adult mortality' is least in the affluent middle-class residential districts such as Eastwood or Bearsden and Milngavie which are as healthy as any districts in the surveyed countries; the other side of the coin is represented by the peripheral public sector housing estates such as Blackhill, Drumchapel or Pollok where the risk of death is nearly double. These are the areas with high male unemployment, many single adult households and most of the inhabitants in social classes IV and V. Despite the public pressure to restrict smoking, the wives of unskilled Glaswegians continue to smoke more, a clear indication of higher than average stress within this group and of the limited regard for health education. No real blame can be ascribed to public health facilities; an extensive health centre building programme is under way but existing provision is amongst the best in Britain.

The Department of Community Medicine (formerly headed by Gordon Stewart) has made a particular study of children admitted to hospitals. Those living in deprived districts were nine times more likely to be admitted to hospital than those from other areas. Stewart believes that admissions are most closely correlated with unemployment and overcrowding. In some parts of Glasgow — the north and east — unemployment of parents was about 33 per cent and overcrowding (more than 1·5 persons per room) of households varied between 20 and 25 per cent; from this environment children at risk to a disease or condition likely to lead to hospitalisation exceeded those from non-deprived districts by over a hundred times. Although the number of children from these adverse home circumstances was less than a third of the total child population of Glasgow, it accounted for over two-thirds of all hospital admissions. Child neglect is central to this analysis for when neglected children are exposed to illness they are more likely to require hospital treatment. More energetic development of health education is clearly necessary, but the Greater Glasgow Health Board Report (1984) instances one clear example of child neglect: only half the children from the poorest areas of the conurbation attend for important medical examinations such as visual screening; of those found to have possible visual or hearing defects up to 25 per cent do not return for further treatment. Later sessions and expensive treatment could be much reduced, and personal health much improved if such problems could be solved. At the more general level the Region still lacks an adequate programme to bring the lead content in its domestic water supply down to health levels prescribed within new national regulations, and its director of water supply estimates that £20 million would need to be spent over a ten-year period to achieve that end.

Positive discrimination to offset deprivation in educational opportunity is also a feature of regional policy. Generally, as Bone shows, the senior secondary sector has become increasingly concerned to widen educational opportunities for all pupils, and reform of the curriculum has been designed to that end. When the Region examined educational provision in APTs, it was found that staffing standards were poor, turnover being a particular problem. Schools had poor reputations and often some very large classes where discipline presented particular problems. Much the same situation prevailed in social work; the recruitment and retention of staff for difficult areas was a major issue. Both the Education and the Social Work Departments have improved the ratio of staff to users of their services in APTs in recent years. The effect of declining rolls and the availability of regional staffing resources through the Urban Programme and Circular 991 has led to better pupil/teacher ratios in APT schools. The Urban programme has also led to a development of community education services, and adult basic educational facilities have been provided on a greater scale. Improvement has also been possible in nursery and primary education (Louden, 1985).

Whereas the Region's Education Department has faced already some problems of contraction, the Social Work Department has continued to grow. Staffing has increased and in consequence it has been possible to devote more resources to the APTs. Community work and welfare rights staffing have particularly benefited, and special needs, such as the single homeless, have been more favourably treated. Yet new problems continue to arise, particularly in the area of drug abuse, and pressure on scarce resources does not ease.

Part of the Region's strategy to improve the quality of life in the APTs revolves around the idea of community participation. Local communities are aided by Development Teams, and Community Councils and other groups encouraged. Council premises such as schools are increasingly used for wider community purposes, and some schools, for instance Whitehill in Dennistoun, represent a community facility with all age-groups using the school's facilities for recreation as well as education.

Despite the expansion of numbers of students in Higher Education the access rate for the cohort of school-leavers, particularly for those wishing to enter universities, has tended to decline. Universities have responded to cuts in real income from government by greater economy in the use of resources, especially staffing. At the same time competitive entry standards have risen, making it more difficult for potential entrants to be successful in their applications. There remain a number of schools in the Region who supply few or no entrants to university, and a policy of positive discrimination, although presently difficult to justify, will have to be considered. Educational inequality is most obviously present in the realms of Higher Education.

Leisure as an element in the quality of life depends more on public facilities than on private income. Strathclyde Region is exceedingly well placed for public parks and open spaces: the development of Strathclyde Country Park is well advanced, and Loch Lomondside has recently been proposed as a Regional Park. The Clyde coast and the islands of Bute and Arran are major tourist attractions and local amenities of considerable value.

Sporting facilities and community participation have been greatly extended. New towns such as Irvine have major Sports Centre complexes, and in Glasgow facilities for athletics and a range of sports varying from swimming to badminton exist in a healthy competitive state. The Glasgow Marathon is now a major event in the sporting calendar and a source of income for a number of worthy causes. Professional football is a less compelling spectator activity than it used to be, but the Region still has many football teams operating at a variety of levels.

The heritage as Auld and Hume demonstrate provides many opportunities for leisure activity. Glasgow with Kelvingrove, Pollok House and the Burrell Museum is particularly well endowed, and there are specialist museums devoted to the history of Glasgow, transport and childhood which attract many visitors. Smaller burghs such as Paisley, Ayr and Greenock have their local collections, and the National Trust operates major attractions such as Culzean Castle. The conservation movement is strong but not oppressively so, and Strathclyde Region still lacks a major museum devoted to the history of the industries which once made its economy so strong.

Leisure, entertainment and tourism also provide new economic opportunities for the Region's population as well as facilities for personal use. These service industries are representative of a new economy which is in the process of creation. Heavy industry has sharply contracted; the Region's economic buoyancy and its capacity to generate the employment, income and purchasing power, which will make APTs less necessary and the quality of life much better, depend upon services, information technology amongst other new technologies, biotechnology and other applied sciences.

Economic regeneration must have a high priority but it has implications for the quality of life arising from changes in the nature of work. Higher levels of basic education will be necessary, and if artificial intelligence and robotics enter production on a significant scale, the work ethic will depend less on physical activity involving little discretion in the workplace and more on freedom of action and flexitime. These changes will provide great opportunities as well as presenting massive challenges.

REFERENCES

Abrams, M. (1973), Subjective social indicators, *Social Trends, 4*, 35–50.
Allardt, E. (1973), About dimensions of welfare: an explanatory analysis of a comparative Scandinavian Survey, *Helsinki University Research Group for Comparative Sociology* Report 1.
Andrews, F. M. and Withey, S. B. (1976), *Social Indicators of Wellbeing — Americans' perceptions of life quality*. New York.
Bateson, G. (1972), *Steps to an Ecology of the Mind*. San Francisco.
Butt, J. (1983), Working Class Housing in the Scottish Cities 1900–1950. In Gordon, G. and Dicks, B. (Eds.), *Scottish Urban History*. Aberdeen University Press, Aberdeen, 233–267.
Butt, J. (1985), Employment in the Scottish Cities since 1900. In Gordon, G. (Ed.), *Perspectives of the Scottish City*. Aberdeen University Press, Aberdeen.
Campbell, A., Converse, P. E. and Rodgers, W. L. (1976), *The Quality of American Life*. New York.

Campbell, R. H. (1980), *The Rise and Fall of Scottish Industry 1707–1939*. John Donald, Edinburgh.

Checkland, S. G. (1981), *The Upas Tree*. University of Glasgow, Glasgow.

Danson, M. (1984), Poverty and Deprivation in the West of Scotland. In Pacione, M. and Gordon, G. (Eds.), *Quality of Life and Human Welfare*. Royal Scottish Geographical Society, Norwich, 23–34.

Gordon, G. (1984), The Concept of Deprivation. In Pacione, M. and Gordon, G. (Eds.), *Quality of Life and Human Welfare*. Royal Scottish Geographical Society, Norwich, 15–21.

Greater Glasgow Health Board (1984), *Report*. Glasgow.

Holtermann, S. (1975), Areas of urban deprivation in Britain, *Social Trends*, 6, 33–47.

Howe, G. M. (1984), Aspects of Social Malaise in Scotland. In Pacione, M. and Gordon, G. (Eds.), *Quality of Life and Human Welfare*. Royal Scottish Geographical Society, Norwich, 91–102.

Johnston, T. L., Buxton, N. K. and Mair, D. (1971), *Structure and Growth of the Scottish Economy*. Collins, London and Glasgow.

Kreiger, M. H. (1969), Social Indicators of the quality of individual life', *Institute of Urban and Regional Development Working Paper 104*. University of California, Berkeley.

Pacione, M. (1980), Differential quality of life in a metropolitan village, *Institute of British Geographers, 5*, 185–206.

Pacione, M. (1984a), Evaluating the quality of the residential environment in a high-rise public housing development, *Applied Geography, 4*, 59–70.

Pacione, M. (1984b), The Definition and Measurement of Quality of Life. In Pacione, M. and Gordon, G. (Eds.), *Quality of Life and Human Welfare*. Royal Scottish Geographical Society, Norwich.

Pacione, M. and Gordon, G. (1984). *Quality of Life and Human Welfare*. Royal Scottish Geographical Society, Norwich.

Payne, P. L. (1979), *Colvilles and the Scottish Steel Industry*. Clarendon Press, Oxford.

Scottish Development Department (1973), *Investigation to identify multiple deprivation areas*. Central Research Unit Paper No. 7.

Slaven, A. (1975), *The Development of the West of Scotland 1750–1960*. Routledge & Kegan Paul, London.

Stewart, G. (1984), Health in Glasgow: The Influence of Behaviour and Environment. In Pacione, M. and Gordon, G. (Eds.), *Quality of Life and Human Welfare*. Royal Scottish Geographical Society, Norwich, 103–109.

Strathclyde Regional Council (1976), *Urban Deprivation*. Glasgow.

Strathclyde Regional Council (1981), *Demographic Indicators 1976–78: An analysis of vital statistics by post code*. Chief Executive's Department, Glasgow.

Strathclyde Regional Council (1984), *Report on Unemployment*. Glasgow.

Wedge, P. and Prosser, H. (1973), *Born to Fail*. Arrow, London.

Wingo, L. (1973). The quality of life: towards a micro-economic definition?, *Urban Studies, 10*, 3–18.

Yates, K. (1984), Strathclyde's Strategy to Combat Deprivation. In Pacione, M. and Gordon, G. (Eds.), *Quality of Life and Human Welfare*. Royal Scottish Geographical Society, Norwich, 35–47.

CHAPTER EIGHT

THE ECONOMY OF STRATHCLYDE REGION

A. G. Nairn and F. X. Kirwan

Introduction

The Strathclyde economy is on the downward phase of an economic cycle which last peaked in the 1920's. The likely duration of the downswing is unknown, its amplitude without precedent this century. The mid-1980's do not furnish an auspicious perspective on the regional economy.

Yet in the first two decades of this century the economists surveying the Region would have painted an altogether different picture. The 'second city of the Empire' presided over a thriving, highly integrated regional economy. Locally mined coal fuelled the steel mills which supplied the shipyards and locomotive makers. These in their turn sustained a broad-based engineering sector. The pull of a prosperous region attracted immigrants in large numbers, swelling the population of Glasgow alone to over 1·1 million in 1931.

Half a century later Glasgow's population had fallen to 765,000, Strathclyde suffers persistent net migration, and large parts of the Region's industrial structure lie in ruins. Post-war regional policy failed to re-create the integrated economy of the pre-war years. Transplanted industries failed to spawn downstream activities, and themselves proved unviable in the long run.

This diagnosis is not new. The Clyde Valley Regional Plan of 1946 in many respects reads like an analysis of the Strathclyde economy in the 1970's and 1980's. Forty years on the same issues dominate the regional economy; the run-down of the Lanarkshire coalmines, the relocation of steel production to the coast, persistent net outmigration and continuing high unemployment. Government intervention, in the shape of the active regional policy of the late fifties, sixties and first half of the seventies, created substantial numbers of additional jobs, but proved incapable of balancing the labour market. The outlook for the non-interventionist market-oriented 1980's is not auspicious for a region in secular decline. The long-term success of policies designed to improve the attractions of the Region as a location for investment remain crucially dependent on a sustained upturn of the U.K. and world economies.

This chapter is in three parts. The first reviews the Clyde Valley Regional

Plan of 1946, and remarks on the relevance of the Plan's analysis and recommendations. The West Central Scotland Plan of 1974 forms the subject matter of the second part. Completed just before the onset of the world-wide recession, it provides a comprehensive review of the structure of the regional economy. The final part of the chapter describes the experiences of the Strathclyde economy over the recessionary period 1973–84.

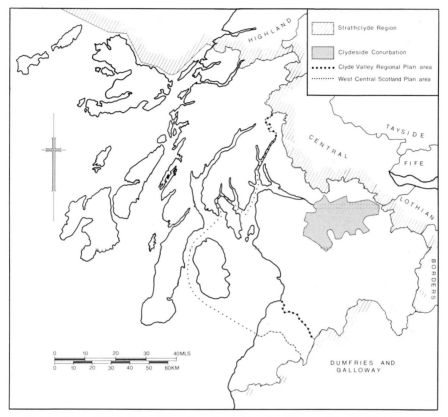

Fig. 1   Area of Clyde Valley Plan, West Central Scotland Plan and Strathclyde Region.

A characteristic feature of the development of the economy of Strathclyde Region was the degree of flexibility and innovation which fostered the cotton, textile and chemical industries out of the accumulated capital and expertise of the tobacco trade. This pattern of rapid technical progress and structural change was also a feature in the rise of the shipbuilding and capital good sectors which brought to Clydeside unparalleled economic prosperity. The external economies associated with these industries created a highly integrated regional economy both in the economic and the corporate sense. The economy at the beginning of the twentieth century was not, however, completely dominated by shipbuilding and heavy engineering and their suppliers; the coal industry for instance was supplying buoyant overseas demand and the textile industry remained an important employer. In addition there were already examples of American inward investment in the form of Babcock and Wilcox and the Singer sewing machine plant at Clydebank. Finally, the tradition of innovation and structural change which had characterised the Region from the outset of the industrial revolution appeared to be continuing, as instanced by the Argyle automobile and the movement by Beardmores, the giant steel and shipbuilding company, into automobile and aircraft production.

The aftermath of the war and the depression of the mid-twenties marked a sea-change in the fortunes of Strathclyde. By the late 1930's Clydeside had become 'Red Clydeside', the male unemployment rate for the former 'second city of the Empire' was over 25 per cent and unemployed rates had reached 40 per cent in some of Strathclyde's towns. The attempt to diversify into newer industries such as automobile and aircraft construction had manifestly failed. The former strengths of the regional economy, its massive export base of shipbuilding and heavy engineering and its highly integrated economic structure, became, under conditions of reduced world trade and protectionism, a source of weakness since the export base in question was highly cyclically sensitive.

The Analysis and Prognosis of the Clyde Valley Regional Plan (1946)

The Clyde Valley Regional Plan is notable in two respects. It was the first authoritative document concerning the economic and physical structure of Strathclyde, and it was distinguished by the resilience of the proposals contained within it, to the extent that, even today, it would be 'premature to think that its influence is over' (Wannop, 1984, p. 41). The Clyde Valley Plan, an advisory document, was preceded by the Greater London Plan, headed also by Abercrombie, and by the Royal Commission on the Distribution of the Industrial Population (the 'Barlow Report') of which Abercrombie was also a member. However, the Clyde Valley Regional Plan did not simply follow prevailing conventions but rather reaffirmed from first principles the conclusions of the Barlow Report. In addition, the Plan provided comprehensive coverage of the issues to be faced in the West of Scotland and prescribed what it considered appropriate remedies. Six major conclusions and proposals concerning the spatial and economic structure of the Region can be summarised as follows:

1. A 'Regional Planning Authority' should be created with the strategic powers necessary to implement and revise the plan as required.
2. A 'green belt' should be preserved in order to ensure that the conurbation possesses 'essential' fresh air and recreation facilities, that prime agricultural land is protected, and that any further outwards spread of the conurbation is prevented.

3. That the maximum permissible urban population should not exceed 140 persons per acre with a maximum of 250,000 persons to be rehoused at peripheral sites within the green belt boundary. In terms of the Clyde Valley as a whole, some 700,000 persons would require to be rehoused from the existing urban sites.

4. In order to provide accommodation for the overspill population of Glasgow existing towns should be allowed to expand, as should other parts of Scotland, to relieve the congestion of the industrial Central Belt. However, the Plan was quite explicit about the integral part in the decentralisation of population played by an accompanying movement of industry. Perhaps the most obvious expression of this can be found in the final strand of decentralisation: the proposed new towns at East Kilbride, Cumbernauld, Bishopton and Houston.

5. The two most important factors influencing industrial change in the Region which the Plan identified were the decline of mining in Lanarkshire and the reorientation of the steel industry. For this reason and to achieve a 'balanced' industrial structure the Plan emphasised the Region's urgent requirements for new industry. Consequently the Plan advocated the provision of strengthened negative *and* positive powers over the location of industry.

6. Further inducement to incoming industrialists should be provided in the form of 'suitable' modern advance factories. The need to remove the disincentives associated with dereliction and decay through an environmental improvement programme was also stressed.

In addition to these major conclusions and recommendations, the Plan recommended schemes to preserve the Region's architecture and amenity, and also improvements to the transportation network including a ring road network, motorway to Edinburgh, and road and rail links to Prestwick airport.

The proposals for the redistribution of population were based upon a number of factors. Firstly, the Plan assumed that the population of the Region would/should remain virtually the same for the succeeding half century. This assumption was based upon the view that the Clyde Valley had reached 'saturation point' and that any further concentrations of Scotland's population within the Clyde Basin would prove extremely detrimental to the development of Scotland as a whole. A more accurate interpretation might be that the Plan saw the existing population as representing the desirable maximum both in economic and social terms. As Table 1 shows, the Plan was correct in its view that the population of Strathclyde would remain around the two and a half million mark, although whether this has occurred for the reasons expected by the Plan is another question.

The strategy proposed for the industrial problems of Strathclyde was the introduction of new 'light' industries to diversify and provide a more 'balanced' industrial structure for the area. This was the case because the Plan viewed the unbalanced industrial structure of Strathclyde as the major factor

TABLE 1   POPULATION OF STRATHCLYDE
REGION AND GLASGOW CITY 1891–1981

Year	Strathclyde	Glasgow*
1891	1,757,508	
1901	2,079,017	950,000
1911	2,269,840	
1921	2,409,832	1,056,000
1931	2,400,223	1,093,000
1939	2,504,706	
1951	2,523,548	1,090,000
1961	2,584,068	1,056,000
1971	2,575,514	980,000
1981	2,404,532	681,000

* Note: the population for Glasgow City for the years until 1961 refers to 1951 Glasgow boundaries whilst that for 1971 and 1981 are for 1971 boundaries.
Source: 1981 Census of Population Small Area Statistics, Robertson (1958), 1971 Census of Population.

contributing to the decline of the regional economy since World War I. The concentration of shipbuilding and heavy industry on Clydeside was held to have prevented the emergence of the new industries necessary to sustain economic growth in the Region. The traditional industries such as shipbuilding were no longer able to hold their share of the world market as a result of the development of competitive industries in other countries and the rise of protectionism. Although the total tonnage of ships produced on the Clyde had decreased consistently since 1919, the proportion of total U.K. output of shipping built there had actually increased. In part this was due to continued innovation in propulsion methods, but more importantly was accounted for by the fact that the majority of the Clyde yards specialised in liners and warships rather than the declining cargo ship sector (Lythe and Butt, 1975, p. 219).

It was not only the decline of the traditional industries which affected Clydeside but also their suffocating effect on the emergence of the 'new' industries. The Plan noted that the major industries of mining and specialised iron and steel production were not natural precursors to the new light industry plants then in evidence in the Midlands and South of England and which were taking advantage of the external economies which previously had been so beneficial to the development of Strathclyde. In addition, there was in the West of Scotland a lack of suitable premises for light industry partly resulting from the impossibility of converting premises designed for the traditional industries to new uses. Conversely large numbers of firms had been established where suitable 'modern' premises, such as those at Hillington, had been provided.

The Plan also noted the psychological role played in the Region's decline by preconceptions both within and outwith Strathclyde. Within the Region the attitude that traditional heavy engineeering industries were both better than other trades and inseparable from the character of Clydeside did not encourage potential incoming industrialists. The view of militancy and 'Red Clydeside' held outwith the Region also served to detract from the potential of the area. Finally, it was argued that the dereliction left by the basic industries had seriously reduced the amenity of Clydeside and would act as a deterrent to the inward migration of both industry and population.

The critical question left unanswered was to what extent the industrial structure of Strathclyde militated against the emergence of new industries *relative* to the other industrialised areas of the United Kingdom. Similarly unanswered was the question of whether or not the physical problems of Strathclyde were in relative terms significantly different from other comparable industrialised areas. This is not to say that the industrial and physical structures of Strathclyde were not possibly the two single most important factors in the economic decline of Strathclyde, but rather that the descriptive nature of the analysis contained within the Plan permits only intuitive rather than substantive conclusions. It is fair to say that the Plan was primarily concerned with the spatial structure of the Region, with what would now be termed 'conventional' physical planning, that is: zoning, rehousing, overspill, the countryside and green belts, and new and expanded towns. The apparent lack of interest among economists of the time in regional economics contributed to the absence of appropriate analytical techniques. The fact that only one economist provided a part-time input to the Plan perhaps explains the tenor of the analysis. However, these criticisms must remain somewhat muted given both the Plan's comprehensive coverage of the Region's economic, social and spatial conditions and its continuing relevance and influence.

It is perhaps appropriate to conclude this section by reiterating one finding which, although not highlighted, was to prove extremely ominous. The study concluded that Strathclyde's economic prospects would continue to depend critically upon the traditional industries which in turn would depend upon the level of both capital investment and world trade. Whilst the long-run role of the 'new' industries might be to replace declining traditional industries, in the short run their role at best could be to absorb only a small proportion of the surplus labour of Clydeside.

From the Clyde Valley Plan to the West Central Scotland Plan

The post-war general election of 1945 produced a Labour Government committed to both an active regional policy and intra-regional dispersal measures. The Distribution of Industry Act 1945, the New Towns Act 1946 and the Town and Country Planning Act 1947 provided the powers to implement the proposals of the Barlow Report on regional policy, overspill and new towns. It was consequently feasible to act upon the recommendations of the Clyde Valley Regional Plan.

Despite initial opposition from the city of Glasgow, an overspill policy for Glasgow was endorsed by the Scottish Office and East Kilbride New Town was designated by the Secretary of State for Scotland in 1947. By 1952 Glasgow Corporation had withdrawn its opposition to overspill policies with the recognition that some 400,000–500,000 Glaswegians would require accommodation outside the city. In addition to population overspill the Corporation sought to encourage, where appropriate, movement of industry out of congested sectors of the city to the reception areas. In particular, industrial concerns likely to be affected by the city's redevelopment programme were encouraged to consider the overspill areas as potential relocation sites.

Redevelopment in Glasgow accelerated with the twenty-nine Comprehensive Development Areas (CDAs) proposed in the 1960 Development Plan being subjected to large-scale clearance and then redeveloped as high-rise residential locations. The regeneration of the CDAs, which constituted one of the most ambitious slum clearance programmes in Europe, was hampered by a lack of funds on the necessary massive scale. As a result, by 1977 of the twenty-nine Comprehensive Development Areas, only nine were completed or nearing completion with consequent problems of dereliction and decay throughout the period (Randall, 1980). The overspill policy was further hampered by the reluctance of industry to move out of Glasgow to the available reception areas (Farmer and Smith, 1975). This applied to industry generally in Glasgow and not just that located in the CDAs. One final point to note about the overspill policy is that whilst the population of Glasgow has declined by around half a million since World War II, only approximately one-quarter of the figure migrated to the official overspill areas (WCSP, 1972). This unanticipated migration was related to the continued relative decline of the Strathclyde economy throughout the post-war period.

Recognition of the problems faced by a number of Britain's cities had led central government to extend regional aid to them in 1945. As a result Glasgow was added to the area of Central Scotland eligible for regional assistance as a Development Area. National balance of payments problems in 1947, however, severely restricted the implementation of an active regional policy by the Labour Government for the remainder of its term of office. In 1951 a Conservative Government ideologically opposed to regional policy was elected. With the decline of unemployment rates, both national and regional, it was politically feasible to slacken the application of regional policy (McCallum, 1979). Consequently, between 1947 and 1958 regional policy fell into abeyance. The economic picture of the decade immediately after the Clyde Valley Regional Plan was one of overall employment growth for Strathclyde Region, with regional employment rising from three-quarters of a million in 1939 to just about the million mark in 1959. The majority of this employment growth, as may be seen in Table 2, resulted from the growth of the service sector which increased its share of employment from 37·8 per cent in 1939 to 44·5 per cent in 1959.

The unemployment rate for the West of Scotland averaged between 3 and 3·5 per cent in this period, more than twice the U.K. average. Whilst the

TABLE 2   PERCENTAGE EMPLOYMENT SHARE IN STRATHCLYDE 1924 TO 1978

Sector	1924	1930	1939	1959	1968	1978
Primary	12·0*	7·4*	6·2	4·6	1·6	1·8
Manufacturing	53·3	51·5	47·7	44·3	42·5	33·8
Construction	5·0	6·0	8·3	6·6	8·5	7·3
Services	29·7	35·1	37·8	44·5	47·4	57·1
Total employment (000's)	600·2**	529·8**	726·5**	996·9	986·6	981·1

* For the years 1924 and 1930 the percentages for the Primary Sector exclude agriculture.
** For the years 1924, 1930 and 1939 the total employment figures relate to the West of Scotland and are approximately 3–4 per cent smaller than those for 'Strathclyde' of 1968 and 1978.
Sources: 1924, 1930, 1939: Clyde Valley Regional Plan 1946, Appendix 9 p. 369. 1959, 1968: West Central Scotland Plan 1974, The Regional Economy p. 130. 1978 Department of Employment ERII Records.

immediate post-war years represented a period of success on Clydeside compared to the unemployment rates of the 1930's, changing attitudes and expectations and the Region's continuing inferior performance relative to the U.K. as a whole were interpreted as failure and grounds for recrimination (Checkland, 1981). Thus pressure was exerted on central government to reactivate regional policy and reduce inter-regional disparities in unemployment rates while at the same time reducing a major cause of the new outward migrant flow. An immediate result of this pressure was the establishment of the Ravenscraig integrated strip mill in 1958 and, later, the 'guiding' of the Rootes motor plant to Linwood in 1961. However, it was the recession of the late 1950's which prompted the major governmental responses; with the 'Toothill Report' in 1961, the 'Central Scotland White Paper' in 1963, and the return to strong regional policy in 1964.

The 1958–59 recession decimated U.K. employment in coalmining, shipbuilding and railway equipment, to the extent that together these three industries shed over 250,000 jobs in the five-year period 1958–63. The impact of the national recession on the Strathclyde economy where these industries were major employers was particularly severe. Between 1959 and 1968 over 20,000 jobs disappeared from the coalmining industry, a further 20,000 from shipbuilding and, with the demise of the former giant of the industry, North British Locomotive, in the early 1960's, the railway equipment industry all but disappeared from Clydeside.

The 1961 'Inquiry into the Scottish Economy' (the Toothill Report) and later the White Paper on Central Scotland (a Programme for Development and Growth, 1963) produced similar plans for the revitalisation of the regional economy. Overspill of population and industry was to be continued and aided by sustained financial incentives for the reception areas. In addition, it was proposed that financial aid should be provided to areas with growth potential. The concept of 'growth areas' represented a departure from the previous philosophy of directing funds to areas of need in favour of one of directing funds to areas of potential. This change in emphasis increased the role of new towns in redeveloping Strathclyde's spatial and industrial structure, and resulted in the designation of Irvine in 1966 and Stonehouse in 1973. However, quite apart from social considerations, the political difficulties involved in a non-needs based strategy precluded its extension since the Labour Government's voting strongholds were in the most deprived areas. Aside from the emphasis on 'growth areas' the main conclusions of the Toothill Report and the 1963 White Paper followed those of the Clyde Valley Regional Plan. These proposals stressed the need for continued overspill of population and industry, improvement in the environment and image of Clydeside, and for change in the Region's industrial structure which, despite the large employment loss in the traditional industries, was still dominated by industries with little prospects for growth and deficient in the growing 'scientific' industries.

The remainder of the 1960's and early 1970's saw the continued redevelopment of Glasgow and the application of 'strong' regional policy. However, both housing conditions and unemployment rates in Strathclyde remained substantially worse than the U.K. average in general and the West Midlands and Southern Regions in particular. Despite the policy measures of the post-war period the 1971 Census of Population revealed that Clydeside stood out from all the British conurbations in terms of its disproportionate level of housing deprivation and unemployment (Holtermann, 1975). This is not to say that policy had no impact. Regional policy in the 1960's, for instance, has been estimated as creating approximately 60,000 extra jobs in Scotland (Moore and Rhodes, 1974) of which 30–50 per cent may have been situated in Clydeside (Randall, 1980). Indeed, the impact of regional policy in the attraction of branch plants, added to the increase in external ownership through mergers and takeovers, represented a substantial shift away from indigenous ownership and control. This process, which was in existence in the early part of the century, became particularly marked in the decades following the Clyde Valley Regional Plan. The problems of the traditional industries continued into the 1970's, coming to a head with the confrontation at Upper Clyde Shipbuilders. Following intervention by the Labour Government in the form of grants and loans and an attempt at rationalisation, the failure of UCS was signalled with the appointment of a liquidator in June 1971. The result of a work-in and allied political pressure was to force the then Conservative Government to make a U-turn and advance further aid to the Clyde yards.

It was in this context of multiple deprivation, industrial decline and unrest that the West Central Scotland Plan Team was established. Unlike the Clyde Valley Regional Plan, the West Central Scotland Plan from the outset had a primarily economic focus. It also had the advantage of greater availability of social and economic data, although to a considerable extent the dearth of regional and sub-regional statistics identified by the Plan still remains. Also available to the Plan team were a number of previous studies of the causes of economic decline on Clydeside. One such study was by Cameron (1971), who estimated that approximately half the employment decline of Clydeside could be attributed to its adverse industrial structure. The remaining employment loss required alternative explanations. The West Central Scotland Plan Team concurred, arriving at broadly similar conclusions.

The Plan showed that Clydeside possessed a local economy in which much of manufacturing industry was uncompetitive as a consequence of the preponderance of labour-intensive methods, low productivity and consequent high unit labour costs. These characteristics were shown to exist relative not only to the U.K. but also to the other British conurbations. The peripheral location of Strathclyde Region and consequently higher transport costs was not considered by the Plan to be a major factor in the Region's decline, although it was noted that in certain industries transport costs could be of paramount importance. Local considerations such as the availability of suitable labour, industrial sites, special natural resources, and local factor costs were not thought to have exerted any significant influence on the performance of indigenous industry.

The Plan concluded that the quality of the local physical environment was likely to have exerted an adverse influence, possibly major, on the evolution of the regional economy, through its effect on morale and selective migration patterns. However, whilst greater provision of quality industrial sites within the Region was required, the absence of such sites was incapable of explaining the relatively poor economic performance of Strathclyde. The average size of establishment in Strathclyde proved similar to that of the U.K., whilst the relatively high level of external ownership and control was discounted as a contributory factor to the Region's decline on the basis that externally owned firms had actually performed better in employment terms than indigenous ones. Finally, the Plan found little evidence that there existed failings in the capital market to which the poor performance of the Strathclyde economy could be attributed.

The main explanation, according to the West Central Scotland Plan, for the 'non-structural' economic problems of Strathclyde lay with poor industrial relations and management. Local management was considered to be 'conservative, inflexible and lacking in dynamism' (WCSP, 1974b, p. 235). In addition to the economic analysis, the conclusions of which are briefly detailed above, the West Central Scotland Plan also discussed the associated issues of the social, demographic and physical structure of the Region. The proposals of the Plan based on analysis of these aspects of the region and its economic structure are detailed below.

1.   That an economic development corporation (SEDCOR) should be set up to aid the existing industry within Strathclyde so as to improve the quality of management and industrial relations.
2.   That regional aid should be increased so that West Central Scotland could enjoy an increased differential over other Development Areas and attract mobile industry. To this end a range of industrial sites and advance factories should be prepared.
3.   That Central Government should widen regional policy to include inducements to encourage office relocation, and should itself relocate at least 10,000 civil servant jobs from London to Glasgow.
4.   That an Environment Improvement Task Force should be set up to undertake the task of providing Strathclyde with a better physical environment.

Other proposals within the Plan included new housing by 1981 for 204,000 people; improvement to surroundings of 120,000 or one in six of the Region's dwellings; spending of £675 million on environmental improvement by 1981; and the postponement of Stonehouse, Strathclyde's fourth new town.

The influence of the West Central Scotland Plan on post-regionalisation Strathclyde is not difficult to see. In the Scottish Development Agency there exists both the concept of SEDCOR and the 'Environmental Improvement Task Force', although for Scotland rather than Strathclyde alone. Stonehouse new town has been cancelled. Regional policy, on the other hand, has faded from sight and been replaced by a different form of spatial policy in the shape of the SDA's area initiatives and Central Government's Enterprise Zones, and the programme of civil servant dispersal has been drastically reduced.

The 1970's and 1980's — Recession and Recovery?

Having peaked at almost half of Scotland's total population in 1961 and then remained broadly steady during the subsequent decade, Strathclyde's population fell by over 6 per cent in the intercensal period 1971–81. The decline in population was particularly marked in Glasgow city, whose population has fallen by over one-third during the last twenty-five years, with the bulk of the decline taking place in the period since 1971. From a peak population of 1·1 million in 1931, the city's inhabitants numbered only 765,000 in 1981 (even less when allowance is made for boundary changes), having fallen by an estimated 170,000 during the preceding decade alone.

Glasgow's contraction has been only partially offset by population growth in areas adjacent to but outside the city boundaries, even though the rate of population increase in some overspill districts, such as Cumbernauld and Kilsyth, and East Kilbride, which encompass new towns, has been exceptionally rapid. The decline in Strathclyde's population does not reflect an unfavourable age structure relative to the rest of Scotland, or a lower rate of natural increase, but is the product of a markedly higher rate of net outmigration, which in turn is caused not by a particularly high propensity among residents of the Region to emigrate, but by the reluctance of outsiders to move in. The pace of net migration from Strathclyde, at a decennial rate of eight per thousand inhabitants during the period 1971–81, was more than twice the corresponding rate for Scotland as a whole.

The most recent disaggregated employment data for the Region relate to 1981, but are inevitably somewhat misleading as an indicator of the structure of the regional economy in the mid-1980's given the heavy experience of redundancies in Strathclyde in the early years of that decade. Compared to Scotland as a whole in 1981, the Region had a smaller proportion of employment in primary industries, less than 2 per cent compared to more than 4 per cent nationally, and a marginally smaller proportion engaged in the provision of miscellaneous services. The share of engineering employment in the Region was markedly higher than in Scotland as a whole, reflecting the industrial tradition of Clydeside, with shipbuilding, mechanical, vehicle and marine engineering particularly to the fore. Strathclyde also had a somewhat greater than proportionate share of Scottish employment in clothing and footwear industries. These were generally industries where the incidence of redundancies was particularly heavy during the course of the recession.

Manufacturing employment in Strathclyde fell by over a quarter in the four

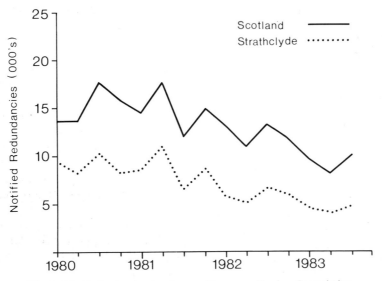

Fig. 2   Notified redundancies. Source: Manpower Services Commission.

years to 1981, a rate of contraction almost twice that experienced in British manufacturing as a whole and somewhat faster than that in Scottish manufacturing. This pattern changed somewhat in subsequent years. Although the phasing of redundancies in the Region moved in step with that in Scotland as a whole, Strathclyde's share of the total during 1983 was much closer to its share of Scottish employment than it had been in the early stages of recession.

Official protestations notwithstanding, the recession-induced contraction in Scottish industrial output was no less severe than that experienced in British non-oil industry as a whole. The timing was, however, somewhat different, with the descent into recession slower and therefore more prolonged, and the upturn to the end of 1983 markedly less vigorous. No separate industrial production figures exist for Strathclyde, but the general similarity of its employment structure to that of Scotland as a whole, coupled with its preponderance of traditional metal-bashing industries, suggest that its experience of recession was unlikely to be more favourable than that of Scotland as a whole.

The only regular source of information on industrial trends in Strathclyde is the West of Scotland Business Survey (undertaken till Autumn 1984 by Glasgow Chamber of Commerce and thereafter subsumed within the Scottish Business Survey undertaken jointly by the Fraser of Allander Institute and the Chambers of Commerce of Glasgow, Edinburgh and Aberdeen). Survey results suggest that industry in Strathclyde did not begin to emerge from recession till the close of 1982, with the stimulus coming primarily from home rather than export sales. The survey suggests that recovery was slow and had gained little momentum by mid-1984.

Strathclyde's marginally less favourable employment structure and its experience of recession are reflected in the unemployment figures for the Region, both in absolute levels of unemployment and in the rate at which workers flow onto and off the unemployment register. Though Strathclyde accounts for less than half of Scotland's population and workforce, it contributes well over half of Scotland's registered unemployment. In the spring of 1981, 77 per cent of Scottish males aged 16–64 were in full-time employment, the corresponding figure for Strathclyde was 73 per cent and for Glasgow only 67 per cent. At the same time 13 per cent of Scottish males aged 16–64 were out of employment, the corresponding rate was 16·5 per cent in Strathclyde and 21·5 per cent, or more than one in five, in Glasgow. For females the picture in 1981 was somewhat different, with the proportion aged 16–59 who were in employment almost identical to that for Scotland as a whole. Strathclyde, and Glasgow in particular, had greater proportions of women in full-time employment and smaller proportions in part-time work than recorded Scottish-wide — a reflection of the greater incidence of male unemployment in the Region and the consequent necessity for full-time female employment to supplement household income.

The areas with the highest unemployment rates are to be found almost

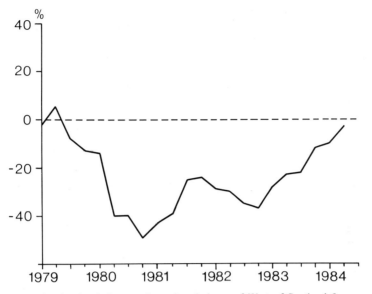

Fig. 3 (a)   Production levels in manufacturing; balance of West of Scotland firms reporting higher production than in previous quarter. Source: Glasgow Chamber of Commerce.

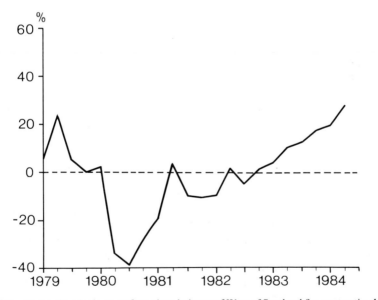

Fig. 3 (b)   Domestic sales in manufacturing; balance of West of Scotland firms reporting higher sales than previous quarter. Source: Glasgow Chamber of Commerce.

without exception within the boundaries of Glasgow. Besides the peripheral post-war overspill housing estates, the areas where the incidence of unemployment is currently greatest are precisely those identified as unemployment black spots in the Clyde Valley Regional Plan of 1946 — Bridgeton, Dalmarnock, Springburn and Maryhill. At the trough of the economic cycle in mid-1981, these areas had registered unemployment rates similar to those of the 1930's. By 1984 the position had worsened further with male unemployment rates of 40–50 per cent not uncommon in parts of the city.

On most conventional indicators the labour market in the Region is amongst the most depressed in Scotland, though as the recession deepened Strathclyde's position relative to Scotland improved much as the latter's position relative to the rest of Britain became less unfavourable. In April 1984, 17·5 per cent of the Region's workforce were unemployed, compared to a Scottish rate of just over 15 per cent. However, while total unemployment in Scotland showed a marginal fall over the twelve months to April 1984, Strathclyde's total actually increased. Unemployment-vacancy ratios in the Region remain amongst the highest in Scotland with between 25 and 30 registered unemployed for each notified vacancy during 1983/4, compared to a Scottish ratio of about 20.

Strathclyde's unfavourable unemployment-vacancy ratio is reflected in other measures of unemployment experience. The median duration of completed spells of unemployment in Strathclyde is generally several weeks longer than that for Scotland as a whole, with the disparity most marked for males. During the final quarter of 1983, males in Strathclyde leaving the unemployment register had typically been on the register for just over thirteen weeks, while the corresponding figure for the Scottish register during the same quarter was under twelve weeks. (In a region such as Grampian with substantial oil-related employment, the median duration of completed spells for males during the fourth quarter of 1983 was under seven weeks.)

Those leaving the register are fortunate. A broader measure of unemployment experience, focusing on the length of time those currently unemployed have already spent on the register, again highlights the relative weakness of Strathclyde's labour market. During the final quarter of 1983, unemployed males in the Region had on average already spent more than forty weeks on the register. The corresponding figure for Scotland was under thirty-seven weeks. Focusing on particular age groups heightens the contrast. While the typical 30–39-year-old male on the Scottish register at the end of 1983 had already been unemployed for just under forty-six weeks, a person of similar age on the register in Strathclyde would already have been unemployed for over fifty-six weeks. The experience of the female unemployed in Strathclyde is less unfavourable than that of their male counterparts, but the general pattern still remains one of a labour market relatively weaker than Scotland as a whole, and of one in which the probability of becoming unemployed is higher than in most other regions, and where having become unemployed, the probability of leaving the register during any one quarter is markedly less than in most of the remainder of Scotland.

The discussion of unemployment to date has focused on those registered as unemployed. Never an adequate proxy of the excess supply of labour, this particular indicator has become even more inadequate in recent years with the inclusion on the register only of those who are eligible for unemployment or social security benefits. Making allowance for those consequently excluded from the register, for those who had withdrawn discouraged from the labour market and for those employed on various official 'special measures', Strathclyde Regional Council estimated the underlying actual rate of joblessness in the Region at 24 per cent of the labour force in April 1984 (Strathclyde Region, *Economic Trends*, June 1984, p. 3).

Though the regional council administers some of central government's 'special measures', such as the Youth Training Scheme, specific regional measures to alleviate unemployment are necessarily limited. Foremost amongst local initiatives directed at the long-term unemployed has been the Region's 'Employment Grant' scheme. Jointly funded by the Region and the European Community, the scheme essentially provides a marginal employment subsidy for a period of six months to firms recruiting additional employees from the register of long-term unemployed. The scheme had subsidised the employment of over 7,000 in the two years since its inception till June 1984. Follow-up surveys suggest that almost three-quarters of the subsidised jobs continue to exist twelve months after payment of the subsidy has ceased.

Strathclyde's weak labour market prompts an obvious question: if the Region's population and employment structure were not markedly dissimilar to that of Scotland as a whole in 1981, why has Strathclyde's experience of recession been so severe? Part of the answer lies in the fact that the differences in employment structure between the Region and Scotland as a whole lay in traditional industries, such as engineering, where the impact of the recession has been particularly severe. But that is not the full explanation. Short-time working was not used in Scotland to anything like the same extent as in Britain as a whole during the course of the recession. For reasons which are not clear, Scottish, and Strathclyde, firms seem to have reacted to a downturn in demand with closures rather than gain a breathing space by means of measures such as short-time working. In addition, while no separate figures are yet available for Strathclyde, the growth of self-employment in Scotland since 1979 has been markedly slower than that in Britain as a whole. Indeed, if this type of employment is treated as an indicator of entrepreneurial activity, Scotland remains one of the lagging regions of the British economy.

While labour market and aggregate industrial trends within the Region have been far from encouraging since the last cyclical break in mid-1979, considerable effort has been expended by central, regional and local authorities, by the Scottish Development Agency and the business community to enhance the attractions of the Region as an industrial location. Such policies are in keeping with the comments of the Secretary of State on the Regional Report produced by Strathclyde Regional Council in its first year of operations in 1974. This report identified the Region's prime problems as unemployment and urban deprivation. The former has proved much more amenable to policy initiatives than the latter.

The Regional Report proposed three policy goals:
(a) strengthening the economic base of the Region;
(b) improving the performance of existing industry;
(c) increasing the attractions of the Region for inward investment.

The onset of the world recession in 1979 frustrated attainment of the first objective and makes assessment of the extent to which the second has been achieved difficult. On the third, there has been substantial progress. Land renewal programmes have transformed the dereliction wrought by traditional industries into attractive industrial estates and recreational facilities. The GEAR (Glasgow Eastern Area Renewal) project is the largest urban renewal programme in Europe, covering over 4,000 acres and more than 45,000 inhabitants. The proposed St. Enoch development will be amongst the largest inner city shopping complexes in Western Europe.

In a reversal of previous policies, private residential investment has been encouraged in the heart of Glasgow, while simultaneously considerable resources have been devoted to the rehabilitation of traditional tenement housing. The Region's already good communications infrastructure continues to be upgraded with further improvements to the Central Scotland motorway network. The latter has in turn been used to influence the location of industry, the SDA's food park at Motherwell being a prime example.

SDA area initiatives and integrated projects, such as those at Clydebank, Motherwell, Cambuslang and Glengarnock, and local enterprise trusts under the auspices of Scottish Business in the Community, have aimed to provide a fertile nursery for indigenous small firms and a pole of attraction for footloose investment. Indeed it is largely through such inward investment that Strathclyde's electronics industry has attained its present size. The designation of Clydebank as an Enterprise Zone, Prestwick as a Freeport, plus the construction of the Scottish Exhibition and Conference Centre at Queen's Dock, further enhance the attractions of the Region.

Nonetheless, any realistic assessment of the regional economy in the mid-1980's cannot ignore the continuing symptoms of economic stagnation such as declining employment and population, high and chronic unemployment, low per capita incomes and persistent net outmigration. While it would be foolish to pretend that these features are amenable to dramatic improvement in the short term, current policies to improve the attractions of the Region must eventually pay dividends. Its success, and the time horizon within which such success is achieved, is crucially dependent on a sustained upturn in the British economy and the world economy in general.

REFERENCES

Abercrombie, P. and Matthew, R. (1949), *The Clyde Valley Regional Plan 1946*. HMSO, Edinburgh.

Cameron, G. C. (1971), Economic Analysis for a Declining Urban Economy, *Scottish Journal of Political Economy*, Vol. 18.

Checkland, S. G. (1981), *The Upas Tree, Glasgow 1875–1975 . . . And After*. University of Glasgow Press.

Farmer, E. and Smith, R. (1975), Overspill Theory: a Metropolitan Case Study, *Urban Studies*, Vol. 12, No. 2.

Henderson, R. A. (1974), Industrial Overspill from Glasgow: 1958–1968, *Urban Studies*, Vol. 11, No. 1.

Holtermann, S. (1975), Areas of urban deprivation in Great Britain: an analysis of 1971 Census data, *Social Trends*, No. 6. C.S.O.

Lythe, S. G. E. and Butt, J. (1975), *An Economic History of Scotland 110–1939*. Blackie.

McCallum, J. D. (1979), The Development of British Regional Policy. In Maclennan, D. and Parr, J. B. (Eds.), *Regional Policy — Past Experience and New Directions*. Martin Robertson.

Moore, B. and Rhodes, J. (1974), Regional Policy and the Scottish Economy, *Scottish Journal of Political Economy*, Vol. 21, No. 3.

Randall, J. N. (1973), Shift-share analysis as a guide to the performance of West Central Scotland, *Scottish Journal of Political Economy*, Vol. 20, No. 1.

Randall, J. N. (1980), Central Clydeside — a case study of one conurbation. In Cameron, G. C. (Ed.), *The Future of the British Conurbations — policies and prescriptions for change*. Longman.

Robertson, D. J. (1958), Population, past and present. In Cunnison, J. and Gilfillan, J. (Eds.), *The Third Statistical Account of Scotland: Glasgow*. Collins, Glasgow.

Scottish Development Department (1963), *Central Scotland: a Programme for Development and Growth*. Cmnd. 2188, HMSO, Edinburgh.

Toothill Committee (1961), *Report of the Committee appointed by the Scottish Council (Development and Industry); Inquiry into the Scottish Economy 1960–61*. The Scottish Council (Development and Industry), Edinburgh.

Wannop, U. A. (1984), Clydeside in Transition: Three questions on the significance of metropolitan strategic planning, *Town Planning Review*, Vol. 55, No. 1.

West Central Scotland Plan Team (1972), *Components of Change Technical Memorandum 4*. Glasgow.

West Central Scotland Plan Team (1974a), *West Central Scotland Plan — A Programme of Action, Consultative Draft Report*. Glasgow.

West Central Scotland Plan Team (1974b), *The Regional Economy, Supplementary Volume 1*. Glasgow.

CHAPTER NINE

THE UNIVERSITY OF GLASGOW:
AN HISTORICAL PERSPECTIVE

A. A. M. Duncan and M. S. Moss

'Poor and proud' is a human condition long familiar in Scotland, both among its rulers and the ruled. The search for employment and prosperity was as hard in the fifteenth century as today but it took men even then to universities for the training which fitted them for any job requiring literacy and administrative competence. To meet that need scholars had gathered to teach at St. Andrews which became a university between 1410 and 1413. By 1450 authorities in the West were looking at a second university as a means of attracting local development. The burgesses of Ayr were beaten to the post by William Turnbull, Bishop of Glasgow for a brief and otherwise undistinguished term (1447–54). In January 1451 papal authorisation was given to create the University of Glasgow, and teaching began that year.

The University was to have the privileges of Bologna, a fairly meaningless phrase in the context of Glasgow, but suggesting an intention to specialise in arts and law (balancing arts and theology at St. Andrews); law was taught in the early decades. The intention mattered less than the means and these were woefully inadequate. Bishop Turnbull gave nothing but a blessing, no college was founded to maintain the lifestyle of the regents (teachers), and in truth no one of distinction stayed to teach at the tiny and struggling institution for material rewards. One of the great Scottish scholars of his time, John Major, was induced to return from Paris to become Principal in 1518; he brought a high reputation and student numbers exploded. After eight years Major was tempted away to St. Andrews, and a hundred years after its foundation, the University was in a sorry condition. Its buildings on the High Street below the Cathedral were dilapidated; its income probably suffered from a general reluctance in the last decade before the Reformation to pay the Church its dues; it had perhaps one teacher and he part-time; the students numbered perhaps forty. But it survived.

Recovery came first in the 1570's, when Andrew Melville as Principal reformed the curriculum to suit the needs of a society which held elementary education for all children as one of its ideals. He, too, left for St. Andrews but not before the *Nova Erectio* of 1577 reformed the finances of the University as well as its teachings, specialist professors replacing omnicompetent regents. Curiously, for most of the seventeenth century this reform was reversed, at a time when the developing commerce of the city was supporting expansion in the University. New buildings around two quadrangles housed a flourishing student body — albeit young by any standards, for many came up aged twelve to fourteen — and the wealthier citizens were anxious to send their sons to its classes as part of their training for a working life in the family business or for a career in one of the professions. Religious debate caused ups and downs in the University's reputation after 1660, but from 1690 a sounder devotion to learning alone was rewarded by the foundation of chairs in specialised subjects, beginning with Humanity (Latin) in 1682 and Mathematics in 1691. By the beginning of the eighteenth century the reputations of the Universities of Edinburgh and Glasgow had overtaken that of St. Andrews.

Glasgow's rise to prominence can be attributed to the growing wealth of the city, first as the centre of the tobacco trade between the American colonies and Great Britain, and then after the War of Independence as the home of fledgling industries like textiles, shipbuilding and engineering. The University benefited. Its benches were crowded with students most of whom declined to graduate as all they wished to do was to learn a skill. Glasgow, always a broad church, welcomed all and sundry, non-conformists as well as members of the Church of Scotland, providing they could pay. The Professors (thirteen by 1760) built up a flourishing trade in extra-mural teaching, charging fees which they pocketed. New-found wealth gave them time to reflect on what they taught and to innovate.

There is a tendency to dwell on the famous names: Adam Smith, Professor of Moral Philosophy, 1752–64, and James Watt who serviced the model Newcomen engine and contributed directly to industrial innovation. But the truth is that their great work was done away from Glasgow University and the city itself. The corporate contribution of the University in strengthening the bounds of knowledge and teaching was more important than that of the most distinguished individual.

In the early and mid-eighteenth century a number of Regius Chairs were established, funded by the Crown, which laid the foundations for later expansion. Medicine swiftly vied with Divinity as the most important subject, attracting students from throughout Great Britain, particularly from Ireland. They came to learn from the greatest medical scientists of their generation, William Cullen and Joseph Black. The speedy departure to Edinburgh of these rising stars created a vacuum until the late eighteenth century when James Jeffray became Professor of Anatomy, a position which he retained until 1848. A powerful medical politician, Jeffray was adept at persuading Faculty to his point of view, however unreasonable.

Throughout these developments the administration of the University remained curiously conservative. The professors of the old foundation resented the largesse showered by the Crown on the new regius professors.

Even amongst the ranks of the professors of the old foundation there was disquiet. One of their number — John Anderson, Professor of Natural Philosophy — fought a pitched battle with the Principal and the factor, the finance officer of the day, about the way the books were kept. A spectator, the Reverend William Thom of Govan, commented in a refrain with a contemporary ring:

> 'Long speeches were made and huge volumes were writ
> And still as their noddles were puzzled, they got
> Swarms of book-keepers clerks to unravel the knot
> There after rewarding with thanks and with plate
> They let loose on their steward a tempest of hate.'

The bitterness of this confrontation contributed to Anderson's decision to provide in his will for the foundation of another university in the city. Although he died £55 in debt, his intentions were ultimately carried and his institution prospers as the University of Strathclyde.

During the first half of the nineteenth century, Glasgow's industries flourished and the city grew rapidly. The University did not always respond willingly to these stimuli, particularly in the industrial sector. Its greatest contribution in the first half of the nineteenth century was in the development of medical services. Several prominent University figures had been instrumental in the foundation of the Glasgow Royal Infirmary in 1787, Glasgow's first voluntary hospital, which opened its doors in 1794 for the treatment of those who could not afford to pay for medical care.

The presence of the Infirmary permitted for the first time the provision of clinical teaching. Relations between the Infirmary managers and the University authorities were often strained over the question of control and management of these resources. The issue was further complicated by the emergence of extra-mural medical schools (notably at the Andersonian University) and a prolonged dispute with the Faculty of Physicians and Surgeons of Glasgow. Since its foundation in 1599 the Faculty had held a monopoly over the right to license surgeons in Glasgow and the West of Scotland. The introduction in 1817 of the University degree in surgery challenged this authority and posed a severe threat to the prestige and finances of the Faculty. The legal proceedings lasted into the 1840's and the matter was not fully resolved until the passage of the Medical Act of 1858.

The University had a role in the advance of a number of the other professions. Its importance as a training centre for divinity students diminished after the Disruption of the Established Church in 1843 and the speedy creation of theological colleges by the Free Church of Scotland. In the secular and commercial spheres it retained its importance in the education of lawyers, who were responsible for providing the financial framework which was a major influence in Glasgow's success.

The major omission of the University was its failure to respond to the needs of the local engineering and shipbuilding trades which in the second half of the century were to be such a major force in world markets. It was left to other organisations to fill the gap, like the Mechanics' Institutes and the Andersonian.

In 1840, under pressure from the Crown, the University, grudgingly, accepted the establishment of the first Regius Chair in Engineering in Britain. The first incumbent, Lewis Gordon, one of I. K. Brunel's assistants, was badly treated, as his new colleagues resented his links with industry and his income from private practice. When he arrived he was not even given a blackboard, let alone a lecture room. When six years later one of his pupils, William Thomson, later Lord Kelvin, became Professor of Natural Philosophy, the University had come to recognise the links between the physical sciences and technical developments in industry. Thomson demanded and got better resources for both teaching and research, which he used for his pioneering work. Gordon's successor, William Macquorn Rankine, undoubtedly one of the most talented theoretical engineers of the nineteenth century, played a leading part in the invention of the compound engines and wrote a series of engineering textbooks used throughout the world.

Despite the brilliance of Kelvin and Rankine, their achievements, like those of Adam Smith and James Watt almost a century earlier, were more outside than inside the University. They preserved extensive consultancy and business interests while attracting large numbers of extra-mural students to their classes, often from distant parts of the world such as Japan.

By the middle of the century the University was again making a significant contribution to the life of the city, especially in the field of medical care where its staff played an active part in tackling the appalling public health problems of a grossly overcrowded urban society. The engineers, Gordon, Thomson and Macquorn Rankine, were called on to lend their particular expertise in bringing piped water to the city in the 1850's. In the following decade W. T. Gairdiner became Professor of Medicine and combined this for nine years with a part-time appointment as Glasgow's first Medical Officer of Health. Above all, Lister's priceless gift of antisepsis and Macewen's role in achieving the transition to the aseptic era of surgery, brought international renown to the city.

After much searching, the University in 1870 abandoned its old buildings, reputedly the finest example of vernacular architecture in Scotland, for a new Gothic building in the fashionable West End, far from the slums and stench of the city centre; the old building was demolished. Although there were insufficient funds to complete the new University, the Principal and the thirteen professors who controlled the purse strings saw to it that they were each provided with a large house on campus.

Easy access for clinical teaching was an essential ingredient in the continued success of the Medical School, a goal achieved in 1874 with the opening of the Western Infirmary on a site adjacent to the new University. Without a great internal debate on 'relevance' but against a background of deep concern about the quality of British technical education, the University recognised the distinctiveness of scientific enquiry and method when it moved to Gilmorehill by providing facilities for experimental work and teaching.

In 1872 a separate degree of B.Sc. was introduced and in 1893 a Faculty of Science which at the same time was allowed to award the B.Sc. in Engineering. Isabella Elder, the widow of John Elder, one of the greatest shipbuilders of mid-Victorian Britain, used her legacy of £500,000 to augment the endowment of the Chair of Civil Engineering and to establish in 1883 a Chair of Naval Architecture. At first these initiatives produced few men of business, nearly all the graduates becoming civil servants either at home or overseas. In 1889 Archibald Barr, a Paisley man who had been a professor at Leeds, was appointed to the Chair of Civil Engineering. With enormous energy and enthusiasm he propelled the whole Science side of the University into the twentieth century, introducing such unheard of novelties as visual aids, certificated evening classes and sandwich courses. Barr recruited overseas students paying economic fees to help the University's finances and raised funds from industry to pay for a new engineering laboratory. This was quite apart from establishing his own business called Barr and Stroud, famous for its range finders and optical equipment. He was behind moves to build closer links with the Royal Technical College (incorporating the Andersonian University and the Mechanics' Institute) with its long tradition of training practical engineers and men of science.

Isabella Elder joined with other well-to-do women, notably Mrs. Campbell of Tullichewen, to pioneer the higher education of women in the foundation of Queen Margaret College in 1881 — a development greeted with less than enthusiasm by the University. After eleven years male chauvinism bowed to the inevitable and the College amalgamated with the University, which acquired its endowments. Initiatives within the University to increase the spread of subjects on offer also required wealthy patrons. There was a plentiful supply of suitable candidates for the University to touch in late Victorian Glasgow. In 1896 Andrew Stewart, a Glasgow merchant, endowed the Chair of Political Economy and in 1907 James Dixon, a coal owner and property developer, the Chair of Mining Engineering. Sometimes funds came from less conventional sources. The Chair of Scottish History and Literature, for example, was established (inadequately) from the proceeds of the Glasgow Exhibition of 1911.

By the end of the nineteenth century more undergraduates took the trouble to graduate, reflecting an increase in demand for qualified professionals in all the walks of life. No longer was it good enough just to have attended a university. In the Medical Faculty and the medical-related sciences, like Botany and Zoology, large numbers of students attended lectures but took their qualifications more cheaply at one of the three other medical schools in Glasgow, St. Mungo's, the Western Medical School and Anderson's College of Medicine; consequently the Professor of Anatomy was the richest man on the campus, earning almost twice as much as the Principal! By the First World War medical and scientific enquiry had become more sophisticated and required expensive equipment, both for teaching and research. It soon became clear that this could only be financed realistically by central government. In 1919 the University Grants Committee was established to co-ordinate and make permanent the previous system of *ad hoc* Treasury grants. With this security the University expanded rapidly after the First World War, multiplying its building on Gilmorehill. Despite swingeing increases in personal taxation, it also managed to win endowments from the citizens of Glasgow to open up new subject areas.

The Modern Faculties

During the last decade several new Chairs have been established in the Medical Faculty, reflecting new developments in cardiac surgery, neurosurgery and genetics. In addition there have been further initiatives of a broadly interdisciplinary character.

One of the few UGC new developments last year was the allocation of three lecturers to Glasgow for teaching and research in behavioural science. This interdepartmental group will begin by contributing to the new 'Environment, Behaviour and Health' course for medical and dental students. With the MRC Medical Sociology Unit moving from Aberdeen to Glasgow, we become the only place outside London and 'Oxbridge' to have three MRC Units. Since the Department of Community Medicine is also moving to Gilmorehill close to the Social Paediatric and Obstetric Research Unit, interest in the social setting of health disease and health care should come to critical mass.

The teaching of medical ethics is another current area of development, which the GMC has been urging since 1967. At a national level the Nuffield Foundation has set up a Working Party to discuss over a two-year period the teaching of medical ethics. Locally in Glasgow discussions between faculties have resulted in the establishment of an Institute of Law and Ethics in relation to Medicine. The intention is to co-ordinate not only teaching but also research in a field in which there is already considerable activity in the Faculties of Medicine and of Law as well as in the Department of Philosophy.

Even before 1950 the University had affiliated to itself the Dental College, instituting a dental degree in that year. Since then the College has been once rebuilt and is again being refurbished, though the school remains part of the Medical Faculty.

The Veterinary College, largely as a result of the efforts of one man, Sir William Weipers, was similarly integrated, but transferred to a new rural-suburban campus and in 1968 recognised as a separate Faculty. Its undergraduate intake is as strictly limited as that of the Medical Faculty but to only one-third the number. One of five Veterinary schools in Britain, its research work has achieved considerable recognition. Much of the pioneering work on open-heart surgery was conducted here, in co-operation with the Medical Faculty. A further example is found in the recognition of a relationship between virus and cancer. The researchers involved in this area have contributed to our understanding of feline leukemia. A great deal of attention has been given to parasite disease in farm animals, and members of the Faculty were the first to introduce a vaccine against this type of disease.

The science departments have always been very active in research. Physics has a long tradition of expertise in nuclear structure and gravity waves whilst Chemistry. has a range of excellence from radio-chemistry (isotopes were discovered in Glasgow) to Organic Chemistry (two Nobel Prize-winners associated with Organic Chemistry). The Mathematical sciences have recently been strengthened with new Chairs in Computing Science, Applicable Mathematics, and Astro-Physics to reinforce a long-held expertise in the subject. The Biological sciences, which shade into Medicine, have always been a strength with interests ranging from the ecological to the most modern applications of biotechnology. It is significant that the Faculty of Science brought the first computers into the University and have always been major users.

Engineering has similarly expanded and adapted to meet changing demands. We no longer need to train men to build railways and steam reciprocating engines, but motorways and wide-bodied jets. New Chairs were established in Electrical Engineering in 1921, and Aeronautical Engineering in 1950. In 1980 the title of the Chair of Naval Architecture was extended to include Ocean Engineering, reflecting the oil-related needs of modern-day Scotland.

Marine technology has emerged as an area of excellence. The University enjoys the advantage of one of the best towing-tanks in the country for work on ships and off-shore structures. There have been notable developments in Electronic Engineering, with opto-electronics as a specialism.

A large Faculty such as Arts can incorporate many interests, and this is reflected in the range of historical departments (Archaeology, Medieval, Modern and Scottish History, and the History of Science) and in the variety of languages taught. In this latter field there have been many changes as a result of innovations in secondary schools. The Faculty has responded by offering beginners' courses in several languages. A new Language Centre is at present being established, which is intended to become one of the most advanced facilities of its kind in Europe. The study of English and Scottish literature flourishes in the Faculty, while there is an increasing demand for relatively new courses in drama and film and television studies. A century ago, the academic study of literature in the English vernacular was just beginning; now the vernacular media of the late twentieth century are demanding their share of scholarly attention.

More traditional arts are not neglected. The old Hunterian Museum has been partly refurbished. A selection of William Hunter's priceless coin collection can now be seen, and the paintings and prints are displayed in a new gallery beside the University Library along with the reconstructed interior of Charles Rennie Mackintosh's house: a contribution to Glasgow's claim to be a major European centre of the visual arts. The Faculty also collaborates with other institutions in the city. The Professor of Architecture teaches not in the University but in the Mackintosh School of Architecture; and departments in the Faculty participate in degree courses in music and drama at the Royal Scottish Academy and in education at the Jordanhill College of Education. The 1984–85 session has seen a reversion to one of the University's original functions. Under an agreement with St. Peter's College, candidates for the Roman Catholic priesthood are once again (for the first time since the Reformation) studying for the M.A. at the University of Glasgow.

Divinity has been most transformed. Since its first increase in size by the merger of the Free Church College and the Faculty in 1929, it has shrunk to become a vigorous two-department school, a large proportion of whose students are mature.

The Faculty of Law has added a flourishing accountancy degree to the qualifications offered in Law. Still wider concerns are reflected in a new title: the Faculty of Law and Financial Studies. Close contacts with the professions are maintained in the employment of local solicitors and accountants as part-time tutors.

In 1977 the subject areas of politics, sociology, economic history and economics hived off to form the Faculty of Social Sciences with a well thought-out degree structure which now also admits honours study in one of these subjects with a subsidiary language. Social Sciences are both traditional and innovatory. A research department has undertaken social and economic studies for government and private agencies since the Second World War. While the philosophical tradition of Adam Smith continues, students are now introduced to the microcomputer as an instrument of analysis and forecasting.

The Glasgow Division of the Business School is a graduate institution federated in the Scottish Business School as well as being a member of the Faculty of Social Sciences. The staff have established for Glasgow a particular excellence in industrial and managerial studies and attract an expanding number of executives to study for the M.B.A. degree.

This sketch of the modern Faculties is designed to give no more than an impression. But it should be clear that a University which has been in existence for more than five hundred years has, in the main, successfully adapted to changing demands. However, in company with others, we now face uncertainties which are not merely financial, and which will require as great, if not a greater, capacity for change and adaptation as that shown in the past.

Fig. 1   Professor John Anderson (1726–96). A contemporary portrait by an unknown artist.

CHAPTER TEN

THE UNIVERSITY OF STRATHCLYDE

Ronald Crawford

The Anderson Legacy

> Except what is contained in the Painted Chest, with three locks ... I
> Give, Grant, Dispone and Convey the whole of my other property, of
> every sort, to the Public for the good of Mankind and the
> Improvement of Science,[1] in an Institution to be denominated
> 'Anderson's University' ... in the course of time perhaps from these
> small beginnings, this Institution may become a Seminary of Sound
> Religion; Useful Learning; and Liberality of Sentiment ...

(From the Will of Professor John Anderson F.R.S., Glasgow, 7th May 1795.)

There are two especially important factors to be kept in mind in considering
the historical establishment of the University of Strathclyde. The first is that it
should have been born out of a plan conceived by a single individual and
meticulously set forth in, of all things, his Will. And the second is that the
author of the Will — testator and progenitor rolled into one — was himself a
university professor. Probably no other university can claim such a bizarre
inception. More cynically, that a university of acknowledged world standing
should owe its origin to the impecunious dreamings of an irascible, litigious
and idiosyncratic crank seems scarcely credible.

John Anderson has been described as 'neither a great man nor a great
scientist' (Coutts, 1909). But then Robert Burns, who died in the same year as
Anderson, was described in a poem published in that very year as a 'worthless
bard ... insignificant and void of sense ...' (Maxwell, 1796). Clearly, Burns's
subsequent fame and influence are ineradicable. So, too, the traditional
dismissal of Anderson as 'a foolish, fond old man' is, it might be thought,
equally perverse and just as drastically in need of reappraisal.

---

[1] Anderson is using 'science' to denote simply knowledge or learning, a sense that according to
Raymond Williams in *Keywords* continued in use into the early nineteenth century. Curiously
enough, Williams gives an example from 1796 of a closer approximation to its modern sense.
('Mineralogy, though tolerably understood by many as an art, could scarce be deemed a Science.')

If it is true that it is to John Anderson and his Will that the University must go to acknowledge its beginnings, it is also easy to exaggerate. There is of course no doubt that Anderson is archetypally an apostle of the Enlightenment and that he was often misunderstood simply because, paradoxically, many of his ideas were ahead of his time. And it is certainly true that like many who defied in their lifetime the conventions of their age, Anderson at times dismayed and outraged his contemporaries. Yet in one important respect the Will is solidly, disappointingly orthodox. Strathclyde became Britain's first technological university when it received its Royal Charter in 1964 but it would be wrong to discern in Anderson's Will any heady prescription for a new kind of university rooted in applicable science. Instead, true to convention, the four named Faculties are Arts, Medicine, Law and Theology. [Anderson actually went further, describing 'the Mechanic Arts', as taught in a 'College' as distinct from a university, as within the provision of 'many other things totally different from learning'.] One cannot, therefore, ascribe to the Will *per se* a vision of a future powered by the white heat of technological change.

Where the Will is memorably radical is in its comment on *orientation, access* and *community*. In emphasising 'useful learning' Anderson conceptualises a purposeful function for his university that, as he sees it, places it apart from the other universities of the day and, especially of course, from the University of Glasgow of whose authorities he had so often fallen foul.

Secondly, Anderson desired to open up his university to persons conventionally denied admission to, or employment in, the established universities. He laid down a scheme, for example, for an annual course of lectures in the physical sciences for ladies who, it was envisaged, would be imbued with 'such a Stock of General Knowledge . . . as will make them the most accomplished Ladies in Europe'. He wished, too, that Anderson's University would build on his own courses for 'Manufacturers and Artificers in Glasgow' who had, in consequence of their studies, 'become distinguished in a high degree for their General Knowledge, as well as for their Abilities, and Progress in their several Arts'. Most preposterously of all, it might seem, Anderson, *ex sepulcro*, appointed by name the first professors in his university, none of whom was by careful design a recognised teacher in, or connected in any way with, the University of Glasgow.

Less obviously perhaps, the Will represents the finest exposition we have of Anderson's philosophy of education that defined knowledge and learning as a means of 'improvement' of the human lot and, therefore, as something that ought not to be reserved and exclusive but open to all who may benefit from it. In removing the mystery of higher education, Anderson, more than even he could have foreseen, had anticipated the ethos of the modern university. In leaving his putative institution 'to the Public for the good of Mankind', Anderson boldly and irreverently threw out the notion of the ivory tower, replacing it by the idea of a university that could not nor should be separable from the society it was created to serve. That is the real message of the Will and establishes overwhelmingly the essential continuity of the Anderson legacy.

The Royal Charter and Amalgamation

In his memoirs *A Time to Remember* (1983), the Chancellor, Lord Todd, does well to remind his readers that the University of Strathclyde, the first new university in Scotland since the reign of King James VI, was not a creature of the Robbins Report (as is sometimes mistakenly claimed) but was assured of its Charter before Robbins saw the light of day in October 1963. In an important and neglected footnote Robbins observes that 'the Royal College of Science and Technology, Glasgow . . . is treated as a university throughout the Report'. And, of course, the former Director of the Royal College of Science and Technology, Sir David Anderson, who retired in 1960, was a member of the Robbins Committee.

If, however, Robbins did not create Strathclyde there is no doubt that it set the seal on the Royal College's special contribution to higher education in Scotland by recommending that it, together with Imperial College and the Manchester College of Science and Technology, receive the accolade of designation as SISTERs ('Special Institutions for Scientific and Technological Education and Research'). To these three were to be added a brand-new foundation and one of the CATs, making five SISTERs in all.

It is scarcely surprising that the SISTER concept was not adopted. The creation of a limited number of what were to be centres of excellence by another name rankled with those established universities that were at least as strong in 'scientific research' as the favoured three which, inevitably, would have been regarded in certain circles as, at best, upstarts and, at worst, cuckoos in the nest. But, in a sense, the failure of the idea mattered little. It was enough, by way of tribute to the Royal College's reputation, that Strathclyde had been singled out for special treatment in this controversial way.

In an important section dealing with the future of the central institutions in Scotland the Robbins Committee had urged 'some form of academic association' between appropriate neighbouring colleges and the Royal College of Science and Technology. With the Robbins formula in accord with their own intentions, the Governors of the Scottish College of Commerce promptly sought integration with the Royal College and, remarkably, in little over six months the necessary formalities were completed and amalgamation of the two Colleges took place, almost literally on the eve of the granting of the Royal Charter in May 1964.

The full significance of the integration of the Scottish College within the Royal College goes far beyond the immediate statistical benefits of an overnight accession of over one thousand full-time students and the interpolation of new disciplines and departments including Commerce, Law, Accountancy, Modern Languages, Librarianship, Hotel Management and Secretarial Studies. Viewed at a comfortable distance of over twenty years, the amalgamation can now be seen as a powerful extension of the new University's claim to authenticity and as a springboard to viability and recognition. That is not, of course, to say that the Royal College would not have succeeded and fared well without the Scottish College. Together, however, they accelerated the appeal of the new University in the eyes and minds of the public at large — potential applicants and their parents, the teaching profession, business and industry.

Despite that, as its anonymous author points out, *A Decade of Progress*, published in 1974, shrewdly observes that 'there were those within the walls who saw in this development a possible threat: the University might forsake its original purpose and the technology upon which it had built an international reputation.' That tension, some would say, heightened to some extent by externally imposed financial pressures, has never entirely been relaxed.

Useful Learning: (a) Science

It has already been stated that it would be foolish to misapprehend Anderson's Will in one important respect — 'the Improvement of Science' so-called — even though he was prudent enough to designate the Professor of Physics as Dean of the Faculty of Arts. The University Charter, on the other hand, is entirely unequivocal:

> 'The objects of the University shall be to advance learning and knowledge [which is precisely what "the Improvement of Science" meant] by teaching and research particularly into the basic and applied sciences and to enable students to obtain the advantages of a liberal university education.'

In *The Glasgow Region* (1958), published on the occasion of the British Association's last annual meeting in the city, Charles Wood documents most capably the astonishing record of distinguished scientists who taught and researched in the Royal College of Science and Technology and its antecedent institutions, among them, of course, Anderson's University — some indeed of the most illustrious names in nineteenth-century science, including such as Thomas Garnett, George Birkbeck, Thomas Graham, Sir Thomas Thorpe, William Dittmar and many others.

More recently, however — and particularly in the years immediately prior to university status — proper recognition of the Royal College's distinctive work in pure and applied science was not always in evidence. Although since 1913 the Ordinances of the University of Glasgow had provided for Royal College students to matriculate, and sit the examinations for, first degrees in engineering and, subsequently, in applied chemistry and metallurgy, it became a source of great irritation to the College that in the basic sciences — mathematics, physics and chemistry — whereas Honours Associateship (ARCST) courses had been successfully offered for many years, no comparable Honours Glasgow degree (B.Sc.) was available to 'Tech' students. Instead, the College — at least in the case of mathematics and physics — had to settle for the administratively cumbersome Bachelor of Technological Science Degree (B.Sc.Tech.).

It is also worth mentioning that when the British Association last visited Glasgow, several of what would now be regarded as key technologies in *any* modern university simply did not then exist — information technology, microelectronics and biotechnology to name but three.

The Faculty of Science was formed in 1982 out of four Schools of Study:
   The School of Mathematics, Physics and Computer Science
   The School of Chemical and Materials Sciences
   The School of Biological Sciences
   The School of Pharmaceutical Sciences
and comprises ten Departments as follows (discrete sections in brackets):
   Mathematics (Pure and Applied Mathematics; Statistics; Numerical
      Analysis)
   Physics
   Applied Physics
   Computer Science
   Pure and Applied Chemistry (Physical; Organic; Inorganic; Chemical
      Technology; Fibre and Textile Research Unit)
   Metallurgy
   Applied Geology
   *Bioscience and Biotechnology (Food Science; Applied Microbiology;
      Biology; Biochemistry)
   Pharmacy (Pharmaceutical Chemistry; Pharmaceutics; Drug Metabolism
      Research Unit; Forensic Science Unit)
   Physiology and Pharmacology

Useful Learning: (b) Engineering
   Although the University of Glasgow rightly claims the oldest Chair of Engineering in Britain (1840), it is to the Glasgow Mechanics' Institution, founded in 1823, where both William Thomson, later Lord Kelvin, and his elder brother, James, were both students, that the Royal College, and now the University of Strathclyde, owe the sound base on which was established their subsequent worldwide reputation in engineering. This was the first Mechanics' Institution in Britain and it continued as a separate foundation until its incorporation (as the College of Science and Arts) within the Glasgow and West of Scotland Technical College in 1886.

   It is curiously ironic that today, at a time of great change for engineering education with many — prompted by the Finniston Report — looking back wistfully to a bygone era when the study of engineering was a judicious mingling of practice and theory, it should be recalled that sandwich courses

* A partner, with the Department of Chemical and Process Engineering, in the Biotechnology Unit.

were first conceived in Glasgow and were only abandoned to suit the requirements of independent degree-granting aspirations. *A Decade of Progress* (1974) puts it well: 'The abandonment of the sandwich course for the engineering degree and the adoption of a three-year term created difficulties for the College which had to follow the new degree pattern while maintaining the traditional pattern for the College associateship.'

Sandwich courses may have all but disappeared at Strathclyde but the clamant need for practical instruction remains and the University's Engineering Applications Centre (opened 1983) stands as evidence of a determination to supply that need. Sir Monty Finniston, an alumnus and a former member of staff of the old Royal College, clearly approves. And so, surely, would John Anderson.

Architecture, now incorporated within the Faculty of Engineering where, for example, computer-aided design is just one obvious common strand, has also a distinguished history at Strathclyde. Here again, however, it is possible to argue that, in the short term, university status was something of a mixed blessing. Until 1964 the Royal College, through the agency of the Glasgow School of Architecture, had co-operated with the Glasgow School of Art in offering a widely recognised Diploma in Architecture. The institution of the new Bachelor of Architecture degree (later conjoined with the degree of B.Sc. in Architectural Studies) meant that such an arrangement was no longer strictly necessary and the partnership was dissolved, leaving the Art School to seek a new association with the University of Glasgow leading to the eventual establishment of the Mackintosh School of Architecture.

Until 1982, when the Faculty of Engineering was constituted, there were three separate Schools of Engineering, viz.:

The School of Mechanical and Chemical Engineering and Naval Architecture

The School of Civil and Mining Engineering and Applied Geology

The School of Electrical and Electronic Engineering

and a School of Architecture, Building Science and Planning, also now incorporated within the Faculty. There are thirteen departments or quasi-departments, a National Centre and a Special Board of Study as follows:

Engineering Design
Dynamics and Control
Mechanics of Materials (including the Materials Testing Service)
Thermodynamics and Mechanics of Fluids
} Mechanical Engineering Group of Departments

Production Management and Manufacturing Technology
*Chemical and Process Engineering
Bioengineering Unit
National Centre for Training and Education in Prosthetics and Orthotics
Ship and Marine Technology

* A partner, with the Department of Bioscience and Biotechnology, in the Biotechnology Unit.

Electronic and Electrical Engineering (including the Industrial Control
Unit)
Civil Engineering
Mining and Petroleum Engineering
Architecture and Building Science (including the ABACUS and ASSIST
units)
Energy Studies Unit
Special Board for Degrees of B.Sc. B.Eng. with Honours in Manufactur-
ing Sciences and Engineering

Useful Learning: (c) Arts and Social Studies
Though the roots of Arts and Social Studies may be traced in the teaching of
'General Studies' in the Royal College to undergraduate engineers it would be
more realistic to date their inception from the College's decision in the early
1960's to set up, in anticipation of university status, a 'Faculty of Industrial
and Social Studies'. The first professors — S. G. E. Lythe (Economic History),
K. J. W. (later Sir Kenneth) Alexander (Economics) and A. M. Potter
(Politics) — were actually in post in January 1963, some eighteen months
before the Charter was received. It is a great tribute to the sheer energy and
resourcefulness of these men (and the staff they gathered round them) that the
College was able to accept its first student intake for the B.A. degree in
October of the same year. The amalgamation, in May 1964, of the Royal
College with the Scottish College of Commerce provided, as has already been
noted, a dramatic irruption of enlarged student numbers and enhanced
academic goals.

The wisdom of the proto-Board of Study in choosing not to ape the
traditional M.A.-type structure of the four older Scottish universities but to
opt instead for a flexible, unit-based structure requiring students to pursue a
greater number of subjects over a shorter period with the option of Honours
specialisation in one or two has borne fruit in ways that even the Board did not
foresee. To begin with, at a time when wasteful duplication is ever in the
forefront of Government and UGC thinking, it is comforting to be assured
that for the most part the two universities in Glasgow complement one
another most effectively in Arts and Social Studies, the one often helping to
supply the other's needs across a remarkable variety of disciplines. Then
again, it is fashionable today to criticise the study of a discipline *per se* where
perhaps it is not immediately apparent that the discipline is relevant or useful
to society at large. The Relevantines of the early 1960's, however, stressed —
as one of the early prospectuses put it — that the subjects taught were 'chosen
with regard to the needs of modern society'. One cannot really quarrel with the
judgement of *A Decade of Progress* (1974): 'By any statistical yardstick —
demand for places, employment of graduates, pass rates — or by the less
quantifiable yardstick of human relations — the rise of the non-science sector
... has been a success story.'

When the University abandoned Schools of Study in favour of four Faculties in 1982, the School of Arts and Social Studies became the Faculty of Arts and Social Studies. There are nine Departments in the Faculty:

History

English Studies (incorporating Philosophy, Drama and the John Logie Baird Centre for Research in Television and Film)

Geography

Librarianship

Modern Languages (comprising sections in French, German, Italian, Russian, Spanish and the Language Centre)

Politics

Centre for the Study of Public Policy

Psychology

Sociology

Sub-Board for the B.Ed. degree (in association with Craigie College of Education)

Useful Learning: (d) Strathclyde Business School

Throughout the 1950's and 1960's, 'Chesters' (Chesters Residential Management Centre, Bearsden) became a household word for residential management courses in Scotland, a unique provision at the time. Indeed, Chesters produced many managers and entrepreneurs whose subsequent careers owe something at least to the soundness and originality of instruction they received from such distinguished practitioners as Christopher Macrae (later Principal of Ashridge College), Paul Hanika, Allan Gay and Professor Tom Paterson.

In 1970 when the Scottish Business School was set up it was undoubtedly the impeccable Chesters pedigree that set the University of Strathclyde apart from the rest, leaving the UGC and CIME (the Council of Industry for Management Education) in no doubt that Strathclyde should be the principal benefactor of new funding, allowing a vigorous expansion in Scotland of residential, post-experience work, albeit within the curiously ill-defined tripartite structure conceived for that organisation.

Of course, the fact that Strathclyde could (and does) play what is by common consent the leading role in the Scottish Business School was simply a reflection of its rapid growth in undergraduate and postgraduate work in a whole range of subjects germane to business administration. Some of these developments emerged from the Royal College's 'Faculty of Industrial and Social Studies', many out of the amalgamation with the Scottish College of Commerce and others could trace their origin to Chesters and Industrial Administration as taught to undergraduate engineers and applied scientists.

The Business School is a rare phenomenon in the university world these days. Large and still growing, it has its eyes set firmly on the future. In so many different ways — from the exciting new possibilities of distance learning to the teaching company and the success attending the 'TBS' degree (B.Sc. in Technology and Business Studies) — the Business School, given an unequivocal vote of confidence by the UGC, is the new jewel in the crown of the University in the view of many. Certainly it is important to Scotland that it should succeed. There is every reason to believe that it will do so.

The Strathclyde Business School, as reconstituted in 1982, comprises the former School of Business and Administration and the Advanced Inter-disciplinary and Post-Experience Programmes (the latter activity alone having been termed the Strathclyde Business School until 1982). The School also represents the University of Strathclyde Division of the Scottish Business School. There are ten Departments and several research units in the School:

Accountancy and Finance
Administration (including the Centre for Police Studies)
Economics (incorporating the Fraser of Allander Institute for Research on the Scottish Economy)
Industrial Relations
Law School
Marketing
Office Organisation
Operational Research
Scottish Hotel School
Urban and Regional Planning
Employment Relations Scottish Resource Centre
Pay and Rewards Research Centre
Strathclyde International Business Unit
Public Sector Management Unit
Steering Board for Opportunities for Women
David Livingstone Institute for Overseas Development Studies
Sub-Board for the Degree of B.Sc. (Technology and Business Studies)

An important organisational feature of the Business School is that, uniquely in the University, it has a Council consisting of academics and a number of distinguished businessmen from the public and private sectors who have the right to offer comment to Senate and Court on any matter affecting the School's policy in teaching, research or resources (human or physical). The first three chairmen of the Council (formerly the Steering Board) were Lord McFadzean, Sir Campbell Fraser and the late Sir William Duncan. The University has been handsomely served by such men.

'Liberality of Sentiment'

It is a commonplace that in the same way as universities exist to serve the needs of society, so, too, they have a duty to be critics of society and of themselves. Newman thought that they made for enlargement of the intellect in the medium of a community in a manner that a foundry or a mint or a treadmill did not (Lyons, 1983). At the present time, not since Newman's day has there been such a restless questioning of what universities ought really to be doing and of their quantifiable service to the community. Do universities need to do everything in the old spirit of 'Universitas'? What is the proper relationship between teaching and research? Should not — indeed *can* — admission become more open? Is *the degree* too much of a sacred cow?

When the British Association last came to Glasgow, astonishing though it may seem, little thought was given to the employability of graduates in considering the introduction of a non-vocational degree course. Today that is the first consideration. Again, in 1958 how many universities gave a fig for their public image? How many bothered to publish a prospectus, or saw any need to? How many Courts made provision for Senate, let alone non-professorial staff, or, horror of horrors, student representation? In the whole of Scotland in 1958 there were relatively few professors and among them no women and no visiting professors. Most remarkable of all, if a schoolboy in Glasgow were denied admission to his local university it was by no means extraordinary to find that the idea of applying elsewhere never entered his head. These were the days of the Entrance Board and the Certificate of Attestation of Fitness, of unrestrained autonomy, the Tech, conversaziones and undivided second-class honours.

If a capacity for fresh ideas and open-mindedness be the criteria, it is certainly not far-fetched to claim a perceived continuity between Anderson's 'liberality of sentiment' and the university that was ultimately created from the Will of 1796. One can easily, however, go too far. There was nothing particularly remarkable in the structure of the B.Sc. courses that were formed out of the old Associateships (ARCST). What was distinctive and almost revolutionary was the University's transforming, and wholly benevolent *attitude* and *style*. In, for example, such important matters as entrance qualifications, mature and National Certificate students have cause to be grateful to Strathclyde's pioneering policies. In a wider context, there is amongst the majority of the Scottish universities today a more consciously relaxed attitude to admission that derives in large measure from Strathclyde's early determination to dispense with the requirement that candidates must have secured a pass in a language other than English. Strange as it may seem, the abolition of the language barrier so-called was a battle not easily won. Access and opportunity were not then, of course, the emotive terms that they have become in the 1980's.

With the benefit of hindsight, however, perhaps the most profound demonstration of 'liberality of sentiment' was to be found in a number of imaginative ideas that are attributable to the first Principal, Sir Samuel Curran. Curran had great vision but his other great quality was his ingenuity. His unorthodoxy (which had nothing to do with eccentricity) was of incalculable value at a time when the University, expanding fast and capitalising on the Royal College's enviable industrial links, sought to forge even stronger bonds with the 'real world' of business, manufacturing industry and technological development. Curran, impatient of the slow pace of change in much of academic life, discerned that what was wrong with too many of the 'old' universities was that they had distanced themselves from, and had become incomprehensible to, the office and the factory.

It was Sam Curran who conceived the highly successful scheme of visiting professorships which has flourished to such an extent that today Strathclyde has over fifty such posts spread over the four Faculties. He knew very well from his own experience at Aldermaston both the advantages of sensible relationships with those in whose hands power lay, and, by the same token, the ultimate danger facing all academics — of becoming backroom boys whom nobody takes very seriously.

Curran's presence and influence were immense and pervaded the whole university scene in Scotland in his day. At heart a shy man, he ruled Strathclyde with formidable authority. A great admirer of John Anderson, he would have identified himself with most of Anderson's ideals and with the concept of 'useful learning' above all. He championed the cause of subjects such as Food Science and Hotel Management which then tended to be looked down on by other institutions, pointing out that it was absurd for universities *not* to become involved in human activities that were of such common concern throughout the world. As ever, it was impossible to deny the simple logic of his argument.

'To the Public, for the good of Mankind'

From Disraeli to Edward Parkes there have been two fundamental questions, overshadowing all others, that have perplexed those pondering the role of the modern university: first, the relationship of the universities to government and, second, their relationship to the community. With both considerations, and within a remarkably short period, there has been a profound shift of attitude. We are more concerned here with the second of these conjunctions — the universities' relationship to the community.

Particularly in the United States many are now calling into question the received wisdom of a hundred years that either put universities on a pedestal and assigned to them near-exclusive academic goals or else characterised them in the words of Clark Kerr (an honorary graduate of Strathclyde) as assemblages of faculty entrepreneurs held together by a common grievance over parking. Less cynically, as Ernest Boyer has put it: 'The hope remains that institutions of higher learning will retain *a social mission* that goes beyond their own self interest and the immediate goals of students' (*Times Higher Education Supplement*, 1983). In other words, the university that fails to heed the importance of constructing (i.e. *re*constructing) its educational provision so as to concentrate its energy on how students may fit themselves most appropriately to the needs and aspirations of the community is, at best, not to be taken seriously and, at worst, in danger — deservedly so — of extinction.

If involvement be a valid touchstone, some impressive examples of the University's conscious involvement in the community are not hard to come by. To begin with, Strathclyde is unambiguously part of city life in Glasgow. This is much more than the frequently pretentious contrivance of town and gown lectures (although, as it happens, these *are* given). In the late 1950's the Royal College Governors had seriously considered the proposition that the campus (if at that time it could be so dignified) remove itself, lock, stock and barrel to a green-fields site at East Kilbride. The idea was resoundingly dismissed. No one today regrets that decision. In possibly the densest of all city-centre campuses in the U.K., the University has not found it easy to reconcile the notion of an expanding institution (for there is, of course, substantially more to expansion than student numbers) with a packed, some would say cluttered, site. Even though great problems remain unresolved, wonders have been wrought through a combination of skilful physical development planning, purposeful intrigue and sheer expedient. Here the secret of success has been recognition of the need to cultivate a partnership with local authority, District and Region, and other relevant agencies, especially the SDA.

Furthermore, it would be wrong to ignore how fortunate the University has consistently been in the advice and expertise freely rendered by a few individuals of great distinction who have served on the Court since its inception in 1964. Men like W. F. Robertson, J. Percival Agnew, Hugh Stenhouse, Alexander Turnbull, John Holm, Isidore Walton, Sir Patrick Thomas, Sir John Atwell, F. O. Thornton and Gavin Boyd have been glad to identify themselves with what Strathclyde stands for, and the University, in her financial, estates and staffing policies and actions, is immeasurably in their debt for their outstanding contribution.

Finally, if, as is probably (sadly) incontrovertible, Britain still lags behind North America in terms of the roles that universities seek for themselves in their relationships with industry (there are not yet any 'corporate campuses' in Britain), Strathclyde is ahead of most in giving full rein to its bid not just to achieve strong links with industry but, more seminally, to try to adjust itself — and to go on adjusting itself — to meet the changing nature of the actual needs of industry as perceived by industry itself. That is an important distinction. Many universities claim sturdy industrial ties. But few can proclaim with conviction, as did a recent Strathclyde poster: 'We're in business too!'. The University has come far since the Ministry of Technology of Harold Wilson's day. The Centre for Industrial Innovation has given way to Strathclyde Limited, to the establishment of a realistic infrastructure for research and development with the emphasis unequivocally on *development* as described elsewhere in this volume. Paradoxically, it seems that only by a single-minded commitment to serving industry in this uninhibited way can an institution of higher education face up to the unyielding pressures of the so-called post-industrial society.

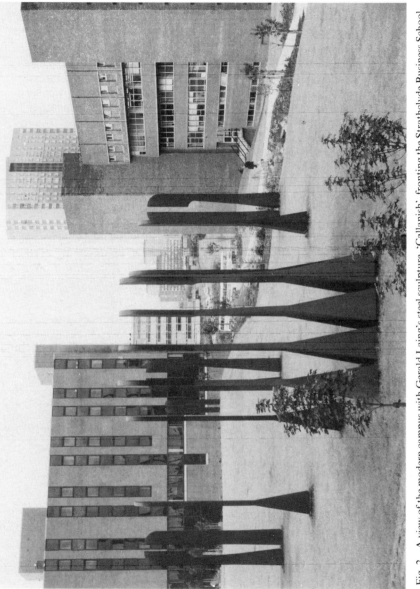

Fig. 2   A view of the modern campus with Gerald Laing's steel sculpture, 'Callanish', fronting the Strathclyde Business School.

Towards 2000

Little over a year ago as these words appear on the printed page, *The Times* (12th March 1984) attempted an assessment of the contribution of universities to society:

'They cultivate a critical intelligence in which the world may see itself reflected to its benefit. They are agents of cultural transmission and enlightenment. They innovate. They civilise. They serve the values implicit in the obsolete expression "seats of learning". These are not quantifiable attributes. They cannot be calculated. But they can be recognised and regarded or disregarded. They constitute together a high view of the place of universities in society. If they are to carry public conviction, if they are to attract the resources they need, the universities themselves must be seen to believe in them and to be aiming for them.'

Precisely. The university world in Britain is in turmoil — in crisis many would say. It would be facile, absurd even to attempt pat solutions or glib prophecies. Nevertheless, it is safe to assume that an institution will continue to earn respect that, by tradition as much as by internally imposed self-discipline, takes in its stride service to the community in all its varying aspects, in prosperous times as well as in adversity. Nothing less will do. Relevance, usefulness, diversification, ingenuity, a spirit of open-mindedness have been instilled into the University of Strathclyde ever since John Anderson's day. That is perhaps the abiding continuity.

REFERENCES

Coutts, James (1909), *History of the University of Glasgow, 1451 to 1909*. Glasgow.
Lyons, F. S. L. (1983), The Idea of a University: Newman to Robbins. In Phillippson, N. (Ed.), *Universities, Society, and the Future*. Edinburgh.
Maxwell, James (1796), *A Second Caution Against Infidelity; soi disant* 'Poet in Paisley', Paisley.
The Times, 12th March 1984.
Times Higher Education Supplement, 25th November 1983.
Todd, Lord (1983), *A Time to Remember*. Cambridge University Press, Cambridge.
University of Strathclyde (1974), *A Decade of Progress*.
University of Strathclyde: Campus Development 1964 to 1984 (1984).
Williams, Raymond (1976), *Keywords*. Collins, London.
Working Together (1983), published by Glasgow University and Strathclyde University.

CHAPTER ELEVEN

DEVELOPMENTS IN ENGINEERING AND SCIENCE

D. H. Brown

It is only when one attempts to review the current research work of a university that one realises the multitude of interests involved. Thus, any report of this type must involve an element of selection limited by space and the author's ignorance. If I have borrowed others' words and not acknowledged them, then as Donatus said before, 'Pereant, inquit, qui ante nos nostra dixerunt . . .'

Introduction

Man's interest and involvement in engineering, science and mathematics has extended virtually from the beginning of recorded time. The Ebers papyrus, found at Thebes and thought to have been written about 1500 BC, contains descriptions of natural products and medicines. Subsequent papyri and wall paintings of the ancient Egyptians showed that they had a depth of appreciation of civil engineering, medicine, physics, mathematics and chemistry. Vitruvius, a Roman architect of the first century BC, wrote descriptively about architecture and civil engineering and the materials best suited for particular tasks. Diosiorides, a Greek physician of the first century AD, compiled a *Materia Medica* in which he described the natural and artificial substances then in use as medicines. Running parallel with the technologists but at a safe distance were the theoreticians. For them, the continuing problem was what was the nature of matter? Most agreed that there must be some primordial, indestructible basic substance. Thales considered it to be water, Anaximander a hypothetical principle called 'apeiron', Anaximenes thought it was air and Heraclitus, fire. Empedocles compromised with the four elements, earth, air, water and fire.

Many of these early philosophers and technologists were great teachers and perhaps also a few had profitable side-lines as well. Just as they were products and advanced thinkers of their time, so too are the staff of an active university like Strathclyde. Then, as now, research should attempt to satisfy the interests and needs of the community as well as providing the fundamental intellectual stimulus required by teachers to motivate themselves and their students. The choice of original work can be a personal thing and often becomes too specialised to be appreciated by others. However, as Virgil said, 'Felix qui potuit rerum cognoscere causas'. More succinctly, Sherlock Holmes described such work as a 'three-pipe' problem.

Such work is often used by critics of universities, unfairly in most cases, to further the currently acceptable 'ivory tower' image. However, in a predominantly science- and engineering-based university such as Strathclyde, a high percentage of its research output is relevant to the immediate demands of the community, in particular to Shelter, Energy, Technical Development and Health and Food. The relative interest in these can alter over the years, with currently the greatest emphasis on health and technical development. In these areas, industrial and governmental purse strings seem a little slacker and this is reflected in research involvement in the University. When Isaak Walton said that 'health is a blessing that money cannot buy', he had not heard of Research Councils!

Strathclyde University attracts externally sponsored research grants and contracts amounting to about one-eighth of its total annual income. In 1982–83, for example, some 250 grants and contracts were awarded with a total value of £10·4 million and an annual value of over £4 million.

The sources of funding vary from year to year according to the current economic climate and Government policy and, from the accompanying chart of the 1983 grant/contract sources, it will be seen that the Research Councils and Government Departments account for almost two-thirds of the total funding, with industry lagging in third place.

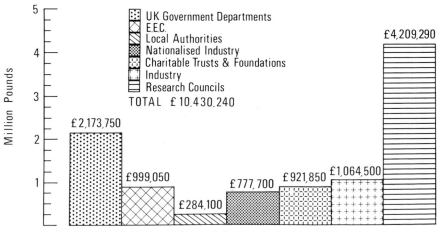

Fig. 1   Sources of research funding 1st January 1983.

As an encouragement to staff to initiate new projects, the University has created its own Research and Development Fund, providing modest pump-priming finance to encourage researchers to take ideas beyond the initial stages to the point where external support can be sought. The University has been keenly aware for many years of the importance of bridging the gap between academic research and development and the introduction by industry of new products based on this research. It has been our experience that the initiative for this transfer of technology has had to rest mainly with the University as an exercise in 'selling' its research output.

Strathclyde has taken the initiative by approaching the problem in a variety of ways, including:

(i) the creation, in 1968, of its Centre for Industrial Innovation to act as an interface between academic researchers and industry. The University, with the Scottish Development Agency, has recently re-examined the role of the Centre and we have formed an Industrial Liaison Company to continue and expand activities in this field;

(ii) a positive policy of patenting, licensing and actively marketing inventions and innovations emanating from the University; and

(iii) encouraging and pursuing collaborative research and development projects with industry and providing a framework for staff to undertake industrial consultancies.

As nearly one-half of the University's sponsored research work is funded by the U.K. Government through its Research Councils and as, until recently, a condition of this funding required commercially exploitable results to be offered to the National Research Development Corporation (now part of the British Technology Group), it is hardly surprising that the University has established a firm relationship with the BTG.

With other developments, the University practice is to seek patent protection wherever possible as a prerequisite to negotiation with industry. This has been found necessary not only to protect the University's interest but also because it has been evident that industry is generally prepared to treat proposals for exploitation seriously only if the University can demonstrate a level of commercial realism in its approach.

The University would normally seek to have its inventions exploited by means of a licence agreement or by assignment of patents, sometimes accompanied by a collaborative development agreement. There have, however, been cases where the University itself is prepared to participate actively in exploitation, either by taking equity in a company to be run jointly with an industrial partner or to go into partnership with an enterprising academic to establish a new business. Such cases have, in the past, been the exception rather than the rule but the facilities now being offered by the recently established West of Scotland Science Park may well encourage more academic entrepreneurs to go down this road and make the move from academe to industry.

The road is not easy and can be a very long one. What is not always appreciated is the lengthy timescale which can be involved between original innovation and the realisation of a marketable product. This is particularly true in the pharmaceutical field, where drugs must go through exhaustive tests before a product licence is issued. A typical example is the development of the new muscle-relaxing drug, Atracurium, where the development stage spanned a period of almost ten years. Even in the case of non-pharmaceutical products, however, the gap can be considerable. The University's own soy-sauce project, now Bean Products Limited, took between six and seven years to come to fruition from the time of the original development to the launching of the company.

There are many obstacles to be overcome and the University does not claim a unique record in successful technology transfer. Nevertheless, it *has* had its successes and has learned much from its less successful ventures. By encouraging its staff to participate in these ventures, the University is richer by the experience. Although many in industry perhaps would not agree with Francis Bacon in saying 'Riches are a good handmaid but the worst mistress', it is hoped that industry, too, could be enriched by seeking benefit from the considerable body of expertise residing in the University.

Fig. 2   West of Scotland Science Park.

Shelter

'Houses are built to live in and not to look on.'
Francis Bacon (1561–1626)

Perhaps more than most departments, those of Architecture and Building Science, and Civil Engineering must be concerned closely with the needs of the local community. This is reflected in their research, some of which is described below.

ASSIST

The stranger to Glasgow is always struck by the quality of the city's architecture. It may be that it is the rich inheritance of high Victorian or Edwardian city-centre building — banks, offices, warehouses — which captures his attention, or the 'turn-of-the-century' *Art Nouveau* of Mackintosh and the so-called Glasgow Style. Or perhaps it is simply the still ubiquitous presence of the tenement, which so dominated the city's way of life, both up-market and down, that makes the most emphatic and memorable impression.

In 1972 ASSIST was established in the Department of Architecture and Building Science as an action/research unit studying techniques for the rehabilitation of Glasgow's tenements and translating theory into action by organising the necessary architectural and building work, actively involving residents in the improvement process. ASSIST's pioneering work in Govan from 1972–74 led to the adoption of community-based Housing Associations as the prime agent of the city's rehabilitation programme, backed by both the District Council and the Housing Corporation. ASSIST also carried out many environmental improvement schemes for tenement backcourts, again working in close collaboration with residents. Latterly ASSIST has turned its attention to devising schemes for the re-use of redundant buildings, emphasising the possibilities of creating low-cost industrial and commercial work space; the principal scheme of this type has been the restoration of the old Glasgow Fish Market (which has a fine galleried interior with a cast-iron structure) and its proposed conversion into the 'Briggait', a complex of retail shops, markets, offices and light workshops. In November 1983 ASSIST became an independent architectural practice but the research aspects of its work will be continued by the newly established Housing and Rehabilitation Research Unit in the Department.

Dampness in Scottish Housing

Perhaps the biggest current problem in housing in Scotland is that of dampness. There are two main reasons for this — the Scottish weather and increased energy costs. The former is common to all, but the latter particularly affects people with low incomes and hence little to spend on fuel. Once the temperature of a room with minimal or no heating falls below the 'dew point', condensation occurs, wallpaper and paint deteriorate, curtains and furnishings rot, black mould appears and living conditions become unacceptable.

The physical, economic and social factors which combine to produce cold and damp homes, however, are highly complex as every local authority has found out to its cost. If the heating systems, especially the electric ones, are or are perceived to be too expensive to run, occupants will often change to other forms of heating, such as paraffin and low-pressure gas. These produce a good deal of water during combustion and add to the condensation problems. If the condensation is fought by increasing ventilation through windows and fans, then the already cold house will be even colder. If, on the other hand, openings are sealed — and many of the modern houses no longer have the natural ventilation which used to be present when there were open flues — the house may remain warmer but the build-up of moisture is much more rapid. Many of the activities in the household generate high levels of moisture, especially cooking, washing and clothes-drying; a number of these activities can occur anywhere in the house, and the moisture they generate can be distributed widely. A number of related studies have been carried out in the Department, and one study on a difficult housing estate in Glasgow has surveyed several hundred houses in general terms and monitored in detail, over two heating seasons, nine houses. In these, three spaces have continuous temperature and humidity records; there are daily diaries of the occupants; fuel consumption and income have been monitored and an outside climatic station recorded the major meteorological variables. This project is currently drawing to a close and analysis of the data is being completed, to produce hopefully some answers to this depressing social problem.

Design of Brick Buildings on Poor Ground

Developers are often forced to build houses on ground that is only marginally suitable for construction. For example, the underlying soil may consist of very soft clay deposits or fill material which is notoriously variable in stiffness. Such problems can be solved by the use of piled foundations but this is often too expansive in the circumstances. The most common solution is to provide a raft foundation and if this is made stiff enough (e.g. by using a cellular raft of perhaps one metre depth) satisfactory performance is usually achieved. However, the stiff raft may also be too expensive and a flexible solid raft is more common. Such foundations alleviate the problems but often give rather unsatisfactory results. More economical means of providing strength and stiffness to resist settlement are needed.

A brick structure (for example a two- or three-storey housing block) is inherently stiff but does not normally have sufficient strength to cope with settlement. It is not uncommon to provide bed-joint reinforcement in the brickwork to enhance its strength but very little is known about the behaviour of such a material.

Designers would like to be able to take account of the structure in their calculations when considering settlement but the problems of doing this are significant. It is well recognised that the supporting soil is difficult to model for long-term deformation predictions and in fact the structure poses no lesser problem in this respect. Thus to make a combined model of the structure and the soil is no easy task.

Professor MacLeod of the Department of Civil Engineering is presently supervising research work in this area funded by the Science and Engineering Research Council. The aim of the project is to provide structure designers with guidelines as to the best course of action to adopt when settlement may be a problem with brick buildings. The type of recommendation which might be made is to give a series of options as to the appropriate measures in given circumstances. For example, if bed-joint reinforcement is to be specified where will it be most effective and how much should be used? How much can the bed-joint reinforcement reduce the requirement for foundation stiffness? Such questions are often asked but may seldom be satisfactorily answered due to lack of knowledge of the true behaviour of the reinforced brickwork and of the interaction between the structure and the soil.

The study includes a testing programme on reinforced brickwork, numerical modelling of the structure and the soil and cost comparisons of different options.

Energy

'The energies of our system will decay.'
A. J. Balfour (1848–1930)

The recent energy crises of 1973 and 1978 emphasised the fact that modern economies and intensive agriculture are driven by fossil and fissile energy. Thus, the problems associated with energy-saving and of finding new fuel deposits are of considerable importance and are included in the research programmes of several departments. Two examples are given below.

Saving on Fuel Consumption

Recent statistics show that oil provides about 43 per cent of the nation's energy requirements, and road transport is responsible for approximately one-quarter of the total oil consumption. The escalating cost of fuel, coupled with the limited global reserves, underlines the importance of ensuring the efficient operation of road vehicles.

In national terms, a 1 per cent improvement in drive-line efficiency, i.e. the efficiency of converting energy in the oil to useful effort at the driving wheels, would save 230,000 tonnes of oil per annum. At a personal level, any reduction in the cost of owning a car would make a welcome change to the normal facts of life. Thus, much effort is being devoted in industry and the universities to exploring methods for reducing the fuel consumption of motor vehicles.

There are many methods for achieving fuel savings. For example, a reduction of vehicle weight and drag pays appreciable dividends and this explains vehicle manufacturers' preoccupation with mystical drag coefficient. There are also less publicised efforts being made to reduce vehicle weight by the use of fibre composites, etc. However, the research being conducted in the Department of Dynamics and Control is focused upon achieving reduced consumption by increasing drive-line efficiency.

It is well known that fuel consumption can be decreased if the standard manual or automatic stepped-ratio gearbox is replaced by a continuously variable transmission (CVT), which is like having a gearbox that can achieve all of the ratios required to match the engine speed to that of the driving wheels. With such a device, the object is to operate the engine at a point of minimum specific fuel consumption consistent with the power demanded by the driver. If this can be achieved for a range of driving conditions, then it is possible to obtain fuel savings of 20–30 per cent and perhaps more, compared with the fuel consumption with a stepped-ratio gearbox.

Various designs of CVT have been proposed. Much developmental effort has been devoted to belt and chain drives. Rubber-belt transmissions have been used in DAF and Volvo cars and Fiat recently announced their intention to introduce a chain-type CVT in production vehicles. An alternative design is based upon the use of rolling traction elements as developed by Perbury Engineering from the early Hayes Transmission. It is this latter type of transmission which is being studied by the Department of Dynamics and Control under Professor C. R. Burrows. This programme is being undertaken in collaboration with Perbury Engineering Ltd. whose managing director, Forbes Perry, is a visiting professor. The work is being funded by the British Technology Group and is concerned with the development of new control strategies for maximising overall efficiency consistent with acceptable vehicle-handling characteristics.

A longer-term programme involves the study of hybrid vehicles, that is, configurations in which propulsion power during specified operation of the vehicle is available from two or more different types of energy stores, sources or converters. Theoretical and experimental studies have been undertaken for flywheel-electric hybrid configurations with the objective of overcoming the well-known disadvantages of battery-electric vehicles.

Other hybrid configurations have been investigated, e.g. internal combustion engine/flywheel configurations have been analysed in detail. The main thrust of this work has been to minimise the capacity of the energy-storage unit consistent with the attainment of certain design goals. This, in turn, has led to a fundamental study of the design constraints imposed on CVTs when used with a flywheel energy-storage unit.

Thus, the work on vehicle-transmission control in the Department of Dynamics and Control ranges over the whole spectrum of problems associated with emerging practice and more speculative long-term developments. The unifying theme in this activity is provided by control theory. Also, there is the desire to help maintain the availability of personal transport without the profligate use of resources which was tolerated without question until the crisis of the 1970's focused attention on our economic and social need to conserve oil.

Resources and Rifting: Understanding Continental Drift Helps the Search for
    Metals and Fuels

That North America, with Greenland, split apart from Britain and the rest of Eurasia in the geological past, so producing the North Atlantic, is now beyond dispute. The questions are, when and how? If 100 million years ago the Atlantic opened in a single stage, the chances of finding major oilfields to the west of Scotland similar to those in the North Sea are minimal. This is because the rocks that produce and harbour the oil in the North Sea are about 175 million years old and they would, of course, be absent to the west. Research in the Department of Applied Geology points to an early stage of rifting and Atlantic Ocean formation about 300 million years ago.

A theory emanating from the Department and first propounded in 1972 predicts a thick development of submarine oil source and reservoir rocks on and beyond the continental rise west of Scotland. Already a large oilfield, the Clare, has been discovered by Elf and BP west of Shetland but the oil is viscous and difficult to extract from the rocks. As efficient extraction is also a problem in marginal oilfields in the North Sea, the Department has just initiated a project financed by and in conjunction with Britoil which seeks to understand how rock porosity affects extraction.

Major ore deposits are also related to the rifting and drifting of continents. The stresses that eventually caused the Atlantic to open started to operate 350 million years ago. These stresses caused some cracking in the single super-continent which allowed saline sea water to circulate convectively in the hot crust of the Earth. The updraughts of these thermally driven convection cells were guided by major fractures formed or reactivated by the extensional stresses that eventually pulled the super-continent apart to allow the formation of the early Atlantic Ocean. Metalliferous orebodies were precipitated from these solutions in Ireland on what was to become an Atlantic Margin.

A 'prediction' made on the basis of the hypothesis adumbrated above successfully anticipated the presence of a major orebody at a fracture intersection near the town of Navan, 50 km from Dublin. Navan currently contributes 40 per cent of the EEC's zinc requirement. From the dimensions of these convection cells, it is further predicted that major orebodies will be at least 20 km apart; that is to say, it is not worth exploring the intermediate ground. A huge deposit of baryte (a mineral used in drilling for oil) with some zinc, lead and silver, has been discovered near Aberfeldy in Scotland and is related to an earlier phase of rifting.

The Department has developed chemical methods for use in the search for additional deposits, techniques that are now employed by many exploration companies on a worldwide basis. These techniques rely on the fact that after base metals have been precipitated on the sea floor around hot springs, transition metals, such as manganese, precipitate more slowly and therefore travel farther from the hot-spring site. Nevertheless, they pollute the sea and sea bottom for a radius of about 10 km. Subsequent analysis of sediments, now occurring as rock, allows us to draw concentration contours for manganese and iron, the bull's eye of which may contain an orebody. Such submarine hot springs are now found in the Red Sea and the East Pacific. Associated recent mineral deposits are soon to be mined in the Red Sea by Preussag. In the East Pacific, hot (350°C) water is building and issuing from metal sulphide chimneys. A team from the Department was the first to discover such chimneys as fossils in the 350-million-year-old Silvermines orebody in Ireland.

Continued stretching of the super-continent led to the formation of deep hollows throughout the aptly named Carboniferous period (from 350 to 290 million years ago) and coal accumulated in their basins along the margins of what was to become the Atlantic Ocean.

North Sea oil has played a central role in the U.K. economy over recent years but it is now at peak production. Research in the Department of Applied Geology is concerned with future prospects, not only to the West of Scotland but also all along the North Atlantic Margin at least up to the Barents Sea north of Norway. Scotland, with its new-found experience of the oil industry and with the added advantage of being free of packed ice the whole year round, will remain a base for the oil industry for the foreseeable future.

Technical Development

> 'They are each of them, contributions to human development.'
> Matthew Arnold (1822–88)

The impact of science and engineering is often related to the progress, both theoretical and practical, of technical developments in areas of importance to the community. From the many examples available, the following six have been chosen to show the diversity of research taking place.

Lasers

The advantages claimed for laser rather than traditional light sources include their directional and narrow-beam properties, their single colour or frequency of operation and their high energies and powers. In reality, it is very difficult to get all these properties in one laser type, and in the Laser Kinetics Group of the Physics Department there is a programme to improve the output frequency characteristics of one of the most powerful and successful laser types: the laser based on the gas carbon dioxide in the infrared part of the spectrum. In practice, most of the problems encountered are similar in other electrical discharge excited-laser media and already some of the solutions obtained with the carbon dioxide system are being applied to other laser types.

The output of a laser is generated by the stimulated downward passage of a molecule from a high-energy level to a lower one, releasing the surplus energy at the specific energy difference between the two levels and, since (as is well known) it is rather difficult to alter the energy of a level, it is usually argued that the output of a laser is naturally at a single energy or frequency. Unfortunately this is only crudely true, because each energy level is not absolutely sharp but covers a small range of energies, so the frequency of the emission resulting from transitions between two levels is uncertain (but not usually indeterminate) by a small amount. The exact frequency of output at any moment within this range of uncertainty (or linewidth) is not controlled by the carbon dioxide gas itself but by the laser feed-back cavity surrounding the gas and providing the stimulating field. Such a cavity usually consists of two mirrors, one at each end of the excited gas volume. These mirrors must be aligned accurately parallel to each other to provide the maximum stimulating field and their exact separation must be controlled to an accuracy of ten milli-micro-metres, or less than one-thousandth part of the traditional engineer's 'thou' or 'mil'. Since the mirrors may have to be one or two metres apart to allow room for enough excited laser gas between them, a two-stage solution is required. First, the mirror mount and separation system is made very rigid and from materials with very low coefficients of thermal expansion, such as invar. Normal constructional materials such as steel, brass or aluminium are totally unsuitable because even small temperature fluctuations in the laboratory or factory will cause huge frequency changes. Second, the exact fine-tuning separation is obtained by mounting one of the mirrors on a piezo-electric tube and varying the exact position of the mirror by varying the dc electric voltage applied between the inner and outer walls of the tube. This fine adjustment is electronically controlled and fully automatic. Any error in the mirror separation is detected as a change in the loading of the electrical excitation discharge on its power supply (the Opto-Galvanic Effect) and the error is amplified and used as a correction signal to slightly change the voltage applied to the piezo-electric and, hence, the exact mirror separation.

Professor A. L. S. Smith and his group have been able to frequency-stabilise devices with up to thirty watts laser-beam power for many hours at a time to a precision of one part in 100 million (equivalent to knowing the distance between Glasgow and London to an accuracy of a few millimetres!) Stabilisation systems based on this work are now commercially available from a Scottish firm and applications include high-resolution spectroscopy, optical pumping and atmospheric pollution monitoring.

Liquid Crystals

Although now a familiar term due to digital watches and calculator displays, until a short time ago liquid crystals were known only to a relatively small number of scientists, and even fewer knew anything of their strange properties. Since their discovery towards the close of the last century by an Austrian botanist, Reinitzer, they had aroused interest as a fourth state of matter, but few actively pursued the topic as a field of research. Initially there was controversy as to whether or not these materials were solid, liquid or some intermediate state, but gradually it was established that they exhibited properties of both the solid and liquid states. For example, optically they behave as a uniaxial crystal, but equally flow readily when subjected to shear. As a result the term 'liquid crystal' was coined and it has stuck despite its inherent contradictory nature. Due to the efforts of several dedicated scientists many fascinating properties of these strange anisotropic liquids were slowly unravelled, but they largely remained something of a scientific curiosity until the late 1960's. Then it became apparent to research groups in one or two laboratories that these peculiar liquids had potential for applications in display devices, and almost overnight it seemed the esoteric academic research topic became one of relevance and importance to modern technology. Their capacity to provide suitable displays in wrist watches and pocket calculators with very low power consumption has now been well established, and shortly it seems likely that they will feature prominently in automobile instrumentation and on a larger scale in information displays at airports and the like. Indeed liquid crystal research is a very good example of the merit of pursuing knowledge for its own sake in that ultimately it proves of value to the community at large.

Uniquely among Mathematics Departments in the U.K. there is a small but active group of mathematicians at Strathclyde University engaged in research into theoretical aspects of liquid crystals under the leadership of Professor Frank Leslie. Essentially this group employs the concepts of Newtonian mechanics, linear and angular momentum and energy to model through continuum mechanics. Of particular interest in these anisotropic liquids is the alignment of the anisotropic axis which reflects the mean orientation of the long, relatively rigid, 'rod-like' structure of the molecular groups of which such materials are composed. Using generalised continuum mechanics one can obtain phenomenological equations to describe flow and alignment, and thereby successfully predict and analyse the response of these liquids to electric fields, flow and thermal gradients. For example, in the electro-optic display devices one switches the alignment of the anisotropic axis or average orientation of the molecules by using electric fields, and it is now clear that this switching of the alignment induces flow, and moreover, that this induced flow affects the alignment. Such effects can be demonstrated experimentally and successfully modelled by the partial differential equations of the continuum theory. Thus switching in devices is not in general a simple process. More recent theoretical work has predicted associated instabilities that may occur and some of these have been confirmed experimentally. This latter work has been carried out in conjunction with the Physics Division at the Royal Radar and Signals Establishment at Malvern in England.

Flow and transient effects in liquid crystals are of course dominated by the viscous properties of these materials, and the continuum equations that model the behaviour of these anisotropic liquids contain five independent viscosity coefficients. A precise knowledge of these material parameters is important in order to predict accurately the stability or otherwise of the switching processes in devices. As a consequence a joint research programme was started a few years back at Strathclyde University between the Departments of Mathematics and Pure and Applied Chemistry aimed at devising means to measure accurately and efficiently the viscosity coefficients of liquid crystals. This interdisciplinary research programme is jointly supervised by Professor Leslie and Professor Richard Pethrick and forms an important element of a larger interdisciplinary activity in material science currently getting under way in the University.

The Motion-Controlled Offshore Workbase

Safety at sea, with particular reference to the offshore industry, lies behind an exciting piece of work currently in progress in the University.

It is acknowledged by all concerned that in hostile seaways it is vital to have a working area with minimum vertical motion for such activities as drilling and handling of subsea equipment. Over the years a number of methods of achieving this have been tried, with varying success. One major advance was to alter the geometry of the traditional ship form to that of the semi-submersible, which has a working deck supported by a series of vertical columns connected to large buoyancy members well below the sea surface. This adaptation greatly reduced vertical (heave) motion in particular, but the solution is an expensive one because of the high cost of construction and limited load-carrying capacity of semi-submersibles. Ideally we want to retain the good features of the conventional ship form, such as mobility, and to incorporate into this a 'motionless' workbase. In other words, to make it possible for the distance between the workbase and the seabed to be held constant regardless of the motion of the vessel. It sounds utopian, perhaps, but the Department of Ship and Marine Technology has produced a revolutionary idea which seems to meet just this specification.

The concept was developed from earlier research into the launch and recovery of tethered submersibles between support vessels and subsea locations. The most popular way to perform this operation is via a moonpool — a vertical 'tube' giving direct access from the deck to the sea through the bottom of the hull. Unfortunately the oscillation of the water inside a moonpool can be very severe and it was essential to reduce this in order to minimise the forces acting on the submersible. The damping down of this oscillation was brought about through the application of the team's theoretical insights and careful manipulation of the design parameters of the moonpool. Once this was achieved a workbase supported by a float could be placed on the calm water within the moonpool. The motion of the workbase can then be isolated from the motion of the vessel by controlling the movement of the water inside the moonpool. This concept of a motion-controlled offshore workbase (MOW) is now being realised on ship models up to $1\frac{1}{2}$ metres long — the first step towards the ultimate goal of a full-scale installation.

The potential of the concept has already found support from such bodies as

Britoil, Houlder Offshore, Shell and the U.K. Department of Energy. Once it has been fully realised, the possible areas of application are almost unlimited provided implementation can be justified on a sound economic basis. It may, however, not be too long before work conditions on vessels offshore will be as motion-free as those on land!

Improving the Interface between Man and the Computer

A decade ago, the user of a computer program usually had to know something about computers and programming in order to derive the maximum benefit from using a computer. At that time, the relatively small band of computer users was prepared to invest considerable effort in understanding the computing aspects of the problem. Often the user was a research scientist or development engineer who had an intrinsic interest in machines and devices. Today, however, the applications of microtechnology have resulted in an explosive increase in the use of computers in all fields, so that the majority of today's users of computing systems often have no interest in the way in which a computer system works or how to program. The computer, to such users, is merely a means to an end — a convenient way of solving a commercial or industrial problem. As a result, non-computing professionals and unskilled workers now form the major part of the computer user population.

The problem of usability has thus become increasingly important during the past five years and the ease with which computer applications programs can be used by non-computing professionals in their daily activities is now an important issue. This group of users includes managers, dentists, doctors, travel agents, accountants and secretaries. Unfortunately, programming design techniques have not kept pace with the rapid widening of this user base. Too often a program will give incomprehensible or (even worse) misleading messages to the user. Sometimes the mechanics of the computing operations, which form no part of the users' view of the problem-solving operation, will show through, causing confusion. The quality of the interface between the user and the computer has a major impact on the degree of success achieved. Poor interfaces cost time and money.

Providing good interfaces between computers and their users is not simple. An interface which is ideal for a novice is usually unsuitable for an experienced user. Furthermore, most applications involve some operations which are carried out frequently (and therefore learnt quickly) and others which are used only rarely (and therefore forgotten). The experienced user may, therefore, actually behave like a novice when using the latter type of operation. Thus, a uniform level of interaction for all aspects of an interface cannot normally be achieved, even for one type of user.

The man-machine interaction group at Strathclyde University under the direction of Professor J. L. Alty has designed a series of software tools to ease interface design and to provide a degree of adaptability. The system is called the CONNECT system (after E. M. Forster, '. . . only connect'). The system separates out the dialogue aspects of the interaction (i.e. the screen messages and user replies) from the computational aspects (i.e. the updating of salary records, calculation of salaries, etc.). This separation of the dialogue and task domains has two important advantages:

(a) the dialogue can be changed without altering the tasks. This is usually not easy in a standard computer program;

(b) the dialogue can be monitored and thus provide the system (or system designer) with a history of user experience with the application.

The dialogue between the user and the computer is handled by a special program — or interface processor. It converses with the user, finding out his requirements and providing him with results. It also converses with the computer application, providing it with the necessary inputs and interpreting its outputs. Thus, different user interfaces can be provided from the same application program. Technically, the dialogue is represented as a network consisting of a series of nodes with arc connections between nodes. Nodes converse with users (or the application program) and one of a set of possible exit arcs is chosen, depending upon the user or computer reply. As a user communicates with the system, a path is traced out through the dialogue network. From this trace the interface program can assess how far the user is achieving his aims and, if necessary, alter the network to provide a more appropriate interface.

Very little is known about the design of good interfaces. The CONNECT system will, initially, be used to study users accessing a number of well-known application programs. Their interactions will be monitored and will provide important clues both for pragmatic improvement and for the long-term deduction of generally applicable design rules. Where possible, experimentation will be carried out in real user environments so that the results obtained will be of immediate relevance to commerce and industry.

Fast Reactor Piping

Research at Strathclyde is helping to pave the way for the United Kingdom Atomic Energy Authority to develop a safe and successful Reactor. Theoretical work is supported by experimental facilities in the Department of Mechanics and Materials set up with funds from the UKAEA in conjunction with the National Nuclear Corporation. Under the direction of Professor J. Spence and Dr. J. T. Boyle, the work aims at developing and validating analytical techniques for the design and the strength assessment of high-temperature piping systems.

Despite recent public attention on the safety of nuclear power plants, nuclear energy has already earned itself a vital role in the generation of electricity world-wide. It is likely that continuing increases in nuclear output will occur to offset decreases in power from oil and gas. However, uranium itself is a non-renewable source and its reserves finite, whatever the improvements in the efficiency of conventional reactors. The next generation of nuclear reactor — 'breeder reactors' — utilising fast neutrons, produce more fuel than they use and have the potential to multiply the fuel seventy-fold compared with conventional reactors. However, fast-breeder reactors convert uranium to plutonium and there is consequent fear of proliferation of nuclear weapons: indeed, breeder development is currently stalled in the U.S.A. Controversies about these side-effects must be solved politically and publicly. Nevertheless, the breeder reactor presents a number of challenging technical and engineering design problems. Heat raised in the reactor core is transmitted through the 'primary' heat-transport system to a heat exchanger which relays the heat to a secondary system which, in turn, transports to steam generators and turbines. In the fast reactor the transport medium ('coolant') in the secondary circuit is water but in the primary circuit is liquid sodium, hence the name Liquid Metal Fast Breeder Reactor (LMFBR). Consequently, there is the danger of a sodium/water reaction and the structural integrity of the heat-transport piping is, therefore, crucial. The engineering problems are compounded by the fact that the pipework is at elevated temperature so that the strength of the material deteriorates in time.

More than a decade ago, Professor John Spence began directing his research to providing design information to help in the assessment of pipework at high temperature and pioneered the basic theoretical analysis of piping components under inelastic conditions. Over the years this basic information has been used by the UKAEA, and to some extent by the U.S. Department of Energy, the French Commissariat de l'Energe Atomique and the Japanese Power Reactor and Nuclear Fuel Development Corporation in research associated with the pipework in the current generation of prototype and commercial fast reactors. Later joined by Dr. J. T. Boyle and with funding initially from the Science and Engineering Research Council and the UKAEA, the further development of these analytical tools has continued, with emphasis being concentrated on simplified methods of system design which might be of assistance to designers. The most recent grant from the UKAEA has made it possible, with the help of a number of research staff, to carry out an experimental investigation into the applicability of these design tools. About twenty 1/5 scale piping assemblies have been tested, each continuously over a period ranging from one to nine months at elevated temperature (570°C). At the time of writing these results are still being assessed, although the initial indications are encouraging. The results will be of assistance to the design personnel in supporting the analytical methods employed for the civil LMFBR piping as well as of use in other high-integrity situations.

Self-Adaptive Control Systems

Rapid progress has been made over the past ten years in the development of adaptive control strategies and the University has established an Industrial Control Unit, headed by Professor M. Grimble, with a specific remit to produce developments in systems theory and control engineering. The most common, developed at Lund in Sweden and at Oxford in the U.K., involves an identification and control scheme termed a self-tuning system. In this type of algorithm the process is identified using a least square procedure and the controller is calculated using the estimated process model. The resulting control system finds application in any problem where the process is unknown or has characteristics which are likely to vary slowly with time.

Existing self-tuning systems have several disadvantages, mainly because of the poor properties of the controller algorithms involved. When these systems were originally developed, computing power was expensive and the simplest control strategy was necessary. The recent advent of very powerful cheap computing devices removes this constraint and hence a major study was undertaken into the most appropriate design methods. Two basic routes were taken, involving LQG (Linear Quadratic Gaussian) and WMV (Weighted Minimum Variance) cost functions. In the former case, an unconditional cost function involving tracking error and control energy terms was minimised which produced a very robust controller with good stability properties. The latter (WMV) approach represented a controller design which was less complicated than the LQG controller, but was rather more difficult to compute than the older minimum variance strategies. The cost function being minimised involved a conditional expectation operator which was also similar to earlier approaches. As might be expected, some improvement in stability and other properties was achieved, but these were not as good as for the LQG design.

A theoretical study on the development of polynomial systems theory was also pursued to support the adaptive controller design work. This analysis was necessary since, for identification purposes, the plant must be represented in this form. Various approaches to the solution of optimal control problems, using related system approaches, have been taken by researchers in the U.S.A. and Czechoslovakia. The theories were rationalised and useful links between them were established. Numerical algorithms for the solution of polynomial system equations have also been assessed and developed, particularly for the solution of diophantine equations. Further work in this area is foreseen.

The above theoretical and design studies were partly undertaken in response to the needs of industrial control projects. For example, an adaptive ship positioning system was developed for oil rig drill ships which must operate in a range of environmental conditions. Industrial partners (GEC Electrical Projects Ltd., Rugby) were, of course, mainly interested in the system to be marketed. However, the Marine Technology Directorate of SERC supported further, more fundamental, studies on this subject.

Health and Food

'All are parts of one stupendous whole, Whose body nature is.'
Alexander Pope (1688–1744)

Over the past few decades, there has been a tremendous expansion in scientific knowledge. To cope with this expansion, scientists have, of necessity, become more specialised. Ironically, this has resulted in many traditional interdisciplinary boundaries being breached, with the result that now research groups in different departments can find themselves working in the same field although generally from quite different approaches. One of these areas is that of health care and, although Strathclyde University has no medical school, its contributions to this field are wide and varied. Included in this section are related developments in biotechnology.

Monoclonal Antibodies

Modern medical science creates a demand for substances such as protein hormones, blood-coagulation factors, lymphokines and antibodies — required in ever-increasing quantities for the treatment of patients with a variety of diseases. Unfortunately the source of many of these substances is severely limited, as they come only from the tissues and organs of animals — and donors, particularly human donors, are always in short supply. Work by molecular biologists and genetic engineers over the past decade has made it possible to isolate the genetic material responsible for the secretion of these factors from animal cells but a problem has been that animal cells in culture tend to die in a few days.

Over the past six years, a research team led by Professor Stimson of the Biochemistry Division has been developing methods of genetic manipulation which not only immortalise animal cells but also make it more likely that they will grow in suspension cultures. The research has taken two directions, using cell fusion and transforming gene-insertion procedures.

The desired animal cell, say an antibody-secreting lymphocyte, is immortalised by growing it in culture by fusion with a cell which already has the property of immortality, such as a cancer cell. The resultant hybrid cell thus possesses the desired characteristics of immortality and antibody production. The use of transforming viruses for the production of animal cell lines has also been studied as an alternative to the fusion system. Problems of the possibly infectious nature of such techniques have been overcome, and the production of monoclonal antibodies by inserting the genetic material into animal cells using bacterial plasmids is now in operation.

The prospect of large-scale production of monoclonal antibodies opens up the possibility of many major medical advances and the Strathclyde team is involved in some of these; for example, immunotoxin therapy, the targeting of drugs to the affected tissue, is already being tested with animals.

At the same time, the development of research on human monoclonal antibodies by the Strathclyde team together with Professor Alan Williamson (formerly of the Biochemistry Department at the University of Glasgow, now Research Director at Glaxo, Greenford) and Visiting Professor Heather M. Dick (Consultant in Clinical Immunology at the Royal Infirmary, Glasgow) forms the basis for work now being carried out by Monotech, a private company set up by Coats Patons.

Rheumatoid Arthritis

Arthritis is one of the most common diseases in the world today and there are, in Scotland alone, about 500,000 people who suffer from it. One of the most crippling forms, and one that can affect the young as well as the old, is rheumatoid arthritis. Little is known as yet about its cause, what factors govern the severity of the disease and how to treat it. For inorganic chemists like Professor D. H. Brown and Dr. W. E. Smith, the frequent references in articles about it, to two chemically related metals — copper and gold — seemed a strange coincidence of sufficient importance to merit further investigation. Because of its relative abundance in the biosphere and its ease of undergoing reduction-oxidation reactions, many living species have developed enzyme systems that utilise copper in their catalytic centres. Recently, considerable interest has arisen concerning the role of copper in inflammatory conditions, particularly rheumatoid arthritis. Three observations have contributed to this: (a) patients with rheumatoid arthritis have abnormally high serum copper levels; (b) copper complexes of anti-inflammatory drugs have shown greater activity in animal models than the drugs themselves; (c) lurking in the boundary of popular belief and scientific knowledge is the possible beneficial effect of the copper bangle — acting via the absorption of copper-amino acid complexes through the skin.

The favourable report of the Empire Rheumatism Council in 1961 encouraged the use of gold drugs in the treatment of rheumatoid arthritis. Since then, however, medical enthusiasm has waxed and waned. The fact that the drugs can effect a remission of the disease in some cases, has been a source of optimism and the significant occurrence of toxic side effects, of concern. However, since there are still no more successful drugs available, gold is still regularly used in the treatment of severe cases of rheumatoid arthritis.

The Strathclyde group, in collaboration with Dr. R. Sturrock and Dr. H. Capell of the Centre for Rheumatic Disease, Glasgow, are examining copper levels in different blood fractions of patients and also the activities of some copper-containing enzymes such as superoxide dismutase. These results are being monitored for patients on different drug regimes, including gold therapy, and the results compared with standard clinical parameters. The work is currently being extended to look at the metabolism of different gold drugs. Thus, hopefully, the interdisciplinary collaboration of the clinician and the inorganic chemist will help to give a greater understanding of this widespread and, as yet, intractable disease.

In some cases, drug therapy (combined with natural healing) fails to restrict the course of the disease — leaving, as a last resort, joint-replacement surgery. This is often able to provide patients with a useful range of movement and some relief of pain. The Bioengineering Unit of Strathclyde University, in collaboration with Mr. W. A. Souter, FRCS, of Princess Margaret Rose Hospital, Edinburgh, has developed a replacement elbow joint for appropriate patients, because other models on the market frequently give rise to clinical difficulties in the long term, due to the loosening of the implanted components from their fixture within the bone. The 'Souter-Strathclyde' elbow joint replacement is covered by patent and is at present marketed by the international company Howmedica. More than one hundred and ten patients have received this treatment and some implants have now been in place for over five years without any major clinical problems. Collaboration is continuing in the assessment of patients with the replacement elbow.

Degenerative Eye Diseases

Many diseases can cause loss of vision or blindness in adulthood; these include glaucoma, diabetic retinopathy, retinal detachment and cataracts, among others. But one common cause of blindness in adults, retinitis pigmentosa (RP), is almost unknown to the general public. Retinitis pigmentosa is a family of hereditary diseases of the retina (the light-sensitive layer at the back of the eye where the process of 'seeing' occurs). These diseases are characterised initially by night blindness and tunnel vision and, while the degeneration is very slow, often occurring over twenty years or more, they may lead eventually to total blindness.

Several years ago the Strathclyde group discovered that a number of RP patients were hyperlipidaemic, that is, they had higher levels of lipids (fats) in their blood than do most people. Since then it has been involved in a U.K.-wide survey of lipids, working directly with the patients, who are enlisted through the BRPS Newsletter, and who supply the genealogical information so that family trees can be constructed and the course of the disease charted in each family.

The hyperlipidaemia in RP is essentially a new finding and it is not entirely clear yet what its significance is to the aetiology of the disease. It is known that the retina requires several lipids (poly-unsaturated fatty acids) in particular and that experimental animals deprived of these lipids will have reduced vision. The hyperlipidaemia may be the consequence of a defect in how the body handles lipids, and this defect may also show up in the retina and cause retinal degeneration. All this is speculation at this stage, so the clinical studies continue, collecting data on patients' lipid titres and statistically evaluating it, as well as conducting basic research on the functioning of the retina, to attempt to determine whether hyperlipidaemia is, perhaps, a clue to what goes wrong in this baffling family of diseases. In any case, hyperlipidaemia is known to be associated with ischaemic heart disease in later life, so it is important to identify those RP patients who might be at risk from heart disease, so that preventative measures can be initiated.

The New Neuromuscular Blocking Drugs: Vercuronium and Atracurium

Since the introduction of the use of a curare extract into anaesthetic practice about forty years ago, the safety of major surgical operations has been greatly increased by the concurrent administration of a relatively small dose of an anaesthetic agent to render the patient unconscious, together with a neuromuscular blocking drug (i.e. a curare-like drug) to prevent reflex movements and to facilitate the passing of a tube into the trachea via the mouth, so as to maintain a clear airway into the lungs. Although skilled anaesthetists have been successfully making use of a range of synthetic neuromuscular blocking drugs for many years, such drugs have not been free from unwanted side-effects. However, as surgical techniques become more advanced, anaesthetists have come to regard any side-effects as less acceptable.

The Department of Physiology and Pharmacology has long shared research interests with Organon Laboratories. On the basis of this long interaction, chemists at Organon designed and synthesised a large number of potential new neuromuscular blocking drugs and passed them for testing to Dr. I. G. Marshall and Dr. N. N. Durant of the Department of Physiology and Pharmacology. They selected one of them, now called vecuronium, as worthy of further trials in human beings. Subsequent clinical trials by anaesthetists all over the world confirmed Marshall and Durant's prediction that vecuronium is a highly potent neuromuscular blocking drug that is free from unwanted effects.

While Dr. Marshall and Dr. Durant were working on vecuronium, Professor John Stenlake, with his collaborators in the Department of Pharmacy, was independently achieving his long-held aim of synthesising neuromuscular blocking drugs with a built-in self-destruct mechanism. The importance of this concept extends into many therapeutic fields, for it means that the patient eliminates the drug from his body no matter what the circumstances. Even in the absence of liver and kidney function the drug disintegrates, when its task is completed, into inactive products. Professor Stenlake's neuromuscular blocking drugs were tested by pharmacologists at the Wellcome Research Laboratories and one of the drugs, now called atracurium, was selected for clinical trials and proved successful.

Both vecuronium and atracurium were approved by the U.K. Committee on Safety of Medicines and other European drug-regulating authorities in late 1982 and they are now being widely used in anaesthetic practice. They are both free from unwanted effects and, although chemically quite different, are remarkably similar in their properties.

It is worthy of note that, after several quiescent years in this research field, two new drugs should appear simultaneously and gain approval by the licensing authorities. The fact that it was the same University that was involved in the simultaneous and independent early development of both drugs (the only two new ones in the world) is an outstanding coincidence.

Research in this field provides a prime example of the commendably close and synergistic relationship that should and does exist between industry, university and clinical medicine. Atracurium was designed and synthesised by Strathclyde pharmaceutical chemists and first tested pharmacologically in industry (by pharmacologists at Wellcome), whereas vecuronium was synthesised by industrial chemists at Organon and first tested pharmacologically by Strathclyde pharmacologists. Research in the field produced another important consequence, for it has led to the formation of an international muscle-relaxant research group involving chemists, pharmacologists and anaesthetists from Europe and the U.S.A., in which Strathclyde plays a prominent role.

Genetic Engineering with Yeast

Painstakingly, more of the genes (the biochemical units of inheritance) in yeast are being identified. Of particular significance are those involved in maximising yeast's use of sugars and other raw materials to convert them into alcohol and other constituents of the wide range of beverages consumed by mankind. Identification of relevant genes permits a less empirical, more rational approach to the development of new strains of yeast. For example, new hybrid strains for whisky fermentations have recently been constructed by incorporating a gene controlling utilisation of a minor sugar from a commercial beer yeast. This hybridisation has been achieved by fusing together yeast cells which have their outer walls removed by enzymes (spheroplast fusion technique). In the near future, construction of much more closely defined hybrids of this type will be attempted by genetic engineering (transformation technique).

Another important property of certain strains under intensive study is the aggregation of large numbers of free yeast cells into clumps or flocs during a late stage of fermentation processes. This flocculation results in rapid sedimentation of yeast, thereby clearing most of it from the fermentation liquid and product. This natural property allowing easier separation of yeast is an important economic consideration. In this connection, strains developed at the University of Strathclyde under the direction of Dr. J. R. Johnston, in association with Allied Breweries of Burton-on-Trent and the major Canadian brewers, Labatt, carry defined genes controlling the flocculation characteristic. In an exciting extension of international collaboration, these strains have been used in making new hybrid yeasts for the massive programme of fuel-alcohol production from sugar-cane juice in Brazil. As part of a research project supported by a considerable grant from the Science and Engineering Research Council, the genes determining flocculation are now being cloned, i.e. isolated and purified. In this way it is hoped that the property of flocculation can be specifically introduced into new commercial yeasts when it is required to improve a particular fermentation process. Research collaboration in genetical aspects of industrial yeasts have also been initiated with academic colleagues in New Zealand and Poland.

Soy Sauce

The work in this field of the Department of Bioscience and Biotechnology is interesting from both commercial and scientific viewpoints in that it is an example of purely academic research being developed into a commercial enterprise under the auspices of the University.

Two types of produce are sold as soy sauce in Europe, first, fermented products which would be recognised as soy sauce by S.E. Asians and, secondly, chemical hydrolysates. Soy sauce has many effects on the flavour of foods to which it is added — increasing saltiness, enhancing the natural flavour of food and adding soy sauce's own aroma and beef flavour. Chemical hydrolysates can bring about these effects to some extent but fermented soy sauce has unique properties which make it highly desirable for most culinary uses, so that it is now being increasingly valued in Occidental as well as Oriental cuisine. The fermentation process is ancient (over three thousand years old), highly traditional in the countries of its origins (although undergoing rapid and extensive modernisation in some areas) and remarkable to Western eyes in its use of moulds which we associate with decay.

As the work at Strathclyde University on soy sauce began to be reported in the scientific literature, the group received a steadily increasing number of requests for information and about the possibility of our supplying sauce for commercial use. A feasibility study supported by a grant from the Wolfson Foundation was favourable and the decision was taken to set up a company 'Bean Products Limited' in Cumbernauld, a new town near Glasgow.

The soy-sauce project now had a name, a home and a fair amount of knowledge but this was just the end of phase one, as was soon discovered. No matter how good the technology is on a laboratory scale, the handling of tonnes of material, especially if that material is fermenting and, even more especially, if that fermenting mash is a slimy slurry containing 18 per cent salt and with a pH of 4·5, represents totally new problems. A lot had to be learned — and fast — about pasteurisation and its limitations and about filtration and its difficulties, especially if sterility is the desired objective. The somewhat bitter lesson had also to be learned that there was a huge gulf between a company expressing interest in the concept of a soy sauce made in the U.K. and that same company actually parting with money for a tonne of the finished produce. However, these technical and marketing problems are now being overcome and a store of knowledge built up about the process of setting up a small business.

This work, however, highlights the vexed question as to the role of universities in the commercial world. External financial pressure may force the issue and hopefully the financial returns will reward the effort and applications of the Departments concerned. Perhaps, however, the greater reward will be to enhance for research workers in the University as a whole, an awareness of the outside commercial world where prosperity is so closely allied to that of the University itself.

CHAPTER TWELVE

THE HERITAGE

(a) THE ARTS

A. A. Auld

The West of Scotland would at first sight seem an unlikely breeding ground for the arts. However, the last two hundred years have seen a burgeoning of painting, architecture and general appreciation of the arts which has largely gone unnoticed by those outwith Strathclyde. The 'Auld Alliance' enabled an artistic environment to be established which allowed the influence of the French court to be disseminated through certain sections of Scottish life, and it is fascinating to see how down the years Scotland has bypassed England and looked to France in the main as its cultural benefactor.

It would be wrong, however, to imagine that this artistic paradise was allowed to flourish unhindered. The strong Calvinistic influence prevalent in Scotland since the Middle Ages made it difficult, indeed almost impossible, for the arts to be looked upon as part and parcel of everyday life by the ordinary citizen. The arts were frivolous at best and downright evil at worst.

Not an encouraging picture but gradually with enlightenment dawning literature became acceptable as a means of expressing emotions, however restrained these may have been. In its wake, architecture, painting and music started to develop and expand until by the mid-nineteenth century a definable Scottish artistic culture could be discerned although still constrained by the morals of the time.

Once contact had been firmly established by artists with the outside world a new found confidence inspired artists and performers to experiment and extend their horizons. They found a receptive and expanding audience. Established institutions such as the Royal Scottish Academy in Edinburgh and the Royal Glasgow Institute of the Fine Arts in Glasgow gave wonderful opportunities to both artists to show their works and viewers to purchase them. The RSA founded in 1826 predated the Glasgow Institute by thirty-five years, but the latter proved to be an excellent vehicle for artists, particularly from the West of Scotland, although throughout its long years it has attracted works by artists from all over Europe who realised the worth of exhibiting in

198

Glasgow where there were many potential buyers. This in turn gave painters who could not travel, the opportunity of seeing something of what was happening in the artistic centres of Europe.

It was, however, a two-way success. Not only did painters and printmakers visit the Continent, the artists and institutions of Europe knew what was happening in Scotland and particularly in Glasgow and the West of Scotland. A deputation from Germany visited Britain in the 1880's and discovered that the most exciting painting was being done by a local group of painters known as the Glasgow Boys, a title adopted by themselves as they considered they were anti-establishment. The work of Charles Rennie Mackintosh and his contemporaries was also known outside of Scotland and complemented the work of the movement known as Art Nouveau or Jugendstil. The Glasgow Style was not just a watering down of Continental ideas but a distinct and separate style largely home grown.

The more formal institutions, such as the Art Gallery and Museum, Kelvingrove, whose collections had been formed in the middle of the nineteenth century, were not slow to react to modern movements and the first work by James McNeil Whistler to enter a public collection, 'Arrangement in Black and Grey' (Portrait of Thomas Carlyle), was purchased by the Town Council in 1891 for the then huge sum of 1,000 guineas.

The Banqueting Hall of the newly built City Chambers was decorated with murals by Walton, Guthrie and Lavery and the architecture of the city in the second half of the century was noted, for example by the works of 'Greek' Thomson, Burnet and Mackintosh. Much of the glory of the work of these and other architects has come to life once more with stone-cleaning and refurbishment. The Victorians were conscious of their lack of provision for the finer things of life for those worse off than themselves and created parks, concert halls and cultural centres, including the People's Palace on Glasgow Green in the east end of the city where exhibitions and permanent displays could be provided for the huge and largely deprived population.

Throughout the area now known as Strathclyde Region this provision was established through the generosity of benefactors either aristocratic or, more usually, wealthy industrialists who, for whatever reasons, provided land and buildings. The founding of, amongst others, the Art Gallery and Museum in Paisley, the Dick Institute, Kilmarnock and Greenock Museum, all testify to the awakening interest in the cultural heritage in their respective districts. Local clubs and societies such as the Glasgow Art Club, the Lady Artists' Club, The Royal Philosophical Society and the Andersonian Society also played an important part in establishing the right atmosphere for these various cultural activities to grow and prosper. Commercial dealers and auction rooms dealing in artefacts of value and importance allowed the more affluent to collect paintings and antiques of all kinds to furnish the large houses rapidly springing up all over the West of Scotland in the fashionable resorts, such as Helensburgh, Rhu, Largs and Wemyss Bay, and in the suburbs of Glasgow. This still pertains today, although in a slightly different way. Architects were given the opportunity of designing individual styled homes for the increasing number of middle and upper class families which the increased wealth of the Region was producing through trade and industry. This growth and artistic awareness was particularly strong from the 1880's to the 1920's, but after the First World War there was a period of relative stagnation. Signs of reawakening in the late 1930's manifested themselves in the Empire Exhibition held in Bellahouston Park in 1938. Again a major war hindered this come-back, and it was a long time after the Second World War before Glasgow and the West of Scotland began to find its feet on the cultural map once more.

The reputation of the West of Scotland, with in particular 'Red Clydeside' and Glasgow, as a dangerous place in which to live, was difficult to overcome. Many people, especially those in spheres of influence in the media, time and again dragged up its past and seemed to ignore the great strides the area had made to abolish poverty and chronic sickness and make the West of Scotland an attractive place in which to live and work.

The last twenty years has seen the establishment of a permanent home for Scottish Opera and Scottish Ballet, the explosion of music groups of all types, the foundation of further exhibition centres and picture dealers, the growth of museums and galleries of every kind and the greater influence of the media — Radio Clyde, BBC and STV. New industries and commercial enterprises have chosen Glasgow and the West of Scotland as their headquarters and they in turn have, through direct and indirect sponsorship, supported and strengthened the cultural life of the area.

The opening of the Burrell Collection (Figure 1) in October 1983 has had a major impact on Glasgow and the West of Scotland. Specialists in the various forms of arts and crafts which make up the Collection have of course known of its existence for many years and have visited it when in store. They along with thousands of visitors who have little or no knowledge of the cultures and techniques displayed have now come to see it in its permanent setting. Their appetites have been whetted by the television and newspaper coverage lavished on the building and the Collection and they have found the experience of visiting it so rewarding that many have made repeat visits or visited other museums in Glasgow. It would appear that the opening of this museum has made the local population of Glasgow and Strathclyde more aware of their cultural heritage.

The sales of paintings, prints and *objets d'art* for private collections and galleries have grown enormously over the last decade and the increase of purchases of reproduction postcards, greeting cards which are specifically 'cultural' in their content, is quite remarkable.

The number of visitors to all museums and country houses in the area has increased many times. If I can give more precise details for the establishments for which I am responsible — the number of visitors visiting Glasgow District's museums and art galleries has risen from 388,000 in 1954, 600,000 in 1964, 936,845 in 1974 to 2·6 million in 1984.

Fig. 1 Exterior of the Burrell Collection from the south. Opened October 1983.

This can be attributed in part to the growth of Glasgow as a tourist attraction but also to the increased awareness of the local population who make up the bulk of the numbers. It has become a way of life for many people to visit and revisit galleries, museums and country houses as well as attending concerts, opera, theatre and other artistic events, all of which would have been unthinkable a short while ago. Scottish Opera each year sell 85 per cent of their available seats and the Citizens Theatre 70 per cent of theirs. Such attendances and encouragement cannot be sustained for long by the presentation of the odd spectacular performance or by subsidies by official bodies but only by the deep commitment and support on the part of the populace who feel the need for such revitalising of their minds and senses.

Perhaps the most important of the recent manifestations of a cultural explosion in the West of Scotland is Mayfest, a festival of music, drama and the visual arts which has dominated Glasgow each spring for the last few years. This is not just in competition with the long-established and highly successful Edinburgh Festival — although it contains similar elements — but a spontaneous response by the people to the growing awareness of the arts which have surrounded them for so long.

There are also, within different parts of Strathclyde, individual festivals and events which have led to more permanent results, the most noticeable being the marvellous mural in Easterhouse which is the work of those who live in the area.

Thriving painting clubs, music societies, dance studios, choirs, brass bands, pipe bands and youth orchestras all point to a healthy and expanding movement which lives alongside the more formal institutions and both of them are mutually interdependent.

Glasgow School of Art still maintains its role as a producer of the best of designers and artists. In the spring of this year, 1984, a major exhibition of their recent work was shown by invitation in Milan — the cradle of design — and was enthusiastically received. Pupils are responding more and more to the challenge of commercial needs in industrial design which in time will achieve a much higher standard being demanded by manufacturers and shoppers. All in all, despite the grim economic situation we are in at the moment, we can truthfully say Glasgow and the West of Scotland are miles better than they were and as Her Majesty the Queen said on the opening of the Burrell Collection — in matters artistic, Glasgow leads from the front.

THE HERITAGE

(b) THE VISIBLE HERITAGE

John R. Hume

Introduction

The term 'heritage' is somewhat vague. For this purpose it is taken to mean physical survivals from the past. This definition excludes explicitly tradition and individual memory, and omits books, manuscripts and smaller artefacts. Buildings, structures and landscape features therefore form the core of what is here discussed, though these other aspects of 'the heritage' give meaning to the 'hardware', and indeed colour the comments made. A small number of places have been selected where features occur that give the flavour of the 'heritage' of the Region as a whole, balancing the exceptional and the typical and attempting to give some historical and geographical perspective, although space does not permit a description of the prehistoric remains.

Paisley Churches

The Christian Churches in Scotland have been characterised by a pattern of schism and reunion for more than two centuries. The resulting proliferation of denominations, coupled with the relative cheapness of building in the nineteenth century, resulted in the construction of large numbers of church buildings in Scottish towns and cities. To cope with increasing population, churches were commonly rebuilt on a larger scale, and competition between denominations encouraged architectural exhibitionism. Within Strathclyde, Paisley has in its central area perhaps the finest and most varied group of church buildings, illustrating in a unique way the ecclesiastical history of Scotland since the twelfth century.

The oldest structure is the nave of the Abbey Church which was founded in 1163 by Walter, High Steward of Scotland, for monks of the Cluniac order of Benedictines. The nave was built between the twelfth and fifteenth centuries, and was used as the parish church of Paisley after the Reformation in 1560. The rest of the building fell into ruin and was used as a quarry by local people. The nave was restored in 1788–89 and again between 1859 and 1862. The success of the thread trade in the later nineteenth century renewed Paisley's confidence, and the Abbey became a symbol of civic pride. Between 1898 and 1928 three of Scotland's most distinguished architects, Sir Robert Rowand Anderson, P. Macgregor Chalmers and Sir Robert Lorimer, re-created the Abbey Church and cloisters, incorporating some seventeenth-century houses as the 'Place' of Paisley. Set in an area cleared of housing and industrial buildings in 1874, the Abbey became, and remains, a striking feature of the town centre.

Next in age are the eighteenth-century churches, built by the established

203

Fig. 1   The High Church, Paisley, exemplifying the solid worth of the town's business
community in the eighteenth century

Church of Scotland to accommodate more worshippers than could the Abbey nave. The first of these was the Laigh Kirk, built in 1736–38, with its crow-stepped gables harking back in style to sixteenth- and seventeenth-century local vernacular building. It was designed, as was then customary, by master masons, in this case James Baird and John Hart. Next came the High Kirk (Figure 1), the body of which was built between 1754 and 1756, at about the same time as similar churches in Glasgow and Greenock. The fine steeple was added in 1770 to a design by John White. Continuing growth in population, associated with handloom weaving of silk, encouraged the building of the Middle Church, just below the High Church, in 1779–81. This plain but handsome structure was designed by its builder, Samuel Henning, a wright. A Gaelic church was added in 1793, but is now secularised.

This burst of activity in church building was succeeded by a lull. In 1810 Oakshaw West Church was built, a very plain structure, and this was followed by the magnificent St. George's Church of 1819, originally intended to have a spire. There followed the South Church (1836), built to cater for new southerly suburbs. Where the established Church had dominated, other denominations now began to build on a large scale. The Episcopal Church in Scotland, survivor of the general return to Presbyterianism after 1689, and the United Presbyterian Church, amalgamation of eighteenth-century secessions, built large new buildings in 1828 and in 1826. The East U.F. Church was designed by John Baird, a noted Glasgow architect of the period.

The religious vicissitudes of the seventeenth and eighteenth centuries, however, paled into significance beside those of the nineteenth century. Most cataclysmic was the Disruption of 1843, when the established Church split. The breakaway group, calling itself the Free Church of Scotland, had to provide itself with new church buildings. One of the first Free churches in Paisley was Free High, at Orr Square, a rather forbidding Romanesque structure with a square south-east tower. The nineteenth century also saw the importation of sects originating in England. The Methodists, as elsewhere, built their church and halls above commercial premises, opposite the Abbey. The Baptists were fortunate in securing the allegiance of Thomas Coats, a member of the leading firm of thread makers in Paisley, and on his death a magnificent Gothic memorial church (Figure 2) was built, of cathedral-like proportions. It was completed in 1894 to designs by the Edinburgh architect, Hippolyte J. Blanc, who had earlier designed the more conventionally French-Gothic St. James, Underwood Road (1880–84), for the United Presbyterians. Roman Catholicism gained adherents in west central Scotland mainly through migration from Ireland and from parts of the West Highlands. The first Roman Catholic church in Paisley was St. Mirren's (1808). To provide for growing numbers, a series of large red-sandstone Gothic buildings was constructed throughout the West of Scotland, all designed by the London firm of Pugin and Pugin. Paisley's example, St. Mary's, was one of the earlier specimens, dating from 1891. Other denominations built churches on a smaller scale.

Fig. 2   Coats Memorial Church, Paisley, a marvellously rich and impressive building.

In a final flourish of building just before the First World War, two very fine and original churches were constructed in Paisley. Wallneuk (1913–15) is a marvellously calm, assured composition by T. G. Abercrombie. St. Matthew's (1908), on the other hand, is a much more idiosyncratic design by William McLennan, incorporating Art Nouveau detailing.

The town of Paisley, then, has still a range of church buildings within its central area which illustrates, on the one hand, the denominational diversity of the Church in Scotland over eight hundred years and, on the other hand, the richness of architecture such complexity produced. There are close parallels between the desire for display of the builders of original, medieval Abbey Church, and of the creators of such churches as the renewed Abbey and Coats Memorial. Both saw a need to express religious fervour in masonry and to create a sense of awe among worshippers. In contrast, the eighteenth- and early nineteenth-century buildings are more modest, though basic simplicity is in most cases complemented by richness of detail and fineness of construction. Throughout Strathclyde, town and city churches are an important part of the heritage: in Paisley they are of dominant significance. Most are listed, but they are still vulnerable; they should be cherished.

Auchindrain and Inveraray

Situated within a few miles of each other, these two communities illustrate complementary facets of life in Argyll over two centuries. Auchindrain, a remarkable survival of a method of farming once common throughout Scotland, is a museum; Inveraray, built as a showpiece, still functions as such.

Auchindrain was the last example in Argyll of a co-tenancy, an area of agricultural land worked jointly by a group of families. This system of farming was common throughout Britain until consolidation of land-holdings became usual. From the seventeenth century there was a steady erosion of the method as enclosed farms, worked by single tenants with paid help, demonstrated advantages to the landowner. The system persisted longer in the highlands, with their small patches of arable land, than in more fertile lowlands, but even there it was displaced by sheep farming and subsistence single tenant crofting from the early nineteenth century. The anomalous survival of Auchindrain is probably due to the sympathy of successive Dukes of Argyll, who have had a strong historical sense. By the middle of the twentieth century even this residual vitality was not strong enough to resist external pressure. The houses of eighteenth- and nineteenth-century construction had become, in the light of modern standards, unfit for human habitation. It was at this juncture in 1962 that a group of historically minded people came together to save the township from decay or demolition. Led by Miss Marion Campbell of Kilberry, they formed a Trust in 1964, whose composition reflected the cultural climate of the period, with representatives from the Universities of Glasgow and Edinburgh and from the National Museum of Antiquities of Scotland, as well as the local Antiquarian Society, the Argyll Estates and Argyll County Council. The intent of the Trust was to restore the township to its earlier condition, and to demonstrate older methods of agriculture. Inevitably, the modern intruded: a bungalow was built for the Curator, and a museum/tearoom housing gallery displays of artefacts and illustrations. Beyond this, however, the ideals of the founders have in some measure been achieved. Several buildings have had their replacement corrugated-iron roofs returned to thatch. Interiors have been restored or conserved. Livestock of traditional types are being reared. The foot plough and other implements characteristic of marginal highland agriculture are again being used. Poverty has, however, appropriately, curbed ambition, and the very partiality of restoration, the unevenness of achievement, brings out an essential element in West Highland living, an essence that could so easily have been lost in a hygienised folk museum. For life in a marginal highland township did have elements of squalor, of makeshift substitution, of real hardship, mitigated by the warmth of human relationships and the richness of Gaelic folk culture. Alas, no museum can keep these alive.

Inveraray is the other side of the coin. It was created by the Campbells, Dukes of Argyll, to serve as their administrative centre and principal seat. The assimilation of Scottish culture with those of England and Continental Europe proceeded rapidly during the late seventeenth and early eighteenth centuries. The ideals of order, dignity, propriety developed by the European aristocracy spread through Scotland, penetrating the lowlands first, then moving to the highlands. By the time they had reached Argyll, however, taste had been subtly modified, so that the new Inveraray Castle, designed by Roger Morris in 1744, was not a Palladian mansion or some other neo-classical synthesis. Instead it was a four-square 'gothick' pile, with round corner towers, a plan redolent of the ancient Comyn stronghold of Inverlochy, near Fort William, though inside all was classical. Construction was slow, and the building was not completed until the 1760's. For a time the new castle co-existed with the old, a typical fifteenth-century Scottish tower house, but in the interest of order and decency the old was removed in 1775.

A similar fate overtook the old burgh of Inveraray, which had grown higgeldy-piggeldy on the shores of Loch Fyne from medieval times. A new town, first suggested in 1743, was created from 1750 to the south, on a promontory, with a front street facing the castle, a main street of middle-class houses and shops, a central square with a church in the middle and court-house and prison to the east, and a continuation of the main street lined with blocks of working-class housing. Basic facilities, apart from these, included a pier for communication by sea; improved roads to Glasgow and to North Argyll; a town house; an inn and a factory for woollen manufacture. Rationality of concept was strong; though architectural uniformity was not imposed, the general proportions and detailing of buildings was carried through. The church (1793–1802) was built with a central division. On one side, services were held in Gaelic, the language of the poor; on the other in

English, which was beginning to supersede Gaelic in Argyll. The two main blocks of working-class housing, Arkland and Relief Land, were designed by Robert Mylne after the manner of contemporary barrack blocks, and may well be the link between, say, Fort George and New Lanark, and ultimately be progenitors of the classical Glasgow tenement. The new Inveraray was an elegant creation, in some ways more than the castle itself, but with a cold formality in complete contrast to its predecessor, which was, simply, eliminated. The concept of order was indeed carried through the countryside for miles around. Planting, woodland walks, summerhouses, elegant bridges, lodges, a fenced deer forest, model farm steadings all created an oasis of calmness and rationality in striking contrast not only to what had gone before, but also to the wild highland scenery of much of the area to the north and east.

The orderly elegance of Inveraray is still with us, owing to the care taken by successive Dukes of Argyll, and more recently to the effects of central government (through the Scottish Development Department and the Historic Buildings Council) and of Ian G. Lindsay, pioneer conservation architect, and his colleagues. From the late 1950's a programme of restoration and rehabilitation was undertaken which has kept almost unchanged the external form of the town. Most recently, the court house has been restored by the Scottish Development Department, and now appropriately houses the archives of Argyll and Bute District. Though the logic of the town has altered, its castle and its grounds (maintained by the present Duke of Argyll) remain as outstanding monuments to the 'Enlightenment' in Scotland, certainly among the finest examples of integrated town and country planning in Scotland.

New Lanark

So well known as to be almost hackneyed, New Lanark is the outstanding monument of the Industrial Revolution in Scotland, and owing to its association with Robert Owen it has an international reputation. New Lanark was founded in the 1780's, when industrial ventures of all kinds seemed attractive to West of Scotland businessmen. The immediate stimulus came from Richard Arkwright's brilliantly conceived package of textile inventions, which allowed any businessman with a few thousand pounds and a suitable site for a water-powered mill to produce strong, even cotton yarn commanding a high price both in home and export markets. Arkwright paid a visit to Glasgow in 1784 to seek licensees for his patents, and found ready acceptance from David Dale, prominent linen-yarn merchant and banker. New Lanark was chosen as a site after a visit by Arkwright and Dale: by the time the first mill was in production Arkwright's patents had been quashed.

What we see at New Lanark today is largely the creation of David Dale. The main ranges of houses were his, as is the plan form of the mills and the water course leading to the now-vanished wheels. Built up quite steadily over some fifteen years, New Lanark was the largest cotton mill complex in Scotland, and among the largest in Britain in 1799, when Dale decided to sell out to a partnership formed by his prospective son-in-law, Robert Owen. After nearly ten years of consolidation, Owen embarked on a programme of enlarging and improving the facilities. To clear Dale's fourth mill for spinning he constructed an apprentice house (Nursery Buildings) and a complex for machine-making and repair, consisting of a three-storey mechanics shop and a range of brass and iron foundry buildings. He built a counting house on to the end of one of the rows of housing. Behind the mills he added a range of two-storey buildings covering a new tailrace leading to an outfall at the lowest point, behind mill one. These were used as stores and blowing houses, for preparing cotton for carding. Owen's most distinctive contribution, however, and the one that made New Lanark world-famous, was his construction of the 'New Institution for the Formation of Character' as a centre for the education of both children and adults, followed by the building of a 'School for Children', accompanied by the establishment of a large general store, the profits from which defrayed the cost of the schooling provided in the new buildings. Owen's community buildings also contained 'public kitchens', where food could be cooked for lunch-time consumption in the homes of the workers.

The shells at least of all these buildings have survived the vicissitudes of, in some cases, nearly two hundred years. Only the mills have undergone significant change. The first two were of a type widely used for Arkwright's method of spinning. Number one was cut down from its original five storeys to three in the 1940's, but retains the Palladian windows found in all four mills in their early form. Number two mill was more radically altered about 1906 when the front wall and interior were removed, and a new brick skin erected over a 'fireproof' interior. The rear wall, however, survives to its full height. The third and fourth mills were larger than the first two, and were designed for mule spinning. Number three was destroyed by fire in 1819, and the remains were completely demolished. About seven years later the present number three mill took its place, with, significantly, a 'fireproof' interior. Number four, the largest of the group, also met its end in a conflagration, this time when it was being re-equipped with new machinery, in 1883. It was not replaced.

The physical heritage of New Lanark is thus rich intrinsically. It presents, externally, a clear view of an Industrial Revolution factory village, despite the need to introduce middle-class restorer-purchasers to ensure the survival of the fabric. On the other hand, it has not been fossilised. The mills show features of styles of factory building spanning more than a century, though one can lament the disappearance of David Dale's uniform Palladianism. Similarly, the housing, community and ancillary buildings have been and are being modified to suit current views of the value of historic buildings, from outright, 'purist' restoration, as in the School for Children, through the retention of existing shells, like the foundry-dyeworks, converted to an interpretation centre for the Scottish Wildlife Trust, to thoroughgoing reconstructions, with only the walls surviving, as in the case of most of the housing. The strong element of constructive re-use is very much 'of the 1980's', but the alternative seems to be at best the 'picturesque ruin'. New Lanark indeed highlights the problems associated with an historic fabric that has outlived its original use.

Oban

The town of Oban is unique, not least because it still fulfils the function for which it was designed. 'Its natural situation, its accessibility, and its safe and commodious bay have splendidly fitted it to become the capital of the West Highlands and "the Charing Cross of the Hebrides" ... Oban is a place of passage and not of rest. Tourists go to Oban simply for the purpose of getting to somewhere else.' This was written in the 1890's, and is just as true today. It is the correspondence between function and form that makes Oban a singularly satisfying place.

The town became a trading centre in the early eighteenth century, and an unsuccessful attempt was made, from 1786, to develop it as a fishing station. Its real growth began when steamboats began to ply up the west coast of Scotland. The romantic character of the Hebrides became widely known through the publication of Boswell and Johnson's Tour through the Hebrides, of the (spurious) poems of Ossian, and of Sir Walter Scott's poem 'Lord of the Isles' in 1814. All these created a market for travel, which was catered for by steamer services from about 1820 for which the first proper pier, the still-surviving South Pier, was constructed. The activities of David Hutcheson & Co. and later David MacBrayne & Son, created a high-class tourist trade, with steamer services from Glasgow via the Crinan Canal — known as the 'Royal Route' after Queen Victoria traversed it. Hotels and guest houses grew up to accommodate tourists, who used the town as a base from which to visit Mull, Staffa, Iona and other islands by sea, and the hinterland by coach services. The first large hotel was the Great Western (1863) and this was followed by a steady stream of new and palatial buildings, especially after the opening of the Callander & Oban Railway in 1880. Hotel building continued almost to the First World War, with a few extensions subsequently. The result is a waterfront of extraordinary architectural richness. Starting at the south, there are the South Pier and the Lighthouse Depot, then the splendid railway station, 'one of the prettiest buildings in the town', with its associated pier. Next comes the Station Hotel (1881), followed by a sweep of miscellaneous buildings, dominated by the striking Argyll Mansions, a block of flats dating from the turn of the century. Then the Oban Distillery, founded in the 1790's, though the present buildings are mainly late Victorian. Above, on the hilltop, is McCaig's Folly, a circular granite building modelled on the Colosseum, never finished, and constructed by otherwise unemployed masons.

Next there is a grand sweep of hotels, beginning with the modest but old Oban Hotel, then the imposing Columba, the first part of which has superb wrought-iron balconies, and the second is an opulent red sandstone building

Fig. 3   The Regent Hotel, Oban, with the Victorian-romantic original block on the right, and the 1930's extension on the left. Originally known as the Marine Hotel, this establishment was renamed after a fire.

of about 1900. Then comes the North Pier, with buildings dating from 1927. To the rear are the baronial Argyll and Regent Hotels (Figure 3), the latter with a grand 1930's extension. Next comes the imposing office of the *Oban Times* newspaper (1883), founded in 1866, still widely read in the west. A further group of largely undistinguished buildings, punctuated by the delightful 'Art Deco' sun lounge of the Park Hotel, ends in the historic Great Western Hotel. Beyond to the north is the 1960's Corran Rest, then the elegant modern Christ Kirk Church of Scotland, the Alexandra Hotel in French style, the enormous bulk of St. Columba's Roman Catholic Cathedral of the Isles, and then a succession of large Victorian villas leading to Dunollie with its genuine medieval castle and rustic lighthouse. Look out to sea, and the green island of Kerrera and the hills of Mull beckon you. Look up, and tiers of neat villas rise up the hillside, mingled with woodlands. This is a heritage worth keeping.

Dalmellington Ironworks and the Doon Valley

The iron-smelting industry was for roughly forty years from the mid-1830's one of the most dynamic sectors of the Scottish economy. From each blast-furnace plant transport systems radiated to ironstone and coal pits, limestone quarries and slag heaps. Pig iron went by canal or railway for further processing or for shipment. Tens of thousands of men worked underground grubbing out the raw materials for the furnaces, while their wives struggled to bring up large families in tiny, often unsanitary houses, many of them in remote areas. The iron and mining communities drew their inhabitants from many different areas, but especially from Ireland and the Highlands. They developed a character based on shared risk and shared hardship which showed itself in a combination of toughness and tenderness.

As the raw materials were worked out, the ironworks closed, particularly rapidly in the inter-war years. The coalmines and their supporting villages, however, often survived. Post-war housing programmes, followed by closure of older pits, saw their numbers dwindle, until now only a handful of 'traditional' mining villages survive. Of the ironworks themselves, only at Waterside, by Dalmellington, are there substantial remains. Here the 1847 engine house (Figure 4), workshops, offices, furnace bank, and the routes of mineral railways survive to illustrate the scale and ramifications of a typical blast-furnace plant. Up on the hillsides round the works are the grass-grown foundation remains of the ironstone and coalminers' houses — Corbie Craigs, Benquhat, Lethanhill, Burnfoothill — while down in the valley, linked by the lines of cable-worked inclined railways, are the churches, school, company store, railway station, and some of the later rows of houses survive to give an impression of an enterprise employing hundreds of men, set up in a remote valley, dominating for a time, and then retreating.

Superimposed on the remains of the Dalmellington Iron Company's empire are other relics of mineral extraction. On the site of the blast furnace are two

Fig. 4   The former blowing engine house, Dalmellington Ironworks. The last substantial relic of the internationally important nineteenth-century iron industry, the left-hand section of this building was constructed in 1847. It was doubled in size in 1865, and the metal bits and pieces were added when the site became a brickworks in 1936.

brick kilns, built in 1936 by Bairds & Dalmellington, inheritors of the coal interests of the original concern, whose coal washery at Waterside still stands. At Minnivey, beside the remains of mine buildings erected by the National Coal Board, is the depot of the Ayrshire Railway Preservation Group, with locomotives and rolling stock from local lines. Brooding over the village of Dalmellington is the massive conical bing of waste from the Pennyvenie 2, 3 and 6 Colliery, the last deep mine in the Doon Valley, closed in 1979. The Dalmellington and District Conservation Trust now owns much of the former ironworks site, and aims to create an open-air museum, linked to the remote village site by footpaths on the lines of the old railways. Most of Waterside village has been created a Conservation Area.

Greenock Harbour

With the abandonment and infilling of most of the Glasgow docks, the Greenock docks have assumed new importance in illustrating the historic significance of the Clyde as a port. Historically, Greenock's trade was greater than that of Glasgow, owing to its location on the naturally scoured channel of the Clyde. During the heyday of the Glasgow-dominated tobacco trade between America and Europe, Greenock was used by the city's merchants more than the purpose-built Port Glasgow.

The deepening of the Clyde to provide a route for large vessels to Glasgow eroded Greenock's position as dominant Clyde port, a process speeded up by the ease with which steamships could navigate narrow channels. The town, however, fought back to the best of its ability. It had enclosed 'docks' (actually tidal basins) well before Glasgow, and from 1871 launched a series of projects for docks on a scale comparable to the Queen's and Princes 'docks' in Glasgow. Of these only the Garvel Graving Dock and James Watt Dock were completed. The relative remoteness of Greenock from the industrial heartland of west central Scotland ensured that the grandiose 'Great Harbour' remained an uncompleted dream.

What survives at Greenock, then, demonstrates changing significance and response to patterns of trade and transport over two centuries. The East India Harbour, designed by John Rennie and commenced in 1805, reminds us of the great international trading days of Greenock, as does the magnificent Customs House of 1818, designed by William Burn, and the biggest in Scotland. The Steamboat Quay, with its fine iron-framed sheds, dates from the eighteenth century, but was a focal point in the first great period of Clyde steamer traffic. The Victoria Harbour, still the haunt of smaller ships, points to early Victorian expansion (1846–50, designed by Joseph Locke). Now filled in, the Albert Harbour (commenced 1862) was a focus for the tobacco, sugar and spirit trades, and bonded warehouses survive on what was the south quay. Later Victorian megalomania can be seen in the James Watt Dock, with its extraordinary warehouse range (1879–86), in the uncompleted Great Harbour (started 1880), and in the magnificent Dalbeattie granite masonry of the

Garvel Graving Dock (commenced 1871), all designed by W. R. Kinipple. The two graving docks now operated by Scott-Lithgow (1786) and James Lamont & Sons (1818) recall the small size of most wooden ships; the Firth of Clyde Drydock is another reminder of changing technology in shipping. Designed to take the largest vessels afloat, it was never able to match the expectations of its promoters. By their very nature docks are vulnerable to alteration, and the long-term future of Greenock's harbour must be a matter for speculation.

The Great Western Road Terraces, Glasgow
   The inclusion of these blocks of middle-class houses in this discussion is based partly on their high architectural quality, partly on the way they illustrate the patchy fortunes of house-building in the Glasgow area, and partly for what they show of middle-class aesthetic and cultural attitudes in the heyday of a great Victorian city. Great Western Road was projected as a turnpike road in the early 1830's to provide a grand new route into the city, avoiding the squalor that had accompanied the rise of Glasgow as a trading and manufacturing centre. It struck straight, and as nearly as possible level, away to the north-west, with the distant prospect of the Kilpatrick Hills as an apparent goal. On either side of the road was wood and farmland, dotted with small industrial establishments, which were more numerous as one neared the city. Much of the ground opened up by the new road was eminently suitable for house-building, and for that reason the Kelvinside and Gartnavel estates were purchased by a partnership consisting of two Glasgow solicitors and one of their clients, inventor of the hot blast process for iron smelting, James Beaumont Neilson. They had a plan prepared by Decimus Burton, the most eminent English suburban planner of his day, which showed crescents and terraces lining Great Western Road, and detached houses behind, echoing the plan for the nearby Partickhill estate.
   In the event the pattern of development differed markedly from that at first envisaged. The first of the partnership's rather grander terraces, now Kirklee Terrace (designed by Charles Wilson), was in fact not commercially successful, and had to be built in two stages (1845 and *c.* 1860). The need to attract high-class custom to the new estate led the promoters to seek architectural novelty. Kirklee Terrace broke from the basic Georgian style of the period, incorporating projecting porches to each house. Kew Terrace, the next to be built (1849, J. T. Rochead), reverted to a more recognisably Georgian style, but the same architect's Grosvenor Terrace (1855) adopted a highly repetitive Italian style, suppressing the individuality of houses almost completely. Belhaven Terrace, the first part of which was built between 1866 and 1869, was in a solidly comfortable style. Designed by James Thomson, it was a prototype for other, mainly more modest, terraces throughout the West End. At the very end of the first phase, however, the high class again triumphed, with the building of Great Western Terrace (Figure 5) by Alexander Thomson in his distinctive Greek revival style. This was followed

Fig. 5   Great Western Terrace, designed by Alexander 'Greek' Thomson, as it was in the 1930's.

by the idiosyncratic Lancaster Terrace (1875–76) on a more modest scale, with odd details.

Further terrace building followed only from the 1890's. Development along the south side of Great Western Road was continued by the building of Devonshire Gardens and Devonshire Terrace, facing the grand villas built from the 1870's on the north side of the road. Devonshire Gardens was constructed in a sort of French style, and set new standards of luxury. Early residents included Sir William Burrell, accumulator of the Burrell Collection, and the Chairman of the Caledonian Railway, Sir James Thompson. Elegance had, however, gone. On the north side, the death of Sir William Mirrlees freed his Kirklee estate for building. Up to then he had retained it as grounds for his magnificent villa, Redlands, built in 1860. Lancaster Crescent, the only crescent in Great Western Road, was built in the late 1890's. Unlike its predecessors, individual houses, though externally similar, were indeed designed by different architects, James Millar and J. L. Cowan. Patrons included shipbuilders and shipowners. Last of the Great Western Road terraces was Lowther Terrace (*c.* 1904), by James Miller and A. G. Sydney Mitchell, where individuality was carried much further, variety of roofline and building style being varied in a manner undoubtedly influenced by contemporary London thinking. Nonetheless this is a most attractive block, and it is most unfortunate that the building boom of the 1900's collapsed before it could be extended, as was obviously intended.

The end of terrace building marked the end of an era in the West End. The First World War and the ensuing Depression destroyed the way of life that had evolved in the area. When new middle-class houses were built, at Kelvin Court in the late 1930's, they were service flats in 'modern movement' brick blocks. The houses that were built before 1914 do, however, illustrate the problems encountered in developing a large estate for upper- and middle-class residents. At no time were large numbers of houses under construction, and terraces were being built for about sixty years. Only a few blocks attracted the highest class of occupants, other wealthy men preferring detached or semi-detached villas in the area, or on the South Side, generally of much lower architectural quality. Elegance, which reached its apogee in Great Western Terrace, thereafter was of less consequence than what one might call fashionable comfort. Colouring all this, however, was a recognition that, with the temporary exception of the Park area, developed in the 1850's and 1860's, Great Western Road did offer the finest residences in the city. The survival of these terraces in substantially unaltered condition has given Glasgow an outstanding heritage, protected both by listing of individual terraces and by Conservation Area status.

Conclusion

Lastly, three observations about Strathclyde's heritage. One is its richness and variety, existing in much greater depth than might be suspected, which is dependent on interrelationships as much as on the quality of individual elements: the sum is greater than the parts.

The second is that one cannot preserve the heritage without altering it, and that the more the heritage is used the more altered it will be. The challenge facing those in charge of its management is to balance the necessity for alteration with the costs of and benefits accruing from such change. The compromises thus achieved will often be uneasy and require considerable thought, but they are worth making, and making at high level. For the consequences of not making the right decisions are with us for a long time, if not for ever.

Finally, the criticism is often made that concern for the heritage is elitist, that expenditure on it is pandering to the tastes of a few. I believe that this is fundamentally misleading, and that awareness of the significance of the physical residue of the past is essential to the psychological and indeed the spiritual health of the people of any country. Some of the value of the heritage is obvious: a beautiful building; a romantic ruin; fragments of the long-distant past. What is less obvious, and what should be part of the education of every person, is an understanding both of the nature of beauty and of fitness; if you like, a morality of aesthetics, with some level of historical awareness in which the present and the probable future are seen as products of past decision taking, and in which *understanding* precedes criticism. Only then will we make sound judgements about what to keep, and what to let go, and indeed how to build to ensure that our successors can value what we did.

THE HERITAGE

(c) Scottish Men of Technology and Invention

W. W. Fletcher

Invention and the progress of technology belong to no one nation. Like science, they are international in character and it is difficult to predict in what country and under what circumstances the next major developments will take place. Without being chauvinistic, however, it appears that Scotland, particularly in the last two hundred years, has had more than her fair share of inventive genius. The developments that stemmed from discoveries by Scots reverberated round the world, changing the lot of mankind (though not nearly enough of mankind) in so many fundamental ways.

During Professor John Anderson's time at Glasgow University (see Crawford), *James Watt* (1736–1819), a Greenock man aged twenty-one, set up shop as an instrument maker in the University after having spent an apprenticeship in London. It was Anderson who gave him a Newcomen engine to repair and it was the theory of latent heat, as expounded by James Black, a professor in the University, that led him to the idea of the separate condenser. The story of how the idea came to Watt as he walked one Sunday morning in Glasgow Green in the spring of 1765 is well known. Today there is a memorial stone to mark the place.

When James Watt moved to Birmingham to join up with Matthew Boulton, the great industrialist, the partnership thrived. A perfectly fitting piston and cylinder was made. Watt's engine was at first used to pump water from the lead mines of Cornwall (indeed it is said that this is the only thing that prevented their closure), but soon orders were coming in from all over the world and the steam engine was being used to drive machinery in cotton and grain mills (replacing water power), to roll out and hammer iron, to coin money, to stamp metal and to mine coal. Britain roared ahead in a cloud of steam into the Industrial Revolution, powered by Watt's steam engine and fuelled by the coalfields of Durham, Yorkshire, South Wales, Ayrshire and Lanarkshire.

Watt was soon to be joined by another Scot, *William Murdoch* (1754–1839), who was born at Bello Mill in the parish of Auchinleck, where for generations the Murdochs had been prosperous millers. William spent much of his early life at the mill and developed high mechanical skills in wood-working, engineering and stonemasonry. In view of later developments, it is of interest to note that he experimented with the production of gas from cannel coal and lit up a little cave near the mill. In the Scotland of his day, however, there was little opportunity for young men of ability and at the age of twenty-four he followed Watt to Boulton's works in Birmingham. Possibly he had an introduction from James Boswell who owned the estates on which William's father worked. Anyhow, after a short interview, Boulton employed him and sent him to take charge of the pumping engines at the tin mines in Cornwall. It was during this period that, in face of opposition from Watt, Murdoch (who changed his name to Murdock because the English could not pronounce it properly) started experimenting with the production of gas by the dry distillation of coal. He lit up his own house and offices at Redruth in Cornwall in 1792, the first practical application recorded to coal-gas lighting, sending the gas along some seventy feet of pipes. Later, in celebration of the short-lived Peace of Amiens in 1802, he lit up the front of the Soho Works in Birmingham. Other large firms in other cities soon followed suit and adopted gas lighting.

On the water, Scots were using modifications of Watt's engine to create steam boats. The first man to apply steam power to them was *William Symington* (1763–1831), who was born at Leadhills in Lanarkshire where his father was an engineman employed in superintending one of Boulton and Watt's pumping engines in the Wanlockhead lead mines. When in his teens, William constructed a model of a steam road carriage which operated by a chain and ratchet system. This so impressed the manager of the mines, Gilbert Meason, that he invited William to his Edinburgh home to demonstrate his model to a group of businessmen and Edinburgh professors. The roads in Britain were, however, so poor that Symington did not develop his idea of a roadcarriage, but among those who viewed the model in Edinburgh was *Patrick Miller* of Dalswinton, a wealthy banker, merchant and landowner, who had been carrying out experiments on Dalswinton Loch, Dumfriesshire, propelling boats by means of hand-operated paddles. Acting on a suggestion by *James Taylor*, a tutor to his family, that he should substitute steam power for manual power, Miller employed Symington to design an engine for this purpose, and in October 1788 the world's first steam boat chugged along Dalswinton Loch at five miles an hour. Unfortunately Miller, on the advice of Watt, subsequently lost interest and the invention lay dormant for ten years. Then Lord Dundas, Governor of the Forth and Clyde Canal, persuaded Symington to fit out a new barge, the 'Charlotte Dundas', with a steam engine. It was an immediate success. Dundas was so delighted that he introduced Symington to Lord Bridgewater, the great canal proprietor, who ordered six boats of the same construction. Unfortunately the proprietors of the Forth and Clyde Canal were less enthusiastic; they were concerned lest the banks of the canal would be eroded by the wash from the barges and they prohibited all further experiments. To add to Symington's misfortune, Lord Bridgewater died and his order was cancelled. Symington drifted, a disillusioned man, to London where he died in March 1831.

Among the visitors who inspected the 'Charlotte Dundas' was Robert Fulton, an American artist, who got an engine from Boulton and Watt and launched his vessel 'Clermont' on the Hudson river in 1807. Another who knew of Symington's work was *Henry Bell*, born near Linlithgow in 1767, who built and launched his 'Comet' in January 1812, and, driven by a 3 h.p. engine, she plied between Glasgow and Greenock until she was wrecked in 1820.

Communication on land was improving too, due to the work of *John McAdam* (1756–1836). He was born in Ayr, but when his father lost all his money and estates with the collapse of the Ayr Bank in 1772, John, aged only fourteen, left Scotland to join an uncle, William, who had a prosperous mercantile business in New York. Together they later founded the New York Chamber of Commerce — William being president and John treasurer. John married a wealthy young American lady and seemed set to develop his career in the United States. However, in the American War of Independence, John and his wife's family supported the Crown and lost all their possessions. John returned to Ayr where he was appointed Deputy Lieutenant and in this capacity became interested in roads and roadmaking. This interest continued when he moved south to Bristol where he had a post as victualler to the Navy. In 1816 he was invited by the Bristol authorities to take charge of their roads as General Surveyor. Throughout the country the roads were in an appalling condition. McAdam changed all that. He believed that roads should be entirely composed of stone to a thickness of about ten inches, no stone exceeding six ounces in weight. Under pressure of the traffic the sharp angles of the stones unite into a compact mass entirely impervious to water. Roads should be laid as flat as possible with just enough rise in the centre to allow rain to run off it into ditches on either side. He did not believe that the weight of the vehicle mattered — indeed the heavier the vehicle the better it would compact the stones and the more solid the road would be. The size of the stones, preferably of granite, was critical for good compacting, so he issued a two-inch ring for measuring the stones and a six-ounce scale for weighing them. He forbade the use of earth, clay or chalk (all materials which had been extensively used before) in road construction because they would absorb water.

The news of the great success that McAdam had with this system soon spread through the country and his advice was much sought. His three sons moved south to help him. The McAdams, together with Thomas Telford (1757–1834), the famous civil engineer, who was responsible for over 1,000 miles and 120 bridges throughout Scotland, transformed the road network of Britain.

The highways of the world were being opened up, but travel was laborious and painful, for all sorts of vehicles were fitted with solid wood or metal wheels.

John Boyd Dunlop (1840–1921), born in Dreghorn in Ayrshire, had become a veterinary surgeon and was settled in a lucrative practice in Belfast. When he was forty-seven years of age he began to experiment with air tubes to reduce shock from the wheels of his nine-year-old son's tricycle and in so doing he re-invented the pneumatic tyre. Unknown to Dunlop, *R. W. Thomson* of Stonehaven had invented such a tyre in 1846, but it had not been developed. Dunlop, the man who made the motor-car and aircraft industries possible, got little profit from his invention. Angry at the use of his photograph to promote sales by the company which had been formed, he sold the patent rights and retired to Dublin where he lived for many years with no business interests beyond a drapers shop.

Dunlop, of course, was not the first to use rubber for commercial purposes and his invention was possible only because of the work of his forerunner *Charles Mackintosh* (1766–1843) who was an industrial chemist in Glasgow. Mackintosh's waterproofing of materials using rubber established a number of major industries.

Noting that Dr. James Syme, Professor of Surgery at Edinburgh University, had found that naphtha would act as a solvent, Mackintosh dissolved the rubber and using it as a glue he stuck two pieces of cloth together and so the waterproof or mackintosh was born. He took out a patent for the process, established factories in Glasgow and Manchester (where, by the way, one of his partners was Thomas Hancock, a pioneer in the vulcanisation of rubber) turning out coats, capes, inflatable goods, cushions, pillows and beds.

By this time Anderson's University was well established and at the age of twenty-five, *Thomas Graham* (1805–69), a native of Glasgow and educated at Edinburgh University, was appointed the first Professor of Chemistry. Graham's Laws of diffusion and the coining of the terms crystalloid, colloid and dialysis paved the way for the much later introduction of the artificial kidney.

A man of nineteen, the son of a carpenter in the Drygate near Glasgow Cathedral, attended Graham's evening classes and Graham was so impressed with this young man, who had had little formal education, that within two years he appointed him his assistant. This was *James Young* (1811–83). When Graham was appointed Professor at University College, London, he took Young with him and it was while he was in the south that Young's attention was drawn by a former fellow student, *Lyon Playfair*, now Professor of Mines, to a spring of oil on the estate of his brother-in-law at Alfreton, Derbyshire. This was the world's first oil well and it yielded about three gallons a day. Young leased the well, produced the lubricants for Manchester cotton mills and made wax candles from a fraction of the oil. When the spring ran dry, he looked around for other sources and had his attention drawn by another former fellow student, *Hugh Bartholomew*, manager of the Glasgow Gas Works, to the oil shale being used by the people of Armadale and Bathgate in east central Scotland to light their homes. Young, after inspecting the area, bought up much of the surrounding land, formed a company and began mining the oil shale. Within a short time the company was producing lubricants, naphtha, paraffin oil and solid paraffin from the shale. Many other companies operated under licence, not only in Scotland, but also overseas. At the height of activity, 120 works in the Bathgate area were employing 40,000 people and turning over three and a quarter million tons of shale. The discovery of oil in the U.S.A. and the development of the great Drake Oil Well in Pennsylvania cast a shadow over the industry. By 1873 the number of plants was down to thirty and by 1905 to thirteen. The last of the shale mines was closed in 1962. Young retired from active affairs in 1870. In passing, it is of interest to note that another graduate of the Andersonian University remained a lifelong friend. This was *David Livingstone*, the missionary and explorer, and Young helped to finance many of his journeys to Africa and sustained Livingstone's family in this country.

Perhaps we can claim *William Thomson* (1824–1907) as a Scot, or at least share him with our Irish cousins. Later Lord Kelvin, he was born in Belfast, but there is a family tradition of 'Covenanting forebears who were rabbled out of Ayrshire by the Dragoons of Claverhouse in the Seventeenth Century'. William's grandfather, his father and William himself all married Glasgow women and he had many relatives in the Glasgow area. His father was Professor of Mathematics at Glasgow University and William was appointed to the Chair of Natural Philosophy at the age of twenty-two after having studied at Glasgow and Cambridge. Despite many attempts to lure him away from Glasgow (it is said at least three by Cambridge), he remained in the Chair for the next fifty-three years. He was, of course, one of the greatest scientists of any age, but pertinent to this account is that, in the face of many difficulties, he was responsible for the laying of the first telegraphic transatlantic cable in 1866 (for which he was knighted).

It was another Scot who invented the telephone — *Alexander Graham Bell* (1847–1922). Born in Edinburgh, he was taken by his father and mother at the age of twenty-one to live in the 'pure air' of Canada. The Bells had already lost two sons due to ill-health and they feared for the life of their third and last. It was in the United States that Alexander met his wife, Mabel Hubbard, who had been stone deaf from birth. In attempting to develop a hearing aid for her, he invented the telephone by converting sound vibrations from the human voice into varying electrical currents. These were conveyed along an electric wire and reconstituted the original sounds by means of the current affecting a magnet and vibrating a diaphragm. He fitted a transmitter in the attic of his home and a receiver in the room downstairs. His words through the telephone to his assistant have become famous, 'Mr. Watson, please come here, I want you'. One minute later Watson was bounding up the stairs; 'I could hear you, I could hear you!' he cried. Bell was not a businessman, but his future father-in-law was; the invention was patented. By 1878 the telephone was becoming well established in the United States. In New Jersey a switchboard had been set up for one hundred subscribers, so that fires and burglaries could be made known immediately. This was the first telephone exchange in the world. Telephones were soon found in every civilised country in the world.

Following the transmission of sound came the transmission of pictures. *John Logie Baird* (1888–1946) was born in Helensburgh on the Firth of Clyde. He was a fellow student at the Royal Technical College in Glasgow (now Strathclyde University) of John Reith (later to become Lord Reith, the first Director General of the BBC), although they saw little of each other and probably had little in common. From his early days he had a very inventive turn of mind. The idea of television came to him while walking on the cliffs near Hastings and, with the aid of a tea chest, an old hat-box, a lens, darning needles, sealing wax, glue, batteries and transformers, he transmitted the shadow of a cardboard cross two feet across the room. On Friday, 27th January 1926, he demonstrated his invention to forty scientists at the Royal Institution. Immediately there was a flood of interest. In the same year the BBC carried out some experimental transmissions by telephone line from Baird's attic laboratory in Frith Street to the BBC studio and back again to Frith Street. In the meantime Baird, using infrared light, was able to transmit pictures of people sitting in total darkness. This he named 'Noctavision'.

In 1927, using a disc with three spirals of holes, one covered with a red filter, one with a blue and one with a green, he demonstrated colour television to the British Association for the Advancement of Science meeting in Glasgow University. He was also experimenting with and demonstrating stereoscopic television. In 1928, using a short-wave transmitter, he sent a television picture to the U.S.A. and to a ship, the *Berengaria*, in mid-Atlantic. In the same year 'Baird International Television' was set up with a capital of £1 million to exploit television commercially. Following a 'secret' test in 1928 (in which Jack Buchanan — another Helensburgh man — took part), the BBC carried out its first experimental transmission in 1929, when about thirty people in the United Kingdom had receivers — bought from Baird Television. At this time it was difficult to get vision and sound in phase, but this was achieved in 1930. In the meantime Baird had been experimenting with 'big-screen' TV and the first show was put on in the London Colosseum using a screen five feet by two feet made up of 2,100 ordinary filament electric bulbs fronted by a sheet of ground glass. It was a great success. A year later in 1931, Baird televised the Derby — he was now at the height of his fame. In 1932 the Gaumont British Company with its vast resources acquired a controlling interest in the company, and Baird looked set for complete success. But other companies, in particular Marconi-EMI (which had behind it the huge resources of the Radio Corporation of America and the Telefunken Company of Germany), were active in the television market. They had developed a 405 cathode ray scanning system that was said to be superior to Baird's 204 line mechanical system. In 1937, on the recommendation of a Parliamentary Committee, the BBC opted for the Marconi system. This was a bitter blow to Baird and although he attempted a recovery with big-screen television in cinemas, his company was dealt a death blow when war broke out in 1939 and television was closed down for the duration.

The advent of war, however, brought about the development of a new method of communication — radar. *Robert Watson Watt* (1902–73) from Brechin, Angus, who was educated at University College, Dundee (now the University of Dundee) and later became Principal of Edinburgh University, with his invention of radar created what have been termed the 'roadways of the air'. On 26th February 1935 in a field ten miles from Daventry, Watson Watt demonstrated to Air Ministry officials that if aircraft flew through a wireless beam they reflected it strongly. The echo could be picked up on earth and the aircraft could be located. Thus was radio-location (or radar, as it was officially named in 1943) born. By March 1939, a continuous chain of stations round the British coasts was ready for action. Radar also guided airborne invasion troops on D-day, and made the first bomber raid on Cologne possible. Without radar it is questionable if the Allies could have won the war. Without an invention by *Lady Curran* (wife of the first Principal of Strathclyde University), Britain could possibly have lost it. It was she who devised a system of scattering tin-foil — 'operation window' — in the pathway of intruding German bombers, thus disrupting their radar guiding system, so making it impossible for them to locate their exact bombing target. Radar has also, of course, many peacetime applications — civil aviation, radar astronomy and others.

CHAPTER THIRTEEN

PRIMARY, SECONDARY, HIGHER AND FURTHER EDUCATION

This section consists of four contributions. Dr. Bone outlines the structure of, and recent developments in, primary and secondary education in Scotland, whilst Mr. Louden presents a detailed account of secondary education in Strathclyde Region. Sir Henry Wood surveys higher education and introduces the section on further education by Mr. Dougherty, a lecturer at Stow College.

PRIMARY AND SECONDARY EDUCATION

T. R. Bone

Introduction
In almost every industrialised country in the world, education at school level has been suffering since about 1975 from a variety of constraints and pressures of a fairly similar kind. Such developments as have occurred in Scotland, and there have been some that are potentially significant, have had to be achieved against this background.

The most obvious constraint has been an economic one, since the U.K. Government, like its counterparts in many other countries, has been forced to look very hard at spending on education when the costs of other social services were rising steeply, and education in first primary and then secondary schools has been an obvious target for reductions in expenditure because of the falling school rolls which came in the second half of the 1970's and which will continue throughout the 1980's. As a consequence the local authorities, of which Strathclyde is by far the largest, have been forced to prune their education budgets year after year, and the task of their administrators in preserving the quality of their service has not been an easy one.

As has been the case in other countries too, economic changes have been accompanied by, and have themselves given rise to, some loss of confidence in education, since the perhaps extravagant hopes of the 1960's have not been realised, and since widespread unemployment has cruelly mocked the

227

aspirations of youngsters to achieve good jobs through the acquisition of school qualifications. The existence of such feelings, no stronger in Scotland than they have been in England or in parts of North America, has naturally reinforced the realisation of central government politicians that education could not be held exempt from economic restraint.

Inevitably, too, there have been some signs of demand for greater accountability from the professionals, and the Conservative Government of recent years has enacted legislation, usually against the wishes of the predominantly Labour Scottish Authorities, that has given parents greater powers in choosing the schools that their children should attend, with results that have in some areas exacerbated the effect of falling rolls, so that numbers have kept up, relatively speaking, in schools with good reputations, and have fallen more severely than would have otherwise been the case in schools not favoured by parents. Schools have been required to make available prospectuses of information about themselves, with examination results, and in 1983–84 the Inspectorate began to publish reports on individual schools.

Associated with the factors referred to above, there has been a fairly strong reassertion of central government influence on the curriculum, seen as in other countries in a pressure towards a greater measure of science teaching for all, some support for technology rather than technical subjects of the old kind, and for the introduction of micro-electronics, but the process has gone further here because the Scottish Education Department and its Inspectorate could operate through existing agencies of central control. As in other countries too, like Western Canada for example, there has been some reaction from the teachers and their unions, conscious of increased pressure from outside and resentful of inadequate rewards for their work. As will be seen later in this chapter, that has resulted in their using curriculum development and changing teaching methods as bargaining factors in salary negotiations, since their previously strongest argument, the shortage of teachers, has been almost completely eroded by the decline in pupil numbers.

The falling school rolls have had some good effects, in that the shortage of teachers has now almost disappeared, even in secondary subjects like mathematics and physics, and school staffing has a stability which it has not had for thirty years, and which assists the introduction of the changes which this chapter will describe. Nevertheless the stability of staffing is a mixed blessing, since the consequences for the recruitment of young teachers have been severe, with many failing to obtain posts at all, and with others spending quite lengthy periods in temporary appointments before eventually finding a permanent place. Indeed there are fears that the age structure of the teaching profession in Scotland is going to be seriously distorted by the 1990's, but it will take time to show whether that actually proves to be the case. What is certain at present is that schools are receiving relatively little new blood in the form of newly trained teachers, and therefore there is an increased requirement for in-service training and refreshment for existing staff who are finding new skills demanded of them.

Yet if in all these ways life has been difficult in the schools, Scottish education has been far from stagnating in this period, and indeed some of the most exciting changes to take place this century will occur in the secondary schools in the 1980's. Primary education, as will be shown below, has seen less development, partly because expansion across a wide front is not easy in a time of restraint, and the priority has been on secondary education, but even there some useful things have been happening, such as the raising of the qualifications of the teaching force. Educational changes tend to go in waves, and in Scotland the pattern has been similar, if not exactly the same, to that in England, where, if one takes the publication of official reports as a measure, the emphasis in the late 1960's was on the primary school, in the early 1970's on teacher training, in the mid-1970's on secondary work, and in the early 1980's on the sixteen to eighteen age range. But the pace of change has to be much less leisurely now than it once was, and while 1985 sees the implementation of the plans for the fourteens to sixteens that were originally made in the late 1970's, it also sees the implementation of plans for the sixteens to eighteens which were only made two years ago.

Developments in the Primary Schools

The reduction in the pupil numbers in Scottish primary schools has of course been dramatic in this period, falling from a peak of 621,000 in 1975 to 448,010 in 1983, and inevitably the pattern of decline has been an uneven one, with the most severe drops occurring in the inner city areas such as Glasgow, and with a greater reduction in Roman Catholic schools than in others, as Catholic families have become smaller. In Strathclyde for example the primary numbers fell from 313,700 in 1975 to 208,900 in 1983, and in Glasgow from 102,600 in 1975 to 57,100 in 1983. Quite remarkably, one might think, there have been very few closures of primary schools, since, as is everywhere the case, there is strong community opposition to such a step and local politicians strive to avoid it. The Conservative Government, however, closed two and merged a further two of Scotland's ten colleges of education, relating this mainly to the need for fewer primary teachers.

There has been no national report covering the whole range of primary education since 1965, but there was one report produced by the Inspectorate in 1980, concerned with 'Learning and Teaching in Primary 4 and Primary 7'. This was fairly critical in a number of ways, finding that the basic subjects were taught reasonably well, but that very little Science was taught at all, and that little satisfaction could be taken from existing practice in Art, Music and Physical Education, these being seen as 'marginal activities' which received inadequate attention. There was also a disappointment that Primary 7 (age range eleven to twelve) offered children an experience which was little different in its form from that of Primary 4, with insufficient advantage being taken for the greater maturity of the pupils and their capacity for self-directed learning.

In an attempt to remedy some of the deficiencies the Consultative Committee on the Curriculum's Committee on Primary Education has produced documents on 'A Policy for Science in Scottish Primary Schools' and 'Expressive Arts in the Primary School' as well as others on such areas as 'School, Home, Community Relationships', and there are signs that some of these are bearing fruit. The Primary Committee also produced a position paper, 'Primary Education in the Eighties', in the autumn of 1983, but this was generally thought to say little that was new, and its impact has thus far been small. Perhaps it is fair to say that the time is now ripe for some major new initiative in the primary field in Scotland, if only it could be given national priority.

The most hopeful development, however, was the decision of the Secretary of State to take advantage of the improved staffing position to raise the qualifications for entry to teaching in primary schools. The three-year diploma course, which had been the main route to primary teaching since the 1930's, will provide no more teachers after 1986, and was replaced in 1984 by a new four-year degree course of a more rigorous and professionally satisfying kind. The step was overdue, in that Scotland, which had once led the world in teacher education, had fallen behind many other countries, including its southern neighbour, in not making a degree a requirement for primary teachers, but the new course, which is taught in the colleges of education and validated either by neighbouring universities or by the CNAA, will provide teachers better equipped to meet the more demanding circumstances of the mid-1980's and the period beyond.

Developments in the Secondary Schools

It is when one turns to secondary education that one finds developments occurring which are of a rather special and noteworthy kind, since the whole face of Scottish secondary schools is changing in the mid-1980's. Indeed Scotland has moved further and faster than England certainly, and many other countries probably, because of three factors: the homogeneous nature of the system, the directing power of the Scottish Education Department, and the occurrence of a national plan just at the time when falling rolls and improved staffing made it possible to implement it.

The system of secondary education in Scotland is remarkably homogeneous in nature, with a small and relatively insignificant private sector and the rest of the schools being basically of a comprehensive kind, and with all these schools working for the one set of examinations, controlled by the one Scottish Examination Board. Moreover, although the Regional Authorities are strong, and they, the teaching profession and the higher educational institutions expect to participate in national decision-making, there is in Scotland a tradition of decisions coming from centralised bodies, such as the Examination Board or the Consultative Committee on the Curriculum.

The planning began in 1975, when the Government set up two committees (known as the Munn and Dunning Committees after the names of their chairmen) which, working very closely together, produced parallel reports on the ways in which the curriculum for pupils aged fourteen to sixteen might be changed, and recommended that there should be a system of national assessment for all pupils at age sixteen, with a certificate indicating the level of performance achieved at the end of the period of compulsory schooling. These reports were the subject of national discussion on an almost unprecedented scale, and won very widespread acceptance, even though at the time of their publication in 1977 there were still severe teacher shortages in many secondary schools which made implementation look very difficult. The Labour Government asked the Scottish Education Department to conduct feasibility studies, and its Conservative successor set up a development programme in 1980 which allowed the SED to draw in support from other agencies like the Examination Board and the Consultative Committee on the Curriculum, while keeping fairly tight control on the process itself. Gradually the staffing situation was easing, and by September 1982 the Government was able to make proposals for implementation which secured general support. In April 1983 a firm decision had finally been taken to go ahead, and by this time there was a very strong basis of evidence as to what the new syllabuses would be like in the subjects where the programme was starting, and of the shape that the assessment might take. After a fairly thorough process of piloting the courses and assessment instruments, it was possible for the first fourteen-year-old pupils to enter the new courses in August 1984, and they should receive their certificates in the summer of 1986.

The changes involve significant differences in the assessment process in all Scottish schools. Hitherto, as has been the case in many countries, only the more able pupils received certificates, and a large percentage of pupils at the bottom of the ability range (at least as high as 30 per cent and often more) not only went through compulsory schooling without anything to show for what had been achieved, but also were in many ways neglected in comparison with their abler brethren, quite often receiving an education, if it could be called that, which was unbalanced in terms of subject range and lacking in purpose in the way it was taught. Thanks to the Munn Curriculum as developed by the Consultative Committee, all pupils, across the whole ability range, are now receiving a much better balanced curriculum in these two years of secondary schooling, and thanks to the Dunning Report, as developed by the Examination Board and Joint Working Parties set up by the SED, they are all following courses leading to national examinations (standard grade) geared to the level of work which they can be reasonably expected to achieve. There are three broad bands of assessment, at Credit, General and Foundation Levels, but these are overlapped in such a way that credit and general pupils for example, or general and foundation pupils, can be taught together and sit the same examinations, receiving different grades of award in relation to criteria established in advance by the JWPs and accepted by the Examination Board. Four standard grade subjects (English, Mathematics, Science and Social and

Vocational Skills) were introduced in 1984, seven more should follow in 1985, and the remaining fifteen are planned to come on stream in 1986.

The programme makes major new demands on the skills of teachers, particularly in respect of the grade-related criteria, but also in motivating the less able pupils through a more experiential style of learning. An important programme of in-service training, involving the SED, the Local Authorities and the Colleges of Education, was therefore planned. Unfortunately both this and curriculum development work became the target for opposition by the teachers' unions in the winter of 1984–85, since they saw their members being required to undertake new and difficult tasks while being given salary increases which were constantly less than the rate of inflation. A boycott of in-service and curriculum development connected with the fourteen to sixteen and sixteen to eighteen programmes was imposed in the hope of winning Government agreement to an independent salary review, and at the time of writing this chapter no decision had been reached on that. As a result it came to be possible that the implementation of the Munn/Dunning reforms might be quite seriously damaged.

One can only hope that this will not happen or that, if there is a slowing up in the programme, the loss will be purely temporary. An enormous amount of work has been done, and the reforms are capable of bringing about greatly needed improvements. Teachers will have to work hard, but there was every sign that they were ready to do so, and even enthusiastic for the changes, so that they themselves will not wish to postpone them for too long. Indeed by the time of the British Association meeting the problem may be resolved.

The fourteen to sixteen age range is at the heart of the secondary school, but naturally there also has been a spilling-over of development on either side. The twelve to fourteen age range has been the subject of considerable attention too, especially in the Strathclyde Region where local politicians have given it some priority, although without the stimulus of national examinations there is inevitably more variation in what is being done. The sixteen to eighteen age range would have been affected, regardless of other factors, by the results of the Munn/Dunning programme, since the certificate examinations at higher level could not remain the same once the Credit grade certificates had been introduced, but in fact this area of the secondary school has been completely overtaken by another quite separate development, that of the sixteen to eighteen Action Plan.

Produced by the Scottish Education Department in the summer of 1982, the 'Action Plan' set out to co-ordinate the wide variety of educational opportunities available to young people beyond the compulsory schooling stage, and at the same time to increase the flexibility with which a young person could move from one sector to another. Briefly, the system that existed did not make it easy for a young person to move in mid-session from a school to a further education college and to take with him credit for the work he had done in school, nor did it allow him to have credit for what he might have done in one FE college course if he chose to move to another one since there was a wide variety of courses, all separate, and all leading to different kinds of qualification. The Action Plan suggested the bringing together of some of the further education qualifications, through merging of the two FE certificating bodies, SCOTEC and SCOTBEC (now merged into SCOTVEC), while at the same time it argued that courses should be modularised in order to make transfer from one to another easier, and then the system of modules should be taken a step further to affect work done in schools beyond the age of sixteen, so that it would be possible to move from a school course to a further education college course without the young person concerned having to start again. The Action Plan was widely accepted as being necessary in the changed economic and employment situation facing young people today, and by the spring of 1984 the local authorities had taken steps to organise their secondary schools into local consortia, each consortium being linked to a further education college, with the schools having common timetables beyond the age of sixteen so that efficient use can be made of teachers with viable groups of pupils drawn together from different schools, and so that pupils can spend part of each week in the further education college if they wish. These consortia were also opposed by the teachers in the winter of 1984/85, as part of their salary campaign, but the idea is so obviously sensible that its implementation seems inevitable, even if some concessions have to be made on the details.

It is all very complex, and it is too early yet to say how well it is going to work, but even if this plan has not been as carefully piloted and built up as was the case at fourteen to sixteen, and even with the industrial difficulties, it is beginning to be adopted in ways that affect the secondary schools quite considerably — in terms of organisation, autonomy and opportunities for pupils. The higher examinations at school level have not yet been modularised, and there are understandable arguments about that, with opposition coming chiefly from the universities, but the realisation of the very different employment situation for young people is bringing everyone to agree that some further changes are necessary. The position may be a little clearer by the time of the British Association meeting, but certainly Scottish secondary schools have hardly been dull places in which to work in the 1980's.

Secondary Education in Strathclyde

R. C. Louden

Dr. Bone's contribution on primary and secondary education deals with national initiatives on the curriculum and examination system. The present article considers in detail the impact of these initiatives on secondary education in the Strathclyde Region.

As in most other areas, the education service in Strathclyde has been under severe pressure in recent years. The substantial fall in pupil population which affected primary schools in the 1970's has now moved on to the secondary sector, where school rolls in Strathclyde are predicted to drop from an actual figure of 196,256 in 1982 to 132,592 in 1990. While school closures have not taken place to a degree proportionate to the reduction in school rolls, there have been some closures but perhaps of greater consequence has been the uncertainty engendered in the minds of teachers and head teachers by the knowledge that school staffing levels have to be automatically adjusted downwards in correspondence with falling pupil rolls. This will continue to be a factor for the remainder of the decade, though fortunately it has been partially alleviated because Strathclyde Region has been able to identify staffing as one of its priorities at a time of major curricular development and secondary staffing ratios have been enhanced over the last few years.

The decision by the Regional Council to improve secondary teacher staffing is all the more commendable when seen in the context of the fierce financial difficulties faced by local authorities in recent years. As a result of central government's determination to exercise more rigid control over regional and district council spending, the education service in Strathclyde has had to sustain numerous financial cuts, notably in such fields as educational supplies where in a more favourable economic climate the advent of new curricular developments would have produced a substantial injection of additional resources.

Another factor adding to the problems faced by schools has been the drastic rise in unemployment, which in any event has traditionally run at a higher level in Strathclyde than in most other areas. Faced with bleak prospects of employment even if academically or vocationally well qualified, many youngsters have lacked the motivation to apply themselves to their school studies and teachers have often found it difficult to develop in such pupils a more positive attitude.

Against this depressing background of economic decline and falling rolls, Strathclyde's secondary teaching force has shown itself to be hearteningly resilient. This resilience was for a while tested in some schools by a decision of the Regional Council to abolish corporal punishment as from August 1982 but this led in many staffs to adjustments of teaching methodology and reviews of disciplinary systems which have produced worthwhile results. The various curricular innovations originating from national and regional sources have further increased the pressures on teachers and of course these pressures are still far from abating since neither the implementation programme for Standard grade courses at S3 and S4 (S1, S2, S3 and S4 refer to the years of secondary education with pupils normally entering S1 at the age of twelve after seven years of primary education) nor that for the sixteens to eighteens Action Plan is yet complete. Nevertheless, teachers have generally given a warm welcome to these innovations because of their increased relevance to the entire secondary population and the new motivation they are giving to pupils who otherwise would merely have drifted.

It might be helpful to look at each stage of the secondary school in turn, beginning with S1 and S2 and developments arising from a report of a working party composed of Strathclyde elected members and officers. On coming into being in 1975 the Regional Council moved quickly towards a policy of six-year comprehensives and associated with this was an emphasis on mixed ability teaching, especially at the lower end of the school, which was given full advocacy in the S1/S2 report. Co-operative teaching — involving the need for, say, four teachers to work with three classes to the particular benefit of the children with learning difficulties — was also strongly encouraged. In order to avoid excessive fragmentation of teaching and the exposure of pupils to too many teachers, the restructuring of the timetable to provide teaching periods of not less than an hour was recommended. The importance of primary/secondary liaison was underlined — especially in the curricular context, bearing in mind how disappointingly difficult it has proved over the years to arrange mutual visits by teachers and the dovetailing of curriculum content. These and other recommendations of the S1/S2 report are being — or have been — implemented and the support provided by the education department to this process will be described later in the article.

Turning to S3 and S4, the new Standard grade courses were introduced in certain subjects to all S3 pupils in August 1984 and these pupils are due to receive their certification in the summer of 1986. It was in this area that Strathclyde teachers were faced with the greatest burden of preparation and the greatest need for in-service training for August 1984. There were two main reasons for this. Firstly — especially in schools and departments where group teaching and/or individualised learning had not been introduced — teachers were going to have difficulties in adapting to a situation where pupils in the same class might possibly be following different syllabus levels or might be following the same syllabus but be presented for the Standard grade at different levels. Secondly, many teachers — in particular some of longer service — had not experimented with techniques of continuous assessment and since assessment (whether internal or external) was central to the new S3/S4 developments, schools were quick to identify assessment as an area of major priority for in-service training and to take advantage of any expertise available within or outwith their staffs. The extent to which schools required assistance in these two areas tended to bear a relationship to the amount of course piloting in which they had been involved at an earlier stage and this discrepancy proved to be a problem in itself.

It has long been recognised in Scotland that, while the educational system at S3 and S4 offered little encouragement to the many who could not reasonably aspire to 'O' grades, a parallel problem existed at S5 and S6, where many youngsters either continued unsuccessfully to strive after elusive 'O' grades or else — in the case of S5 Christmas leavers — were for a time prisoners of the system by virtue of their age. The S3/S4 developments have now opened up new horizons for many young people and a similar purpose lies behind the introduction of the sixteens to eighteens Action Plan.

The Action Plan as implemented in Strathclyde represents an attempt to co-ordinate all the course arrangements available to youngsters beyond the compulsory schooling age and as such incorporates all school and non-advanced FE college provision including Scottish Certificate of Education courses and the wide-ranging programme of modular courses for which the Action Plan is best known. The concept behind the modular arrangements is the design of forty-hour short courses or modules, available in many subject areas and vocationally orientated, from which a young person can select those which he wishes to take, either on a horizontal or linear basis, either on their own or in conjunction with SCE or other courses. The system is intended to be so flexible that transfer to other courses or establishments is possible with credit given for work successfully completed.

It can be readily imagined that, coming on top of the S3/S4 innovations, the modules presented another formidable challenge to the Scottish teaching profession. When the Action Plan was published in 1983 it was envisaged that around 600 modules would be designed but by mid-1984 the figure had risen to about 1,200 and has continued to rise since then. While the majority have obvious application to the FE sector, many are nevertheless of interest to schools. At national level course outlines or 'descriptors' were prepared but the detailed work of filling out the content of the modules had to be undertaken by working parties and development officers. Since school session 1983/84 was well under way before the first descriptors were ready for distribution, it would have been unrealistic to expect schools to introduce many modules at the start of session 1984/85. August 1985 will see a wider availability of suitable modules in schools. Because of their vocational bias the modules have important implications for the Youth Training Scheme, funded by the Manpower Services Commission to provide an integrated pre-vocational one-year programme of education, training and workshop experience.

Meanwhile, Higher grade and post-Higher work continues in schools but significant alteration is inevitable because of the impact of the introduction of Standard grade syllabuses (particularly at Credit level). It may well be that the revised Higher arrangements will make provision for some degree of modularisation.

It is perhaps time now to look briefly at the support which the Regional Council in Strathclyde has offered to schools preparing for these major changes. The most significant, and most appreciated, improvement has been in the field of staffing. Additional teachers have been appointed to secondary schools, not only to take account of the curricular innovations at S3 and S4, but also to encourage the development of co-operative teaching at S1 and S2 and to provide teachers with more time free of class commitments in which to prepare themselves for the introduction of new courses.

Turning specifically to the S1/S2 stage, where the member/officer report stressed the need for improved primary/secondary liaison, advisers have been given a remit to ensure that proper account is taken of curricular linkage with the associated primaries when they are discussing methodology and course content with teachers. Emphasis has also been placed on the need to assist teachers to acquire skills in assessment and school representatives have been invited to courses where they have been introduced to the various approaches to assessment considered most appropriate for pupils at this stage of their secondary schooling.

However, it was in relation to S5 and S6 that Strathclyde found it necessary to take the most urgent supportive measures because of the comparatively short gap between the announcement of the SED's sixteens to eighteens Action Plan and its implementation in August 1984. In relative terms Strathclyde was better placed than most authorities because a member/officer group had produced in 1981 a report whose major recommendations were highly relevant to the strategy outlined in the Action Plan. Even so, it was immediately obvious that some mechanism would have to be established to prepare and co-ordinate local plans and avoid wasteful duplication of provision. To this end, forty-six area curriculum planning groups were set up, each consisting of head teachers of between two and eight of Strathclyde's 191 secondary schools and of special schools, an FE college principal, an education officer, community education and careers officers and regional councillors. These area curriculum planning groups had the difficult task of initiating arrangements which would ensure that pupils had access to SCE courses and sixteen to eighteen modules in schools and FE colleges, with provision also being made where appropriate for youngsters on the Youth Training Scheme. In order to achieve this, linked timetables had to be arranged so that young people could, with as little travelling difficulty as possible, move from their base establishment to another where centralised teaching of a particular course or module was available.

To assist the area curriculum planning groups in their deliberations, working parties were set up which produced useful reports on the following topics — school day patterns and timetabling arrangements, curriculum choice, transport and insurance and attendance arrangements. Armed with these reports and taking advantage of all the expertise available within their membership, the area curriculum planning groups were able to ensure that the Action Plan started in 1984 despite a multiplicity of practical problems.

An interesting initiative taken by the education department to assist teachers to see in their context the many developments occurring almost simultaneously throughout the secondary school was the production of six fifteen-minute video tapes covering such areas as the S1/S2 developments, Standard grade courses and assessment and the Action Plan. As well as explaining the background to the national developments and the initiatives being taken by Strathclyde, the video tapes were designed to stimulate staff discussion and they made a useful contribution to the general preparation of teachers for August 1984.

The measures described above should, of course, be seen as complementary to the specific in-service training programme offered by the education department in anticipation of the new developments. With limited financial resources available, it was important to define priorities for in-service provision and in this context special attention was devoted to these areas — the S3/S4 developments, the sixteens to eighteens Action Plan and the education of pupils with learning difficulties. In developing its in-service programme in these and other areas, Strathclyde has been fortunate to enjoy a close working relationship with the three colleges of education located in the West of Scotland — Jordanhill, St. Andrew's and Craigie — and through a combination of school-based and college-based provision, it has been possible to reach out to large numbers of teachers in a relatively short space of time. This co-operation with the colleges has also led in recent years to the development of major joint courses including school-focused guidance courses and very successful intensive courses for members of the senior management team in secondary schools.

If all these major developments, spanning the entire twelve to eighteen age range, seem to have presented Strathclyde schools with a powerful challenge, the story is not yet ended. Various specific areas of the curriculum have in the last few years been subject to significant innovation — mention will be made here of only two. Firstly, the increasing national emphasis on computer education has been accurately reflected in Strathclyde, where secondary schools now have a wide range of microcomputer equipment, and interest among pupils — and teachers of various disciplines — is intense. Secondly, in the field of religious education, a working group of elected members and officers produced a report which reminded schools of their obligations in this area and is gradually leading to the employment of more RE specialists in schools as they become available. A significant number of promoted posts were created early in 1984 and all schools were asked to designate a member of staff as co-ordinator of religious education. To assist schools three study groups were set up (one each for the primary, secondary and special education sectors) for the purpose of examining existing material and producing guidelines which schools could adapt and supplement for their own use.

While the concentration in all of this has been on providing a satisfying and relevant curriculum for the twelves to eighteens, the concept of continuing education has been assuming greater importance in Strathclyde and adults have been encouraged to participate in our courses in secondary schools. Many adults have taken up this offer and are sharing classes with fifth- and sixth-year pupils. They have negotiated their own timetables and are attending, usually on an agreed part-time basis, to take either SCE or other courses or a combination of the two. They have fitted easily into the existing structure of the schools and it is to be hoped that more and more of them will take advantage of what is seen as an exciting opportunity by those who are already participating.

Finally, associated with all these initiatives is one of the central policies of the Regional Council — its commitment to discriminate positively in favour of its most deprived areas (known as 'areas for priority treatment'). A continuous effort is made to try and compensate for the serious effects of social deprivation by the application of additional resources and professional expertise. Strathclyde suffers more from deprivation — particularly urban deprivation — than any other region north of the border and it is fitting that professionally trained staff in the departments of education (community education officers, careers officers, etc.) and social work should spend a proportionately high percentage of their time working with and for those resident in areas for priority treatment. In the field of secondary education this positive discrimination is most obvious in enhanced levels of teacher staffing and educational supplies but in fact it permeates all aspects of the education department's work and, for example, the professional officers whose function it is to provide curricular support to secondary schools (subject advisers and staff tutors) devote a high degree of attention to those schools which serve areas for priority treatment.

So much has happened in our schools in the last two or three years that the time has come to take stock and to set about establishing a comprehensive curriculum rationale spanning the entire S1–S6 range. This is now being done at national level and its successful completion will add the final touch to an ambitious programme which will have made our secondary schools more relevant to the needs and aspirations of young people in the mid-1980's.

HIGHER EDUCATION

Sir Henry Wood

The basic structure of Higher Education in Scotland, outside the universities, was established in the early years of this century. In 1901 four colleges were designated as 'Central Institutions' — Dundee Technical Institute; Heriot-Watt College, Edinburgh (now a university); Glasgow and West of Scotland Technical College (now Strathclyde University); and the Glasgow School of Art. The Committee of the Council on Education in Scotland considered that these new institutions 'might be regarded as industrial universities' and that from them 'distinct advantage to the industries of the country, in so far as that is dependent on education arrangements' was to be looked for. The continued creation and development of Central Institutions right up to the present day explains why there are no Polytechnics in Scotland. The 1905 Regulations for the Training of Teachers led to the establishment of four provincial Training Centres (now Colleges of Education), one in each of the main cities, governed by Provincial Committees which were in effect Area Training Organisations. The Centres were responsible for all forms of teacher training, for what is now called in-service training and for the official 'recognition' of teachers from furth of Scotland. Thus, in 1905, any direct university responsibility for teacher training was ended. The ancient universities retained education departments whose main work after 1916 was to teach graduate teachers for the degree of B.Ed. (now M.Ed.) and the products of these courses, especially those conducted by Godfrey Thomson in Edinburgh and by William Boyd in Glasgow, played a considerable part in the pre-war development of education in Britain and the Commonwealth. Now, Stirling University is an exception to the general rule — it has seven semester and nine semester courses including education as a main subject which lead to a teaching qualification and from which about fifty students graduate every year.

There are now fourteen Central Institutions, three of them Agricultural Colleges under the Department of Agriculture and Fisheries in the Scottish Office, and the others directly financed by the Scottish Education Department. The colleges are managed by independent boards of governors which include representatives of appropriate educational, professional, industrial and other bodies. Until the 1960's the colleges, essentially monotechnic in nature, conducted many part-time courses, some at a relatively low level, and it has been argued that this retarded the growth of local authority Further Education in areas of concentrated population and good transport. Since Robbins there has been great expansion of the Central Institutions accompanied by much diversification of courses. At the same time the local authority system of Further Education has developed strongly.

In Strathclyde Region the Central Institutions, in order of recognition, are the Glasgow School of Art; the Queen's College, Glasgow; the Royal Scottish Academy of Music and Drama; and Paisley College.

The Glasgow School of Art

The Glasgow School of Art began in 1840 as the Glasgow Government School of Design which was founded to meet the need for trained designers in industry. On its first committee of management was: the Lord Provost, the Dean of Guild, a calico printer, an engineer, a de Laine manufacturer, two shawl manufacturers, an upholsterer, a sewed muslin manufacturer, an engraver, a goldsmith and a sheriff. What modern bureaucrat or advisory council could invent such an appropriate board?

In 1842 it was recognised by the Board of Trade as a School of Design and its official links remained in London when the Board of Trade's functions were transferred in 1852 to the Science and Art Department of South Kensington and even in 1899 when a further transfer took place to the Scotch Education Department, which was an office in Dover House, Whitehall. (The 'Scotch' Education Department did not become 'Scottish' until 1918 and its offices were not totally transferred to Edinburgh until 1939.) Life classes were instituted in 1850. Until 1900 most of the work, including classes for apprentice architects, was done in evening classes or from 7.00 to 9.00 a.m.

The significant developments in the School of Art occurred under two outstanding Directors, Francis Newberry (1885–1918) and Sir Harry Barnes (1964–80). When Newberry came to Glasgow from the Royal Academy, the School of Art suffered not only from a shortage of money but also from the lack of a permanent home. After the Glasgow Exhibition of 1888, the Corporation decided to build an Art Gallery and a School of Art, using the profit of £40,000 as a financial base. In the end the Art Gallery alone was built since it was considered that the presence of an Art School in the same building might lead to disagreements. The Corporation made a grant of £5,000 to the School of Art which Newberry used to start a building fund; this, with aid from various trusts — including the gift of a site above Sauchiehall Street from the Bellahouston Trust — reached £14,000 by 1896. Newberry prepared a schedule of accommodation, described nowadays as 'brilliant' or 'demanding', and instituted a competition for architects. The winning design was by the young Charles Rennie Mackintosh, and, as Newberry was not only his former teacher but also his friend, patron and admirer, there was something of a furore in architectural circles. The first phase of the building was completed in 1899 and the second, which had to wait for lack of money, in the period 1905–09. This remarkable building, which still functions without any major internal change, is possibly better appreciated by visitors from Europe and America than by Mackintosh's own countrymen.

The School became a Central Institution and began to enrol more and more full-time students and to issue its own Diplomas. A course for architects was established in 1903 in co-operation with the Technical College. Newberry did everything possible to improve the standing of the school — he employed teachers from Europe and expected them to continue their own work as well as teaching. He also encouraged his vigorous and talented students to exhibit abroad. His support for the 'craft' movement did not preclude the flowering of painting and sculpture.

The next decisive period of change was from 1964–80 under the guidance of Sir Harry Barnes who spent thirty-six years in the School. After the war the Diploma courses flourished and produced painters, workers in a variety of crafts and teachers, though critics asserted that the School was still operating under the 'Beaux Arts' tradition of fifty years earlier and that not enough attention was being given to Design. Architecture had suffered a set-back since the new University of Strathclyde decided to conduct its own courses without the Art School link.

Barnes set himself the tasks of expanding existing programmes, of developing new fields of activity and of acquiring the physical resources for staff and students in an expanding school. He was also determined to improve the nature of the qualifications awarded so that the standing of the School and of its students abroad should be enhanced.

New buildings were erected near the Mackintosh building — Foulis, Newberry Tower, Bourdon — which provided accommodation for developments in Design, Planning and Architecture. Old buildings of distinction in the vicinity were acquired and transformed to provide both for teaching and student amenities.

Discussions with universities and the C.N.A.A. led to the decision, taken with great reluctance, to replace the standard Scottish Diploma Courses by Degree Courses. The necessary changes in departmental structures and groupings was effected so that four main departments were created: Fine Art Studies (painting, printmaking, sculpture, murals and stained glass, photography); Design Studies (ceramic, graphic, furniture, interior and product design, embroidered and woven textiles, printed textiles, silversmithing and jewellery); Planning; and Architecture. The courses in Fine Art Studies and in Design Studies led to degrees of the C.N.A.A. and those in Planning and in Architecture to degrees of the University of Glasgow.

The School, which is one of the largest in the country, now has over 800 full-time students of whom 500 study Fine Art or Design and 40 are in post-graduate courses. It is a School justifiably proud of its history, proud of its contribution to painting and the arts in Britain and proud of its share in the cultural development of a very art-conscious city.

The Queen's College, Glasgow

The Queen's College acquired the present title from its patron, Queen Elizabeth, at the centenary in 1975. It has been known as the Glasgow and West of Scotland College of Domestic Science since it was recognised as a Central Institution in 1908, when it was created by a forced marriage of the Glasgow School of Cookery and the Western School of Cookery. Until 1975 it was a women's college developed by those who fought for the education of women in Victorian times, many of whom believed that great social benefits would accrue if working-class women could be taught to cook. The two Glasgow schools of cookery were founded by groups of academics, clerics and philanthropists and their wives, with the financial backing of businessmen of all grades. They were developed by two very determined Principals, Grace Paterson and Margaret Black, both of whom found very soon that working-class women did not want evening classes in cookery even when they were free. As a result of this discovery, the Principals concluded that the important thing was to train teachers of cookery. An emphasis on preparing teachers, eventually of housewifery, needlework, millinery and dressmaking as well as of cookery, remained with the college until very recent times. The tradition begun by Miss Paterson and Mrs. Black was maintained and the College was served by a succession of very able, indomitable and far-seeing Principals who, as time went on, introduced courses in dietetics, institutional management and social work. They tried in 1921 and in 1946 to interest the University of Glasgow in degrees in Home Economics and Dietetics, but without success.

The college is now co-educational and, under the present Principal, who has a staff of almost equal numbers of men and women, the work has been organised under four main departments: Applied Life Sciences; Home

Economics and Management Studies; Physiotherapy; Social Sciences and Communications. By now almost half the students are taking C.N.A.A. degree courses. In a recent Report the Principal wrote:

'The 1982–3 academic session began with the first enrolment of undergraduates to the new C.N.A.A. degree programmes in Home Economics and Physiotherapy. The College has now the largest Home Economics and Physiotherapy degree intakes in the United Kingdom and it offers the only three-year physiotherapy degree course. The Queen's College, Glasgow, alone offers the Higher Diploma in Consumer Studies and it has the only Scottish one year post-graduate Social Work Course outside the university sector. The three year Social Work Diploma for mature students with family commitments is also unique in Scotland, whilst the two year post-graduate Diploma in Dietetics is available at only one other United Kingdom polytechnic. A new part-time Home Help Organisers Course offered in collaboration with the Strathclyde Region is the sole course of its kind in Scotland. This uniqueness of the course portfolio offered by the College is a distinguishing feature of a Scottish Central Institution.

Another feature of College courses is diversity. It is no small achievement (for a college of about 800 students and 76 teaching staff) that eleven courses are currently on offer at higher diploma, under-graduate and post-graduate levels. In addition, staff have become increasingly involved in a variety of in-service and post-registration courses and in research in many fields.'

The College also offers a four-year B.Sc. course in Dietetics in collaboration with Paisley College of Technology as well as a great variety of part-time courses.

The Royal Scottish Academy of Music and Drama

The Academy had its origins in the Glasgow Athenaeum, a centre for subscription lectures which was established in 1847, after an inaugural banquet presided over by Charles Dickens, to provide a further education for adults in the fields of commerce, science and the arts. The Athenaeum, which had as many as 2,500 part-time students in its Victorian heyday, moved to the present site of the R.S.A.M.D. in 1888 and gradually the scientific, commercial and fine art functions were transferred elsewhere leaving a school of music which became the National Academy of Music in 1928. Then the link with Glasgow University was established when the office of Principal of the Academy was combined with that of the Professor of Music. The Academy became a Central Institution in 1939 and accepted the new College of Dramatic Art into its orbit in 1951.

Though the combined posts of Principal and Professor lapsed in 1953, the link between the Academy and the University departments of Music and of

Drama has become stronger since the R.S.A.M.D. degree courses are validated by the University. The Academy offers courses for the degree of B.A. in Music and Performance; Music Education; and in Dramatic Studies, as well as Diploma courses for performers and professional actors. There are also advanced fourth-year courses in instrumental music and opera and a special one-year course for students wishing to work backstage in the theatre professionally, leading to the award of a Technical Certificate.

Orchestras and choral societies flourish in the Academy and this type of work is enhanced by Visiting Artists in Residence, at present the Alberni String Quartet, and by Master Classes conducted by distinguished visitors.

The opera course provides comprehensive coaching and instruction both in works from the standard repertoire and also in the more rare or even new works. Classes are held in stage production, movement, fencing, languages and dialogue. A course for repetiteurs is also available and one student each year may be selected for training as a conductor. Performances are given of operatic excerpts under workshop conditions and of productions of complete operas fully staged with orchestra and with all the necessary technical backing provided by the staff and students of the School of Drama. The emergence of Scottish Opera has stimulated every aspect of the work of the Academy which in its turn has contributed to the burgeoning of Music and Drama in Scotland in recent years.

At present the Academy has 250 students in the School of Music and 130 in the School of Drama. In 1964 the Scottish Education Department promised support for a new building to house 470 students. After years of frustration the problems have been resolved and on 27th September 1984, Dame Janet Baker, the President of the Academy, laid the foundation stone for the new building. In a foreword to a booklet about the new building, the enthusiastic and justly proud Principal wrote:

'It is both exciting and appropriate that the Scottish Education Department has decided to endow the Royal Scottish Academy of Music and Drama with an entirely new purpose-built building. Having occupied its present site since 1888, the Academy fostered the growth of the arts in Scotland throughout its distinguished history. The RSAMD fully deserves the special position that it enjoys as one of the four Royal Schools of Music in the United Kingdom. In Drama the role of the Academy in Scotland is comparable with the Royal Academy of Dramatic Art in England.

We shall be sited close to the Theatre Royal, the home of Scottish Opera, with whom we have common ideals and, more practically, a most fruitful working relationship. Glasgow's resident symphony orchestra, the Scottish National Orchestra, has an international reputation and this is shared by the Scottish Chamber Orchestra, the Scottish Baroque Ensemble and the BBC Scottish Symphony Orchestra. Productions at the Citizens' Theatre and at the Tron Theatre are of the highest standard. In

1983 the Burrell Collection was given a magnificent home in Glasgow and this has added greatly to the already considerable artistic riches of the City. Glasgow has a wealth of fine Victorian architecture and several splendid Art collections.

Now, too, the RSAMD will have a first class building, exceptionally well designed and equipped where students of music and drama will be taught to achieve the highest standards.

A rare moment, then, in the history of the RSAMD but one that we believe, will prove to be of immeasurable importance to the cultural life of Scotland.'

Paisley College of Technology

Paisley College became a Central Institution in 1950. For over fifty years previously it had been an independent and traditional technical college which survived with the aid of benefactors and the vigorous support of local industry and commerce. Though it presented students for the external degrees of the University of London, the main thrust of its work was vocational and locally directed.

The greatest development and expansion came in the 1960's when Edwin Kerr, now the Chief Officer of the C.N.N.A., was Principal of the college. The college is now organised in three 'schools' — Engineering; Science; Social Planning and Management — which prepare the students mainly but not entirely for C.N.N.A. degrees. The heads of departments in Science and Engineering, as well as in Economics, Politics and Society, and Management, are all designated as Professors.

Apart from its full-time degree courses, many of the 'sandwich' type, the college provides specialised M.Sc. courses in fields like Analytical Chemistry and Pressure Vessel Design, together with a variety of courses leading to 'graduateship' of the Institute of Physics, the Institute of Biology and the Royal Society of Chemistry.

The present Principal has stressed and expanded the industrial bias of the college and this is nowhere better expressed than in the long list of industrial and specialised units, only a few of which can be described here. The Centre for Liaison with Industry and Commerce provides a range of services to industrial and commercial organisations in Scotland. It also links with companies in the rest of the United Kingdom and abroad. The Centre supports college departments and specialist units in developing and promoting their contacts with industry and commerce. It provides a useful focus for innovation in industrial liaison within the college, providing support services to academic departments, establishing new industrial units and similar industrially orientated activities, e.g. the establishment of a Small Business Centre sponsored by the department of Economics and Management. The Centre is also responsible for the organisation and administration of the programme of short courses and conferences operated by the college. This Centre organises what are described as PACE courses — Programme of

Advanced Continuing Education. These have been established to meet the growing needs for the in-career training and education of the community. An important feature of PACE is the specific design of appropriate courses to meet the requirements of companies even when small numbers of delegates can attend.

A great variety of courses is provided by the Microelectronics Education Development Centre which was established at the request of the Secretary of State in 1980 to provide short courses for industry and commerce, to give general assistance to Scottish Education and to disseminate information. Paisley also houses one of the twenty centres in the United Kingdom sponsored by the Department of Trade and Industry — Strathclyde Microsystems Centre — which aim to foster the more widespread and effective use of microcomputer systems in business and commerce, especially in small businesses. The Centre provides impartial advice on the selection and use of microcomputer hardware and software together with access to training systems and a workshop of representative hardware which can be used 'hands on' by interested businessmen or for demonstration purposes, without pressure from salesmen.

This thriving college, which occupied its present buildings in 1963, now has 2,700 full-time students and a full-time equivalent of 300 part-time students. It hopes to increase these figures to 3,000 and 500 when the present building programme is completed.

In 1959 the four provincial training centres, Glasgow (Jordanhill), Edinburgh (Moray House), Dundee and Aberdeen, along with Catholic women's colleges, Notre Dame (Glasgow) and Craiglockhart (Edinburgh), and the Dunfermline College of Physical Education, were designated Colleges of Education. Representative Boards of Governors were established for each college with a statutory number of teachers on each board. The colleges were funded directly by the Scottish Education Department in the same way as the Central Institutions. By then the four city colleges, mainly non-residential, were already large by English standards and they all expanded in the period 1959–75 when, for instance, Jordanhill had 3,720 students. To reduce the pressure on the older colleges, three new colleges were established for the training of primary teachers in the standard three-year Diploma course for women — Craigie College (Ayr) and Callendar Park (Falkirk) in 1964, and Hamilton College in 1966. Unfortunately, Callendar Park and Hamilton Colleges were closed by government diktat in 1981. All the colleges eventually established B.Ed. courses in the post-Robbins period, though the ancient Scottish universities co-operated with considerable reluctance and the degrees created tended to be copies of the traditional ordinary M.A. Notre Dame and Dunfermline worked with the C.N.N.A., Hamilton and Craigie with Strathclyde University, and Callendar Park with Stirling. By now the total student population in the Scottish colleges is about 4,500 — only one-third of the peak in the mid-1970's.

The recognition of teachers is now a matter for the General Teaching Council for Scotland established in 1966 to operate like a G.M.C. for the teaching profession. The Council maintains a register of all qualified teachers and has certain disciplinary powers in relation to the profession. The G.T.C. acts as the principal adviser on teacher training to the Secretary of State for Scotland. Qualified teachers are in a majority on the Council and, because of that, and their membership of college Boards of Governors, they have more say on teacher training than teachers anywhere in the world.

In the Strathclyde Region the remaining colleges of education are Jordanhill, St. Andrew's (a recent combination of Notre Dame and Craiglockhart) and Craigie College, Ayr.

Jordanhill College of Education

The origins of Jordanhill College lie in the work of David Stow, one of the pioneers of teacher training in Europe. In 1828 he opened a school in the Drygate near Glasgow Cathedral which accepted students to learn Stow's system of instruction for work in schools in other areas. In 1837, largely through Stow's initiative, the Glasgow Normal School was opened at Dundas Vale — the first institution specifically provided in Britain for the training of teachers. The Normal School along with a Free Church equivalent (Stow College, 1843) trained the teachers for the schools of the West of Scotland throughout the nineteenth century. The two colleges were taken over by the Glasgow Provincial Committee in 1905 and functioned until the opening of Jordanhill in 1921 which had been delayed because of the war. Dundas Vale College is still in use as a Teachers' Centre. The original Stow College, from which John Adams went in 1899 to be the first Professor of Education in London University, was pulled down in the 1960's to make way for a motorway.

Jordanhill, which has now about 2,000 students, conducts all forms of preservice training for primary and secondary schools, except physical education for women which remains at Dunfermline College. The national centre for the training of staff in Further Education is an integral part of Jordanhill and fulfils the function of colleges like Bolton except that the courses are all inservice. The Scottish School of Physical Education for men has been at Jordanhill since 1931, and the students take three- or four-year courses for C.N.A.A. degrees. The School of Speech Therapy prepares students for the degree of B.Sc. in Speech Pathology of Glasgow University. There are also departments concerned with the training of social workers and of staff for youth and community work.

The original post-Robbins B.Ed., which led to primary and secondary teaching, was replaced in 1984 by a four-year B.Ed. solely for primary training. The degree is validated by Glasgow University and the course has been very carefully structured for the primary teacher instead of being merely an M.A. course with elements of education and psychology.

Jordanhill was one of the first institutions in Britain to have a department of In-Service Training. Now, this department has a full-time staff of twelve and is entitled to call on staff from other parts of the college to make up the total number of lecturers involved in this work to seventy-two 'Full-Time Equivalents'. The extent of the commitment may be judged from the following figures for 1983–84: 238 courses were conducted for 5,517 teachers — 109 courses being wholly in school time and the remainder being wholly or partly out of school time in evenings, weekends or vacations. Of these courses, twenty-one led to awards or qualifications.

In terms of staff commitment, about 25 per cent of the work is in the college, 10 per cent in assisting such bodies as the Consultative Committee on Curriculum Development and nearly two-thirds on school-focused in-service work, i.e. work with teachers in their own schools or in a Teachers Centre in the Region. Traditionally, many of the courses were concerned with primary education, Special Educational Needs and Early Education. The balance is now tending to swing towards the secondary school, especially because of the so-called 'Munn and Dunning' developments described elsewhere. Award-bearing courses vary from Diplomas in Educational Technology and Computing to a new in-service B.Ed. for primary teachers which enrolled forty-seven students in 1984.

St. Andrew's College

In its present form as the national Catholic College of Education, St. Andrew's College, Glasgow, was established as recently as 30th November 1981. 1981 was the year of college closures in Scotland and, presumably in an attempt to stem the tide, the Scottish Hierarchy agreed to a merger of Notre Dame College, Glasgow, and Craiglockhart College, Edinburgh, which had both begun life as residential colleges for women founded by religious orders in 1894 and 1918 respectively. By the late 1960's both colleges had expanded, had begun to admit men students and had ceased to be almost entirely residential. Notre Dame had moved to an entirely new building at Bearsden and was therefore in every way equipped to become the national college. It was announced in 1984 that pre-service training at Craiglockhart was to cease but that the campus would continue to be used as a Centre for In-Service Research and Development.

Apart from Business Studies, Home Economics, Technical Subjects and Physical Education, St. Andrew's College conducts the same pre-service courses as Jordanhill, but as teacher-training is the only activity numbers are greatly reduced and are now about 600. A new four-year B.Ed. for primary teachers was negotiated with C.N.N.A. and the first students were admitted in 1984.

The college has developed strong in-service departments with an 'F.T.E.' staffing of thirty-five. The Glasgow department makes an important contribution to the programme of courses issued by the National In-Service

Committee — known as National Courses — especially in the field of Guidance. (The National In-Service Committee was introduced fifteen years ago to co-ordinate in-service work and to assess national needs. More recently another Council, SCOVACT, has been established, composed in the main by university and college representatives, to validate in-service courses for teachers.) School-based and school-focused in-service work is a feature for which the college offers 'consultancy' in a wide variety of subjects. At Craiglockhart there has been an emphasis on mathematics and micro-computing.

Craigie College of Education, Ayr

Craigie College is the sole survivor of the three colleges which were built in the 1960's to meet the demand for primary teachers. They were built to accommodate altogether 2,100 students and in the peak period dealt with over 3,000. It is a measure of the enforced contraction that Craigie at present has less than 250 full-time students.

All these colleges were extremely successful from the very beginning, partly because they had a single objective — primary training — partly because they began at a time of great curricular change in the primary school, New Mathematics and so on, but chiefly because they brought support and sustenance to teachers in areas where that had not existed. Craigie could help teachers in the south-western counties — Ayr, Dumfries, Kirkcudbright and Wigtownshire. However willing to help, colleges like Jordanhill could only offer summer vacation courses which involved long journeys and often residence. The new colleges could identify with their localities and could encourage subjects like music and drama where provision had previously been sparse. However desirable on economic grounds, the closure of the two colleges was a serious blow to the teachers and schools they served.

At present the main course at Craigie College is the four-year B.Ed. which is validated by the University of Strathclyde. Other courses include a post-graduate primary course, a variety of courses on Early Education and an in-service course on Social Care.

The college has gained a reputation as a conference centre and it has a very extensive in-service commitment to the south-west of Scotland which involves the equivalent of twelve members of staff.

Concluding Remarks

Critics of the Scottish system complain that the Central Institutions and the Colleges of Education, which deal with about 40 per cent of the students in Higher Education in Scotland, plod on much as before, ignoring develop-ments in the south, and that the Scottish Office has soothed everyone into thinking that the present structure of Higher Education can continue for ever.

It is true that there have been no forced marriages in Scotland between

Technical colleges, Art and Music colleges and Colleges of Education to create polytechnics. But the Central Institutions have developed and diversified as much as could be expected given the resources at their disposal. The range of courses, the quality of the work done and especially the commitment to industry and commerce are as good as anywhere. Three Central Institutions — Robert Gordon's (Aberdeen), Dundee and Paisley — are as polytechnic as could be, given the Scottish reverence for university Faculties of Arts. Two education authority Further Education colleges — Napier College (Edinburgh) and Glasgow College of Technology — were deliberately developed on polytechnic lines and both are to become Central Institutions in 1985. Glasgow College of Technology, opened in 1971, is organised in three Faculties — Life and Social Sciences, Business and Administrative Studies, Science and Engineering — and it already has 3,000 full-time students and 4,000 on part-time courses.

The Colleges of Education, too, have diversified as much as regulations and political pressures would allow. There has been no development of General Degree courses as in Colleges of Higher Education in the south — the teaching profession has always been very strongly against such innovations. Those in the Scottish colleges who weathered the storms of coping with the teacher shortage were always buoyed up by the hope that, in some ideal future, there would be enough teachers to allow adequate release for in-service training and for enough remedial teachers to be employed where the need was great. This could have happened, but governments have decreed otherwise.

It could be that there is violent change on the way. In 1984 the Secretary of State for Scotland established a new Scottish Tertiary Education Council (STEAC) with thirteen members of whom only three are educationists. The Council's terms of reference are:

> 'To consider and report on the future strategy for higher education in Scotland, including the arrangements for providing institutions with financial support and the general principles which should govern relations between universities and other institutions; to advise the Secretary of State on such other matters as he may remit to the Council; and to collaborate as necessary with the University Grants Committee, the National Advisory Bodies for local authority higher education in England and Wales, the Manpower Services Commission and other appropriate bodies.'

The new Council is expected to report before the end of 1985 and it would seem at first sight that the references to the U.G.C., to bodies in England and Wales and to the Manpower Services Commission, indicate an elimination or a reduction in the 'Scottishness' of the present system.

The fundamental problem is the same on both sides of the border — political control, especially of finance. In Scotland the Colleges of Education have been ruthlessly pruned, financial support cut to the bone, and buildings less than twenty years old sold for a song instead of being given to local authorities and communities for education purposes. The return to central control in Scotland is now so definite that colleges have little discretion over the size of their intakes to courses.

To some extent, but not wholly, Central Institutions have escaped from such a marked squeeze on student numbers and finance because of their relationship with industry and commerce. They have of course suffered from the fall in demand for teachers of Art, Home Economics, Music and Drama. They must wonder sometimes whether a buffer between them and the government might not be better than the present system. It is already clear that Sir Keith Joseph expects higher education to be reshaped and to coalesce more conveniently with the requirements of an innovative industrial and exporting nation . . . but that the costs to the exchequer must not be enlarged. Is it too much to expect that the Scottish Office will be allowed to promote and financially support a clear strategy of its own?

FURTHER EDUCATION

Hugh Dougherty, with a foreword by Sir Henry Wood

Foreword
At a time of great concern about the state of education generally, about reductions in staffing, resources and finance, it is refreshing to look back to the tremendous development in post-school public education between 1956 and 1976. Nowhere was the achievement greater and more significant than in Scotland — two new Further Education colleges were opened in nearly every year of that period, and in one year seven. Before the war local authority involvement was almost entirely restricted to evening continuation classes — in 1939 there were 850 centres, mainly in schools, dealing with 164,000 students. Determined students attended these evening classes for many years before being able to travel to Central Institutions for three or four more years of evening work for qualifications such as H.N.C. Stow College of Engineering in Glasgow (Figure 1) was one of the first purpose-built colleges. Opened in 1934, it enrolled very few full-time day students until it was taken over for war-time purposes. Even in 1956 there were only 4,400 full-time students in local authority establishments in Scotland, and of those only 1,400 were taking courses lasting longer than two years. The Central Institutions were still enrolling more than 20,000 evening students.

The Strathclyde colleges range from the large and prestigious Glasgow College of Technology to small colleges (seven) with less than 500 full-time students.

The Glasgow College of Technology was founded in 1971 and has now about 3,000 full-time and 4,000 part-time students. It offers a range of full-

Fig. 1   Stow College.

and part-time C.N.A.A. degree courses, Diploma, Certificate and Professional qualifications through courses which cover a substantial part of the spectrum of subject areas, including Biological and Physical Sciences, Engineering, Social Sciences, Humanities, Business, Finance and Management Studies. Recently approved C.N.A.A. courses include a degree in Risk Management, an evening course for a B.A. in Social Science and a new postgraduate Diploma in Public Administration and Management for overseas students. There is also a long-established B.Sc. Honours degree in Ophthalmic Optics.

Besides offering a wide and developing range of research and consultancy activities, the particular thrust of the college in these areas is aimed at the local community. The Policy Analysis Research and Trade Union Research Units were leaders in this field. The recently developed Community Resources Project (supported strongly by an Urban Aid Grant from the Strathclyde Regional Council) and the Local Enterprise Development Unit (established with grants from the Scottish Industry Department and the Manpower Services Commission) have made college expertise available to local community and business interests. The college has also developed links with Uganda and Indonesia.

Two other colleges in the Region are officially regarded as centres of Advanced Study — Bell College, Hamilton, and the Glasgow College of

Nautical Studies which deals with every possible aspect of the training of Merchant Navy personnel, with departments of Navigation, Marine Engineering, Communications and Power Plant Practice. There are five other large institutions in Glasgow with regional and national functions — the Central College of Commerce, Glasgow College of Building and Printing, Glasgow College of Food Technology, Springburn College, which is unique in its provision of engineering craft courses, and Stow College, the major national centre for the provision of technician education in science and engineering.

The remaining colleges, including Ayr and Kilmarnock in the south, Greenock and Paisley in the west, Coatbridge and Motherwell in Lanarkshire, and Clydebank and Cumbernauld in Dunbartonshire, serve mainly but not exclusively local needs. They have been projected as community colleges which will not only fulfil their traditional technical/business college roles, but will look also to the education of the whole adult community. Most of these colleges already conduct a great variety of courses described as Community Education-Leisure both during the day and in evenings.

All colleges which do not conduct courses for degrees of the C.N.A.A. teach students for qualifications awarded by SCOTEC (Scottish Technical Education Council) or SCOTBEC (Scottish Business Education Council) as well as the older established qualification awarded by the City and Guilds of London Institute and the Royal Society of Arts. They have all played their part in contributing to Y.T.S. and other schemes promoted by the Manpower Services Commission or by Industrial Training Boards.

Further Education in Strathclyde Region
It would be simple to describe the Strathclyde Region Further Education Service by jotting down its vital statistics, for with some 85,718 students attending twenty-one colleges, taught by 3,500 full-time staff, and accounting for a budget of nearly £96·5 million, the operation is clearly impressive in its very scale. But to do that would be to fail to put across the climate that the service operates in, both socially and economically, and although the figures quoted are for session 1984–85, they fail completely to convey the spirit of change and challenge which pervades the service today. Further Education in Strathclyde is, quite simply, responding to meet the very real needs of the wide community that it serves.

The County Councils and Glasgow Corporation had developed further education services with regard to papers such as the 1956 White Paper, 'Technical Education', and policies dictated by the 1964 Industrial Training Act. When the Strathclyde Regional Council took over the service it decided to weld the twenty-one colleges into a more unified system, and by October 1979 the Region had set up its Member/Officer Group on FE, which took a wide variety of evidence from all interested parties. That included education, industry and community interests, so that the Group could formulate policy for the FE service which would truly reflect the needs of its client groups.

In 1981 the Group reported back with its findings and recommendations and, after discussion of the Report, a Statement for Post-Compulsory Education was issued in 1983. The statement saw that provision extending throughout adult life, and envisaged a flexible system which would be able to adapt itself to the changing needs of the community. An important consideration was the position of the sixteen to eighteen age group and, along with the subsequent developments of the Scottish Education Department's Action Plan, the Region sought to make a wider choice available to the over-sixteens. With the Youth Training Scheme and interaction with schools and community education, it was clear that the new provision would have to be less college based than before, and outreach classes in the community, and close contact with schools through regional consortia, were all envisaged.

The market for traditional FE has, of course, been changing and the vocational elements which were traditionally the bread and butter of FE colleges are no longer of primary importance, especially in the craft area, where the demand for certain trades is waning as the economic base of Clydeside has changed from heavy industry to the age of the microchip.

Colleges have become much more responsive to the needs of the technician student (Figure 2), where the demand is growing in industries such as micro-electronics, and it is all-important to meet the needs of local employers such

Fig. 2   Technician needs.

as Motorola in East Kilbride, or IBM at Spango Valley, by providing appropriate education at accessible FE centres.

Hand in hand with the demands of the new technology, the service must still meet demand in all other sectors, and colleges such as Springburn in Glasgow, have adapted to meet the needs of the wider community, by providing courses in a variety of disciplines which are appropriate to their local market. That could mean teaching anything from basic computing to local history modules, and leisure classes, organised in many cases with Community Education, are not forgotten either. A college is a community resource, and must be seen to act as such, especially when its catchment area has special needs.

Dealing with special needs takes a variety of forms in Strathclyde. There are specialist units such as the Glasgow Arts Centre in Washington Street, technically the Region's smallest college, and the Home Craft Centre in Glasgow's South Side also carries out a specialist function. Beyond these units are the community colleges which have adapted to the needs of the handicapped by supplying special facilities and classes to meet the needs of a section of the community which traditionally found that its educational provision came to an abrupt halt when schooling stopped in mid-teens. Now, with initiatives at colleges such as Cardonald, Clydebank, Kilmarnock and Motherwell, where residential accommodation is available, FE is opening its doors to meet the needs of the handicapped and, by including them in ordinary classes in many cases, and by helping them to integrate with other students, barriers are being broken down to the benefit of society at large.

With a policy decision taken in 1975 that fees would be waived for unemployed persons, courses were made available which helped to sharpen up job-seeking skills, allowed better and more relevant qualifications to be gained, and provided many people with a sense of purpose that was absent after employment ceased.

Closely related to work with and for the unemployed, is the provision of education and training for the sixteen to eighteen age group. In concert with the Manpower Services Commission, with whom the Region enjoys a close relationship, the Region provided 3,317 Mode B1 training places, while a further 565 Mode A places were approved during 1984–85. YTS has come to be a major consideration of the service, and with thirty-one training workshops and two ITECs, the Region is heavily involved in schemes which are seen as part of its overall strategy of employment initiatives. With a total budget of some £20 million MSC money, to include some £13 million on Mode B1 and Mode A schemes, and around £7 million spent on Community Programmes, the Region has a major management task on its hands.

With the issue by central government of 'Training for Jobs', presented to Parliament in January 1984, it is clear that YTS will continue to develop, and that the Region's involvement will continue to be considerable (Figure 3). The involvement with adult training will also develop and Open Tech will play a larger part in the adult provision.

Open and distance learning projects are already being used to effect to make

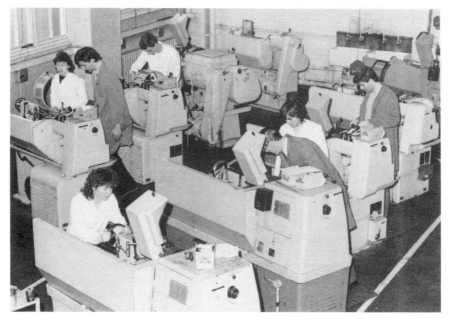

Fig. 3   Teaching skills in Further Education.

the service more accessible to adults who, for a variety of reasons, cannot attend classes at traditional times and places. Already there is a flexistudy scheme run by Ayr Technical College, while Community Education courses run by the Lanark Division include everything from Life and Social Skills and Basic Arithmetic to a special course for Travelling People, taught by a Traveller himself, using Open Learning Techniques.

These, and the Argyll homestudy scheme, are just a few examples of the flexibility of the service. To help staff develop schemes in these directions, there are links with the Scottish Council for Educational Technology (SCET) and the Strathclyde Open Learning Experiment, funded jointly by the Region and the Open University in Scotland. The latter is based at the former Adelphi School in Glasgow which also houses part of the community initiative of the Glasgow College of Nautical Studies.

Also housed in Adelphi is the EEC Social Fund Adult Education Project, which has moved away from providing basic adult education towards a more vocationally biased initiative, by providing back-up to tutors working in the field. As a Regional Resource, the Unit provides training and help to tutors who may be providing courses in Argyll designed to help craft workers set up traditional cottage businesses, or who may be working in Glasgow, setting up courses intended to give women the confidence to go back to work.

The Careers service gives valuable support by working in close co-operation with FE and Community Education, using the very latest methods, such as the Lanark Division's Computer profiling system, and their Careers Outreach Bus, the only one of its type in Britain, which has done much valuable work in re-introducing young people to the potential of FE and YTS schemes. With such involvement from Careers and from the Youth Enquiry Service, known locally as YES, every step is being taken to ensure that the post-school student knows exactly what is available in terms of educational opportunity.

Also aiding that process is Community Education with its own integrated initiatives. In Glasgow's Castlemilk housing scheme, for example, Community Education has pioneered a Support Team for the Young Unemployed, which has provided broad-based educational opportunities in an Area of Priority Treatment.

The picture that emerges is one of constant change on all fronts, and the Region has been faced with further change in the shape of the Scottish Tertiary Education Advisory Council (STEAC), which is conducting a review of higher education strategy for the Secretary of State for Scotland. As a provider of higher education courses at Glasgow College of Technology, Bell College, and other centres such as Stow College, the Region has a clear interest in the future of higher education, although Glasgow College of Technology has already been identified as a Central Institution and will pass from regional control.

But that does not mean to say that Strathclyde will cease to be interested in GCT, for relations with the universities and the existing Central Institutions are good, and help all the institutions to work for the maximum good of industry and the community. Already the Strathclyde Access to Higher Education Scheme, organised jointly by the Region, Strathclyde and Glasgow Universities, provides courses for overseas students needing pre-university training to allow them to enter a university, while the universities and CIs are fully involved with the Region's schemes for retraining teaching staff.

Bell College of Technology, for example, has been providing courses in electronics, aimed at teaching staff from FE colleges, who find that their original disciplines, such as engineering, have less relevance in the high tech 1980's. There are plenty of similar examples, for staff development is an important aspect of the Region's policy for FE. However, in this field there is a growing threat from private training agencies, who have made the world of post-compulsory education competitive in a way that few would have thought possible when the Region took over its twenty-one FE colleges in 1975.

Any review of the work of Strathclyde Region's FE and training work would be incomplete without a mention of the very diverse work of the Community Programme Agency. With schemes for counselling newly unemployed people, teams painting village halls in Argyll, and projects aimed specifically at Vietnamese Boat People who became residents of the Region, not to mention many projects designed to help the handicapped, the Region is one of Scotland's biggest managers of the Community Programme, and the Education Department is responsible for some 1,400 places on such schemes,

all designed to provide temporary employment for the long-term unemployed, with the ever-present theme of helping the community to help itself.

Further Education in Strathclyde is all about going further. That means
going further into the community, further exploring the links and
relationships with industry, and furthering the aims and objectives of
education and training by opening up new approaches, whether it is for the
sixteens to eighteens, the handicapped or the microchip makers of Spango
Valley. It means being further aware of the change and challenge of the
Region's post-shool population, and it means further strengthening the links
with schools, Community Education, Careers, universities, Central Institutions and external agencies, to provide an education service which continues
to be relevant to the needs of the last quarter of the twentieth century and
beyond.

CHAPTER FOURTEEN

THE WAY AHEAD

Sir Kenneth Alexander
Principal, University of Stirling

'The Way Ahead' implies what can be achieved as a result of conscious policy, a man-made future, and not the projection of existing trends or the assumption of drift. What follows concentrates on the policies and actions necessary for the attainment of my desired future for the Strathclyde Region. Tempting as it would be to pitch the target date so far into the future that rationality and belief could be suspended, the time-span I have chosen is twenty-five years, taking me up to the end of the first decade of the twenty-first century.

Looking at the names of my fellow contributors to this section suggests that scientific and technological forecasting and policy will be very well covered. Most of what I have to contribute is socio-economic and cultural. However, some expectations regarding our technological future are necessary as underpinning to my thoughts on the socio-economic future as I see it — and wish to see it.

Perhaps I may be allowed to recall a personal involvement in an earlier attempt to forecast 'the way ahead' for the Strathclyde Region. As economic consultant to the steering committee which commissioned the West Central Scotland Plan, I had to explain the basis of forecasts of a decline in manufacturing employment between 1968 and 1981 of approximately 50,000 or $12\frac{1}{4}$ per cent, a common reaction being that the Planning Team were over-pessimistic, even exaggerating to strengthen the case made for the establishment of a Development Agency for the Region. The actual decline has been at nearly three times the forecast rate — with the secular decline in U.K. economic activity proving to be a factor additional to the aspects of regional weakness to which we were drawing attention. Fortunately, the rise in unemployment has not been in step with this remarkable rate of decline in manufacturing employment and the continued expansion of service industry employment is one assumption made in forecasting the next twenty-five years.

Does this mean that manufacturing is being written off, with a continued rate of decline taking it towards elimination, and to being a fairly unimportant segment of the total regional economy? It need not. Even in heavy engineering there are opportunities related to new materials and an emphasis on quality control. Ravenscraig is now recognised as in the same quality league as the several Japanese steel manufacturers who have been taking the lead in recent years. The experience of oil-related work has helped some Scottish firms to establish excellent reputations for innovation and for quality control. The continued expansion of 'Silicon Glen' presents new opportunities not only for direct employment and skill acquisition in the electronic firms, but for the development of many medium-sized suppliers to these firms. An as yet unanswered question is the extent to which the growth of electronics will become linked to other branches of manufacturing production and help to establish a more general application of automatic and robotic processes. The role of higher education is probably crucial in this connection — with more emphasis now being given to process manufacturing techniques. I believe that the future of much of manufacturing industry now depends on the links established between companies and researchers. The potential for new materials with a fibre component is now widely recognised, but this potential is very far from being realised in Scotland at present. Efforts must be made by industrialists and academics together to change this, only one of several examples of opportunities lost because research talent is not being deployed effectively and its importance overlooked even when the work done is of direct relevance to particular industries. The importance of research and the follow through to the development of new adhesives may also be cited.

These sketchy references are offered to underline the importance I attach to research as the determinant of the future of manufacturing industry. I believe that Scotland has research resources which could underpin a healthy growth of 'the new manufacturing' if companies and tertiary education would jointly devote resources to achieve this. I feel confident that there will be a continuing place — and probable growth — for manufacturing industry. What is at issue is whether Strathclyde will play a major part.

The educational sector has an even more direct contribution to make to a region's economic future, through training for employment. Technological change is already placing heavy demands on education — not for small adjustments to the character and content of training, but for fundamental changes, emphasising the increasing importance of flexibility and the performance of several roles and also the need for greater emphasis on deductive reasoning and analytical skills generally. If it is accepted, as it seems to be, and if it becomes an objective of policy — which is overdue — that technological change demands a shift of emphasis from employment to leisure if a majority of those who want to contribute to and benefit from economic activity is to have an opportunity to do so, then this too has its social and educational implications. Changes in work organisation, emphasising human factors, will take place — for example the positive encouragement of semiautonomous groups in many branches of employment. Education for leisure as well as for participation in work will have to be given much greater attention and encouragement. As one commentator has put it, the knowledge revolution and the increasing importance of skill will smash the hierarchical pyramid approach to management and possibly to government also. Exaggerated? Possibly, but the trend is there already and I believe that the societies which adjust to it rather than try to frustrate it will take the lead in the exploitation of the benefits which the new technologies make possible. Not all of education is vocational and work-related, and the growth of leisure raises the issue of how will it be used. Already in Strathclyde there is a major exhibition centre being built, and there are many examples of leisure centres in being or being planned which reflect the need for enhanced opportunities for recreation, for participative and spectator sport, and for new approaches to the use of such facilities as museums and aquaria. The view that only the physical production of goods provides a secure base on which prosperity can be built is no longer in vogue. The creative development of leisure businesses can contribute to employment and prosperity, particularly when these businesses attract tourists, and add to the ability of a region to enjoy the beneficial multiplier effect of earnings derived from 'exporting' services to spenders from outwith the Region.

The interaction of a rising level of education and culture and the adaptation to and exploitation of technological opportunities will be the driving forces behind the economic and social development of Strathclyde over the next twenty-five years. Despite the grim contraction of manufacturing industry, there is a resilience here which, linked with the strong educational infrastructure, leads me to believe that the West of Scotland now has a real chance of changing its position in the league table of the economic strength of regions within the U.K. For it to do so, well within the next twenty-five years, will require concerted action from the Region — and the present leaders of industry, education and regional government have the major responsibility to act. Government must react, but I would not expect a regional policy strongly favouring the West of Scotland to be a feature of the next twenty-five years. The main thrust must come from the Region, linked with policy proposals as to how government should use the resources at its disposal to produce the optimum results.

One thing is certain. If the West of Scotland can move forward as I suggest, it will not be to a position of permanent superiority. There must be no renewal of the old over-confidence that being Clyde-built is a guarantee of orders, jobs and prosperity. Under conditions of technological change and in dynamic economies, swings and roundabouts are inevitable. Strathclyde has suffered a period of decline and now has an opportunity not only to recoup but perhaps to go ahead. There are, however, no guarantees.

COUNCILLOR JAMES BURNS
Convener, Strathclyde Regional Council

The British Association's visit to Strathclyde in 1985 takes place a decade after Strathclyde Regional Council came into being under the provisions of the Local Government (Scotland) Act 1973. The Council, which I have served as Convener since 1982, is responsible for a population of approximately 2·4 million, almost half the total population of Scotland, and for a geographical area of 5,348 square miles, extending from Ballantrae to Appin and from Tiree to Biggar including rural and remote upland and island areas: indeed, Strathclyde includes more inhabited islands than any of Scotland's Island Area authorities.

The first ten years of Strathclyde Region's life have been difficult years for local government, and as well as coping with the challenge of establishing a new structure and the problems of financial and manpower cutbacks and a worsening economic climate, the Regional Council has had to deal with a range of inherited problems as well as with the scepticism and at times outright opposition of those who considered that a local government unit on such a scale would be remote and unmanageable. Such criticism is now much rarer, and I feel that the Regional Council has by its actions and policies over the past ten years been able to demonstrate that it can make positive and effective use of the resources which size brings with it, while at the same time seeking to ensure the sensitive and responsive delivery of services through the involvement of local communities and groups and through positive initiatives in areas of special need. In all of this the 103 elected members of the Regional Council, who in most cases represent around 20,000 constituents, have a vital role, and it is a tribute to the calibre and dedication of the Council's local members, of all political persuasions, that within the short time the Regional Council has been established, three of Strathclyde's current MPs, and one of the Region's MEPs, have been drawn from its ranks.

What, then, of the way ahead? Ten years of experience give no grounds for complacency, and some of the problems facing the Region are more acute than a decade ago. British figures which treat Scotland as a single entity for employment purposes disguise the fact that Strathclyde has a level of unemployment which compares with the worst of the English regions. There are parts of Glasgow with male unemployment rates in excess of 30 per cent, while unemployment among school-leavers remains an intractable problem. In many parts of the Region, not just the Clydeside conurbation, there are acute problems of multiple social deprivation: the Regional Council's last review of the indicators, early in 1984, defined eighty-eight areas for priority treatment throughout the Region, with a further 123 areas at risk. These economic and social problems are also reflected in physical dereliction and the need for environmental treatment and renewal not only in older tenemental and industrial areas but in some post-war developments.

In responding to these problems, however, the Regional Council can bring to bear policies and strategies which have been developed since the Region's establishment to meet the particular needs of Strathclyde. These include a land-use policy, expressed through the structure plan, which is designed to support the regeneration of Glasgow and other established centres in the Region, the effectiveness of which can already be seen in the demand for private housebuilding in parts of the city which a decade ago had been virtually written off, and in the surge of commercial development in Glasgow city centre; a series of economic initiatives, undertaken in partnership with district councils and the Scottish Development Agency, which have transformed areas such as the Garnock Valley, Clydebank, and parts of Motherwell and Coatbridge; and a social policy which is based on acceptance of the need for positive discrimination to overcome multiple deprivation and a strong area focus to rebuild community confidence and self-reliance. In support of these policies essential infrastructure is being modernised, new provision is being made for particular client groups such as the pre-school age group and the disabled, and the Council has devised mechanisms to involve members and officers more directly in targeting the tactical as well as the strategic response to the undeniable needs of the Region. It is perhaps a little early to judge the success of these policies — in parts of the Region we have been swimming against the tide of major closures, and many of our efforts are hamstrung by restraints on resources. In many cases the scale of the problems is immense, and the Regional Council is just one among several agencies with a role to play. Nevertheless, there is evidence of progress: for example, the physical transformation of the East End of Glasgow by the GEAR project; the way in which inherited shortages of teachers or social workers in areas of need have been overcome; the analytical and advocacy resources the Regional Council has been able to bring to bear on major industrial issues like the future of Ravenscraig or Scott Lithgows; the success of the Regional Council's employment grant scheme, making direct use of EEC funds. Strathclyde is a Region with tremendous resources as well as severe problems: these resources include the skills and commercial and industrial resources inherited from Clydeside's past, the teaching and research facilities of two major universities, as well as the Regional Council's own network of further education colleges and the Central Institutions; the locational and communications advantages. The Regional Council is anxious to exploit these advantages, as well as its own resources, and, in partnership with other bodies and agencies in the area, to help to build the future of Strathclyde. Ten years' experience have made us even more aware of the scale of the task; they have, however, also given us grounds for realistic optimism that progress can be made, and that the Regional Council has a unique and positive role to play in shaping that future.

SIR WILLIAM DUNCAN
Chairman, Rolls Royce Ltd.

From the beginning of the eighteenth century, Clydeside's fortunes were linked to tobacco until eventually the Industrial Revolution brought it prosperity during the age of steam. It is always tempting to look back to such great days, when the West of Scotland epitomised the excellence of Britain's heavy engineering and when the Clyde in particular stood for all that was fine in shipbuilding.

I spent my early schooldays in Glasgow in the late 1920's and early 1930's when grim unemployment created the atmosphere from which the labour movement earned the description 'Red Clydeside'. Industry was traditional with management autocratic and perhaps even remote. The trade unions adopted a counter-role and inevitably 'the two sides' created divisions of 'them' and 'us'. However, this handbook is about the future of Strathclyde Region, and therefore we should look forward.

Today the contrast is stark, although unemployment is still a desperately serious problem. New industries have emerged led by professional managers with beliefs and values that people count and that customer service and quality products are essential objectives, without which success is unattainable. These firms prove that Scots can work as effectively and efficiently as any. Studying the success of companies such as Babcock Power, Barr and Stroud, Digital, Ferranti, Hewlett Packard, IBM, Motorola, National Semi-Conductor Corporation, Prestwick Circuits, a certain pattern can be identified in their beliefs, values and practices.

My introduction described the relative prosperity which accompanied the West of Scotland's transition from an agricultural to an industrialised economy. What is needed now is to ensure that the further shift to an economy in which service becomes more important brings to the Region more jobs and greater prosperity. The polarising of political attitudes in Scotland with a strong Conservative Government at Westminster but with a substantial Labour majority in the Strathclyde Region makes it imperative that individuals act in a cohesive way to promote the Region's prosperity.

The Universities and the Business Schools in particular can help by ensuring that our managers are given every opportunity to learn from the best practices wherever they are used, and Strathclyde University's Business School's 'Distant Learning' project is a splendid example of how extensive and comprehensive our management teaching can be, and how far it can reach, if the student is committed enough.

As Chairman of the Council of Strathclyde University's Business School, I am pleased and proud to write about the largest concentration of business teaching from undergraduate to post-experience MBA courses in Europe today.

The Rolls-Royce name stands for excellence in engineering, and as

Chairman of Rolls-Royce Ltd., an important employer in the West of Scotland over many years, I am proud of the high quality work we do in aero engine component manufacture at Hillington and aero engine design as well as aero engine overhauls at East Kilbride.

The Strathclyde Region is ready for a fundamental change in its fortunes with a first-class infrastructure and the range of skills and experience needed to attract even more high technology companies. A fusion of academic, civic and business commitment would help to make the Region much more prosperous and I believe that commitment will not be lacking.

The Editors regret to inform readers that Sir William Duncan died on 5th November 1984.

SIR MONTY FINNISTON
Chancellor, University of Stirling

It is becoming increasingly borne upon the population and particularly upon those already launched in their career that although the direction the future may take can only be dimly discerned, one way ahead which nobody can avoid treading is clear. From now on and for the indefinite future everybody will have to participate consciously (even formally) in assimilating the continuing output of information and knowledge which epitomises and conditions the developing world; and this will have to be done not just to survive economically (though that would be justification enough) but to appreciate (if not enjoy) a better way of life. Understanding the new technologies and their impact upon industrial and domestic life and their social implications nationally and internationally can only be gained by a process of education. The computer, the robot, the optical fibre and genetic engineering are but four of the many technologies which have already changed our modes of thought and action in some way or another directly or indirectly, and since these technologies and many others are themselves changing to higher levels of complexity and performance, there will be further consequential and radical changes upon our ways of living before the end of this century. As the old pop song had it, 'You ain't seen nothing yet'!

The way ahead has to cater for this increase in demand for knowledge and this implies that established and traditional formal systems of education may — probably will — have to be modified to accept the numbers (which far exceed the present undergraduate population) and provide the greater diversity of disciplinary information, conceptual and practical, through new techniques for continuing education and training beyond the graduation stage. Not that as a nation we are all that progressive in our provision of tertiary education. The age participation rate for higher education after eighteen is 42 per cent in the U.S.A., 39 per cent in Japan, 25 per cent in

France, 19 per cent in Germany but alas less than 13 per cent in the U.K. — and that before the university cuts of 1981!

Thankfully, the very conditions which have created the demands for continuing education have also generated the technological solutions for its provision. As example, the Open University and now the Open Tech with television and radio, cablevision in due course, satellites, the audio-visual cassette, etc., all provide channels of communication between those who have knowledge and can transmit it and those who wish to gain it. The sources of such knowledge are to be found in the expertise in universities, polytechnics, colleges of further education, professional institutions of all kinds — learned societies, qualifying bodies — trade associations and even particular industries and companies; in fact, the input of knowledge is changing and expanding constantly. All forms of professional expertise must take account of this if their future development and success is to be ensured.

But the formal educational establishments (schools, universities, polytechnics) will not be able to confine their efforts to teaching by the classical tuition methods — lectures, book study, tutorials — but will have to supplement these and other external forms of education by short or long courses in association with our industrial society — manufacturing, service industries, commerce — and even public life — government, the civil service, Parliament and local councils. Already something is stirring. The universities and the polytechnics or Central Institutions in Scotland, for example, are developing more direct association with industry through teaching companies, joint ventures, consultancies and other mechanisms, enabling academics and industrialists to exchange their complementary expertise to advance the interests of both parties. The creation of Science Parks is an expression of this new environment attracting academics from their so-called ivory towers.

The way ahead will see a proliferation of methods by more institutions to provide more and more information and knowledge, more and more quickly to meet more and more needs of a changing society. Even the British Association with its long and proud history may well have to change the techniques by which it has provided a needed service to society over these many years. Why, for example, once a year? Why national and not regional? Why not special arrangements with our forty-four universities and our thirty polytechnics? The BA has already done much with its BAYS and other schemes but it wants a rethink to accommodate the needs of the changing world. Perhaps Glasgow will inspire it.

Finally, take the special case of Scotland — because it is special — Scotland has more universities for its population than any other country in the world and having always shown initiative in its educational systems, one hopes that Scotland will continue to show that leadership in education it has always held. As the sages said, 'If you are not for yourself who will be for you? And if you are only for yourself what are you? And if not now when?' Could the BA Annual Meeting of 1985 in Glasgow herald those innovations in continuing education of which we are sorely in need now?

GRAHAM HILLS
Principal, University of Strathclyde

The University of Strathclyde was born out of the Industrial Revolution and the Age of Enlightenment. Perhaps not surprisingly, its fortunes have followed closely the ups and downs of Scotland's economy and especially that of the West of Scotland. It seems to me that for some time to come the University's future will be influenced by these same external influences and rightly so.

Economic historians point to three stages of the Industrial Revolution, the first replacing water power by steam, the second replacing fingers by machines and the third replacing the brain by the computer. This third, electronic revolution, which has only just begun, is visibly beginning to lift the economies of Glasgow and of the Scottish lowlands into another bout of success and prosperity, and it is likely that again the universities will reflect this new surge of innovation. But with a difference, for whereas the mill owners, the iron masters, the engineers and shipwrights were largely non-university men, their successors will, for good or for ill, have been caught in the meritocratic net from which the only escape is by way of the system of tertiary education.

The universities must therefore be careful that their great traditions of scholarship and of the search for truth wherever it may lie will not entrap the minds of the young to the point of turning them away from productive industry. We have somehow, and not too slowly, to Nipponise our culture, to make the practice of design-and-make as worthy of esteem as purely intellectual pursuits. There is always room for intellect and intelligence but they flower best in the world of doing because only by doing can we afford as a country to support those who do not.

This will present no problem to Strathclyde, the ethos of which has ever been in support of the doers as well as of the thinkers. If it be true that Newton combined the mind of a mathematician with the hands of a carpenter, then it follows that at least in technological universities we should encourage the development of those practical skills of hand and mind deemed essential to the well-trained graduate. They may be the skills of the mechanical or electronic workshop; they may be the skills of the market place or board room; they will certainly be the skills of exercising judgement, and of communicating that judgement in clear and simple language.

Thus it seems to me that the university courses of the future should not be confined to the subject-based, departmentally owned single Honours courses which have dominated the British scene for nearly a century. Rather, they should be, and almost certainly will be, academic pathways of considerable lateral and longitudinal diversity to match the equally wide variety of talents and aspirations in every cohort of university entrants. We need not fear incoherent courses. Students, their parents and their mentors are, in my opinion, surer and swifter guides than most of what is best. The well-informed customer is the only reliable guide to any enterprise. Our democratic institutions depend upon it.

Other skills once essential but lately discarded need to be restored. The skills of writing and speaking clearly on one's feet and in the face of others were a feature of the Scottish tradition of rhetoric. They need to be brought back, as in some courses they already have been. This implies the penetration of the technologies by the humanities. How else are the technologists, the scientists and the architects to feel the obligations of the social framework in which they work? How else are the analytical niceties of independent scholarship to be married to the mission-oriented requirements of everyday life and work? The tool kit of the modern graduate must therefore contain as many different kinds of social soft-ware implements as can conveniently be fitted in. Even they are unlikely to last for long and the once-for-all education must give way to the continuing education already a necessity of medicine, pharmacy and other professions where the need to keep up with change is paramount. This has long been the practice in the United States.

The adaptation of the modern university to the needs of its time will, like every other change, be driven by necessity. The necessity now in Scotland is to assemble a gifted, well-trained workforce well able to spear-head this country's economic revival. It is true that universities stand for more than that but arguably not much more. Their view of themselves as timeless repositories of ancient, unchanging wisdoms is Arthurian in its charm and is yet another left-over of our imperial past. 'Brideshead Revisited', 'The Jewel in the Crown' and even 'Strangers and Brothers' evoke deep feelings of past glories, of detached dons and lost causes. They are used to defend all manner of educational anachronisms which I hope Strathclyde will bundle into the archives as soon as humanly possible.

The modern university will still remain faithful to the pursuit of truth and knowledge, but it will be primarily a teaching institution where undergraduates and postgraduates master the arts of learning, of how to confront and organise new information, of how to criticise and evaluate the content and significance of new experience and of how to present and defend the conclusions of that analysis. The ancient skills of rhetoric and logic would be restored and the more recent emphasis on fact gathering be put firmly in its lower place.

Thus we would prepare a new generation of men and women able to comprehend the world they go into and able to protect it against the unrelenting forces of instinct, of greed, power and aggression. They themselves must not perpetuate, as they do now, that derivative instinct of aggression, namely the desire to compete. For the future to be bearable, it will need to be more concerned with co-operation and conservation. It will need to eschew the adversarial antics of competition between people, between companies and between countries. Humans will continue to strive, and so they should, but their pursuit of excellence has to be within, where there is infinite room for it. The phrase that 'competition brings out the best in a person' needs to be put into context. It should be put in its place by the imperative that we learn to 'live and let live'. And that embraces the animal kingdom, the plant kingdom, indeed the entire lithosphere.

Research will remain as a professional training activity of universities. It needs no stimulus and should be written in the lower case. It is one of the most pleasurable and satisfying of activities; its rewards are also within. In some subjects it may be best done when one is young. In others it is certainly best done much later and against a background of experience. The same will be true of education itself. To be educated at any time is a privilege, not a right. I therefore look forward to post-school education of the widest and most open kind, treasured and at least partially paid for by a grateful clientele of all ages. I hope that the purpose of education at all levels, but especially at the tertiary level, will be to encourage the wide diversity of talents latent in all of us. I also hope that, in fulfilling this purpose, university education will let go of its twentieth-century preoccupation with degrees, certificates and the other forms of grading. The qualities of life are by definition not to be quantified. In a world as rich as our own, there is no case that they should be. Merit remains its own reward.

ARNOLD KEMP

Editor, *The Glasgow Herald*

The great days of grievance have gone from Scottish politics. The song of relative disadvantage was sung by successive Secretaries of State: whether it was the girning *basso profundo* of Willie (now Lord) Ross or the suaver voice of Lord Maclay, the message was the same.

They worked on two assumptions that were generally credible in Whitehall: first that Scotland was worse off than the rest of the United Kingdom, and, second, that the nationalists were at the gates. This second proposition acquired considerable force in the 1970's: the SNP doubled its votes in three successive General Elections when the wealth of the North Sea lent hard economic conviction to the hitherto rather romantic case for Home Rule.

This brief spring and summer in Scottish politics ended in 1979 with the indecisive devolution referendum. The considerable political energy that had been generated died as suddenly as it had appeared. Mrs. Thatcher was that year elected to Downing Street with little debt to Scotland, and for the first time in many years the nationalist card looked blank.

Nevertheless, Scotland retained certain legacies of this period, particularly the Scottish Development Agency and its substantial programme of urban renewal (in association with the local authorities) in the East End of Glasgow. Mr. George Younger has been able to retain a surprising amount of influence in Cabinet, standing somewhere between the Wets and Dries; it is perhaps the secret of his success that his precise degree of dampness has been hard to establish. Ravenscraig and Scott Lithgow were saved, and he has, for the moment, fought off the attack on the SDA from forces at the Department of Trade and Industry who would like to see Scotland's efforts to attract overseas investment absorbed into the consular services. The litany of decline remains extensive, of course. Achievements of previous Secretaries of State have fallen like green bottles off the wall: British Aluminium at Invergordon, Leyland trucks, Peugeot at Linwood.

Economic statistics, too, have shifted to show Scotland apparently well off in comparison with most English regions outside the still pre-eminent South-East and the dynamic London–Bristol corridor. Government Ministers and officials have been at pains to explain that Scotland is no longer a special case. Indeed, a high official said recently that the divide in Britain was no longer north–south but east–west.

If oil were to be abstracted from the Scottish economic performance, one suspects that the results would not be so favourable. Nor is the east–west argument entirely true. Tyneside languishes, resentful of Scotland. Bathgate, at the heart of central Scotland, has, at 21·5 per cent, unemployment matching the worst examples in the west, and there are other black spots like Dundee. Yet there is a general conviction that economic development in Scotland, involving new technology, services and oil, will favour the east.

For Strathclyde, this trend, together with the prospect of reduced regional aid and the Government's preoccupation with such areas as Merseyside, Tyneside and the West Midlands, is somewhat worrying. Strathclyde remains eighth from the top of the EEC's poverty league, outranked (if that is the word) in the U.K. only by Merseyside. The regional authority has shown some skill in securing grants from Brussels. This is encouraging, for Strathclyde's future will depend on winning the struggle for external investment and building up its appeal as a centre for services and as an attractive place in which to live.

It has a great deal to live down, since its record of poverty and deprivation is so thoroughly known; and the key to its future must be the successful rehabilitation of Glasgow. This extraordinary city, whose cheerful reality belies its reputation for poverty, violence and grime, has suddenly begun to believe in itself. Dr. Michael Kelly's remarkable 'Glasgow's Miles Better' campaign demonstrated impressively the enormous dividends that could flow from quite a modest investment in the city's image. Now the SDA has produced a plan for Glasgow's continuing development which contains a number of populist and apparently extravagant ideas — like moving the Greek Thomson church from the Gorbals to form a dramatic upper perspective for the very fine Buchanan Street, or opening an aquarium in the manner of Baltimore. To charges of extravagance the reply must be that such activity would yield enormous returns in publicity and popular appeal, improve the city's morale and generate further investment.

The plan, reflecting much of the thinking in the city's planning department, also relies on the continued growth of private housing in the inner city. Nothing in the last few years has more transformed Glasgow than the modest family homes which have sprouted up in unprepossessing gap sites, bringing vigour and commerce back to areas that seemed lost in perpetual twilight. Rehabilitated tenements live handsomely again; the irreplaceable grace, whether Venetian or in the Scottish vernacular, of abandoned commercial buildings in the Merchant City to the east of Queen Street has been most successfully pressed into domestic use. In the West End, late-night delis add a cosmopolitan flavour to the more typical urban Scottish landscape of pub, newsagent, betting shop, travel agency and video library. Here, one senses, is a city ready for a leap forward.

Problems of political leadership remain. The SDA, for fear of upsetting the local authorities or arousing regional jealousies, prefers to work in the background. Under the two-tier system of local government, the District Council is the custodian of civic pride and enterprise but the Regional Council of Strathclyde has responsibility for strategic planning. Luckily the Region also recognised the supreme importance of Glasgow's revival. Indeed, the Council, not without discord, has come out in favour of Glasgow as Scotland's international airport at the expense of Prestwick, which is also in Strathclyde, and, more significantly for its security, in Mr. Younger's constituency.

The key figure is probably the Lord Provost of Glasgow, who although nominated by the District Council's Labour group can to some degree stand above the battle and mediate between the various factions in the city — a delicate task since the commercial sector, because of its extremely heavy burden of rates, has little goodwill for the Labour administration which, in turn, is not free of Militant tendencies. Skilful leadership of the Labour group has so far prevented a lurch into defiance, Liverpool-style; and after some alarms caused by declaratory passages in Labour's manifesto in this year's District Council elections, the administration is resuming its partnership with private builders. Sluggish demand, rather than doctrinal distaste, seems to be holding things back.

Mr. Robert Gray, the new Lord Provost, has picked up the 'Miles Better' campaign and, in his own style, seems ready to carry it on. The new exhibition centre opens soon; Glasgow has been successful in its bid for the garden festival. In this new climate of Government scepticism and reduced regional aid, Strathclyde will depend on a willingness to work fruitfully with political opponents, and an imaginative approach to the increasingly intense competition for scarce resources.

GAVIN H. LAIRD
General Secretary, Amalgamated Union of Engineering Workers

Present-day Strathclyde is a progressive and dynamic force in Scotland and has established itself as one of the major industrial and business centres of Europe. The diversity of the Region, its varied geography and resources, its financial and occupational interests, the aptitude and skills of its workforce provide extensive opportunities for investment in many fields. The Region boasts 7,700 miles of roads, an extensive railway system, two major international airports, with Prestwick being a Freeport — and the highly successful Scottish Development Agency is based here. It also has outstanding educational facilities which have considerable links with industry — and an enviable cultural heritage.

At its centre is Clydeside, the industrial heartland of Scotland, accounting for 50 per cent of those employed in manufacturing. A reputation of craftsmanship earned through decades of leadership in engineering, shipbuilding and steel has been handed down through generations and has produced Clydeside's highly skilled, present-day workforce.

Scotland has a history of inventiveness and engineering expertise second to none. A catalogue of inventors would include such people as Alexander Graham Bell, who invented the telephone; John Logie Baird, television; James Bowman Lindsay, the electric light bulb; James Watt, steam engine; Kirkpatrick Macmillan, the pedal bike; James Gregory, the reflecting telescope; and Sir Robert Alexander Watson-Watt, who developed the radar system used in World War II.

Determination to remain at the forefront of industrial development is reflected by the performance of the Region's two, highly acclaimed, universities. The University of Glasgow and the University of Strathclyde have both won a tremendous reputation within world-wide academic and industrial circles. Both universities have continuously channelled their human and technical resources, in conjunction with industry, into the research and development of new industrial projects. The physical expression of this commitment has been the establishment of the Science Park by the two universities and the SDA. Opened in September 1983, it is already beginning to flourish. Another joint venture is the creation of the private company Kelvin Technology Developments Limited, which is designed to provide financial support necessary for innovative projects to be realised as marketable products.

Facilities for attracting new industries have been greatly improved in recent years by the selection of Clydebank as Scotland's first enterprise zone. The enterprise zone, the most successful in Britain, was established in 1980, and already it has attracted over two hundred companies into the area.

We have much to be proud of in our past and present achievements, and are fortunate to have flourishing growth areas, such as oil and gas activities and rapidly expanding electronic companies. In fact, North Sea oil and gas related industries now account for 100,000 jobs in Scotland. Britoil, based in Glasgow, announced a successful year for 1983, with pre-tax profits increased to £586 million; the volume of sales had risen to 56 million barrels of oil, and exploration activity cost a total of £122 million on the United Kingdom Continental Shelf.

Electronic companies have been attracted to the Region by the resources available, including the fact that it is easier to find skilled engineers and graduates in Scotland than in most other major electronics centres around the world. This, coupled with the back-up services which the universities can provide, has made Strathclyde a major electronics production centre. There are now dozens of well-known electronics companies throughout Strathclyde, including a high proportion of American multinational companies like IBM, Honeywell, NCR, Motorola, and Burroughs. In the last four years, over £300 million have been invested here in the semi-conductor industry. Six companies produce nearly 80 per cent of Britain's output of this product, and account for 21 per cent of Europe's capacity.

Since 1975, the United Kingdom's electronics industry has grown by 18 per cent. In Scotland, during this same period, the electronics industry has grown by 88 per cent. As a result the electronics industry in Scotland now employs more people than the shipbuilding, steel manufacture and heavy engineering combined.

Establishing good industrial relations and eliminating factors which contribute to friction and conflict is becoming increasingly important for the future development of the Region. Red Clyde is a myth! The vast majority of working people in Clydeside have never been on strike, and continue to work in harmonious conditions. Witness to this is the vast investment by industrialists in older basic industries and the influx of new high technology industry. Negotiation around a table is a far better way to resolve problems than building up an explosive situation with the workforce. It is also important that there is full disclosure of information and workforce involvement in the implementation of technological change.

The question of harmonisation and single status is another burning issue which must be resolved in the near future. The distinctions between white and blue collar workers, which affects the thinking of both management and labour alike, are increasingly untenable due to the impact of new technology.

Some progress is already being made and the results are becoming increasingly recognised as mutually beneficial to both workers and management. This has been witnessed in the agreement reached with Cummins Engine Company Limited in Shotts, which aims 'to reduce or eliminate the historical areas of differential between work groups and encourage mutually supportive effort'.

The roll call of the firms who grew up within the Region generations ago and are still well established today is impressive. Firms of world-wide renown include: John Brown, the Weir Group, Anderson Strathclyde, Rolls-Royce,

Babcock Power, Barr and Stroud and Yarrow. Many of these firms are involved in providing a range of technologically advanced products, and have introduced high technology systems into their own plants. The flexible manufacturing system at Anderson Strathclyde, for example, required £6 million in investment.

The Region has a workforce with the skills, adaptability and innovative talents that we need for wealth creation — to expand new industries and to modernise and successfully develop older ones. I am convinced that Strathclyde is setting the pace and is making British industry once again a dynamic, competitive nation, taking a leading role in the world economy.

DR. IAN MACGREGOR
Chairman, National Coal Board

Scotland is richly endowed with primary sources of power, having at her disposal solid fuel (coal and peat), petroleum (oil, oil shale and natural gas), hydro and nuclear power.

Coal has played a significant part in the development of Scotland and, since the year AD 1500, a total of 3,655 million tonnes of coal have been mined from Scottish coalmines. The National Coal Board estimates that a further 275 million tonnes can be extracted from mines that are in business and there are probably about another 200 to 250 million tonnes of reserves that may qualify for extraction at an economic cost. The principal coal measures lie in Ayrshire, in Fife and Midlothian, with a number of small isolated reserves such as those near Campbeltown and Brora. There are also fairly substantial tonnages of coal in the Moray Firth offshore, in the Firth of Forth, the Upper Forth basin and the Solway Firth, but the cost of obtaining it would make it uneconomic at the present time.

The principal market for coal is to supply the electricity generating stations of the South of Scotland Electricity Board at Longannet and Cockenzie. The SSEB bought nearly 6·5 million tonnes of coal and slurry in 1982/83, over 90 per cent of which was supplied by the National Coal Board. Electricity sent out from the SSEB's power stations in 1982/83 totalled 19,338 million units, a decrease of 20·4 per cent compared with the previous year which reflected output from the gas-fired power station at Peterhead and the loss of the Invergordon smelter load. The coal-fired plant at Longannet and Cockenzie provided 9,844 million of the units sent out compared with 15,980 million units in the previous years.

Electricity produced in Scotland by nuclear power stations in 1982/83 was 9,948 million units representing 38·8 per cent of the electricity consumed in Scotland. A further 5,883 million units were sent out by the North of Scotland Hydro-Electric Board. So the variety of power generation in Scotland is diverse and highly competitive.

The history of hydro-electric power stations is closely related to the production of aluminium. The first hydro-electric developments in the Highlands were started in 1896 although the first large project for the public supply of electricity at Rannoch did not come into operation until 1930. Although various attempts at legislation were made between 1928 and 1941, it was not until the Hydro-Electric Development (Scotland) Act 1943 (which established the North of Scotland Hydro-Electric Board) that developments were co-ordinated and organised in a proper manner. The Board's prime task was to harness the water energy in the more remote parts of northern Scotland in order to provide electricity to the remote settlements in that area. As hydro schemes were constructed a 132,000 volt transmission system called the Highland Grid was built to link them together and carry their power to centres or transformation into the expanding distribution networks. Growth in demand has made it necessary to upgrade the Highland Grid and in addition to overland cable, submarine cables link island settlements.

There is no doubt that hydro-electricity has stimulated the economic development of the north of Scotland, increased agricultural production, helped the tourist trade and, by making it possible for industries to set up in any part of the north of Scotland, hydro-electric power has also contributed to industrial expansion.

The most recent energy source to be discovered and exploited in Scotland is North Sea oil and gas. Since the discovery of the West Sole field in 1964 the role of natural gas in U.K. primary energy consumption has undergone a dramatic rise from almost negligible amounts in the late 1960's to over 11 per cent of the total in 1982. Since the Forties strike was announced in October 1970, other substantial discoveries of oil have been found in offshore Scottish waters. For an industry as technically demanding and economically risky as the oil business, the Scottish people responded with enthusiasm and vigour in building up a highly successful industry from small beginnings. Within a decade of the early discoveries of North Sea oil in 1969 and 1970, Britain became self-sufficient in oil.

The energy industries are a major source of employment in Scotland. The coal industry employs about 13,000 men and the offshore oil and gas industry directly supports about 60,000 jobs in Scotland with a further 40,000 in partly related activities. However, while the north-east of Scotland has flourished in the oil boom, more than 100,000 jobs in manufacturing industries have been lost in Strathclyde and there are forecasts of further decline. These job losses reflect the decline in traditional industries such as shipbuilding, marine engineering and textiles.

Although the Grampian, Highland and Islands regions are the best geographical locations for service bases, for platform construction sites and land terminals for offshore pipelines for the North Sea oil market, about 30 per cent of all direct employment in the North Sea oil industry is in the Strathclyde Region. These are jobs created by firms that have devoted part of their business to supplying equipment for offshore operations.

The history of North Sea developments, as projected by one of the U.K.'s major North Sea producing companies, shows that U.K. oil demand declined from a level in the early 1970's because of the recession and the more careful use of petroleum. It is expected that the U.K. is rapidly approaching its peak production from the North Sea and within another decade the production rate may decline below the U.K. demand rate. A similar forecast is given for the natural gas supply from the North Sea which at the present time consists of two components: gas produced from fields in the United Kingdom and gas which comes into the United Kingdom from other parts of the North Sea or is imported as liquids. It is expected that the U.K. will still have an escalating projected demand for natural gas in the future but it is difficult to see a continuation of supplies at the current level of demand after the end of this decade.

This information clearly indicates that at some time before the end of this century we will probably see opportunities for expanding the use of coal as an alternative source of energy to petroleum and natural gas and Scotland, once again, will be well placed to exploit her indigenous resources.

SIR ALWYN WILLIAMS
Principal, University of Glasgow

The forecast in the Government's expenditure plans to 1986–87 of yet another round of cuts in our recurrent grants, is a reminder to everyone in British universities of the completeness of our dependence on that source of income. In the early 1970's, Treasury grants accounted for about four-fifths of the revenue of all universities. Indeed with over 80 per cent of the tuition fees and most of research contracts also being met from the same source, private incomes would have kept the average university going for less than one week.

The well-being of any university, then, is at the mercy of the fiscal policies pursued by the political party in power. Under the previous Labour Government, university incomes dropped in real terms as infra-inflationary cash limits were imposed and student numbers were increased without any compensatory improvement in the recurrent grants. But our vulnerability was not really exposed until the Conservative Government of 1979 began cutting public expenditure on higher education. The introduction of economic tuition fees for overseas students enrolling after 1979 followed by the cuts in recurrent grants beginning in 1981, reduced university revenue from public sources by about 14 per cent over a period of four years.

The next round of economies seems set to be at least as traumatic as that just experienced. It will certainly be more profound than the annual fractional 'efficiency cuts', as Sir Peter Swinnerton-Dyer so euphemistically described our dribbling losses of Treasury funds from one year to the next. According to well-orchestrated leaks from high places and ministerial musings, it is nothing less than the 'privatisation' of another slice of university revenue, a large-scale replay of what happened when overseas students were required to pay economic tuition fees. Behind that ugly word is, of course, the assumption that Treasury grants to universities can be drastically cut without affecting teaching and research because means will instantly be found to make good the losses from other sources. Sir Keith Joseph has been especially enthusiastic in his support of 'privatisation' and is said to entertain hopes that up to one-third of the revenue of universities will eventually be so derived.

An increased privatisation of our funding would certainly help universities to exercise greater control over our financial affairs and to ward off academic dirigisme. It would, of course, involve all universities in quickly raising very large sums of money from private sources. Doubts over our ability to do so have been expressed but they tend to be nullified by irrelevant comparisons with the funding systems of other countries and by a widely held belief that our dependence on public support is a relatively recent development which could be reversed without great harm. Such a belief deserves to be checked. In particular it seems appropriate to assess the extent to which teaching and research have been dependent on grants from the Government, Crown or Church. In that respect the records of the University of Glasgow are as pertinent as those of any other British institution of higher education. The University was founded within a few centuries of the oldest Oxbridge colleges. Yet with its strongly centralised arrangements for study, it is more typical of the country's newer universities than the collegiate system which presently caters for about 8 per cent of all students. Indeed even before most British universities had come into being, this assertion would still have been true. In 1922 when one-fifth of the 45,000 students reading for a degree in the United Kingdom were resident in Oxbridge, one-quarter were attending one or other of the four ancient Scottish universities.

The history of the University of Glasgow is well documented although its finances are poorly known for the first three centuries following its foundation in 1451. This deficiency is partly due to the absence of accounts showing the revenue from tuition fees. Until 1889, fees were paid directly to teachers and one can only guess what was pocketed. The dearth of precise accounts, however, mostly reflects a chronic cash flow problem. Gifts and grants frequently fell short of promises. The revenue from bestowed chaplainries was difficult to assess and even more difficult to collect, while that from tithes varied with the price of grain. In all, the University led a hand-to-mouth existence which was not much improved during the seventeenth century when the Crown displaced the Church as the chief external arbiter in its affairs.

By the latter part of the eighteenth century, reliable annual accounts were being prepared for all revenue except tuition fees. These, however, can be estimated from the total income of the teaching staff as has been done by Paul L. Robertson (1976). Assuming tithes and other leases granted by the Crown to be equivalent to annual allocations from present-day governments, an interesting pattern emerges. In the 1770's, over two-fifths of the University's income came from the 'Government' and the Church and not much more than one-quarter from endowments. By the 1820's, the relative contributions from both sources had fallen behind class fees which by then accounted for over two-fifths of total revenue. This change in funding was not attributable to an increase in student numbers which remained at about 1,000 throughout the period. The additional income came from a sudden rise of 50 per cent in class fees. Since students paid fees directly to their teachers, these increases indicated a significant, if variable, improvement in the living standards of the professoriate.

The constitutional changes which transformed the University into a modern institution for higher education and research were mainly brought about by Acts of Parliament during the nineteenth century, especially those of 1858 and 1889. Yet in the uncertain years between, the University moved to its present site on Gilmorehill and its student population doubled.

By 1889 the final steps were also taken to perpetuate recurrent Government grants which were to account for 30–40 per cent of the annual revenue over the next fifty years. In fact the 1889 Act guaranteed Scottish universities a level of public support which was not enjoyed by sister institutions south of the border until the University Grants Commission came into being twenty years later. By 1900 the Government was spending twelve times as much *per capita* on higher education in Scotland as in England. The main surge in Government funding, however, has occurred since World War II and has been as high as 80 per cent of our total revenue in 1972.

Over the same period, income from endowments has declined steadily from almost one-quarter of revenue to less than 5 per cent. Yet the flow of benefactions has never ceased, averaging nearly £0·7 million per annum over the last five years. But the income generated by this rate of increase has not kept pace with inflation, let alone the expansion of the University as decreed by successive governments. There is, however, another source of financial assistance for academic pursuits which ought to be considered in the same context as endowments. Within the last thirty-five years, contract research has grown rapidly and now accounts for 13 per cent of our recurrent expenditure. It is financed by Research Councils and other government agencies, philanthropic foundations and the private sector. Only a minority of projects, however, afford an opportunity for the University to recover overhead costs and thereby bring this source of income more into line with traditional benefactions.

Throughout the century before the Second World War, tuition fees provided between 40 per cent and 50 per cent of our income and, as the University could vary their value as it wished, they were adjusted from time to time to balance budgets. Since the 1950's, tuition fees have become a minor source of revenue. They are now so completely controlled by the Government that in 1982, home students' fees were peremptorily halved in order to reduce the earnings of universities exceeding their student targets. The greatest change, however, in fee income was the introduction of an economic charge for the tuition of overseas students. Overnight such fees became private revenue earned by the sale of academic skills.

In retrospect it is seen that the University of Glasgow has always subsisted on a mixed economy of public funding, private income and tuition fees. Public funding, whether by Church, Crown or Government, has consistently exceeded private income. Even tuition fees have seldom, if ever, been a wholly private contribution to revenue. By the mid-sixteenth century the Crown and Glasgow Town Council had founded seventeen bursaries, a sufficient number to support well over one-fifth of the students. The bursaries were obviously the forerunners of the modern maintenance grants and fees awarded to home students by the Scottish Education Department and Local Authorities. Such a preponderance of public funding, through grants to the institution and to its students, seems appropriate when one considers the University in its regional context. For over five centuries it has prepared local school-leavers for the professions, primarily to satisfy regional needs. Indeed if one has to justify the investment of public money in universities, the professionalism with which the Industrial Revolution was pioneered in the West of Scotland confirms that returns from higher education are inestimable.

Comforted by this historical evidence for sustained public funding, I can now consider the prospects for a further bout of privatisation of the University's revenue. The accompanying graph summarises our plans for attracting incomes from various sources in relation to those which supported

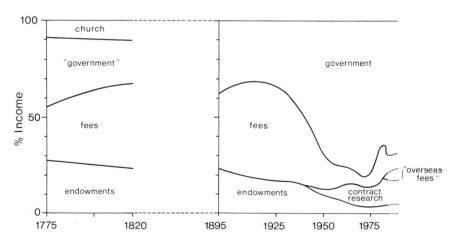

The University of Glasgow
Apportionment of Funding 1775-1820
and since 1895

the University at selected periods in the past. If left alone to our own devices, we should be able by 1990 to reduce our dependence on public funds (Treasury grants and home student fees) to just over three-quarters of our revenue. This apportionment will, in fact, be comparable with that obtaining a century ago if one assumes that research contracts are as private a source of money as benefactions, endowments and overseas students.

The income from endowments and the tuition fees of overseas students should eventually amount to 10 per cent of all revenue, a proportion last achieved in the 1950's. This improvement, however, does not allow for more than a percentage or so of additional privatisation of income. To attempt to go any further would quickly threaten our academic standards. Certainly to go for a three-fold increase in our private income would be folly. Such an attempt would not only destroy the identity of the University and be contrary to the apportionment of its funding throughout its history, but also break our traditional links with the West of Scotland.

REFERENCE

Robertson, P. L. (1976), The finances of the University of Glasgow before 1914, *Hist. Educ. Quarterly*, 449–478.

RT. HON. GEORGE YOUNGER
Secretary of State for Scotland

Predicting social and economic change is not an exact science; and no one can claim to forecast either objectively. Value judgements inevitably colour our perceptions of the future and for politicians it is perhaps right that that should be so.

My view of the future is therefore based on my beliefs about what Scottish people — and particularly Scottish industry — can achieve if the right conditions are there, conditions which this Government is trying to create through its firm control of inflation and by limiting the encroachment by the public sector on economic freedom. A good illustration is the growth of microelectronics in Scotland. This is an area where the rapid pace of development is bringing about major changes from which Scotland is well placed to benefit. We are already involved at every stage from the manufacture of silicon chips to the production of software, and Scotland is becoming increasingly known throughout the world as a place to invest. Health care and biotechnology, which span a number of different industries including parts of chemicals, instrument engineering and electronics, though relatively small scale at present, are other areas where world markets are growing and technical innovations offer the opportunity for rapid development.

Forest products afford the potential to develop one of Scotland's main natural resources although this depends on world timber prices and exchange rates. There is a corresponding potential with chemicals where access to low cost North Sea feedstock is an advantage which has prompted the construction of Esso's ethylene plant at Mossmorran.

North Sea oil is by no means yet exhausted — on the contrary, the latest estimates suggest a higher level of reserves than previously thought. I am optimistic about the continuing prospects for a vibrant oil-related industry provided we in Scotland can develop our potential to serve not only the North Sea but offshore markets worldwide.

Turning to services, we must look to the private sector, especially business and professional services including finance, information, recreation and leisure, to provide more growth in employment. Scotland already has a distinctive insurance and banking sector whose continued growth can be expected. Electronics growth is likely to be accompanied by an expansion in related services such as programming. The general range of personal services and tourism will surely be important, with the impact of tourism being particularly significant in the more remote areas.

To enable the country to adapt successfully to changes in economic and industrial circumstances, a supply of graduates and others with high level qualifications and skills, particularly in relevant areas of science, technology and commerce, will be required. To ensure such a supply, the Government is promoting a change in the balance of tertiary education to place greater emphasis on engineering and technology and is extending teaching and research facilities in natural science through the 'new blood' and information technology programmes for the universities. In the Strathclyde Region we have encouraged the redeployment of resources at Paisley College of Technology in favour of new technology subjects. We have also sought to enhance the close working relationship which the universities and colleges of the Region have long enjoyed with industry. Further developments which consolidate existing collaboration include West of Scotland Science Park and the Kelvin Technology Fund, to help small, high technology companies establish themselves near the two universities. Technology Transfer Ltd., responsible for handling Strathclyde University's links with industry and especially for marketing certain technological strengths within the University, is another important development.

But education for our future industrial needs cannot start in colleges and universities. There is need also for a change of emphasis in schools. It is for this reason that new curriculum and assessment arrangements for fourteen to sixteen year olds are now being implemented in Scotland together with reforms for the education and training in schools and colleges for the sixteen to eighteen age group. The new modular system which the latter embraces will provide greater opportunities for young people, assist employers in the development of skills to meet their employment needs and enable schools and colleges to make better use of available resources. Successful completion of modules by students is to be recorded on a new National Certificate awarded for the first time in the academic session of 1984–85 by a new awarding body, the Scottish Vocational Education Council.

These developments in education are matched by several exciting initiatives which the Government have introduced through the Manpower Services Commission. Foremost amongst them is the Youth Training Scheme which provides work experience and training to help young people to bridge the transition from school to work. Progress continues to be made towards two further training objectives: the reform of occupational training away from time-serving apprenticeships towards a more open, standards-based system, and improved training for adults. The central objective of all these developments is the promotion of training practices which will produce a flexible and adaptable workforce capable of meeting changing skill requirements so that industry becomes and remains competitive.

I believe, therefore, that in the future we will see a much more coherent and cohesive industrial society established. The emphasis will be on developing areas of potential growth, and education at all levels will be more in tune with employment needs. At the same time, there will be increasing cross-fertilisation between industry and commerce on the one hand, and our academic institutions on the other. In this latter regard Strathclyde Region is entitled to feel pride at what it has accomplished.

In saying this, I do not wish to minimise the difficulties which have to be overcome in a Region of tremendous diversity embracing such contrasts as the worse extremes of urban deprivation and the remoteness of islands and rural areas. This explains why successive governments have devoted considerable resources to the needs of Strathclyde. Public sector initiatives have helped to rehabilitate the housing stock, improve the urban environment, provide new industrial premises and stimulate the service sector by new initiatives such as the Scottish Exhibition Centre. These improvements have been reflected in a dramatic slowing down in the rate of population loss from Glasgow, and the city has seen substantial new private sector investment in service industries such as insurance, banking, offices and hotels. At the same time, other urban areas in the Region are coming increasingly to benefit from area-targeted initiatives, such as the Motherwell Project, the Ardrossan, Saltcoats and Stevenston Enterprise Trust (ASSET) and Cumnock and Doon Valley Enterprist Trust (CADET) and others.

Furthermore, the Highlands and Islands Development Board has done much to improve economic and social conditions of Argyll and Bute, Arran and the Cumbraes by building advance factories and workshops, as well as providing assistance to boat building, food processing, tourist developments, fishing, fish-farming, agriculture, manufacturing in crafts and community co-operatives.

A great deal is happening, therefore, which points to a prosperous future for Strathclyde and for Scotland as a whole. But the future does not build itself. It is a long hard process to adapt the industrial structure of a country to modern conditions. I believe that, as has been demonstrated in Strathclyde, the many agencies involved are coming to appreciate more than ever that the endeavour is a co-operative one.

THE CONTRIBUTORS

Sir Kenneth Alexander   Principal of the University of Stirling.

Alasdair A. Auld   Director of Museums and Art Galleries, Glasgow District Council.

Thomas R. Bone   Principal of Jordanhill College of Education.

Donald H. Brown   Professor of Chemistry, University of Strathclyde.

Councillor James Burns   Convener of Strathclyde Regional Council.

John Butt   Professor of Economic History, University of Strathclyde.

Ronald Crawford   Academic Registrar, University of Strathclyde.

Hugh Dougherty   Lecturer in Further Education, Stow College.

Archibald A. M. Duncan   Professor of Scottish History, University of Glasgow.

Sir William Duncan   Former Chairman of Rolls-Royce Limited.

Sir Monty Finniston   Chancellor of the University of Stirling.

William W. Fletcher   Emeritus Professor of Biology, University of Strathclyde.

285

GEORGE GORDON	Senior Lecturer in Geography and Dean of the Faculty of Arts and Social Studies, University of Strathclyde.
GRAHAM J. HILLS	Principal of the University of Strathclyde.
JOHN R. HUME	Senior Lecturer in Economic History, University of Strathclyde.
ARNOLD KEMP	Editor of *The Glasgow Herald.*
FRANK X. KIRWAN	Scottish Development Agency.
GAVIN H. LAIRD	General Secretary, Amalgamated Union of Engineering Workers.
RICHARD C. LOUDEN	Depute Director of Education, Strathclyde Regional Council.
S. G. EDGAR LYTHE	Emeritus Professor of Economic History and former Vice-Principal in the University of Strathclyde.
DR. IAN MACGREGOR	Chairman of the National Coal Board.
ARTHUR F. MIDWINTER	Lecturer in Administration in the University of Strathclyde and co-Director of the Public Sector Management Unit, Strathclyde Business School.
MICHAEL S. MOSS	Archivist in the University of Glasgow.
ALASDAIR G. NAIRN	Postgraduate Student in Urban and Regional Planning, University of Strathclyde.
MICHAEL PACIONE	Senior Lecturer in Geography, University of Strathclyde.
KEITH SMITH	Professor of Geography, University of Strathclyde.
LORD TODD OF TRUMPINGTON	Chancellor of the University of Strathclyde and Past President of the Royal Society.

URLAN WANNOP	Professor of Urban and Regional Planning, University of Strathclyde
SIR ALWYN WILLIAMS	Principal of the University of Glasgow.
SIR HENRY WOOD	Formerly Principal of Jordanhill College of Education.
RT. HON. GEORGE YOUNGER	Secretary of State for Scotland.

INDEX OF PERSONAL NAMES

INDEX OF SUBJECTS

Fig. 10   Multi-variate classification of non